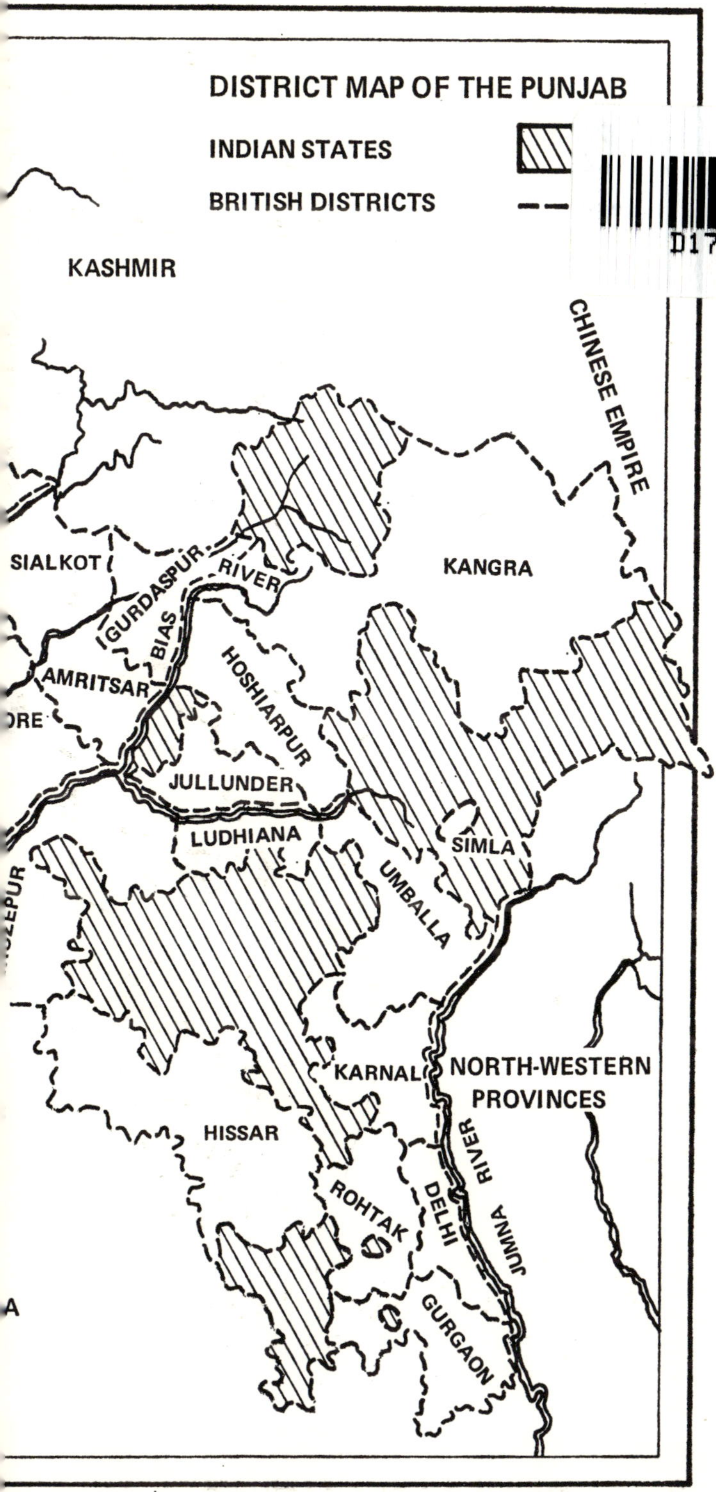

DISTRICT MAP OF THE PUNJAB
INDIAN STATES
BRITISH DISTRICTS
KASHMIR
CHINESE EMPIRE
SIALKOT
GURDASPUR
RIVER
BIAS
KANGRA
AMRITSAR
HOSHIARPUR
JULLUNDER
LUDHIANA
SIMLA
UMBALLA
KARNAL
NORTH-WESTERN PROVINCES
HISSAR
ROHTAK
DELHI
RIVER
JUMNA
GURGAON

WITHDRAWN BY THE
UNIVERSITY OF MICHIGAN

# THE PUNJAB TRADITION

# THE PUNJAB TRADITION

Influence and Authority in
Nineteenth-Century India

by P. H. M. van den Dungen

London · George Allen & Unwin Ltd.
Ruskin House   Museum Street

First published in 1972

This book is copyright under the Berne Convention. All rights are reserved. Apart from any fair dealing for the purpose of private study, research, criticism or review, as permitted under the Copyright Act, 1956, no part of this publication may be reproduced, stored in a retrieval system, or transmitted, in any form or by any means, electronic, electrical, chemical, mechanical, optical, photocopying, recording or otherwise, without the prior permission of the copyright owner. Enquiries should be addressed to the publishers.

© George Allen & Unwin Ltd 1972

ISBN 0 04 954016 5

Printed in Great Britain
*in* 10 *point Times Roman type*
by Unwin Brothers Limited
Woking and London

*To Giedre*

# CONTENTS

| | |
|---|---|
| Preface | *page* 11 |
| Acknowledgements | 25 |
| Abbreviations | 27 |
| 1 Introduction | 31 |
| 2 A Political Dilemma Emerges | 42 |
| 3 The Tradition Transformed | 109 |
| 4 Extending the Conflict | 196 |
| 5 The Shape of Legislation | 247 |
| 6 Triumph of the New Tradition | 283 |
| 7 Conclusion | 298 |
| Notes | 302 |
| Appendix: Divisions of the Punjab | 345 |
| Bibliography | 347 |
| Index | 357 |

# PREFACE

To the historian of British India a reference to the Punjab tradition is likely to bring to mind figures like John Lawrence, seeking political stability in the contentment and well-being of a numerous body of peasant proprietors, or events such as the Jallianwala Bagh massacre and repression of 1919, marked by disdain for educated urban opinion. Apart from the prevalence of such general impressions the Punjab tradition has received little sustained scholarly attention; little more perhaps than the political and intellectual traditions of other Provinces of British India. Yet an analysis of the growth of such traditions would seem mandatory as part of any larger view of Indian political history. Indigenous political forces, nationalist or otherwise, are already the subject of close study on a Provincial basis; and it seems desirable to match this work by studies of the growth of official traditions in the various Provinces.

In a field in which so little is known it appears to be likely that the greatest advances will be made in the attempt to provide answers to interesting questions. The core of the Punjab tradition undoubtedly lay in its reliance on the loyalty of the village proprietors; and an attempt to probe this central feature in depth seems more promising than any treatment of the subject designed to answer merely formal questions. The apparent threat to the viability of the tradition posed by changes in the possession of agricultural land provides a remarkable opportunity for exploration of a vital area. The question to which this theme gives rise is perhaps most clearly visualised in terms of the views of two members of the Indian Civil Service, Arthur Brandreth and John Maynard. In 1869 Arthur Brandreth emerged as the first British officer in the Punjab to take a serious political view of the steady transfer of agricultural land from the landholding tribes to the trading castes. Then and later Brandreth questioned the political wisdom of policies which fostered a process so conducive, in his view, to rural disaffection. The message was a novel and unwelcome one; but by 1909 the only champion of a contrary point of view was John Maynard. In a period of forty years a whole Province had changed its mind about an issue central to its political and intellectual tradition; and in the process the tradition itself had undergone changes both obvious and subtle. To ask why

## THE PUNJAB TRADITION

official opinion in the Punjab was transformed in this manner between 1869 and 1909 is to raise a question which touches the motive forces in the growth of a political and intellectual tradition.

An attempt to answer this question also involves a critique of the fundamental assumptions which at present underlie much research and writing in the field of British-Indian history. That a historian should concern himself, for instance, with members of the Indian Civil Service as undistinguished, so to speak, as Brandreth and Maynard, may in itself appear unusual. Much of British-Indian historiography is characterised by respect for formal authority, both in the political and intellectual spheres. The heads of the Home and Indian Governments are very much to the fore, as are men who combined intellectual eminence or relevance in an English context with senior Indian service. Among British administrators whose whole career and prospects lay in India, few have claimed attention who did not rise to high office. General assessments of the men who ruled India, by those who wrote from the inside, have not sufficed to rivet the historian's attention. All too often the vast majority of British officers in India have remained shadowy figures, lacking all individuality, fortunate to be mentioned by name, and more often admired or abused than studied. The history of British policy has been written without them, and the political history of modern India knows them not. The two most ambitious accounts of recent years in these areas, by S. Gopal and A. Seal respectively, do not even reveal any awareness of the problem. Similarly in dealing with administrative issues a historian like E. Stokes has not hesitated to divide official opinion into schools of thought without taking the views of most British officers into consideration. And even scholars who do not share this preoccupation with formal authority have not brought the British-Indian bureaucracy into sharp focus. They are indeed the forgotten men of British-Indian history.

Yet we know that these men were not simply administrators of an empire, that their responsibilities extended to the formulation as well as to the implementation of policy. We know too – certainly nationalist India knew – that their political traditions provided something very much like the cement of empire. An attempt to redress the balance appears to be in order, therefore, and such an attempt must range as widely as possible, taking into account the parts played by these men at every official level. In attempting to explain the transformation of Punjab opinion between 1869 and 1909 this book shows these men exercising quite decisive influence on the policy of the Government of India and the India Office. It shows the important role played and the influence exerted by successive heads of the Punjab Government, themselves members of the Indian Civil Service. And careful narrative shows the remarkable degree to which a particular legislative measure was shaped by the conflicting counsels of the civilians and military civilians of the Punjab. But above all it is the general movement of Punjab opinion over forty years, which places these developments in context, which comes in for special attention; and it is the extent to which the initiative and driving force in the movement came from below that deserves special emphasis.

There is no intention here of disparaging the role played by those occupying positions of formal authority. Whatever the pressures which British officers might exert on their superiors, whatever the advice they might tender, the formal decision was not theirs to take. The contributions of the heads of the Home and Indian Governments are by no means ignored, therefore; and, as already suggested, a new stress is laid on the contributions made by the heads of the Provincial Government. And it is apparent that these contributions were as often important in the realm of influence as in that of authority, in the realm of opinion as much as in that of decision. But the influence exercised, and the decisions taken, by men in positions of formal authority must not blind us to the fact that great influence was exercised at times by individuals who did not occupy the highest positions at all, and by large bodies of officers. None of these contributions can be studied in isolation, as if they were not part of a larger context. No one, whatever his official position, made decisions in a vacuum; no individual could ignore the fact that the changing views of others, high or low, provided him with certain terms of reference, whether wide or narrow. The respective roles of official influence and official authority mark one sense in which the theme of influence and authority pervades this book.

It must not be imagined that the particular balance struck in this book in these matters possesses general validity. Obviously in different circumstances, at different times, or in relation to different issues, the balance might well have to be struck in a different way. But existing work, preoccupied with the occupants of great offices and the emergence rather than the shaping of policy, has discerned only the tip of the iceberg, and failed to make any attempt to strike the balance at all. The very scope of most work on British-Indian history inhibits any more technically demanding investigations of general trends in official opinion; as does the slavish dependence on sources which enshrine the view from the top.

The present work provides some illustration of the technical challenge which the study of general trends and influences poses. If we wish to speak of general developments we must not be content to cite the opinions of a few distinguished officers at one time or another, and assume them to be representative. If we seek to depict not just the actions and motives of prominent men, but the official atmosphere in which they functioned, we must study literally hundreds of officers over a very considerable period of time. And as far as the evidence allows, these men must be studied as individuals, not as district officers indistinguishable one from the other, and not as adherents of some rigid school of thought invented by the historian. It is only by acquainting ourselves with the particular views of particular men that we are able to trace changes in the character of their opinions; and it is on this basis alone that we can build up a clear picture of general trends in official opinion. This means not only access to as large and varied a range of relevant sources as possible, but also the most intensive analysis of those sources. Quotations from contemporaries are not likely to suffice, for long-term trends do not always attract the attention or understanding of contemporaries. The very changes which take place in the attitudes of individuals over the years are not generally understood by those individuals themselves, or at any rate not generally admitted or recorded. The study of influence is subject to similar problems. To trace individual as well as general trends and influences, therefore, the historian's analysis must reveal what the documents do not say except by careful comparison, often over long periods, and with reference to what may appear to be only details.

The very techniques which are required to elucidate the nature and influence of general trends serve as a reminder that these trends do not represent the views of some undifferentiated body of men but the changing and converging opinions of a large number of diverse individuals. Inevitably, for particular rather than general reasons, some of these individuals played a greater role than others; so that any analysis in terms of general trends must take into account the interaction of these trends with particular contingencies. The advantage of speaking of trends, or alternatively of traditions, is that unlike the more rigid and static concept of schools of thought both these terms enable us to emphasise what is held in common while giving full latitude to individual differences over a period of time. They enable us to preserve that delicate balance between the general and the particular which lies at the root of historical explanation.

PREFACE

Yet to leave an explanation of the transformation of Punjab opinion between 1869 and 1909 at the level of the cumulative effects of individual changes of opinion and particular contingencies is to leave the most tantalising questions unanswered. The steady growth of opinion over a period of decades suggests the need for explanation in terms of larger, underlying influences; influences which will explain not merely how but why so many men came to think alike. And might those influences not be found to radiate from Indian society? We are dealing here, after all, with officers who came to India at an early and impressionable age, and spent up to thirty-five years or more in the country. The very nature of their official duties brought them into close contact with rural society; and they were discussing a social issue, that of the voluntary transfer of agricultural land. It was an issue, too, which struck at the very basis of their political tradition; and one might well ask how one could conceive of any regime attempting to maintain authority over a society without taking into consideration, and without being influenced by, the forces which prevailed, or appeared to prevail, within it. This, then, is the second sense in which the theme of influence and authority figures in this book: with reference to the social influences facilitating and promoting a particular, speculative view of the kind of society and the kind of policy required to perpetuate British authority.

It is understandable that this theme, that of social influence on political and intellectual trends, has received but scant attention from the historians of British officialdom in India. It is not a theme which enters easily into the work of those who are concerned primarily, if not entirely, with a handful of English public men whose senior Indian service represented only one phase of a wider career. Social influence may well be ignored more or less by historians whose main interest relates to men who had the least direct contact with Indian society and the most direct links with European society. To such historians the proposition that the roots of British policy and attitudes lay in Europe also seems natural enough. That proposition, championed by historians like R. Guha and E. Stokes, has influenced a whole generation of scholars. But the tendency to treat social influences as of no more than background importance does not derive merely from a commitment to the role of formal authority; it also derives from a fundamental inability to see the history of the British in India as anything more than a simple extension of certain features of British or European history, or to consider it in any terms other than those which make sense in

European as well as in Indian history. Whatever the merits of this tradition, the tendency of its practitioners to write political and intellectual history as if its links with the society to which it relates were only tenuous, is singularly unconvincing.

It is not contended that the particular conclusions which emerge in this volume regarding the role of social influence are to be taken as establishing some sort of general pattern of explanation applicable to British India. What is contended is that previous studies of the British in India for various reasons have failed to apply those historical techniques to their material which would enable them to elicit such influences. The case for social influences has gone by default.

Books have been written, of course, in which some importance has been attributed to the role of internal developments in the shaping of policy. But as long as the orthodox tradition in British-Indian studies reigned supreme, that attempt had perforce to be confined to influences or events such as those of 1857, the impact of which was immediately apparent in the correspondence of the most elevated individuals. A change in the angle of vision came with R. Frykenberg's work on the Guntur district, revealing the importance of local circumstances to the administrative fabric of British rule in the first half of the nineteenth century. The methods of that study, however, have little to say to the present endeavour; for we are concerned not with acute difficulties in administration which impaired the effectiveness of the British administrative regime (British rule in the Punjab stood on a far sounder administrative footing in any case) but with social influences on the minds of men.

The search for social influences should not be equated simply with the study of social history. The old assumptions retain their hold in as recent a study of social change as R. Kumar's *Western India in the Nineteenth Century*. Here change in the districts provides no more than a simplified and elegant background to matters political and intellectual, which still move at a rarefied level in conformity with the orthodox tendency to stress the primary importance of intellectual trends in Britain. Due understanding of social change, if attained at all, is but the first step to the appraisal of social influence.

To attempt to establish, for instance, some immediate and direct equation between extent of land transfer and official opinion in the Punjab would be to treat society and the British as if they were entities—as if the former were not an immensely varied, complex set of conditions in a state of flux, and the latter not represented by any number of diverse individuals. No doubt some general aspects of Punjab society exerted a fairly steady and important influence on almost all Punjab officers. But land transfer itself exhibited the most remarkable variations from place to place and from time to time; so that we must look for such particular manifestations as proved to be influential. The local experience of Punjab officers varied widely, so that different officers saw different things and generalised on the basis of different data. Hence we must relate the particular experience of an officer to his opinions. This involves an appraisal of his experience, the districts in which he served, the conditions in the villages and tracts which he actually saw, the information gained from the reports of others—a considerable task in itself for it must be done for a large number of officers if it is to provide any basis for generalisation. But even then a further variable remains. The importance which is attached to any phenomenon, or to any aspect of it, is likely to depend on the point of view of the observer; so that factors affecting the individual's perception, such as his personality, official position and preconceived ideas, must be taken into account.

In relating an officer's experience to his opinions it is essential to do so at a particular moment in time; for the experience as well as the opinions of one and the same officer might be very different at different points in his career. And if we have to relate them at more than one point in an officer's career, that is not just because in the interim he may have served in a different part of the country. Over the years continued observation of the same phenomenon, or continued reflection, might produce results not at first apparent. Experience did not necessarily take its toll of opinion immediately; and the fact that the rate at which it took its toll varied among officers involves an appraisal of the capacity of different individuals to absorb experience and relate it to opinion. Having examined all the conceivable inter-relationships between experience and opinion, in as large a number of instances as the evidence permits, we must still direct our attention to the indirect ways in which society exercised influence. The influence exercised by particular reports and statistics, by officers on each other and on their superiors, by ideas permeated by Indian influences—these are all examples of indirect social influence. And they too are traceable only by careful analysis at particular points in time. In view of the techniques required for the study of social influence it is perhaps not altogether surprising that historians have sought explanations in a different quarter.

## THE PUNJAB TRADITION

It may seem strange that the demands made by the study of social influence should fit in so neatly with the demands of narrative history. In fact the two approaches are, or should be, inseparable; and there ought to be no difficulty in reconciling an interpretation in terms of underlying influences with one stressing the importance of a specific succession of events. Characteristically, historians of influence are tempted to overstate their case. Ignoring men and contingencies, or failing to give them their proper due, they tend to attribute to underlying influences an importance which raises them almost to the stature of impersonal forces working towards some definite goal. That pitfall is avoided here; for it should be clear from the very means adopted for the investigation of social influences that such influences can act only through the minds of men. And even then it is only by due appreciation of the interplay of such influences with particular contingencies that a satisfactory explanation of the course of Punjab opinion between 1869 and 1909 emerges.

It is not only by failing to take account of particular contingencies, however, that the historian of influence is likely to err. Equal difficulties are likely to arise if the historian confines himself to isolating one kind of influence, and overlooks the possibility of other kinds of influence. In British-Indian history the classic example of both tendencies is E. Stokes' *The English Utilitarians and India*. But if we criticise the historian of intellectual influence for failing to take sufficient consideration of social factors, we are not likely to overlook intellectual factors. Social influences work through the minds of men; and men are not devoid of ideas or values.

This brings us to the third and final sense in which the theme of influence and authority finds a place in this book: in terms of the influence exerted by ideas and values which occupied a position of authority in Britain. Of all the varieties of influence examined in this book, that of intellectual influence has obtained by far the greatest share of scholarly attention. It is indeed obvious that British officers must have brought the ideas and values of their own society to India; and that the role of ideas and values in history is not to be under-estimated. But this does not mean this book will give much comfort to those who see the intellectual history of British India primarily in terms of formal intellectual influences. Formal ideas, though given their share of attention and emphasis in this book, do not make the showing which they make in the conventional accounts of British ideas and attitudes in India. And the reasons are not hard to discover. Existing methods of tracing intellectual influence are attuned to a historiographical tradition committed to formal authority; and these methods lose much of their force when that tradition is itself questioned. The case for formal intellectual influence has carried such conviction in the past not because of the weight of evidence presented in its favour, but because the only evidence presented was selected according to certain preconceived notions. The personal preference of the scholar for clear, logical thinkers, and the literary methods of analysis which eschew the counting of heads, have combined with a tendency in some instances to examine only those formal intellectual trends which make sense to those who look at Indian history from the vantage point of English history. Historians have found it comparatively easy to identify a few individuals who were in close touch with formal intellectual developments in England; and it has been just as easy to assume that such men were numerous, or that they were the only ones who mattered. A fair acquaintance with a hundred or more officers in one Province gives us some idea how small a proportion of the total these men were in the Punjab or are likely to have been in India. It would be altogether vain to suggest that we can here determine the precise role of formal doctrines in the intellectual history of British India; but it would be equally vain to pretend that a general survey of Punjab officers does not undermine the credibility of assumptions which have not been put to a test of this kind. A recognition of the role of many men leads to an awareness of the power of the commonplace notions of the time, notions which were all the more influential because they were simple and adaptable.

The concentration on formal authority has served to mask another difficulty in the investigation of intellectual influence. Doubtless Viceroys, Secretaries of State for India and members of the Government of India sent out from Britain may be assumed to have had a fair degree of awareness of current trends in Britain. The same assumption cannot be made so easily for British officers who spent most of their adult lives in India, apart from periods of furlough. It seems more reasonable to postulate a time-lag in the transmission of influence than to assume that men as hard-worked as British administrators in India were, would always be in close touch with the latest trends in Britain. Intellectual influence, we must remind ourselves, is no less subject to verification than social influence; and not merely with reference to what officers actually perceived, but also with reference to the viewpoint from which they perceived it. English public men holding Indian appointments might well consider that developments in Britain were relevant to Indian questions; though even some of them looked at Indian questions from an Indian point of view. But the relevance of controversial issues in British politics to those who are often suspected of having little appreciation of or taste for English public life is quite another matter. Such issues may or may not be relevant, it depends on circumstances; but the point is that their relevance must be demonstrated, not assumed.

But even apart from a historiographical bias in favour of formal authority this is to touch the orthodox methods for tracing intellectual influence at their weakest point. Whereas social influences cannot be established at all without detailed analysis, and are therefore apt to be overlooked by most historians, intellectual influences appear to be so easily traceable, by merely reading a document and spotting a familiar idea, that historians are apt to forget to verify them altogether. The tendency has been to assume intellectual influence simply on the ground of similarity and without sufficient supporting evidence to show that a connection really existed. At times the assumption may be justified, at other times not. There is, after all, such a vast array of material in both Britain and India that almost any doctrine could be found to have some counterpart, in some part of India, in relation to something. Such discoveries do not suffice to establish intellectual influence; they merely indicate that such influence is one of a number of logical possibilities. To think otherwise is to deny the possibility of men being able to arrive at similar conclusions independently. Yet sometimes historians have not stopped to look for even the flimsiest documentary evidence necessary to lend an air of plausibility to their conclusions. Thus the gradual decline of *laissez-faire* ideas in Britain has been depicted – on the grounds of apparent similarity alone – as the major intellectual influence behind the Punjab Alienation of Land Act of 1900, an assertion which a survey of the period from 1869 to 1909 does not bear out. While something as fundamental, all-embracing and persistent as *laissez-faire* political economy exerted the greatest influence on British officers, not every adjustment in the British intellectual tradition at home (such as the slow and tentative decline of *laissez-faire* ideas) was likely to exert an equal influence, unless such an adjustment was of the most specific relevance to Punjab problems. And if we look to agrarian issues in England or Ireland for such specific relevance, we shall not find it; for the solutions mooted in these instances, whether relating to entail or the creation of peasant proprietors, had little direct bearing on the Punjab problem of restricting the power of peasant proprietors to transfer their land.

## PREFACE

It is the need for more care and discrimination in the tracing of intellectual influence that is the general point here; and not the particular blend of ideas and values that this book endorses as important to an understanding of Punjab opinion between 1869 and 1909. Yet there is another general point to be made, one which historians could not help but overlook as long as they failed to consider the role of social influence. We have suggested that the influence exerted by a changing society cannot be determined without taking the observer's viewpoint, including his preconceived ideas, into account; equally we must suggest that the role of ideas and values cannot be fully understood unless those ideas and values are examined in their social context. This cannot be done by means of the literary methods of analysis which prevail, for such methods focus on words in the abstract, making it all too easy to assume that the same thing said in Britain and India invariably had the same significance. Consider, for instance, that when *laissez-faire* principles were applied to Indian society in order to deny the need for legislation to deal with land transfer, they served a distinct purpose from that which they served in Britain—and not merely in the sense that they inhibited State intervention of very different kinds in these societies. The very ideas which challenged the *status quo* in England might help to maintain it in India; for in England free trade in land could appear as a cry for reform, but in India, where free trade in land existed, its significance was reversed. This indicates the need to examine the circumstances within which familiar English ideas were applied in India; a need which is overlooked by historians who think that the attitudes of British-Indian officers to British controversies necessarily provide a simple key to their attitudes in India. Even familiar ideas, however influential, had to be adapted to Indian society, and even familiar ideas derived some of their strength and meaning from Indian circumstances.

But the failure of historians to consider ideas in their social context has led them to overlook an even more important dimension in the intellectual history of British India. So great has been the interest in establishing the influence of British ideas in India that the intellectual history of British India has become a mere shadow of British intellectual history. It has been forgotten that if all that was said and done in India was foreshadowed in Britain then one must deny British officers in India any capacity for original thought whatever. But when we look to social influence the balance is restored; for we see men confronted by particular problems, problems for which formal thinkers provided no solution, and we see them drawing on their Indian experience in their attempts to formulate answers. This is not something which will become apparent through the conventional approach of collecting ideas under broad, general themes, and ignoring those which do not fit preconceived categories. The methods of analysis employed in general compilations of British attitudes in India, such as those of G. D. Bearce and F. G. Hutchins, ensure that any conceivable development of this kind is obscured. If we wish to see whether British India had an intellectual history of its own in any sense, we must examine ideas in their proper context. This book shows, for instance, that it was to a more or less indigenous process that the movement of Punjab opinion between 1869 and 1909 owed its intellectual dynamic.

From all this it should be clear that it is not just a matter of investigating and verifying social and intellectual influences, and then deciding that one kind of influence was more effective than another. In the same way as we examine the interplay of general and particular factors, we must study the whole web of inter-relationships between various kinds of influence. When we do this we find that the analysis of influence is far more complex than existing works on British-Indian history would suggest. What emerges is the realisation that particular kinds of influence do not necessarily work in one and the same direction. The same ideas and values, as well as influences emanating from the same society, may be found to have contrary effects. Social influences inhibited as well as aided the movement of Punjab opinion. Some intellectual and cultural influences had something to say to the progression, as well as to the retardation, of Punjab opinion. When we take stock, therefore, we find that social, intellectual and cultural elements prevail among influences which permit or promote and among influences which retard the progression of opinion. As far as underlying influences are concerned, the question thus becomes why one set of influences should triumph over another. If, in relation to this question, this book puts considerable emphasis on social influence, that is not merely because social influences constitute a large part of the whole range of influences at work, but because it is among social influences alone that dynamic elements explaining a steady progression of opinion can be detected.

It will be readily understood that this book should be evaluated not within the existing tradition of British-Indian scholarship, but as a pointer to a new, revised interpretation of British-Indian history. The differences between the old and the new approach are indeed fundamental and inescapable. A new question is asked here, a question which is intended to probe the long-term movement of official opinion as a means of eliciting some deeper understanding of the British contribution to the political history of modern India. But this is only the beginning. Quite vital differences in historical method are involved. The aim is to exploit to the fullest extent, and to reconcile, the kinds of insights which are often confined to the work of particular historians. The insights of the narrative historian are joined to those of the historian of underlying influence; and the role of circumstances is taken into account as well as that of ideas and values. Historical evidence is subjected to intensive scrutiny within its particular context and from a number of points of view. That such scrutiny produces rather startling conclusions suggests that equally interesting results might follow an application of these techniques to other facets of British-Indian history which at present appear to be firmly settled. The difference between the old and the new approach extends to the very criteria for the selection of evidence. Hitherto many historians have ignored evidence that had no bearing on formal authority, political and intellectual, thus slanting British-Indian history in a particular direction. The application of new standards of relevance is bound to lead to new interpretations. The scope for historical revision is immense; and while this work does not pretend to predict the outcome, or to provide a rigid model for future research, it does illustrate some of the relevant techniques. It also indicates that there are levels and dimensions in the history of British India which the historian will ignore at his peril.

# ACKNOWLEDGEMENTS

I owe much to Professor D. A. Low and Dr K. L. Gillion, my mentors in the field of South Asian history at post-graduate and undergraduate level respectively. At the National Archives of India Mr S. Roy, Mr V. C. Joshi, Miss D. Keswani and Mr S. R. Mahajan provided assistance and encouragement on a generous scale. Mian Muhammad Sadullah, the Keeper of the Records at the West Pakistan Secretariat Records Office, was invariably helpful and sympathetic. I am indebted to Mr Fazl-U-Rehman Khan, Secretary to the West Pakistan Board of Revenue; for I believe that it was through his scholarly zeal and good offices that I secured access to the Board's records in 1962. At the Board of Revenue I am likewise deeply appreciative of the aid given by Mr Sultan Maqsood. Much valuable help was provided by the staff of the various offices mentioned above, and by the Librarian and staff of the West Pakistan Board of Revenue Library. Nor can I fail to mention the assistance given by the Department of History of the Punjab University in Lahore. In the final stages of my research the courteous and efficient service provided by the Librarian and staff of the India Office Library enabled me to supplement the material collected in India and Pakistan. In similar fashion my labours were lightened by the efforts of colleagues and others too numerous to mention. Without the financial assistance of the Australian National University the research on which this book is based would not have been possible. Aid and encouragement of various kinds was provided by the Department of History of the University of Adelaide. To Miss A. Haggis of that Department I am obliged for typing the final draft. It is difficult to express adequately my thanks to my wife for her assistance and comments at every stage.

P. v. d. D.

# ABBREVIATIONS

*Official Positions*

| | |
|---|---|
| AC | Assistant Commissioner |
| CC | Chief Commissioner of the Punjab |
| ChC | Chief Court of the Punjab |
| CR | Commissioner and Superintendent of a division |
| DC | Deputy Commissioner of a district |
| DJ | District Judge |
| DLR | Director of Land Records and Agriculture, Punjab |
| DVJ | Divisional Judge |
| FC | Financial Commissioner of the Punjab |
| Govt | Government of the Punjab (unless otherwise specified, e.g. Govt of India) |
| JC | Judge of the Chief Court of the Punjab |
| Jnr Sec. | Junior Secretary |
| LG | Lieutenant-Governor of the Punjab |
| Offg | Officiating (e.g. Offg FC, etc.) |
| Rev. Sec. | Revenue Secretary |
| SC | Settlement Commissioner, Punjab |
| Sec. | Secretary |
| Snr Sec. | Senior Secretary |
| SO | Settlement Officer |

*Official Proceedings*

1 *West Pakistan Government Secretariat Records Office*

| | |
|---|---|
| PP | Proceedings of the Punjab Government |
| Judicial | Judicial Department |
| Revenue | Department of Revenue, Agriculture and Commerce and, after 1881, Department of Revenue and Agriculture |
| (R) | Revenue branch of Department of Revenue and Agriculture |
| (A) | Agriculture branch of Department of Revenue and Agriculture |
| Home | Home Department |
| (J) | Judicial branch of Home Department |
| Foreign | Foreign Department |

(G) General branch of Foreign Department
KW Keep-With to Proceedings

2 *West Pakistan Board of Revenue*

FF Financial Commissioner's Office Files
PF Punjab Civil Secretariat Printed Files, Revenue
KW Keep-With to Proceedings

3 *National Archives of India*

IP Proceedings of the Government of India
Revenue Department of Revenue and Agriculture
(R) Revenue branch of Department of Revenue and Agriculture
(LR) Land Revenue branch of Department of Revenue and Agriculture
(F) Famine branch of Department of Revenue and Agriculture
(G) General branch of Department of Revenue and Agriculture
(HB and AS) Horse-breeding and Agricultural Stock branch of Department of Revenue and Agriculture
Home Home Department
(J) Judicial branch of Home Department
Legislative Legislative Department
Legislative Papers Legislative Department, Papers relating to Act XIII of 1900
KW Keep-With to Proceedings

4 *Commonwealth Relations Office*

IO India Office Records

*Official Documents and Publications*

AR Assessment Report (of one or more tahsils)
Book Circular Orders *Book Circular Orders issued by the Financial Commissioner for the Punjab in the Revenue Department for years 1858 to 1860*, Vol. 3
Circular Orders *Circular Orders issued by the Board of Administration in the Revenue Department during the years 1849 to 1853* (Lahore 1855), Vol. 1

## ABBREVIATIONS

| | |
|---|---|
| *ERR* | Extracts from the Revenue (or Land Revenue) reports of local officers, bound with the Provincial Revenue (or Land Revenue) Report |
| *History of Services* | *History of Services of Gazetted Officers employed in the Punjab* (annual editions appearing under this or similar titles) |
| *LAR* | *Annual Report on the Punjab Alienation of Land Act XIII of 1900* (Lahore 1902–9) |
| *Panjab Castes* | *Panjab Castes. Being a reprint of the chapter on 'The Races, Castes and Tribes of the People' in the Report on the Census of the Panjab published in 1883 by the late Sir Denzil Ibbetson* (Lahore 1916) |
| *PAR* | *General Report on the administration of the Punjab* |
| Parl. Papers | Parliamentary Papers |
| *Public Selections* | *Selections from the Public Correspondence of the Punjab Administration* |
| *Punjab Report* | *Punjab Report in Reply to Inquiries issued by the Famine Commission* (Lahore 1878–9) |
| *RR* | *Annual Report on the Revenue (or Land Revenue) Administration of the Punjab* (Lahore 1861–1902) |
| *Selections* | *Selections from the Records of the Office of the Financial Commissioner, Punjab* New Series No. 11, No. 37, No. LXV Papers on Indebtedness of Agriculturists in the Punjab and Foreclosure of Mortgage (Lahore 1887) |
| *SR* | *Settlement Report* (of a district) |

Note: In regard to official reports all dates given in brackets are dates of publication; all other dates pertain to the year to which the report refers (in the case of annual reports) or to the year in which the report was completed or submitted to authority.

CHAPTER I

# Introduction

At the heart of the Punjab political tradition lay the desire to create and preserve a stable rural base. A study of British attitudes to voluntary land transfer thus illuminates the major problem of political authority in the Punjab as envisaged by the British in the nineteenth century. The story begins, in a sense, with Arthur Brandreth. In his revenue report for 1868–9 Brandreth, at that time Commissioner of the Multan division, stressed the political danger of the voluntary transfer of land from hereditary landholders to the Hindu trading castes. His statements on the subject became more virulent, if anything, in the years which followed. Hitherto there had been nothing quite like it.[1]

No doubt in earlier years a number of senior Punjab officers had expressed their anxiety about agrarian indebtedness and land transfer. In the first decade after annexation (1849) certain measures had even been taken to limit the growth of indebtedness and to restrict the transfer of land. But in all this Punjab officers had been influenced as much by experience in the North-Western Provinces as by what was happening in the Punjab. In so far as the voluntary transfer of land (as distinct from its compulsory transfer by the courts) was considered harmful, it was regarded as a temporary problem, characteristic of the early days of British rule. Arthur Brandreth was the first officer to conceive of the voluntary alienation of land as a major political problem, the seriousness of which would increase with the passage of time.

Yet a few years before Brandreth himself had not held any opinion of the kind. As Settlement Officer and Deputy Commissioner he had shown, like some of his colleagues, his awareness of the problem of agricultural indebtedness; but that was all. The change in Brandreth's views was, in fact, only the first sign of a more widespread change in attitude; a change which cannot be understood without reference to economic and social developments which had their roots in the first twenty or more years of British rule.

Arthur Brandreth's career illustrates some of the major developments of those years. A civilian, he had been appointed in 1851, arriving in India in the following year.[2] As Settlement Officer Brandreth undertook the first regular settlement of the Jhelum district in 1855. In this, as in many other Punjab districts, the summary settlements which had been made a few years before had not always worked well. The transition from a system in which the amount of land-revenue fluctuated with the harvest and was as often as not paid in kind, to one in which the amount of land-revenue was fixed and payable only in cash, had not been an easy one. Insecurity of harvests in some areas, combined with a general fall of agricultural prices in 1851-2, had played havoc with the earliest summary settlements. Revenue reductions had followed in many places. In Jhelum the trouble had not been entirely overcome by the time Brandreth started work. But when he finished, the settlement was a reasonable one. Much the same might be said of most Punjab districts after about a decade of British rule. Of course in the process the Government had surrendered a considerable amount of revenue; and in so far as this was due to insecurity of harvest, the agricultural surplus left to the landholder over a series of years was somewhat greater than it had been before British rule. Yet as long as prices remained low, that surplus was not of great marketable value.[3]

In fixing the assessments at a reasonable level Brandreth had carried out only one part of his duties. In charge of a regular as distinct from a summary settlement, he was obliged to adjudicate and define all interests in land. Broadly speaking the result in Jhelum, and throughout the Punjab, was that the ownership of land was vested in the hands of a large number of small holders cultivating their own land either entirely or partly. Only in some western districts, such as Jhelum itself, was there more than the merest sprinkling of substantial landlords cultivating entirely through tenants or hired labour. The notion of individual, transferable property in land, which was imposed therefore on a large class of small holders, was a novel one in many areas. In parts of the Province in which such notions of landed property had existed before British rule, the regular settlements still brought the greater security which followed in the wake of clear titles.[4]

Brandreth's report on the regular settlement of the Jhelum district was one of the few which was not submitted to Government till the 1860s. It was also the only settlement report in which the Settlement Officer cast serious aspersions on his own handiwork. By 1864, the year in which Brandreth submitted his report, he was fully convinced that his settlement, in common with all the Punjab settlements, had been based on faulty reasoning. Brandreth had become, in fact, for various reasons, including the outbreak of 1857, an adherent of an aristocratic land policy. Revenue reductions and settlements with small holders, which he had favoured at first, he now considered futile. Such settlements wasted the Government's resources while not permitting that improvement of the land which would result from light settlements with large holders. Above all, such settlements did not secure the contentment of the country. The small holders would not benefit economically, or be more contented, he thought, in the long run. In any case they exerted no influence, they were apathetic and would not help the British in a crisis. Only the leading men in society, those who had occupied a prominent position under previous regimes, could be relied upon either to turn against the Government or to secure its continuance in troubled times. Their contentment, therefore, was a prime consideration.[5]

Forty years were to pass before another Punjab officer would speak in such strong terms of the overriding importance of securing the contentment of a minority. Indeed, the Brandreth of 1864, the advocate of aristocratic privilege, became in 1869 the first officer to face the danger of widespread agrarian discontent. In 1864 an aristocratic land policy was a lost cause. Five years later Brandreth was perhaps no less isolated. But he had the future with him.

For by 1869 the long-term effects of British policy were beginning to take shape. Agricultural prices which had fallen in 1851–2, had remained low until the famine of 1860–1. Thereafter these low prices were not touched again. The improvement in communications which was taking place under British rule reached its zenith in 1870 with the completion of the railway. As the century progressed it became clear that average agricultural prices were rising steadily. This was accompanied by a marked extension of cultivation. The British could not take immediate or full advantage of these circumstances, for their assessments were fixed for some twenty or thirty years. With rising prices, an increase in cultivated area, and a revenue demand fixed for long periods, the amount and marketable value of the agricultural surplus steadily increased.[6]

The consequences for the relations between landholder and moneylender were little short of revolutionary. Not that agricultural indebtedness had been unknown in the early 1860s or even before for that matter. Brandreth himself had experience of it in Jhelum and elsewhere.[7] But as the amount and marketable value of the surplus increased, the marketable value of land rose, and a great expansion of agricultural credit ensued. Agricultural indebtedness became possible on a hitherto unknown scale. Land being valuable and transferable, indebtedness assumed unprecedented forms. High rates of compound interest ensured that a debt not quickly repaid, grew rapidly to the point where it could not be repaid from current income. Ultimately only the transfer of land would wipe the slate clean. During the last third of the century voluntary transfers of land in satisfaction of debt or under the pressure of agricultural or social necessity assumed ever more serious proportions. In many places Hindu traders and money-lenders were prominent among the alienees.

Other developments contributed to this process. The British civil courts provided the money-lenders of the Province with regular facilities, of a kind hitherto quite unknown, for enforcing the payment of debts. The results, during the first decade of British rule, were sufficient to alarm the Provincial authorities. This, as well as other evidence, indicates that there is no point in drawing an idyllic picture of the early Punjab judicial system. As agricultural indebtedness grew, however, the role of the courts steadily increased in significance. Besides, during the later part of Brandreth's career, there occurred changes in the system of civil justice which, if their effects have been exaggerated, certainly did not improve matters. In 1869 we find Brandreth complaining about the deficiences of the courts and the rigidity of the British legal system.[8] Three years before, the transition to the new system had begun, with the introduction into the Province of a Chief Court, a strict Civil Procedure Code, and pleaders. It continued in 1872 with the passing of the Evidence Act and the Contract Act. The culminating point (as far as the question of agricultural indebtedness is concerned) was reached in 1874–5, when a separate, sedentary judicial agency, staffed by educated Indians without administrative experience, replaced the executive agency which had handled rural debt cases till then.[9]

The law which guided these courts looked on loose agreements between debtor and creditor as contracts to be enforced without detailed enquiry into the circumstances. It relied on written in preference to oral evidence, a boon to the money-lender who, being the only literate party, kept the accounts or had the bonds drawn up. The law also placed much of the debtor's material assets at the disposal of the judgement-creditor. Though under the new as well as the old system the courts had, and sometimes exercised, some discretion, the system as a whole could only work in the creditor's favour. Civil courts in the Punjab did not order the alienation of

## INTRODUCTION

appreciable areas of land in satisfaction of their decrees; but they were used to bring pressure to bear on the landowner, so that he might voluntarily transfer his land, or otherwise satisfy his moneylender.

While Brandreth's term of service, extending into the 1880s, spans the period in which the transfer of land became a regular feature of the life of the Province, little or nothing was done at this stage. Nor did Brandreth's contemporaries fully appreciate the complexity of what was happening. It was only during the last fifteen years of the century, at the same time as pressure for legislation steadily increased, that a more complete understanding of the intricacies of land transfer eventuated.

These years comprehend the early Indian experience of a man whose views foreshadowed the end of an era much as those of Arthur Brandreth heralded its commencement in 1869. John Maynard joined the Indian Civil Service in 1885, and arrived in India in the succeeding year. He served as Assistant Commissioner in a number of Punjab districts, and in various secretarial positions under the Punjab Government. His early experience included some officiating appointments as District Judge and Deputy Commissioner; but no settlement work. In 1899 he received a substantive appointment as Deputy Commissioner.[10] It was from about this time that he developed into one of the most persistent critics of the legislative measure which had been undertaken in an attempt to restrict the alienation of land. The sort of economic objections he raised had always been one of the main obstacles to legislation; but he was the first Punjab officer to appreciate fully the serious political problem posed by the inhabitants of the towns.

Maynard's career began at a time when not much precise or detailed information about land transfer was available. The uncertain value of the district statistics in the annual land-revenue administration reports had become dramatically apparent a few years earlier. The statistics in the assessment and settlement reports of the 1870s were neither complete nor above suspicion. Only from the early 1880s did there begin to come from the pens of Settlement Officers a steady stream of assessment reports with local statistics of more certain value. By the end of the century these assessment reports covered large parts of the Punjab in considerable detail.

From these reports as well as from some other sources it was apparent that the transfer of land, its extent, direction and consequences, varied widely from one part of the Province to another.

Nor need this occasion surprise. The Punjab itself exhibited the most marked variations. Its agricultural systems varied through a wide range from the most secure to the most insecure. Cultivation was carried on by means of perennial canals, by inundation canals, wells and Persian wheels, by river floods and hill torrents, by heavy or light rainfall, and by various combinations of these sources of irrigation. The pursuits of the landholding tribes and castes extended over most of the range between the purely agricultural and the purely pastoral or nomadic. Various descriptions of crops were raised, chiefly wheat and the inferior food grains, together with varying quantities of pulses, rice, cotton, oil-seeds, sugar-cane, indigo and so on. The landholding castes and tribes were differentiated by distinctions in social status, while the three major Hindu trading castes, Khatris, Aroras and Banias, each associated with a different part of the Province, were not identical in their pursuits or outlook.[11]

Throughout the Province the units of social organisation were anything but consistent; words like 'caste' and 'tribe' perforce meaning different things in different rural areas, to say nothing of other sections of society. By any system of enumeration the number of separate landholding castes and tribes was considerable. The word 'village' had a uniform meaning only in an administrative sense. In social terms the compact and well-preserved village communities of the south-east represented one extreme; the prevalence of hamlets in much of the south-west, the frontier and the eastern hills, another.

In the east the hereditary landholders were Hindu and Muslim, with a Sikh element in the centre. The agricultural population of the west was almost entirely Muslim (though there were hereditary landholders of the Hindu trading castes in the south-west). Culture did not necessarily follow religion. The rural adherents of Hinduism and Islam differed in their customs according to the general tone of different parts of the countryside. Some of the frontier areas stood outside or on the edges of any culture that may be termed Indian.

Bearing in mind that many of the above factors were to be found in a number of combinations, the variations in the economy and society of the Province may be more easily imagined than described. Some of these variations exerted direct and obvious influences on the transfer of land, its extent and direction. Others, particularly those shaping some of the consequences of alienation, were more intangible, not subject to precise measurement and not always easy to assess.

The more obvious variations in land transfer which forced themselves on the attention of the British took the form of regional, local and communal differences.[12]

## INTRODUCTION

In much of the south-eastern Punjab, for instance, agriculture was most insecure, depending as it did on a small and uncertain rainfall, which was liable to fail completely after a series of years. Hence agricultural credit was more restricted, land more limited in value, than in more secure parts of the Province; and this was one reason why alienations, including those to Hindu money-lenders, were less extensive throughout much of this region than in several others.

Contrast this situation with that of the south-western Punjab and parts of the lower frontier. Here a great many conditions served to give a special, almost unique character to the story of land transfer. There had been few restrictions on the power to alienate land even before British rule. At annexation the Hindu trading castes held a significant share of the land. The Muslim landholding tribes lacked skill and thrift to an unusual degree. There were special agricultural systems which placed a premium on capital. These circumstances resulted in the extensive alienation of land to Hindu traders, and very limited transfers to agricultural alienees; a situation which could not be matched in any other region of the Province. Besides, the Hindu traders were often fair and improving landlords here, though almost nowhere else.

The upper frontier again had much to show that was not to be found in many other parts of the Punjab. If anything, the existence of individual landed property before British rule, and the fact that in some tracts transfers were common both before and after annexation, recalls conditions in the south-west and on the lower frontier. Yet outside particular tracts the Hindu money-lenders hardly figured as alienees.

In addition to regional distinctions of this kind, there were, for various reasons, significant local variations. Thus in districts like Gujranwala or Umballa (or rather in large parts of these districts) Hindu money-lenders acquired most of the considerable area alienated. Yet in other districts, as for instance Jhelum, a much smaller percentage of the cultivation was transferred, and more of it acquired by agricultural alienees. There were also striking local differences within districts. One notable example of this was that land transfer often assumed a different complexion in the high lands as compared to the adjoining low lands of a district.

A further distinction which the British noticed was that between different agricultural communities. Other things being equal, semi-pastoral tribes, or tribes and castes claiming high status, such as the Rajputs, often lost most land to outsiders, agricultural as well as non-agricultural. There were groups, like the Hindu Jats of much of the eastern Punjab, and the Pathans of the upper frontier, who, by and large, maintained much of the land transferred within the community. Then there were the Sikh Jats of the central Punjab, not only able to keep outsiders at bay, but manifesting acquisitive and money-lending tendencies to a remarkable degree. Among certain Muslim landholding tribes there was in scattered areas (notably on the frontier and in the north-west) a phenomenon individual rather than communal in form—that of the large Muslim landlord and Government beneficiary adding significantly to the landed possessions of his family.

If to these glimpses of some of the more conspicuous elements of diversity, there be added the varied factors which presumably shaped popular attitudes towards land transfer in different parts of the Province, some idea may be gained of the manifold influences on British officers. Depending on experience, direct or indirect, some officers became acquainted with various forms of the land transfer situation; others, limited in their experience to particular parts of the country, were influenced more especially by distinct manifestations of the problem. Yet it would be idle to pretend that experience in particular parts of the country necessarily led to the countenance of particular opinions. The most limited experience included variegated features any of which might impress different individuals.

The opinion which John Maynard offered on the Punjab Alienation of Land Bill in 1900 illustrates this point with rare precision. Maynard was at this time in charge of the Umballa district. In the four southern tahsils of that district the agricultural indebtedness of the major landholding groups was striking. The transfer of land to professional money-lenders had been more extensive here than in any other compact area of similar size in the eastern Punjab. It was above all this aspect of land transfer in the Umballa district which, in the past, had impressed and worried a number of British officers acquainted with the general state of the district.

Yet Maynard saw much in the condition of the Umballa district which appeared to justify the unrestricted transfer of land. In addition to the alienation of large areas of land to money-lenders there had been, he thought, a parallel process in which land passed from weak to strong agriculturists. The Jats, at any rate those of the two northern tahsils, were frequently acquisitive. The market-gardening castes, whose exertions improved the land out of sight, had been making purchases in several of the southern tahsils. It was sometimes the non-agricultural alienee, Maynard indicated, who served as an intermediary in the transfer of land from bad to good agriculturists. Then there were tracts in the district which were notoriously unhealthy or subject to persistent injury by the action of water or sand. Only intelligent and wealthy men, with large estates, could ever take the necessary remedial measures, or set the required example. Money-lenders might not make improving landlords, but there were certainly men in the district whose acquisition of land was a public blessing. Among lesser arguments against the restriction of the power of transfer Maynard noted that Umballa now shared, to a small extent, in the industrial development which had begun in the Punjab. He feared that British officers, given a veto over land transfer, might well use it in cases where it was proposed to found 'a cotton press on what was once a cabbage garden'. Finally Maynard declared, with regard to the rural economy of the district, that the restriction of credit was likely to have awkward and unexpected results.[13]

If the circumstances of one district could justify different opinions, in the eyes of different officers, the difficulties attending a solution in a large and heterogeneous Province could not be otherwise than formidable. When Maynard referred in 1904 to the 'simple and attractive' problems of rural India, he was thinking in terms of a new order of difficulty. The British, he predicted, would find it infinitely more difficult to win the confidence of an unappreciative urban population, with whom they were not in sympathy, than that of a rustic population. By the early years of the century Maynard, if almost no one else in the Punjab, believed that in the long run British rule would depend on the ability to deal with 'the educated man, the trader, and the townsman generally'.[14]

The wheel had come full circle. In 1864 Arthur Brandreth had emphasised that the aristocratic elements in society were the fundamental sources of political strength or weakness. Some forty years later John Maynard saw the urban population in the same light. Both were impressed by the political role of influential minorities.[15] Again, Brandreth in 1864 had spoken of the beneficial economic results which might have been expected from land-revenue settlements with men of position. Many years later Maynard defended land transfer to large proprietors for the same reason, if not quite as confidently. In all this their views ran more or less counter to the general opinion of the time.

Between them Arthur Brandreth and John Maynard provide some of the major clues for an understanding of the political tradition of the Punjab Province. Sharing an interest in history, and in foreign countries, they were both politically sensitive to an acute degree.[16] In 1864 Brandreth could do little more than mourn at length the British failure to institute a rural society dominated by aristocratic influence. Whatever Brandreth hoped might still be done, whatever concessions the British had made or might make in the future to surviving aristocratic elements, the main chance had passed. In the countryside the political future rested with the small landholders; or so the British thought. It was Brandreth's point in 1869 and after, that this political future was in jeopardy. And this gradually became the major source of official anxiety, leading indeed to a distinct shift in the political thinking of the British. John Maynard's views suggest that this period was coming to an end. Yet he was only the first Punjab officer to foresee something of the problems of the future; and the views which he challenged influenced the British approach to new political problems in the first decades of the twentieth century.

The views of Brandreth and Maynard also illustrate something of the intellectual history of the period. In 1875 Brandreth appealed for a law which he observed had been found necessary for five centuries in England, namely that a man's land should not be liable for his debts beyond his life.[17] The remark was notable because, throughout the land transfer controversy, there was the very general (though not universal) assumption that English experience was hostile to any legislative remedy. Whether that experience was altogether relevant in India was another question. Victorian ideas about society and property, received notions of political economy, the belief in progress or improvement, and evolutionist modes of thought certainly exerted a profound influence on the discussion; for perhaps no man could view questions of this kind without reference to the ideas of his own society. Yet in any particular context, and at any particular time, different officers placed a very different valuation on specific elements in this intellectual tradition. Brandreth, for instance, was preoccupied with the question of political danger, and there is no evidence that he thought that there were any serious economic objections to legislation. If Brandreth represented one extreme, Maynard certainly represented another. To Maynard there was no independent political danger in the countryside; and he gave free rein to economic and social objections to the restriction of the power of alienation, objections which in his eyes were warranted by rural conditions. Not all Punjab officers fitted into either of these categories. The more some officers saw of the voluntary transfer of land, the more they sensed political danger or other harmful effects, the more they were inclined to modify their intellectual heritage. Not only were the absolute convictions of many undermined, but entirely new intellectual convictions, attributable largely to Indian experience, took root.

Brandreth and Maynard further exemplify the phenomenon of the officer who did not hesitate to champion lost or apparently hopeless causes. There were to be many more such men, campaigning occasionally or incessantly against the views of their superiors. In the debate on land transfer they played a vital and creative role, weakening opinion which otherwise would have reigned by default, crystallising and emboldening opinion which otherwise would have remained dormant. Yet theirs was not an easy, or for some, a complete victory; for in the drama which began with Brandreth and ended with Maynard, the stage was crowded with actors who exerted their influence as they saw fit. It is to the multitude of individual officers, to the individual changes in their political and intellectual convictions, as well as to general trends and underlying influences, that this book addresses itself.

CHAPTER II

# A Political Dilemma Emerges

I

'With the knowledge now generally prevalent respecting village coparcenaries', ran the Government of India's instructions to the Punjab Board of Administration in 1849, 'there is no apprehension that our officers will not exert themselves to maintain those important bodies in all their integrity.'[1] The knowledge to which the despatch referred, and the policy which it anticipated, can be appreciated only in the light of British experience in the North-Western Provinces.

That experience was very much in evidence among the members of the Board of Administration. John Lawrence, Charles Mansel and Robert Montgomery (who replaced Mansel on the Board in 1851) were civilians from the North-Western Provinces. The career of Henry Lawrence, the Board's President, had been primarily military and political; but his wide and varied experience included a term of years as revenue surveyor in the North-Western Provinces.[2]

British experience in that part of India was represented, moreover, by a number of civilians, most of them chosen by John Lawrence, and including a number of senior men. They had, however, no monopoly of office; for Henry Lawrence had brought a large number of military officers into the administration. At annexation several experienced officers had been taken from what had been, until then, the north-west frontier of British India.[3]

The system of administration initiated in these circumstances, under influences stemming from the North-West, accorded well with the Government of India's admonition to preserve the hereditary village communities. In the essentials of revenue and judicial administration the Government of India's instructions and the Board's inclinations appear to have been the same. The system of village settlements current in the North-West Provinces was adopted without question. The insistence on light or moderate settlements reflected the difficulties and dislocation which had accompanied heavy settlements in those Provinces. A simple judicial system was adopted in an attempt to by-pass the technical system which prevailed in the older, regulation provinces.[4]

Nor was the attempt to preserve the landed communities confined to general administrative measures. Applications of lessons learnt in the North-West were made in the specific matter of the transfer of land. During the first decade of British rule there developed an official, protective policy in this respect. Of course the major administrative measures inaugurated by the British in these years would lead in the fullness of time and circumstance to the steady transfer of land. Yet of this most of the early administrators had hardly any clear or complete idea. The restrictions which they placed on the transfer of land, limited though they might appear in retrospect, were to them significant protective measures, constituting serious departures from fundamental British principles.

Within the Province the first hint of a protective attitude appeared in 1850 when the Board of Administration prohibited the practice by which villages were sub-let for the purpose of discharging the revenue demand. The prohibition had been advocated early in 1850 by Robert Cust, a civilian of cis- and trans-Sutlej experience, who had been appointed to the Umballa district to restore order in its affairs.[5] After some discussion, and in spite of the opposition of certain other officers, the Board obtained the sanction of the Government of India to prohibition. In issuing their final orders the Board tried to meet the argument of the opposition that sub-leases of the revenue were much the same as mortgages of the land, and that neither the one nor the other could be prevented. The members of the Board thought that the mortgage of a village, by which the management changed hands, was certainly an evil, and particularly where a village proprietary body existed. It was, they considered, 'our true interest to preserve the village proprietary bodies, as far as possible, in their pristine state'. In the Board's view the limits of possibility did not extend to the prohibition of mortgages; but subleases, by which intriguing characters obtained the management of villages and finally their proprietorship, were on a different footing. The land, the Board pointed out, did not belong to the proprietor in an absolute sense; it was subject to land tax, and the Government had an undoubted right to prevent the deterioration of the revenue-paying capacity of the village.[6]

Though the Board felt itself unable to do anything about mortgages, it was prepared to empower the village communities to check the permanent transfer of land to outsiders. To this end the Board issued final instructions in May 1852 in regard to the right of pre-emption. These instructions reflected a mixture of political boldness and economic caution. The Board was aware that economic principles supplied no warrant for any restriction on the transfer of land. But there were social and political reasons; and the Board's circular instanced 'the existing state of tenures throughout the Punjab . . . the constitution of society . . . the experience gained in our older provinces'. In Hindustan, however, the rule of pre-emption had been criticised, as it was frequently evaded by the collusive fixing of prices. Hence the Board prescribed the procedure for determining an equitable price at which any member of the proprietary community, or the community collectively, could purchase. If the property could not be disposed of in this way then, and only then, was its sale to a stranger permissible. All transfers effected under these rules were to be reported to the Commissioner of the division. The rules would apply to all permanent transfers of land (including foreclosure of mortgage and sale to decree-holders by order of court). Temporary transfers were to be excluded from their scope; for the Board believed that such transfers facilitated agricultural credit.[7]

As for the compulsory transfer of land in execution of civil decrees the Board's tenderness was further exemplified by the remark in their first administration report, dated August 1852, that poor defendants were given an opportunity to pay by instalments while 'care is taken that landed property shall not unnecessarily be brought to the hammer'.[8] This was part and parcel of the Board's attempt to prevent the courts from becoming engines of oppression.

That the Board's protective policy in regard to land transfer represented opinions of a kind commonly (though not universally) held, is indicated, among other things, by the views of George Campbell, a civilian whose service dated from 1843. Campbell had spent three years in the North-Western Provinces, followed by about four years in the Cis-Sutlej States. While on furlough in the 1850s he wrote two books about Indian administration, the one delineating the system as it was, the other as it ought to be. Much can be found in these books which, while not identical, does bring the Board's policy to mind; a matter which gains in significance when it is remembered that Campbell was far from being a protégé of either Henry or John Lawrence.[9]

The desirability of preserving the corporate village communities figured as largely in Campbell's works as in the Board's correspondence. In the volume published in 1852 Campbell, unlike the Board, conceived of circumstances in which the sub-letting of the revenue demand, which he took to be temporary in its effects, was preferable to the appointment of farmers of the revenue. But this was a difference in detail rather than principle. The collection of the revenue in the Punjab had been accomplished so easily, Campbell noted, that there had hardly been time for settling the mode of coercion in case of default. The power to sell land for arrears of revenue, which had been restricted in the North-Western Provinces for the past twenty years, had not been exercised in the Punjab (an aspect of the protective policy of which more will be said later). Campbell approved of the policy, current in the North-West, of transferring the land of revenue defaulters to solvent sharers, and avoiding in this and other ways compulsory sale in all but the most extreme cases.[10]

There was one matter, Campbell indicated in 1852, which had yet to be regulated, and about which he was anxious. If the Punjab was ever to have civil courts such as those in the North-Western Provinces, which had transferred land in execution of decree on a large scale, the village communities would be destroyed, for no stranger could ever become part of these communities. In thinking that land in the Punjab was not and should not be sold in execution of civil decrees Campbell, while proceeding along lines similar to those of the Board of Administration, went somewhat further than the Board's policy of restraint. Again Campbell's opinion that land was not so far a separate property that individuals could sell it to a stranger without the consent of the community, and his view that the land of those in difficulties should be transferred to the community, encompassed the essence of the Board's instructions on pre-emption;[11] but Campbell's second book confirms that he contemplated something more than a right of pre-emption.

In this volume, published in 1853, Campbell proposed that in perfect communities the transfer of shares by ordinary proprietors would be permitted only among those who were already members of the community. Transfer to other persons would be allowed only with the consent of the majority, or with that of the Collector as the representative of the superior lord (the Collector's consent being essential, or so it appears from one passage, in the case of the sale of land in execution of civil decrees). Only those holding not less than one-fourth of an estate and paying not less than 200 rupees revenue per annum would be permitted unrestricted power of transfer. When in peaceable and prosperous times inequalities gradually arose, and the more prosperous share-holders began to absorb the less prosperous, the former would gradually become village landholders with

45

unrestricted power of transfer, while the less prosperous would sink into lower occupations or seek other professions. The village system would then merge into a zemindari system; for Campbell did not believe that it was possible in 'a more highly artificial state of civilisation' to maintain the village communities for ever. But his proposals were intended to avert what was 'in every way most undesirable, pernicious, and unfair' to the village communities, that is 'to facilitate their premature dismemberment by laws altogether inconsistent with their previous constitution and rights'.[12]

When it is recalled that in 1850 the Board of Administration qualified their determination to maintain the village communities by the phrase 'as far as possible', it is apparent that Campbell did not stand alone in his view that these communities could not go on unchanged for ever. In both instances the reasons were the same, the economic thinking of the time. In speaking of the attempt to provide proprietors in northern India with a margin of profit Campbell noted that the great object throughout had been the creation of a valuable and marketable proprietary right in the land, so that the revenue would be secure, and capital be obtainable for effecting improvements. The accumulation of capital, especially for investment in land, though it spelled ultimate doom for the corporate communities, was yet an object of which Campbell thoroughly approved. Indeed, he looked on village bankers as not the least useful of men, accumulating capital as they did, and providing the village communities with credit and other essential services. Their profits might be usurious at times, and the British might decry them, but it was after all the pursuit of self-interest which provided the right principles of political economy.[13]

While Campbell showed no less attachment to orthodox economic principles than the Board of Administration, he did produce a scheme which reconciled the pursuit of these principles with a long-term if not indefinite maintenance of corporate communities. The Board, in exercising restraint on the compulsory sale of land, and enforcing the right of pre-emption, had struck its own balance between ambivalent considerations; but without resolving the tensions inherent in any limited departure from fundamental principles.

It was, nevertheless, the Board's policy in regard to land transfer which was confirmed and extended when the Board itself was dissolved (1853), and John Lawrence assumed sole authority as Chief Commissioner.

The first important measure completed under the new dispensation was the Punjab Civil Code of 1854. It was prepared under the immediate direction of Robert Montgomery, one of John Lawrence's closest associates, who had served as junior Member of the Board, and was now Judicial Commissioner. Most of the work was undertaken by Richard Temple, a Settlement Officer, who in 1854 became the Chief Commissioner's new Secretary. As in the measures taken by the Board, the Code revealed the same conflict between social and political considerations, on the one hand, and economic considerations on the other.

The Civil Code indicated a concern with indigenous restrictions on transfer designed to protect the interests of heirs and relatives in ancestral land. Though Muslim law did not restrict transfer, it was thought that custom would prohibit capricious alienations. In regard to Hindus both law and custom were held to have this effect. Hence the courts could set aside unreasonable alienations (that is alienations made to spite heirs or relatives), if challenged by the aggrieved parties within the legal period. Whether these restrictions did or did not accord with political economy, it was observed in the commentary on these provisions, they were an integral part of society as then constituted. The courts were warned, however, that transfers which might facilitate the investment of capital, and which were made for really cogent reasons (even though without reference to the heirs) were to be maintained.[14]

The Code of 1854 also reiterated the rule of pre-emption in regard to permanent transfers of land. Once more the difficulty of defending the rule on economic grounds was admitted, and its desirability on social and political grounds urged. A special point was made on this occasion of its relevance to the sale of land for debt in execution of civil decrees. It was hoped that in this respect the rule would mitigate the hardships arising from a practice which it had been necessary to introduce, but which was not in general force before British rule. The decision to leave temporary transfers unfettered was justified not only in terms of enabling landowners to borrow from the money-lenders, but also to ensure the free circulation of money, and the investment of capital in land.[15]

A further step was taken in 1856 when John Lawrence extended the right of pre-emption to usufructuary mortgages.[16]

Hitherto British experience in the North-Western Provinces had been the major factor in the emergence of a protective policy. It was only gradually and imperceptibly that conditions in the Punjab began to influence this policy. Yet even at this early stage those conditions were not always uniform.

In the south-western Punjab the malfunctioning of the summary settlement in the Alipur tahsil of the Muzaffargarh district attracted the attention of the Financial Commissioner in the mid-fifties. The Deputy Commissioner of the district, when asked for a return of land transferred between 1850 and 1854, attributed the transfers (three-quarters of which were made to Hindu traders) to the severity of the land-revenue. The Financial Commissioner concurred in this analysis. He also expressed his surprise and concern at the number of transfers, and noted that nothing of the kind had occurred elsewhere in the Punjab.[17]

In broad terms this last statement was certainly true. Throughout most of the Punjab the voluntary transfer of land to Hindu traders was hardly apparent. Nevertheless, events in Alipur were only the first acute manifestation of the kind of situation which came to prevail throughout much of the south-west.

Compare Alipur, however, with much of the country round Ludhiana, held by Hindu or Sikh landholders. In the mid-fifties Ludhiana was one of the districts of the Cis-Sutlej Commissionership, and George Campbell was for some time Commissioner. The summary settlements in the Ludhiana district, which Campbell himself had fixed in earlier years, had not broken down despite difficulties. And Campbell recalled in his memoirs that the landholders had very rarely shown any inclination to part with their land. No, they had clung to it tenaciously; and if the opportunity ever arose there were always other landholders in the village ready to add to their fields.[18]

Whatever the regional or local variations in the voluntary transfer of land, they did not attract much attention at a time when transfers generally, let alone transfers to money-lenders, were rare in most of the Punjab. Under Sikh rule voluntary transfers, though not entirely unknown, had not been common, if some areas such as parts of the upper frontier be excluded from consideration.[19] Nor did the early days of British rule bring any fundamental change in this respect (though the summary settlements did result in sales and mortgages in some instances). In 1854 in two tahsils of the Amritsar and Gurdaspur districts it was found that three and six per cent of the area or cultivation had been mortgaged; but in several other tahsils of these districts less than one per cent was under mortgage.[20] Indebtedness was certainly apparent in various parts of the Punjab; but even in districts like Gujranwala and Umballa, where the transfer of land to money-lenders would reach notable proportions in future years, local officers did not appear to attach any particular significance to the indebtedness which existed. The comments of Settlement Officers on the state of indebtedness, the onerous terms on which money was borrowed, and the transfers which had occurred, were either incidental or designed to illustrate the effects, sometimes the unfortunate effects, of particular summary settlements. Where the heaviness of the summary settlement was responsible for indebtedness or land transfer, the reduction of the revenue demand might be proposed, not for this reason alone, but on general administrative grounds. Throughout the 1850s there was no widespread anxiety about agricultural indebtedness as such.[21]

Indeed, many years later Richard Temple (who had served in various local capacities before he became John Lawrence's Secretary in 1854) wrote in regard to the regular settlement operations in John Lawrence's time, that 'Sums began to be advanced' to the peasant proprietors by the money-lending classes 'on the new security afforded by the property in land' but he added 'the privilege was not abused, nor did any extensive indebtedness set in'.[22] This description might not be strictly accurate for every Punjab district; but the optimistic tone is consistent with contemporary evidence which yields no indications of special anxiety.

In one respect a qualification must be made. Agricultural indebtedness in itself may not have worried British officers unduly. Yet just as there was a desire to remove any oppressive aspect of the revenue system, so the bearing of indebtedness on the administration of justice was kept in mind. The Government's reluctance to sell land freely for debt through the civil courts was the most notable though by no means the only example. During the first half of the 1850s a number of the most senior officials, at any rate, were resolved that the courts should not be used by money-lenders to oppress the landholders.[23] In 1856 the period of limitation for debts on bonds and accounts was reduced from twelve to six years; a reduction which was undertaken, according to a later account, in order to reduce the scope and range of money-lenders' claims.[24] There are grounds, therefore, for believing that some senior administrators were concerned to remedy any undue or unscrupulous fostering of indebtedness through the courts.

Then in 1857 came the upheaval in Hindustan. To advocates of the protective policy, who had served in that part of India, the crisis threw a new light on conditions in the Punjab itself. A renewed stress on, and strengthening of the protective policy followed. There was a change of emphasis from protecting the village community from outsiders to protecting landowners from money-lenders. An urgent, political note was sounded, of a kind hitherto lacking.

The Chief Commissioner's review in September 1858 of the civil justice report for 1857 bore witness to the new state of things. Agricultural indebtedness in relation to the courts came to the fore once more. John Lawrence indicated that he shared the general opinion that the courts did not sufficiently protect ignorant agriculturists from unscrupulous money-lenders. He was hopeful that legal measures might remedy the growing evil. It was a significant comment on the economic thinking of the time (as well as on the conditions prevailing in the Punjab) that even now John Lawrence thought only in terms of measures which would not affect the agricultural credit which had developed during British rule. Agricultural credit was still seen as a great benefit to the landowners, thriftless though they might be. Nevertheless, when John Lawrence also proposed to place restrictions on the compulsory sale of land for debt, restrictions which would render such sales a comparatively rare and extreme measure, he was going far by contemporary standards.[25]

The restriction of the compulsory sale of land for debt was now quickly taken up. At the end of September 1858 Edward Thornton, the Judicial Commissioner, and one of John Lawrence's handpicked men, proposed that the compulsory sale, for debt, of ancestral and joint-acquired land be made subject in each instance to the sanction of the Judicial Commissioner.[26] This proposal, made with a view to placing greater obstacles in the way of compulsory alienations to village bankers, was accepted by John Lawrence, who like Thornton stopped short of absolute prohibition. In approaching the Government of India in October 1858 John Lawrence referred to events in Hindustan as something which rendered explanations of Indian attitudes to compulsory sales for debt superfluous. ('From the events of Hindoostan', runs a sentence in a report written about this time under Lawrence's direction 'it is evident that such sales foster hatred between classes who will tear each other to pieces directly the bonds of civil order are loosened.')[27] Compulsory sales for debt, Lawrence continued in his letter to the Government of India, were already rare in the Punjab, being dependent on the sanction of the Commissioner of the division, but it was proposed to make them still rarer.[28] Before the end of October the necessary orders were actually issued in the Punjab.[29] The Government of India accorded its approval early in 1859, suggesting that where a decree could not be executed by other measures, and sale of land was proposed, the debt might be discharged on some occasions by leasing the land on favourable terms.[30] Further instructions in regard to

## A POLITICAL DILEMMA EMERGES

other courses besides sale were issued by the Government of India later in the year.[31]

Measures to check agricultural indebtedness were undertaken by the Chief Commissioner in the belief that the landowners were the ignorant victims who, imposed upon by the money-lenders, the villains of the piece, would retaliate in a time of trouble. To place the borrower on a more equal footing with the lender, action was taken in regard to the registration of bonds and the keeping of proper account books, these measures being introduced in 1859. In an effort to reduce false claims in court, John Lawrence also proposed a reduction of the period of limitation for parole debts and debts on account, from six years to one year. Edward Thornton, the Judicial Commissioner, objected to a period of one year as likely to cause too great an injury to agricultural credit. The period of three years which he favoured was adopted in 1859.[32]

The crisis in northern India also brought the question of the sale of land for arrears of revenue into prominence. Such sales had not been particularly common in the Punjab. Yet in at least one district, that of Gujranwala, where the regular settlement proceedings had met with serious and concerted opposition, an appreciable area of land had been sold at the instance of the Settlement Officer. These transfers were comparable to sales of land for arrears of revenue, though not conducted in the regular manner. Nevertheless, they appear to have been approved by the superior officers who considered them. Then in 1858, about two years after the submission of the settlement report (which recommended the rigid enforcement of all revenue penalties against defaulters), Robert Cust was appointed Commissioner of the Lahore division. He took up the matter of the irregular transfers in Gujranwala, with the result that both the Financial Commissioner and the Chief Commissioner decided that they must be cancelled.[33]

The attitudes of the time to sales for arrears of revenue are reflected in certain contemporary documents which also shed light on the way the voluntary transfer of land was now viewed by some of the highest authorities in the Punjab.

That Robert Cust had been duly impressed by his experience in the North-Western Provinces (he had served there for several years after 1852), and by the fate of auction-purchasers there, is apparent from a letter written in May 1858, in which he strongly objected to the compulsory sale of land of village communities for arrears of revenue. Cust had taken charge of the Lahore division only recently, but in the same letter he apprehended that there was a tendency on the part of landowners to alienate their land voluntarily. There is no indication that he saw this as the beginning of a long-term process. Rather, he wrote in terms of landowners who were flinging away a newly acquired privilege before they appreciated its value. In his view this was one reason why the new settlements required careful watching.[34]

The Financial Commissioner to whom Cust had addressed this letter was Donald McLeod, one of John Lawrence's close friends and nominees. In September 1858 a circular was issued by the Financial Commissioner, addressed to all Commissioners, on the subject of unauthorised transfers during or after assessment. Cust's views on the subject, it was indicated, should be impressed on every revenue officer. The subject of the voluntary transfer of land was also taken up. This time there was no suggestion that the landowners were unaware of the value of their property. Instead it was noted that even voluntary transfers might be made in order to pay an oppressive revenue demand. If land was sold and mortgaged for inadequate sums that would afford the strongest grounds for such a view. Hence even voluntary transfers effected by the parties among themselves should not always be permitted to pass unquestioned.[35]

These views found an echo, at about this time, in the administration report for the years 1856 to 1858, prepared by Richard Temple under the direction of John Lawrence. Sales of land for arrears of revenue would be confined within the narrowest possible limits. Even private alienations of land would be jealously watched. But once again there was no concept of the voluntary transfer of land being harmful except in connection with some special disturbing element.

> By all means let land fetch its value in the market, and let people sell and buy it if it be their interest to do so. But experience shows that such transactions are not frequent when people are prosperous; whenever they are frequent, we may suspect that there is either some distress capable of remedy, or some pressure of the revenue, or some sinister influence at work.

And the report went on to mention the unusual number of transfers in Muzuffargarh, and the irregular transfers in Gujranwala, noting that the assessment was too high in both districts.[36]

This was as far as the protective policy would ever go. In regard to the restriction of the compulsory sale of land for arrears of revenue it went quite far, much having been done already on this head in the North-Western Provinces. The restrictions which were imposed in 1858 on the compulsory sale of land by the civil courts would ensure the almost complete prohibition of such sales, this being perhaps the greatest departure from the established practice of other Provinces, and representing a trend to which the crisis of 1857 made a distinct contribution. But the only prescriptions for the voluntary alienation of land were the right of pre-emption (an attempt being made to ensure stricter enforcement than in the North-Western Provinces by the provision of machinery for fixing prices), the restrictions of custom or law that the courts might impose in individual instances, and finally a stress on executive vigilance which reflected the events of 1857. Economic considerations were set aside to some extent, but not without deference; the need for agricultural credit appeared to be unquestionable. The restrictions imposed on voluntary transfers fell far short of those which George Campbell would have liked to introduce. Doubtless it was difficult to fetter the rights of property at a time when it appeared that these rights were just being created by the land-revenue settlements. At any rate these were the political and intellectual fruits of many years of experience in northern India, including the events of 1857, supplemented in a very general sense by an acquaintance with conditions in the Punjab. And this was not the only, though undoubtedly the most influential current of opinion.[37]

II

From the very beginning of British rule in the Punjab there were officers who did not favour a protective policy, or whose views at any rate diverged, either sharply or by degrees, from those which shaped official policy. That a number of these men had served as civilians in the North-Western Provinces need occasion no surprise. No more than in the Punjab in later years did experience in northern India produce uniform views.

In 1850 in opposing the absolute prohibition of sub-leases of the revenue George Edmonstone, an old civilian from the North-West and now the officiating Commissioner of the Cis-Sutlej States, argued that as long as the British recognised a right of property, they could not and should not interfere with it. This theoretical view of the inviolability of property rights, also held by one of the Settlement Officers in Edmonstone's division, went just a little too far for the Board of Administration.[38]

Richard Temple, who had served for a short period in the North-Western Provinces under Edward Thornton, did not take such an extreme view as this. In the Punjab, Temple, as Secretary to the Chief Commissioner and otherwise, was closely associated with the expression of the protective policy throughout much of the 1850s. On a number of points this policy may well have coincided with his personal views. But as Settlement Officer of Jullunder he wrote in 1851 about the transfer of land to Khatris, the Hindu traders of his district, in a way which indicates that he felt no anxiety whatever on this score.

> They [the Khutrees] are sure to thrive and multiply under British rule; as yet they possess but little land, and that little they have acquired by sale, mortgage, and such like transactions. The increasing landed occupancy of this class has proved an interesting subject of statistical comparison in the North-Western Provinces; many years hence it will be instructive to note whether Khutree proprietorship has or has not increased in this doab.[39]

Richard Temple's successor as Secretary to Government in 1859 was Henry Davies, who had served somewhat longer in the North-Western Provinces. As Settlement Officer in Gurdaspur Davies noted in 1854 that idle, extravagant and pauper communities would not or could not pay a fair revenue. The 'prejudice' which existed in maintaining the peasant proprietors found in occupancy, was one reason why the Government was unable to demand what the land would yield under average cultivation. Though Davies accepted this 'prejudice' as a fact of life, the use of this word (together with his view that mortgages in Gurdaspur were a proof not only of the necessities of the proprietors but also of the mobility and value of the land) hints at the early views of a man who would play a crucial role as Lieutenant-Governor many years later.[40]

Another Settlement Officer, Edward Brandreth (Arthur Brandreth's cousin) saw the power to transfer land in a distinctly favourable light. He observed in 1855 that the proprietor's right to sell or mortgage his land, denied to the non-proprietary cultivator, might appear at first sight to be more a nominal than a real distinction. But the proprietor's right to dispose of his land if he wished to quit the village or for any other reason was sometimes a great advantage to him. It would be more and more valued, he thought, as the rights of landowners were better understood.[41]

Opinions which were adverse to, or not fully in accord with, the protective policy were expressed in the very shadow of the upheaval of 1857. One of the officers responsible had not served outside the Punjab, while the other had been drawn from the army.

## A POLITICAL DILEMMA EMERGES

Philip Sandys Melvill, who had joined the civil service in 1846, had been in the Punjab from before annexation, serving as one of the Assistants to the Resident. Afterwards he completed the regular settlements of two districts in the eastern Punjab, one in 1852 and that of northern Umballa in 1855. In his reports on these settlements he attached no particular significance to existing indebtedness and land transfer, except in so far as they had some bearing on the assessments. He did note in 1855 that as one of the advantages of a reasonable settlement was the creation of a marketable value in land it was desirable to fix the proprietor's demands on the cultivator at such a rate as would offer an inducement to the purchase of land.[42] Then in 1858 he returned to the Umballa district as Deputy Commissioner. By this time land was changing hands rapidly in a tract in one of the northern tahsils. Melvill, after a careful enquiry, decided that the deadly climate from which the tract suffered rendered it inevitable that the village tenures would disappear. In these circumstances the quicker the villages were bought up by capitalists the better. The Government would then have some security for its revenue, while the villagers would be no worse off. Melvill felt so strongly about this that he did not even recommend a reduction of assessment, though he now believed he had assessed the tract rather heavily and in some instances had been far too high. Reductions in revenue would do no good to the villagers. Speculative purchasers, on the other hand, must take the risk of loss; a risk which might lead them to exert themselves to improve the condition of the tract.[43]

The circumstances were, of course, local and exceptional, and Melvill's view of administrative and economic advantage was conditioned by that fact. Yet it is difficult to believe that an advocate of the protective policy could have argued along these lines in 1858 of all times. The Commissioner accepted Melvill's recommendations with some hesitation, though finally it was decided to let events take their course.

It was a military civilian, however, who made what was until then the most direct and uncompromising attack on the protective policy. As Settlement Officer of Gujrat, Hector Mackenzie recorded his opinion in a report made early in 1859, that it was in the interests of justice and policy alike to demand a modification of that part of the rule of pre-emption which compelled an intending vendor to dispose of his land to one of the community at a fair price, even though he should have received larger offers from outsiders. The rule should be effective only where a member of the community offered a price

55

equal to or higher than that offered by any one else. Mackenzie was influenced by the nature of landed society in the district, and more particularly by economic propositions which he believed to be universal in their application. The rule might be considered just, Mackenzie wrote, if the people looked on the land as something held in partnership. But in Gujrat, whatever the situation elsewhere, neither the circumstances of the past, nor the present views of the people, supported the partnership view of the matter. Besides being unjust, the rule destroyed part of the value of the property which the British had tried to create. Mackenzie predicted that sales, hitherto as good as unknown, would become more frequent every day, now that the land had become valuable. The rule of pre-emption might be expedient. But the 'little republics' were the result of a despotic and arbitrary Government and, like George Campbell before him, he thought that they might naturally, perhaps inevitably, break up under enlightened laws and the spirit of improvement. The day would come when village settlements would no longer be expedient, when land would be minutely divided again, and when the land-revenue system would change as well. It was better to face that day boldly, than attempt to fight against destiny by elevating expediency over the operation of inexorable laws.[44]

While Mackenzie would not be heard from again, his point of view would never lack supporters. The stress which those of his way of thinking placed on economic considerations did not permit the qualifications which the advocates of a protective policy were prepared to champion (though even Mackenzie, rhetoric apart, did not really recommend the total abolition of pre-emption). Moreover, officers like Edward Brandreth, Philip Sandys Melvill and Hector Mackenzie looked forward confidently to the day when voluntary transfers would be common; a confidence which those in favour of a protective policy did not always share, or not to the same extent. The views which Melvill and Mackenzie expressed in 1858 and 1859, the views which Edward Brandreth and others would express not long thereafter, suggest that this faith in the orthodox economic thinking of the time was not to be shaken, or not decisively, by revolt and disorder on a large scale.

III

Though John Lawrence left the Punjab in February 1859, the key posts in the Province remained for long in the hands of his closest associates and nominees. Robert Montgomery returned from Oudh, where he had served briefly as Chief Commissioner, to take up the Lieutenant-Governorship of the Punjab. He was succeeded in 1865 by Donald McLeod, who had been Financial Commissioner until then, and who remained Lieutenant-Governor for more than five years. The Judicial Commissionership was retained by Edward Thornton until his retirement in the early 1860s. His successor Robert Cust, though of a later generation, had risen rapidly, and had already officiated as Financial Commissioner. All these men were civilians with extensive experience in the North-Western Provinces. Every one of them had been associated with one or other aspect of the protective policy in regard to land. The first deviation from this general pattern came in 1865 when Edward Lake, a military civilian who had not served in the North-Western Provinces, and who had little regard for the protective policy, became Financial Commissioner.

As Commissioner of the Jullunder division Lake had voiced his opposition to the new restriction on the compulsory sale of land for debt as early as April 1859. Part of his opposition stemmed from what he believed to be the contradiction between the discouragement of the compulsory sale of landed property and the encouragement given to the rapid enforcement of decrees of court. The period of payment of a decree by instalments was limited at this time to two years, and Lake suggested that this period be extended to six years in certain cases. Lake also had more fundamental objections to the new restrictions on the compulsory sale of landed property for debt. He saw these restrictions as no more than delaying tactics, involving much extra work, as well as the harassment of the creditor, and resulting in no benefit to the debtor where there were *bona fide* grounds for sale. Lake was not opposed to restriction in all forms. He would have preferred the prohibition of the compulsory sale of real property except in liquidation of registered bonds, or in other exceptional cases, where a just demand was obstinately withheld. Together with this he favoured a legalisation of temporary transfers of land in satisfaction of decrees.[45]

Edward Thornton, the Judicial Commissioner who had devised the new rule in regard to the compulsory sale of land, defended it against Lake's attack. His reply to Lake in June 1859 gave some indication of the manner in which the new rule was being worked. In the previous year, Thornton observed at one point, there had been ninety-three compulsory sales of land in the Punjab, more than a third of them in Lake's division, and most of these in one particular district, that of Hoshiarpur. Since the new rule had been introduced, eight months ago, only four Commissioners apart from Lake had applied for sales, and then for no more than five sales altogether. Yet Lake alone had applied for ten sales, all of them in Hoshiarpur. Thornton questioned whether any evil was apparent as a result of the general discouragement of compulsory sale, and hence whether the sales in Lake's division were really necessary. In considering these cases, Thornton noted, he would be strongly inclined to avoid sale, and to act on the injunctions of the Governor-General, who desired the substitution of temporary transfers for absolute sales of land.[46]

The rule regarding the compulsory sale of land for debt appears to have been worked in much the same way by Robert Cust, Thornton's successor as Judicial Commissioner. Indeed in May 1862, according to one account, Cust made it clear that his views were fundamentally fixed and that he would never sanction the compulsory sale of hereditary land under any circumstances whatever. Cust's policy had come under fire from Herbert Edwardes, a distinguished military civilian whose civil experience, though confined to the Punjab, dated from the days before annexation. Edwardes, who was at this time Commissioner of the Cis-Sutlej States, wanted to do away with the rule requiring the Judicial Commissioner's sanction to compulsory sales. It appears that one of his objections was to the discretion which successive Judicial Commissioners had in applying the rule, and that he would have preferred compulsory sales to be either legal or not legal.[47]

At Edwardes' request his correspondence with Cust was brought to the attention of the Lieutenant-Governor in June 1862. Robert Montgomery supported Cust, agreeing that it was not desirable to make any new rules on the subject of compulsory sales. In the Government despatch conveying this information to the Judicial Commissioner, Montgomery's decision was justified in terms of a note prepared for him in the Secretariat. This note suggested the more fundamental reasons for Edwardes' opposition and indicated the characteristic defence of the advocates of the protective policy. The decision to maintain existing arrangements, the despatch noted, did not imply any dissent, in the abstract, from the principles advocated by the Commissioner. It merely meant that in present circumstances, political, mercantile and social, these principles would not be enforced except under checks proved to be salutary.[48]

The argument, then, turned on the question of the degree to which, and the manner in which, the orthodox economic principles of the time might be qualified with reference to particular circumstances.

That the area of disagreement between those who took opposing views in this respect, might be quite narrow, is apparent from the view which Cust himself took of compulsory sales for debt in the semi-official Revenue Manual of 1866, first drafted in 1863. Cust was aware of the mischief caused by the civil courts in the North-Western Provinces. As a strong supporter of the policy of not selling land for arrears of revenue, he did not see why the Government should accept the odium of selling land in the creditor's interests when it was not prepared to sell the land in its own interests. Such sales had not been known under native rule, and they were not understood by the people. Nevertheless, Cust was not insensible to the abstract consideration that the compulsory sale of property was the natural and just result of definite property in land. He noted that the restriction on the compulsory sale of land by the civil courts could not be justified in terms of political economy, and thought that this restriction doubtless reduced the value of land, raised the rate of interest, and retarded the improvement of the soil. In spite of this he considered that this restriction was a move in the right direction; but he did not dismiss the possibility of its relaxation in future.[49]

Whereas Robert Cust was ready to set economic considerations aside, at least for some time, Herbert Edwardes chafed under all restrictions on orthodox principles. Of all the restrictions on land transfer introduced by the Government, Cust felt least compunction in regard to the restrictions on the compulsory sale of land for arrears of revenue. Yet Edwardes' ready agreement with certain remarks made by one of his district officers, another military civilian, in 1864, shows that even here he disagreed. Captain Tighe was in charge of the Umballa district, a district not noted for the energy of its landholders, and one in which the settlement of the land-revenue had proved peculiarly difficult. No further encouragement, Tighe recommended, should be given to the idleness of the Thanesur landholders, in the south of the district, whose demoralisation continued despite the good and lightly assessed land lying waste around them. Tighe's solution to the problem, peremptory sale in all cases of balance of revenue, and his desire to see the existing owners thus displaced by better ones, ran directly counter to the official policies of the Province, if only on a local scale.[50]

Though officers like Herbert Edwardes could not or were not likely to challenge successfully the almost complete prohibition of the sale of land in execution of decree, or the limited use made of the power of sale for arrears of revenue, they had more success in regard to the voluntary transfer of land.

In the wake of the revolt of 1857, it will be recalled, it had been resolved to watch even voluntary alienations of land closely. Something of the kind was done in at least a few parts of the Province in 1860–1, a famine year in which an increase in the number of voluntary transfers was recorded in several divisions.

The Commissioner of the Hissar division, James Naesmyth, a civilian of some fourteen years' standing, both now and in succeeding years showed considerable interest in the proportion of transfers to landholders and money-lenders respectively. Naesmyth's division was one of the most insecure in the Province; and though he realised that in time of famine the money-lenders would necessarily press the landholders, he believed that the latter should be protected as far as possible from undue pressure, and should be discouraged from recklessly parting with their land. He had always opposed permanent transfers to strangers as much as possible, he observed in 1861.[51]

Yet in the Cis-Sutlej division, where voluntary transfers had increased as well, another civilian Commissioner was not certain that the discouragement of voluntary sales by the Deputy Commissioner of Thanesur, and the latter's attempts to commute them to mortgages, had been altogether politic. Edward Brandreth, the officiating Commissioner in 1861, thought it better that a man who could not derive an adequate profit from his land should resign it and seek his livelihood elsewhere, particularly in view of the evils of minute sub-division which resulted from the law of inheritance.[52] The opposition of Herbert Edwardes, Brandreth's successor as Commissioner, to the policy of checking private transfers in famine times was based on economic grounds too. Edwardes agreed with the military officer in charge of Umballa who, in criticising this policy in 1862, indicated that the value of land was much increased by its availability as security in time of need.[53]

In assessing the views of a military civilian like Herbert Edwardes, who disagreed so vigorously with so many aspects of the protective policy, it is well to remember that he had not served in the North-Western Provinces. He had no personal experience, therefore, of the situation created by the unrestricted transfer of land in execution of civil decrees or for arrears of revenue. In this respect the revolt of 1857 which heightened the anxieties of a number of civilians from the North-West probably would not have meant as much to Edwardes. Of the voluntary alienation of land Edwardes had some experience as Assistant to the Resident in the days before annexation, when he was troubled by the large areas of land under mortgage in

Bannu and neighbouring parts of the frontier. At that time he had encouraged measures to secure the redemption of this land. But of course those transfers had occurred under an indigenous rule, and had been facilitated by a local law of mortgage which Edwardes considered unjust.[54] Under British administration Edwardes, who had no personal experience of its long-term trends, could give full sway to abstract considerations which appeared to be unquestionable.

In any case even before Edwardes declared his opinion on checking voluntary alienations in famine times the Lieutenant-Governor, who was otherwise a supporter of a protective policy, ranged himself on the opposing side. In August 1861 Robert Montgomery expressed his entire agreement with Brandreth's remarks as to the inexpediency of official interference for the restriction of *bona fide* voluntary transfers.[55]

Nor does it appear that Montgomery stood alone even among those senior officers who supported a protective policy in other respects. In the revenue reports for 1860-1 and 1861-2 Donald McLeod, the Financial Commissioner, made no adverse comments whatever on the voluntary alienations of land which had occurred.[56] As Lieutenant-Governor, McLeod later revealed the ambivalent attitude towards voluntary transfers typical of the prominent advocates of a protective policy. Reviewing the settlement report of the Shahpur district in August 1867, it struck McLeod as most encouraging and hopeful that a certain amount of land in the district had been redeemed from mortgage. And yet like Edward Brandreth he saw the law of inheritance with its excessive subdivision of land as an evil. The most salutary solution to this problem, he indicated in the same review, lay in encouraging the more prosperous landholders to buy out their poorer brethren, who would seek other employment.[57] In the first instance McLeod presumably conceived of voluntary transfers as due to distress, in the second he saw them as a desirable solvent for the economic problems of society.

A similar ambivalence is apparent in the views of Robert Cust. In June 1860 Cust, officiating as Financial Commissioner, remarked in the annual revenue report that he was not certain that the machinery for recording transfers of a voluntary, or ordinary nature, was in every district quite correct. He proposed to regulate the powers of the various officers in this matter. Obviously it was a waste of the district officer's time to trouble him with ordinary transfers which occurred by the consent of the parties, or from the hand of God. Still, cases of a complicated kind did occur; and it was the acknowledged practice of the Punjab, Cust noted, that transfers of land to outsiders (that is the entry in the revenue records of such transfers) required the confirmation of the Commissioner.[58]

This practice, which derived from the right of pre-emption, was reaffirmed in a Financial Commissioner's circular issued in October 1860, while Cust was still Financial Commissioner. (In addition to rules on the subject of recording transfers of land, the circular also contained a warning that if the landowners were driven to sell or mortgage by the pressure of the revenue, the matter must be immediately investigated, and the assessment reduced.)[59]

While this circular found a place in Cust's Revenue Manual, published in 1866, Cust did add on this occasion that perhaps the requirement for the Commissioner's sanction to mutations of names in favour of strangers might be withdrawn. Cust also approved of an amendment, made in 1863, in the working of the right of pre-emption. This amendment was designed to overcome the difficulty, which Hector Mackenzie had represented, of vendors of land being forced to sell at prices lower than those which had induced them to agree to sell. Only where the price offered by a stranger was a fictitious and fraudulent one, Cust pointed out, should the assessors be allowed to fix a lower price in lieu of it. Where a stranger made a genuine offer it was the Collector's duty to overrule any attempt by the assessors to fix a lower price for pre-emptors. This would enable the owner to obtain the legitimate value of his land, according to the law of supply and demand.[60]

Cust still defended the right of pre-emption in the familiar manner, not on economic but on social and political grounds. His inability to reconcile the right with the law of political economy, however, caused him much heart-searching. The consideration that the power to alienate land was the natural incident of property came home most strongly in regard to restrictions on voluntary alienations. Such restrictions depreciated the value of land, they checked the flow of capital to the land, and kept parties in possession of the soil who were unfit for the duties imposed by property, and who in ordinary circumstances would have been swept out of sight. What use then was this 'propping up of an antique, and perhaps falling fabric'? The answer was that if the village communities would melt away and give place to a more modern distribution of property, so much the better; but the measure could not be forced. While the disappearance of a system based on village communities was not unwelcome or unexpected, it was not an immediate prospect. But the discouragement of voluntary transfers was to Cust a measure of a more distinctly temporary character, lasting only as long as owners did not appreciate the value of their land. The right of pre-emption could not be allowed to go on too long or be pressed too far. At one point Cust even listed undue restraints on voluntary transfers as one of the errors, one of the remediable errors, made in the Punjab.[61]

During the second decade of British rule, then, the most prominent supporters of a protective policy did no more than maintain the *status quo* in regard to the voluntary transfer of land. On this head there were no developments comparable to those which took place in the matter of regulating the compulsory sale of land for debt.

From the very beginning, of course, the apprehensions which the most senior officers had expressed about voluntary alienations had been qualified, and the protection which they had been prepared to extend to landholders in this respect had been limited. This was true even in 1858, when official anxieties were generally at their height. Thereafter even partial misgivings regarding voluntary alienations grew less acute among the most senior officers, and no further interference with such alienations was countenanced.

In assigning reasons for this state of affairs, it is necessary to recollect how far the advocates of a protective policy had gone already, by the standards of the time, in such a matter as the right of pre-emption. Their refusal to attempt any justification of such a policy on economic grounds is one illustration of this situation. The fundamental criticism of the law of pre-emption by their opponents is another.

Hector Mackenzie's insistence in this context that there could be no escape from universal and inexorable laws, has been noticed already. Later critics, while approaching this issue from a similar angle, took a different and revealing tactical line.

It was the obsolescence of the rule of pre-emption rather than its total futility which Douglas Forsyth, the Commissioner of the Jullunder division, urged in his revenue report for 1866–7. The rule that land in a village could not be sold to a stranger without the sanction of the authorities, might have been very necessary in the early days of British rule, wrote Forsyth, whose service as a Punjab civilian dated from the annexation of the Province. At that time land had little value in the eyes of the people who, being only too glad to escape the burden of the land-tax, had been ready to part with their property without considering the consequences. In the early days too, Forsyth claimed, it was feared that capitalists from the older provinces might come in and, taking advantage of the ignorance and fears of the people, buy up land and so break up the village system. But whatever the situation then, things had changed;

for the people had become very much aware of the value of their landed property. Besides, Forsyth doubted the district officer's legal power to prevent a purchaser from taking possession, so that it was only a waste of time to ask the Commissioner for a sanction which he could not withhold. Forsyth also referred to a letter on the subject written by Edward Lake, as Financial Commissioner, from which he gathered that Lake was in favour of abolishing this rule as obsolete.[62]

Like Mackenzie and Cust, Forsyth objected to the depreciation in the value of land which he believed resulted from the right of pre-emption. He complained that in its first and most extreme form the rule of pre-emption had obliged a vendor to dispose of his land to a pre-emptor at a price fixed by valuation, even though the vendor had been tempted to sell only by a much larger offer. Even now the rule was that if the pre-emptor agreed to pay the full price offered, the seller could not withdraw from the sale. This caused great hardship and made the transfer of land a difficult business. Forsyth instanced the difficulties which certain European tea-planters in Kangra might experience in their attempt to raise capital by selling a share of their land to another European, if this transaction were challenged by pre-emptors.

Forsyth also cited the objections of the people to the effect that the law of pre-emption had all but put a stop to the sale of land, an evil of great magnitude in the eyes of those who desired to see all restrictions on the employment of capital and the extension of trade swept away. He admitted, however, that there were others who considered the natives of India as still in a state of pupilage. At one point he even conceded that the law of pre-emption might be considered useful perhaps when exercised to a moderate extent. These verbal ambiguities suggest that Forsyth was not quite clear in his own mind about his attitude to the law of pre-emption.

In 1869 Captain Tighe, the Deputy Commissioner of Umballa, who a number of years before had recommended peremptory sale of land for arrears of revenue in Thanesur, criticised the law of pre-emption in much the same way as Forsyth had done. As laid down in the Punjab, Tighe thought, the law of pre-emption was a serious obstacle to the acquisition of land, besides interfering with the rights of property. In his opinion the law was no longer applicable to the improved state of the country. He gave instances of the evil effects of the law of pre-emption, and recommended that property which had once passed into strange hands should not be subject again to pre-emption claims. Also that purchase of land should not

## A POLITICAL DILEMMA EMERGES

bring with it the rights of pre-emption enjoyed by the seller, unless seller and purchaser were descended from a common ancestor whose property it previously was (presumably because otherwise a stranger who once bought into a village would be able to claim the right of pre-emption as if he were himself a hereditary landholder in the village).[63]

The tendency of Lake, Forsyth and Tighe to treat the right of pre-emption not merely as something which was wrong, but as something out of date, provides an index to the great changes which had occurred during the second decade of British rule. The annual revenue reports from 1859–60 bear witness to the steadily increasing value of land throughout the Province. This process rendered the protective attitude towards voluntary transfers of land less and less relevant. That attitude was based on the assumption that voluntary transfers were unhealthy because they occurred under some special kind of pressure, notably that of an excessive revenue-demand, or through the initial ignorance of the landowners about the nature and value of property. The constant increase in the value of land could serve only to weaken these apprehensions. If people no longer sold land for a song, then clearly they were aware of its value. If land fetched a steadily increasing price, then the revenue-demand could not be oppressive. Thus the very basis of the protective attitude towards voluntary transfers disappeared. It is not surprising that a policy which could be justified only by setting aside received economic doctrines, did not develop further when the conditions which had appeared to demand it had ceased to exist.

It is possible to go further. The local revenue reports of the 1860s show that Commissioners and Deputy Commissioners took great pains to ascertain the value of land each year, statistics of alienation providing an obvious source of information in this respect. This was, of course, a matter on which they were obliged to report. Nevertheless, the fact that few did much more than comment on the value of land, year after year, indicates that to many this was the really vital point. While voluntary transfers were becoming an established feature of rural life, administrators focused their attention on one aspect, the price which this land fetched in the market. To them an increase in price was a hopeful sign. It meant the days of excessive revenue-demands were passing, it implied a secure revenue and a prosperous economy, and it fitted neatly into the general anticipation of progress and improvement which marked Victorian thinking.[64]

Nor was there, until the end of the 1860s, any indication of local circumstances which might throw doubt on the assumption that all was well. The settlement reports of the 1850s, some of which were reviewed early in the succeeding decade, spoke of conditions which might appear to be on the mend; and in any case they contained nothing alarming. Fewer settlement reports were completed in the 1860s. Their references to land transfer and indebtedness, where they mentioned the subject at all, were brief. Neither in the settlement nor in the revenue reports of most of the decade does one sense that intimate connection between indebtedness and land alienation which pervaded official thinking in later years. The most that can be said is that a few officers, notably Arthur Brandreth, found existing indebtedness distasteful.[65]

The first twenty years of British rule in fact mark a distinct stage in the history of official attitudes to land transfer in the Punjab. One distinguishing feature of this period, as compared to that which succeeded it, is that there was general agreement on fundamental matters. It would be difficult to find parties more widely separated in their opinions than George Campbell, whose schemes for the restriction of alienation went beyond those officially sanctioned; Robert Cust, who was associated with the policy of the time; and Hector Mackenzie and Herbert Edwardes, who attacked that policy. Yet in the abstract Campbell and Cust had as profound a respect for the laws of political economy as did Mackenzie and Edwardes. Given a difference of emphasis, no one questioned the universality of these laws. That land should be valuable, and agricultural credit good, were not matters for dispute. Nor was it Mackenzie alone who looked to the day, distant though it might be, when the village communities would disappear. That was a prospect which Campbell and Cust had taken into account as well. Improvement, reform and progress was the order of the day; and they were championed by all alike. The notion that Western civilisation should rejuvenate India materially as well as morally was held with equal fervour by Campbell, Cust and Edwardes.[66] It was this disposition to look to the West as the ultimate source of wisdom and experience which provided the fundamental unity underlying official attitudes to land transfer in this period.

Within this framework disagreements arose about the degree to which accepted doctrines might be qualified, or their application temporarily suspended, with reference to particular circumstances. Those who derived part of their attitude from political economy, and part from practical experience, undoubtedly placed themselves in an ambiguous position. Intellectually they were unable to deny

## A POLITICAL DILEMMA EMERGES

the validity of political economy; as administrators they were unable to deny the evidence of their eyes. All those who introduced and supported the protective policy had observed the long-term effects of British rule in the North-Western Provinces; though not every officer from these Provinces agreed with that policy. Conversely some of the most fundamental attacks on the protective policy came from officers who had little or no experience of this part of India, whether civilians like Melvill and Forsyth, or military civilians like Lake and Edwardes.[67]

Yet ultimately the question of whether a particular officer had or had not served in the North-West was not a decisive factor. No drastic restriction of voluntary transfers had been implemented as part of the protective policy; and in the 1860s the rising value of land in the Punjab made such a prospect more and more unlikely. On the other hand, the restrictions on alienation which had been introduced into the Punjab, under the influence of circumstances prevailing in the North-West, tended to perpetuate themselves. A number of those who attacked these restrictions on the most doctrinaire grounds nevertheless did not insist on more than the removal of features which had proved objectionable in practice. For all their fulminations against the right of pre-emption Mackenzie, Forsyth and Tighe did not demand its total abolition; though Lake may have felt that way. In the very act of challenging the restrictions imposed on the compulsory sale of land by the civil courts, Lake and Edwardes were led to propose alternative schemes of restriction. Nor was this mutual, if partial, coming together of opinion limited to a few officers. A debate which took place in 1869–70, on the subject of the restriction of the compulsory sale of land by the courts, shows clearly the extent to which the process had gone.

IV

In 1866 there occurred two changes which necessitated a formal adjustment of the system of restricting the compulsory sale of land for debt. The Judicial Commissioner, who had to sanction such alienations in the case of hereditary or joint-acquired land, was replaced by the Chief Court. And the Code of Civil Procedure, which asserted that all property was liable to attachment and sale in execution of a civil decree, was extended to the Punjab. Sections 243 and 244 of the Code enabled the civil court or district officer to avert the compulsory sale of land when the money due could be raised from the land in other ways. But these provisions, designed to ensure that land was not sold unnecessarily, were much less stringent than the protective system developed in the Punjab.

These difficulties were met by the Government Notification of September 1866, in which it was provided that the sale of hereditary or joint-acquired land in execution of decree could not take place without the sanction of the Chief Court. In the ensuing year the Financial Commissioner, at the request of the Chief Court, issued instructions to Deputy Commissioners, directing that before they applied for sanction to sell ancestral or joint-acquired land, they should satisfy themselves that there was no objection to the sale. Where any objection did appear, they should try to effect a temporary alienation of the land, or make some other arrangement that would satisfy the parties and avoid the sale. Early in 1868 the Chief Court issued detailed instructions, based on the Code of Civil Procedure, regarding the procedure to be observed in applying for sanction, and in conducting the sale of land in execution of decree. So far, then, the transition appeared to have been made smoothly enough.[68]

Yet these changes had not removed an old objection to the system, that of the unregulated nature of the discretion which the superior judicial authority exercised. This time that objection was raised by the Chief Court. In its letter of May 1869 to the Punjab Government the view was taken that since no principles had been laid down to guide the Court in the exercise of its discretion, it really possessed no greater powers than those conferred by the Code of Civil Procedure. To rectify what they considered to be an undesirable situation the Judges, Charles Boulnois and David Simson, expressed their preference for legislation which would provide a substantial check on the sale of land in execution of decree.[69]

The Judges were in close, if not entire agreement. Both spoke of the need to protect the village communities. Simson, a civilian with almost a quarter of a century's experience, referred to the evils which had arisen in the North-Western Provinces from the sale of land in execution of decree. All this might appear to be in the tradition of the protective policy; and to a certain extent it was. But there was this difference, that both the Judges wanted a more precise and definite restriction of the sale of land. Boulnois, a barrister who had joined the Court in 1866, four years after his arrival in India, harked back to Lake's suggestion of prohibiting the sale of land in execution of decree, unless the land was mortgaged to the decree-holder. While Simson did not altogether reject the utility of such a restriction, he desired complete prohibition.

## A POLITICAL DILEMMA EMERGES

This request for complete prohibition was accompanied by a distinct difference in attitude to that which the early advocates of a protective policy had held. The latter had not argued their case on economic grounds, and they had striven for protective measures which would not affect agricultural credit. Simson, writing no doubt in circumstances already very different, went much further in this respect. Indian society was not English society; and however objectionable any interference with freedom of contract might be in England, the complete prohibition of sale of land in execution of decree, in so far as it restricted agricultural credit, would be beneficial rather than injurious. That the limitation of credit would be great, Simson did not believe. Compulsory sales of land had been unknown under indigenous rule, and yet (he argued somewhat doubtfully) the landholders had as little difficulty in obtaining money as at present. Any limitation of credit that did ensue would be beneficial, perhaps imposing some check on the reckless and unnecessary expenditure on marriages and the like. If the restriction of credit made it impossible for landowners to pay an excessive revenue-demand, the reduction of that demand was a duty which Government fully recognised. Nor did the argument that a restriction of credit would prevent the landholder from improving his estate stand up to scrutiny. Such improvement was not general; the mortgage of the improved land would in any case satisfy a debt for such a purpose; and besides Government provided advances for such improvements.

Towards the end of May 1869 the Punjab Government, with Donald McLeod at its head, forwarded the correspondence to the Financial Commissioner who, in addition to being asked to give his own opinion, was requested to obtain the opinion of Commissioners on the proposal made by Boulnois.[70] The Financial Commissioner replied in November, having collected the opinions of eight Commissioners, as well as those of a few comparatively junior officers.[71]

At first glance these opinions might seem to justify a remark which Simson had made, namely that on no question did the ablest of judicial officers vary more completely, their opinions ranging between the entire prohibition of compulsory sales and the absence of any restriction on them. It would be well to remember, however, that the sale of land in execution of decree had not been frequent in the Punjab; and that there were safeguards in the Code of Civil Procedure. The opinions of the officers consulted varied widely enough, but the essential difference lay between those who wanted extra restrictions, and those who thought that nothing further need be done. Five British officers agreed on the complete prohibition of the sale of ancestral land in execution of decree; two others wanted to confine the restriction to land which had not been mortgaged. But among the British officers who opposed further action there was only one, Alexander Benton, a civilian who had joined less than six years before, who ventured to think that almost no restrictions should be placed on compulsory sales of land.[72] Of the six British officers who, like him, took a negative view of the need for legislation, five referred to sections 243 and 244 of the Civil Procedure Code, or to other restrictions, as sufficient. In short, even the opponents of further restrictions, did not question the propriety of some sort of restriction.

This is not to say that officers on opposing sides did not approach the question from very different points of view. To Lieutenant-Colonel Coxe, an officer whose civil experience dated from 1849, and who was now Commissioner of the Jullunder division, the justification for the entire prohibition of compulsory sales of hereditary or joint-acquired land lay in the one-sided relations between landholder and money-lender. The former was entirely at the mercy of the latter, who exploited his advantages ruthlessly. The money-lender could enter into his account almost any amount he pleased; and if his books had been kept according to law (that is, in the technical sense) he was almost certain to win a decree in court. On the other hand the landholder was ignorant and utterly incapable in money matters. As long as this state of things continued, Coxe concluded, something should be done to protect the landholder from the rapacity of the village money-lender.[73]

Of the other Commissioners who supported the prohibition of compulsory sales, Arthur Brandreth and Colonel Cracroft, both old Settlement Officers, had shown their aversion to rural indebtedness in earlier years.[74] In 1869 Brandreth stressed not so much the nature of the relations between landowners and money-lenders as the impact of British judicial and revenue administration on those relations. Brandreth referred in particular to the defects and unpopularity of the inferior courts, and to faulty revenue arrangements which forced landowners to borrow at high rates of interest. He wished to avoid the sort of ill-feeling, roused by compulsory sales of ancestral land, which had manifested itself in the mutiny.[75]

Nor did all the opinions in favour of action come from Commissioners. Lepel Griffin, a district officer, and civilian of nine years' standing, wanted to prohibit entirely the compulsory sale of ancestral real property, though not of joint-acquired real property.[76] One military civilian, also in charge of a district, touched on the familiar theme of protecting the ignorant agricultural classes from the money-lenders; though he did not want to interfere with mortgaged land as such interference was likely to injure the community at large.[77]

The belief that the restriction of the power of compulsory sale represented an injury to society was, however, more characteristic of the opponents of further substantial action. These comprised three district officers, as many Commissioners, and the officiating Financial Commissioner, Philip Sandys Melvill.[78] More than ten years before Melvill, confronted with desperate conditions in a small tract, had not hesitated to advise against any remedial measures. Now, surveying a Province which he believed to be in a sound state and very much improved under British rule, he was no less confident that nothing, or rather very little, should be done.

Indeed Melvill, like the opponents of pre-emption earlier in the decade, and in common with two other officers who opposed further restrictions on compulsory sales, looked less to agricultural indebtedness than to the great improvement which had occurred in the conditions of the landholders. Land, previously of little or no value, had become valuable; this was the unquestionable essence of the position taken up. From this Melvill went on to insist that this had been accompanied by a great development of the intelligence and aptitude of the landowners to look after their own interests. They had shaken themselves free from the unbroken burden of debt which previously weighed them down, he thought, and their obligations were now commonly isolated and contracted with the intention of paying them off in a specific time. Both landholders and money-lenders were, in Melvill's opinion, more precise in their transactions than they had been. The district officer and Commissioner, who had argued along similar lines, had not gone as far as to contend that landowners and money-lenders had become economic men; but they certainly believed that material prosperity encouraged frugality, thrift and foresight.[79]

There being, as Melvill thought, no case for serious action, he harped on the injurious nature of the restrictions proposed; and pointed with some perspicacity to the fact that even those who supported restrictions advocated them only for a time, thereby admitting that the restrictions were intrinsically harmful. Melvill agreed with the objection put forward by most of the opponents of restriction that if unsecured land could not be sold through the courts the moneylender would take more mortgages; but he treated it lightly enough, indicating that if the sale of unmortgaged land were prohibited the same restrictions should apply to mortgaged land. Instead he took up a point already made by Alexander Benton. The restrictions, by sweeping away the security of land for loans, Melvill claimed, would result in a contraction of agricultural credit which could not fail to be harmful, the landowners requiring short-term loans for various purposes. Melvill still clung to the old view of credit, ignoring Simson's arguments on this point.

In short, Melvill drew liberally on the evidence for the increase in rural prosperity, setting aside the spectre of agricultural indebtedness, and insisting on accepted English notions of non-interference with a beneficial economic process. If there was any undue pressure of the revenue-demand, or some other special pressure at work, he wrote, echoing the arguments which advocates of a protective policy had once been able to use with effect, there might be reason for legislation. In the absence of such conditions he recommended only minor alterations to sections 243 and 244 of the Civil Procedure Code to ensure that land was not sold in execution until it had been shown the debt could not be realised in any other way. Occasional forced sales would now and then occur, and they might not be an unmixed evil. In the richer parts of the country they were likely to be rare, and would serve as a warning to landowners to be careful in their money affairs. In wilder parts, as in the south-west, the occasional introduction of a stranger with capital to locate cultivators would be a benefit.

Notwithstanding Melvill's views, the discussion appears to have emboldened an old advocate of the protective policy. At first Donald McLeod's Government had asked only for opinions on Boulnois' suggestion to prohibit the compulsory sale of unmortgaged land. Then, late in November 1869, McLeod expressed his entire concurrence with Simson's views. McLeod's sentiments were those of an older generation, minus the arguments which had become out of date. He referred neither to the reasoning of those who saw agricultural indebtedness as a ground for restricting compulsory sales, nor to that of those who believed that the improvement of the country had rendered further restriction unnecessary. The compulsory sale of hereditary land had never been recognised under indigenous rule, McLeod contended. The *principle* of such sales was abhorrent to the feelings of the people of the Punjab. And McLeod buttressed his argument with a reference which no material improvement could render less relevant, a reference, that is, to scenes witnessed in 1857 by English refugees in part of the North-Western Provinces – villages in flames, auction-purchasers ejected, and so on. The Judges were asked to prepare a draft enactment to prohibit the absolute sale of hereditary or joint-acquired land in execution of decree, and to limit temporary alienations of land under section 244 of the Civil Procedure Code to twenty years.[80]

When the Chief Court replied in January 1870, it did not speak with one mind. A third Judge, Charles Lindsay, recently appointed to the Court, turned out to have opinions resembling none so much as those of the officiating Financial Commissioner. Lindsay, a civilian with twenty-five years' service to his credit, had occupied many judicial as well as other posts in the North-Western Provinces. In his minute on the subject of compulsory sales of land he agreed with Melvill that the Punjab was not in tutelage, and that the people were well able to take care of themselves, knowing the value of land and money. He further agreed that legislation was likely to make matters worse, by depreciating the value of land as security, and hence impairing the landowner's ability to obtain a loan in time of need. The mild expectation of Melvill that in certain parts of the country compulsory sales might result in the improvement of the land became in Lindsay a doctrinaire expectation verging on social Darwinism. There was no point in maintaining a family that had lived its time, that through foolishness had ruined itself. The arrival of a capitalist was likely to infuse new energy, and to give life to the decaying property. As for the expropriated landholding family, Lindsay, like others before him thinking in terms of a mobile society, saw some advantage in sending the family out into the world, where the younger members might do something for themselves. Still Lindsay, like Melvill and indeed almost every officer, did not advocate the indiscriminate sale of land. He thought that, carefully worked, sections 243 and 244 of the Civil Procedure Code would ensure that compulsory sales were rare, being confined to cases in which there was no other way of satisfying the debt; and he quoted several authorities in the North-Western Provinces, among them the High Court, on this point.[81]

Lindsay thought that Boulnois and Simson would prepare a draft bill; but they advised the Lieutenant-Governor that only the submission of the papers to the Government of India would expedite matters. In their joint note Boulnois and Simson tried to buttress their position. The Government of the Punjab, they declared, had closed the question. This did not prevent them from attacking the views of the officiating Financial Commissioner (and hence those of Lindsay). In so doing they provided further evidence of the way in which the Punjab system of restricting compulsory sales had worked. Statistics, to be found only in their office, appeared to establish that the Judicial Commissioners as well as the local authorities had discouraged compulsory sales in a systematic manner. Hence Melvill's assumption (as they saw it) that such sales had been going on for many years, and had not interfered with the prosperity of the Province, could not be substantiated. Such sales had been rendered most exceptional, by means not altogether regular, such as intentional delay in disposing of them. With reference to McLeod's allusion to the mutiny, they appended the opinion of a recent Judge of the Sudder Court of Agra, who had witnessed the evil effects of compulsory sales on the fabric of British power in a district of the North-Western Provinces in 1857.[82]

It did not come off. In addressing the Government of India in February 1870 McLeod's Government observed that as one of the Judges of the Chief Court, the Financial Commissioner of the Punjab, and the High Court of the North-Western Provinces were opposed to the prohibition of the sale of land in execution of decree, the Government of India would hardly agree to legislate in that sense. Nevertheless, McLeod submitted the papers to them, trusting that at least some more stringent provisions against the abuse of the power of sale might be adopted than those contained in sections 243 and 244 of the Code of Civil Procedure.[83]

In any case, constituted as the Government of India was, there was no likelihood of any prohibition of the sale of land in execution of decree. Certainly neither Mayo, the Viceroy, nor a number of distinguished Members of Council, contemplated such a prohibition for a moment. A desultory discussion of other possible remedies, notably some amendment of sections 243 and 244 of the Civil Procedure Code, finally resolved itself into a decision to find out how these provisions had worked in Provinces which had no separate arrangements of their own.[84]

In May 1870, some four months before the Government of India took this decision, the Chief Court again addressed the Punjab Government, hoping that the question might be settled quickly, so that the action of the Court might proceed on a satisfactory basis. In the meantime they were rejecting applications for the sale of land in execution of decree, because they felt it proper, in such an important matter, to act on the view taken by the executive Government.[85] This was intended to be a temporary policy; but given the Government of India's failure to act, it presumably became permanent. At any rate it is apparent that compulsory sales were as rare in the thirty years after the discussion of 1869–70, as they had been in the decade preceding it. Ultimately, in 1885, the power to grant sanction was transferred to the Financial Commissioner.[86] In regard to compulsory sales the early protective policy had contributed a lasting element to Punjab administration.

The debate of 1869–70 provides some indication of why this happened, why the restrictions on compulsory sales were not discarded. Donald McLeod was the last, prominent figure of the old generation to lend his influence to such restrictions, and he would depart in the middle of 1870. Those who wanted a more definite, or total, prohibition of compulsory sales for debt still spoke in terms familiar to the old defenders of restriction, insisting on the need to maintain village communities, and pointing to the North-Western Provinces and the events of 1857. To this extent the ideas of the old protective policy were still alive, not only among Simson and Brandreth, men whose experience dated from the 1840s and 1850s respectively, but also in the case of Boulnois, a relative newcomer from England. There were, however, new elements as well. Agricultural indebtedness, as manifested in the Punjab itself, came into the foreground as a justification for restriction. One officer, David Simson, defended restriction on economic grounds, an intellectual position which hitherto no advocate of a protective policy had been able to assume. As for those who spoke out against further measures, a number of them looked to the improved state of the country. There was, however, less desire to whittle down existing restrictions than had existed among those who attacked the law of pre-emption as obsolete. The point was that the restriction of compulsory sales did not give rise to those practical anomalies and injustices which accompanied attempts to enforce the right of pre-emption. Those who opposed further restrictions on compulsory sales were prepared to accept the continuation of a policy with which they were familiar and which had worked no apparent harm, however much they might profess to believe that that would be the result of new restrictions. There was therefore in 1869–70 no conceivable threat to existing policy. In later years those who apprehended, or came to apprehend, harmful effects from indebtedness would tackle in some instances the far more fundamental question of voluntary alienation, while those who looked to material improvement, in their eagerness to refute the new charges, would fall back on the arguments and measures of the protective policy as an adequate answer. Hence the principle of an almost total restriction of sales of ancestral land in execution of decree ceased to be a matter of serious controversy.

## V

A new era may be dated from 1869 when Arthur Brandreth, the Commissioner of the Multan division, referred to the voluntary transfer of land as a 'political question of extreme importance'.[87] As his remarks in this and succeeding years show, Brandreth believed that voluntary transfers were taking place to a serious extent, and were cumulative in their nature, resulting in the steady displacement of the hereditary landholders by the trading castes. Brandreth thought that this process gave rise to grave agricultural discontent, leading to serious trouble in any future uprising, just as had happened in 1857. While not discounting the misfortune or folly of the agricultural classes as causes of these transfers, he spoke scathingly at times of the rigid exaction of revenue and the pressure of the civil courts. By 1871 he was on the verge of propounding a solution; for he appealed to the sentiment that the British were the real landlords of revenue-paying land, and to the state of England up to 1648, as a warrant for refusing to allow free alienation.[88]

By this time Brandreth was no longer Commissioner of the Multan but of the Jullunder division. It was not entirely fortuitous, however, that a campaign against voluntary transfers should have been begun in the Multan division, that is, in the south-west of the Punjab. In 1869 Brandreth had quoted one of his subordinates, Colonel Fendall, who suggested that the money-lenders were getting exceedingly rich, and were investing their money in land. Fendall pointed to a circumstance which helped to explain why the process was already advanced in the south-west. The money-lenders here were following the lead of Sawan Mal, who had governed much of this area under Sikh rule, and who years before the advent of the British had drawn the attention of the traders to the acquisition of land.[89] Again in 1871, after Brandreth had left the Multan division, his successor noted that in most parts of the country the hereditary holders of land were being replaced gradually by men of a different class, of better business habits and more impressed with the value of landed property.[90] Whatever these officers might think of these changes, they did not doubt their existence.

That matters had not come to the same pass in every part of the country is illustrated in striking fashion by the reports on the revised settlements of the Gujrat and Lahore districts, in the north-west and centre of the Province respectively. The Settlement Officers of Gujrat and Lahore, who submitted their reports in 1870, spoke not of growing agrarian discontent but of prosperity and contentment.

Thus in Lahore the Settlement Officer indicated that when he entered the district, resources and population had increased, the canal had just begun to pour its treasures on adjoining villages, many Sikhs had returned from Hindustan and China enriched with plunder and grants of land, and there was contentment on every face. In both districts the Settlement Officers noted a considerable expenditure on domestic ceremonies, the Settlement Officer of Gujrat believing that the ability to maintain such an expenditure would go far to reconcile the people to British rule. Nevertheless, in Gujrat as well as in Lahore it was recognised that this expenditure led to much indebtedness, and the Settlement Officer of Gujrat remarked rather ambiguously that some attempt should be made to keep marriage expenses in check. Though he noted that a more uncomplaining lot of debtors could hardly be found, and referred to the general opinion that under British rule the long-standing connections between the landholder and the money-lender were becoming weaker every day, he was not entirely sanguine about the increase in registered debt during the settlement and the general extent of indebtedness. The Settlement Officer of Lahore was less hesitant, designating debt as a curse to all men, but to agriculturists in particular. The credit of the landholders was particularly good, he noted, owing to light assessment; while the money-lender used the courts as engines of oppression to enforce his iniquitous terms. Within their respective districts the Settlement Officers were conscious of differences in the extent of indebtedness; the Settlement Officer of Gujrat enlarging on those between one tahsil and another, the Settlement Officer of Lahore contrasting the indebted Muslim Rajputs with the Jats, less dependent on the bankers. While both officers struck a somewhat uneasy balance between prosperity and indebtedness, the transfer of land to Hindu traders received only the briefest and most incidental mention in the report on Gujrat.[91]

It is only fair to add that opinion did not necessarily reflect any precise stage in the process of land transfer. The stimulus given to land transfer in the Hissar division by the famine of 1868–9 drew from James Naesmyth, the Commissioner of the division, much the same remarks about the attempt to discourage land transfers to money-lenders as the famine of 1860–1 had occasioned.[92] Yet many years later, let alone in 1870, the transfer of land in that insecure division as a whole was not great by Provincial standards.[93] On the other hand Captain Tighe, who had criticised the law of pre-emption from the vantage point of the Umballa district, expressed his regret in 1870 that the money-lenders of the district were working themselves into large landed proprietors.[94]

If there were signs that some officers had begun to realise that a distinct change in the ownership of land was taking place in some parts of the country, this was nevertheless a matter which gave rise to varying interpretations. When Arthur Brandreth returned to the attack in rather strong language in 1871, the Financial Commissioner, Robert Egerton, took a rather sceptical view of his conclusions and criticised him for failure to verify his assertions. Egerton doubted whether the voluntary transfer of land resulted in any hatred of Government. It was possible to understand this feeling arising, as it had arisen in other parts of India, when land was sold for arrears of revenue. But voluntary transfers appeared to be the natural result of the creation of a valuable property in land, owing to security and low assessment. They were not likely to be due to the unfair operation of the civil courts. Place a valuable property in the hands of a number of persons, Egerton wrote, the careful would look after it, the improvident would squander it, and nothing the British could do would prevent this.[95]

The Lieutenant-Governor, Henry Davies, who in earlier days probably had little sympathy even for the protective policy, supported his Financial Commissioner. In so doing he upbraided Brandreth in a manner which reflected the novel and startling nature of Brandreth's message. The Lieutenant-Governor expressed his regret, in February 1872, that such prominence had been given to the remarks of the Commissioner of Jullunder, and roundly condemned him, an officer in such a responsible position, for putting on official record opinions which could not be supported by admitted fact or reasonable argument.[96]

Only four months after the Lieutenant-Governor's condemnation of Brandreth, the political danger, as well as the injustice, of the transfer of land from landholders to trading castes was raised by Philip Sandys Melvill, the same man who had been so sanguine in 1869 about the ability of the landholders to take care of themselves. Melvill, on his return from the Central Provinces, where he had officiated as Judicial Commissioner, took up briefly the Commissionership of Jullunder; and the evidence suggests that he became alarmed at the extent to which land was being transferred to money-lenders in the Hoshiarpur and Jullunder districts. One suspects too the hand of Arthur Brandreth, whose place as Commissioner Melvill occupied. At any rate in June 1872 a memorandum of Melvill's, written as officiating Judge of the Chief Court, was submitted to

Government. In this memorandum Melvill took a view of the origins of alienation which Egerton had been disposed to deny. Melvill expressed his belief that civil courts in the Punjab often, and perhaps generally, decreed excessive interest on sums due for the time that passed between the date the debt became due and the institution of suit. He thought that this excessive interest had led frequently to the alienation of land and other immovable property in execution of decree; that sometimes debtors against whom decrees had been passed had transferred their land to their creditors without awaiting the coercive processes of court; and that debtors who had not been brought into court at all were commonly selling and mortgaging their land to their creditors, chiefly money-lenders, in payment of debts swollen by compound interest, fearing that if sued, the court would give no relief from the interest charged. Given that under Sikh rule there had been customary restrictions on the amount of interest, Melvill urged that a somewhat similar restriction might be right now, when the creditor's security was so much better. Accordingly he recommended that an enquiry be made from local officers on all the major issues raised in his memorandum.[97] One of Melvill's colleagues, Charles Boulnois, agreed with Melvill as to the importance of the subject, while Lindsay declined to give an opinion, though he did not object to an enquiry being made.[98] This time the Lieutenant-Governor responded favourably, and he allowed the Chief Court to make the proposed enquiry.[99]

Meanwhile evidence was not wanting that the subject of voluntary transfers was attracting attention in various parts of the Province. Gore Ouseley, the Commissioner of the Umballa division, which contained the district of the same name, remarked in his revenue report for 1871–2 that the changes brought by the British would doubtless promote a change of ownership of land. Like Egerton he spoke of the establishment of property in land, and the general security of property, and while admitting the role of the courts and the law, he did not question their just operation.[100] In districts of the Lahore and Amritsar divisions investigations into the specific causes of voluntary transfers were in progress before or around the middle of 1872, the results being transmitted to the Financial Commissioner. It was the Gujranwala district, heavily pressed in the early days of British rule, and manifesting in later years transfers of notable extent, which was the subject of enquiry in the former division.[101] Colonel Fendall, apparently was responsible for the enquiry in Gurdaspur, a district of the Amritsar division. In addition to causes he tried to ascertain the proportion of land transferred during the year to landholders and money-lenders respectively, his conclusion being that, roughly, the landholders bought two-thirds of the land sold, while the money-lenders acquired the same proportion of the infinitely larger area mortgaged.[102] This investigation did not perturb the Commissioner of Amritsar, a military civilian who had served in the Punjab from the earliest days, for in trying to substantiate the proposition that transfers were due not to heavy assessment but rather to extravagance, he referred to the enquiry in Gurdaspur as showing that landholders were quite as able and ready to buy and take land on mortgage as money-lenders.[103] Nor did the Financial Commissioner, Robert Egerton, who had all these reports, as well as those of an enquiry in Multan, a south-western district, before him, express any apprehension in the Provincial revenue report in September 1872. That he too felt obliged, and not for the first time, to point out that transfers were not due to heavy assessment, is an indication of the extent to which the arguments which had justified the old protective policy retained their hold. At the same time Egerton tried to minimise the extent of transfer of land, referring to statistics showing how very small a percentage of the cultivation had been transferred in the Province during the year.[104]

The situation in the south-western Punjab continued to be brought before Government. In the district of Multan, as we have noted, an enquiry had been undertaken, an attempt being made to ascertain the proportion of transfers to landholders and money-lenders respecttively. As regards the Montgomery district the Lieutenant-Governor considered, in November 1872, a petition from certain headmen and eleven others. They prayed that Government would liquidate their debts from the proceeds of their land, pleading that the river inundations had failed, that the resulting debt had been increased by compound interest, that their land had been mortgaged and even sold, while applications existed for their imprisonment.[105] Then in December 1872, in a memorandum on the Jhang district prepared for the Lieutenant-Governor's perusal during his cold-weather tour, the officiating Deputy Commissioner of the district, G. E. Wakefield, noted the great want of a law to extricate leading families from debt, and urged the introduction of something along the lines of the Oudh Talukdars' Act. The power to interfere in the management of estates, he claimed, would be an answer to the subject of the Chief Court's enquiry, that is the alarming transfers of land resulting from the action of the courts and amounting to twenty-five per cent sold and mortgaged in the Multan division.[106] In both these instances of indebted landholders requiring relief Davies showed some disposition to at least consider the possibility of relief.[107] He was inclined to consider favourably, as we shall see, the remarks made to him by James Lyall, the Settlement Commissioner, about this time, and probably during the Lieutenant-Governor's tour. Lyall may well have referred to the part played by fixed cash assessments in creating indebtedness in areas like Montgomery, dependent on variable river inundations, or such as Muktsar (outside the Multan division), having little rainfall. At any rate he certainly suggested the adoption of variable assessments for these tracts.[108] Similar difficulties of collecting a fixed cash assessment from land with a fluctuating outturn confronted Davies, during his tour, in certain districts adjoining the Multan division.[109]

The accumulation of official opinion that all was not well with the landholders of the Punjab created a distinct change in the Lieutenant-Governor's outlook. In reviewing the Provincial revenue report for 1871–2 in January 1873, Davies struck an alarmist note, the significance of which is readily apparent when it is remembered that this was hardly a year after his forthright condemnation of Brandreth. It was not so much the partial district enquiries which had been made which worried Davies; and here he referred not only to those already discussed, but also to an enquiry in the Jullunder division (a division, it may be recalled, to which Brandreth and Melvill had drawn attention) which showed that in a number of selected villages throughout the division something less than eleven per cent of the land had been transferred since the early 1850s. It was rather the absence of information which made Davies anxious. It was not known whether the rate of transfer was increasing, or what proportion of the soil had been transferred in other parts of the Province. If, as some experienced officers seemed to think, the amount of land transferred to village bankers was increasing each year in a larger ratio; if the tendency of the present system was to allow the land to pass from the peasant proprietors to the moneylenders, then it would be necessary to seek a remedy for an evil which otherwise would be a certain source of future trouble.[110]

The political difficulties which Davies now anticipated were much the same as those which Brandreth had propounded. The British had held the country without any popular uprising mainly, Davies thought, because the rights of the village proprietors (whom he characterised as the great mass of the inhabitants) had been maintained. In times of great confusion, as in 1857, village communities had been known to take up arms against each other for some ancient boundary dispute, which the courts had forgotten, but which the certainty and fixity of rights under British law had invested with a stronger interest. If the Government were to forget the source of its strength, and left the proprietors to be absorbed by the moneylenders, Davies contended, the feeling of the people in times of uncertainty would be in opposition to the Government, and any change would appear tolerable which might allow them an opportunity of recovering what they had lost.

To meet this political danger Davies, like the supporters of the protective policy before him, was prepared to set political economy aside. He looked forward to measures which would strengthen the position of the proprietary body against the money-lenders, notably the regulation of the rate of interest allowed by courts, in regard to which he hoped some substantial reform might be possible. Discussing the probable effects of such a measure on agricultural credit he went further than the old defenders of the protective policy, arguing that careful landholders would be able to obtain loans as before, while the inability of the reckless to do so would be advantageous. Inclining to the view that in some districts of the Punjab the rigidity of the Government demand forced people into debt, he also thought that fluctuating assessments might be practicable for such tracts.

Yet Davies' conversion to the views of officers like Brandreth and Melvill should not be exaggerated. The question, as Davies pointed out, was a complicated one; and he could think of several influences which, if they had been at work, might put his mind at ease. In particular he cited the possibility that growing population and the sub-division of estates in some districts had rendered transfers, which in this case would generally be made between members of the agricultural community, unobjectionable and even necessary. If this proved to be so, then interference would not only be undesirable but ineffective.

It is not altogether surprising, therefore, that when Davies reviewed the next Provincial revenue report, just over a year later, he was inclined to minimise the significance of voluntary alienations of land. This distinct change in tone and emphasis, however, does require explanation.

It requires explanation, in particular, because there are no indications that the change in Davies' opinion reflected any similar shift in the balance of opinion in the Province at large. The extracts from local reports given in the Provincial revenue report for 1872–3 show that three Commissioners, supported by a number of district officers, agreed that voluntary transfers had little or nothing to do with the assessment;[111] but this was something which Davies had taken into account. One of the Commissioners, Colonel Coxe, who had drawn attention to agricultural indebtedness in 1869, opined indeed that in the Jullunder division a large portion of the agricultural community was following the 'road to ruin' by transfers arising from extravagance, litigation and exorbitant interest rates.[112]

Apart from the revenue reports there was the fact that in July 1873, the Settlement Commissioner, James Lyall, urged that it was important to prevent land changing rapidly from the hands of the present holders to those of the monied classes. To this end Lyall wanted legislation to extend the right of pre-emption (recently limited by direct enactment to permanent transfers) to long-term usufructuary mortgages. It was a proposition to which Davies in September 1873 gave a qualified assent, deprecating legislation, but suggesting that an entry in the record of rights might suffice, the question having originated in districts then under settlement. The Settlement Commissioner doubted whether the legal validity of such an entry could be upheld.[113]

Then the question of the relief of indebted landholders in several south-western districts remained a live issue. In his report on encumbered estates in the Jhang district the Deputy Commissioner, G. E. Wakefield, took the opportunity in August 1873 to again represent the need for Government power to manage estates. It was not the extension of such a power to a small privileged class but to the great body of landholders (landlords of a certain status, as he said at another point) which he now considered a great political measure. He alluded not only to the prevailing sentiment that Government was the real landlord, but also to the danger of blind adherence to English theories in dealing with India. The political danger of transfers, he thought, had been manifested in the North-Western Provinces in 1857; and while he believed that in the Punjab they were still on the right side of the hedge, he cited district figures for five years which appeared to show that if transfers continued at the same rate, another twenty years would see the transfer of sixty per cent of the cultivation.[114] The Commissioner of the Multan division, R. Young, who in 1869 had seen no merit in Boulnois' plan to restrict compulsory sales, was annoyed that Wakefield should depart thus from his brief. Yet even Young was impressed by the return of transfers, and he agreed to recommend Wakefield's solution, provided that action was limited to those families or classes which he believed it was particularly important to maintain, and then in limited numbers and only for one generation.[115] In addressing the Punjab Government in September 1873 the Financial Commissioner, Robert Egerton, indicated his entire agreement with this opinion.[116] The belief that only substantial landlords need excite concern was one which Davies came to share.

The matter of relieving the village headmen and others, residents of the Montgomery district, who had petitioned in 1872, contributed towards this result. The Deputy Commissioner had reported in June 1873 that nothing could be done for them under the existing law because only a fraction of their liabilities was in the form of judgement debts, most of their debts being secured by registered bonds, with the creditors in possession of land mortgaged as security. He had advised legislation similar to that undertaken in 1871 for the Thakurs of Baroda.[117] When the headmen petitioned again in November 1873, and the Punjab Government wrote to the Commissioner of the Multan division, the Deputy Commissioner's letter was once more brought to the attention of Government.[118] The new incumbent of the Deputy Commissioner's office in Montgomery, however, advised in December 1873 that instead of a new law, insolvency powers under the Punjab Laws Act might meet the case.[119] In January 1874 the Lieutenant-Governor notified the Chief Court of his intention of adopting this expedient, unless the Judges saw any strong objection.[120]

In addition to the problems of relieving indebted landlords in the south-west, the general views of Robert Egerton, the Financial Commissioner, played a significant part in the development of Davies' attitude. Egerton, still believing that voluntary transfers would not give rise to political danger and that it would be impracticable to check them,[121] continued to play down the significance of these transfers in the Provincial revenue report. In the report for 1871–2 he had minimised the extent of transfer. In November 1873 in the report for the succeeding year he mentioned Fendall's latest enquiries in Gurdaspur, as well as observing that in Hoshiarpur it was found that land was largely sold and mortgaged to agriculturists who had accumulated a little capital. He noticed further that almost two-thirds of the mortgage money and almost half of the purchase money were raised in nine districts, all of which were known to be in a prosperous state.[122]

When Davies reviewed this report in February 1874 he no longer spoke of partial local enquiries or of the paucity of information. Instead, succumbing to a temptation understandable in one responsible for a vast and complex Province, he accepted the Provincial returns of transfers, which he had ignored in the previous year, as perhaps fairly reliable. He stressed the small fraction of the cultivation of the Province which, according to these returns, had been transferred during the year, and noted proudly the great increase in average selling price over the last ten years. In regard to mortgages he echoed Egerton's remark that the loans were taken for the most part in districts known to be eminently prosperous. Davies had returned to a position in which transfers were seen as a matter for congratulation, indicating remarkable prosperity and a moderate land-revenue demand. While he now saw no cause for anxiety in the extent to which or the circumstances under which land was changing hands, he did refer to the problem of the indebtedness of substantial owners of land. In particular he instanced the south-western districts, Multan and Muzuffargarh as well as Jhang and Montgomery, as ones in which individual instances had come under his notice. It was the loss of land by these men that he now believed to be a source of grave dissatisfaction, and it was for their benefit that political economy might be set aside. The extension of insolvency jurisdiction to the rural areas he observed was the answer[123] (perhaps unaware or unconcerned that three days before the Chief Court had expressed its total disapproval of such a measure).[124]

Davies, therefore, had changed his mind before the Chief Court submitted the results of the enquiry into voluntary land transfer sanctioned in June 1872. The opinions submitted by local officers for the purposes of this enquiry are not traceable, but the comments of the Judges of the Chief Court, and later the Lieutenant-Governor, do provide us with some glimpses of what was said.

The Chief Court submitted the minutes of the Judges in April 1874. Charles Boulnois referred to the hardship caused by the short term of limitation for debt. A number of officers and natives, it appears from another minute, had urged the extension of the period.[125] Boulnois also advocated the abolition of imprisonment for debt. The question of the voluntary transfer of land he found too wide to enter upon, confining himself to recommending in an absolute form what he had proposed in 1869 in a qualified form, namely that sales of land in execution of decrees held by moneylenders for debts due by agriculturists should not be permitted.[126]

The opinion advanced by Charles Lindsay, Judge of the Chief Court, showed him to be much the same man as in 1870. The landholders of the Punjab did not require protection, thought Lindsay, though he admitted many other persons held the opposite opinion. Besides, what was the point of maintaining careless, extravagant landlords. Only men who strove to maintain themselves should be maintained. They should be taught habits of thrift, and should come to feel the responsibilities of property conferred on them by British rule. If a limit was set upon the rate of interest recoverable, the bankers would find new outlets for their money, so that the landholders would not be able to borrow in times of scarcity. Under a law limiting interest, a law so easily evaded, the landholder would lose in the long run, at any rate he would not gain.[127] This was an analysis which had many points in common with that which Lindsay gave in 1870 in regard to compulsory sales.

But in 1874 Lindsay had to take cognisance of matters which were far from obvious in 1870. With the local opinions before him Lindsay conceded that the agricultural class was to a great extent in the hands of the village bankers. He accepted the idea that voluntary alienations had taken place to a considerable extent though, true to form, on the basis of some evidence relating to the Hoshiarpur district, he inclined to the view that much land might be acquired by the prosperous brotherhood, not averse to lending money, rather than by professional money-lenders. As to the causes of these transfers Lindsay noted that some agreed that it was due to the apprehended action of the courts, while he himself sided with those who denied this view.

The fact that Lindsay was prepared to recommend certain remedies for prevailing indebtedness throws further light on the development of official opinion in the Province. Lindsay's recommendations were made not with regard to his own view of the matter, but in deference, as he put it, to the opinions of many men of alleged large experience. Some interference might be reasonable, Lindsay thought, in view of the fact that the Government was the chief landlord. Lindsay's view of the political problem, perhaps influenced by his long experience in the North-West, was the same as that which Egerton and Davies had taken up, namely that it might be politic to maintain some of the larger men. Advances of money could be made to large landowners, their debts might be paid, or their estates managed by Government. Land should be answerable for secured debts alone, he added, moving to the position which he had rejected outright in 1870. The debtor who borrowed on the security of his land could be further protected by a law compelling the creditor to produce his accounts yearly. In addition to some such system, it would be well if the courts looked more closely into accounts between creditors and debtors. Perhaps legislation might go as far as to lay down that the interest recoverable at any one time should not exceed the principal. This was the limit of interference which Lindsay thought tolerable to meet opinions which he did not himself share.

The note written by the third Judge of the Chief Court, Philip Sandys Melvill, gave further glimpses of the general trend of official opinion, while indicating that a striking transformation in Melvill's own attitude had been completed.[128]

Melvill noted that the officers consulted were almost unanimous in the view that the existing law regarding interest caused undue hardship to agricultural debtors. A large majority of officers recommended an alteration in the law; their opinions tending to a fixation of a maximum rate of interest that might be decreed by the courts, and the grant of power to the courts to make an equitable adjudication of interest, notwithstanding any agreement made by the parties. Some of the more thoughtful reports, Melvill added, were against any alteration in the law. And Melvill himself thought that a circular of the Chief Court, issued in 1873, had gone far to meet the evil which he had brought to notice in his original minute.[129] He was not prepared to recommend any alteration in the law where the rate of interest had been agreed upon by the parties. All that was required was that the equitable principle laid down in the circular should be applied in going behind the terms of the bond to ascertain the true nature of the transaction.

In Melvill's mind the problem had gone beyond the question of regulating the award of interest. The picture which he now drew of agricultural affairs showed how far he had come since 1869 when he had insisted on the improvement in the condition of the landholders, on the decline of rural indebtedness, and on the advent of rational conduct in the transactions between landowners and money-lenders. Though the statistics of alienation supplied by local officers did not allow any deduction to be drawn as to the extent of transfers, Melvill was convinced that alienations had been extensive, and that they were chiefly due to agricultural indebtedness. A large number of agriculturists were still free from debt, but he thought their numbers would diminish year by year. The landowners were undergoing a gradual but no less certain process of extinction. The value which British rule had given to land enabled its owners to borrow freely, and they had shown a great want of caution in making use of this credit. The professional money-lender, with his superior intelligence, and his rapacity and unscrupulousness, took unconscionable advantage of the landowner's necessity, ignorance and carelessness. Melvill did not share the opinion generally expressed that the main remedy for this state of things was to be found in the better education of the agricultural class. The difficulties of effecting any rapid improvement in their education were so great, that if any remedy for indebtedness were to be proposed it must be looked for in a measure which would restrict agricultural credit. An alteration in the law of limitation for debt was also necessary, if less important.

Agricultural credit could be curtailed only by placing restrictions on the voluntary transfer of the proprietary right in land; and Melvill went on to make definite proposals which in their scope and stringency recall those which George Campbell had made more than twenty years earlier. The comparison with Campbell's schemes is instructive, as showing the very different settings in which these proposals were made. While Campbell had hardly challenged the need for agricultural credit, Melvill, faced with growing indebtedness, saw the restriction of credit as a major part of his scheme. Campbell looked forward calmly to the day when the more prosperous shareholders might absorb the less prosperous. That prospect was already a real one in Melvill's time, he himself noting that landowners had taken to money-lending on the same terms and with the same avidity as the professional lender. He did not think with Campbell that the process was a desirable or inevitable one, nor did he share the views of those of his contemporaries who thought that transfers to the brotherhood deprived the whole business of much of its sting. Unlike Campbell, Melvill was not concerned with cushioning the decline of village institutions, but with checking the evil consequences of indebtedness. Where Campbell had wished to confine the transfer of land by ordinary peasant proprietors to members of the village community, Melvill conceived that the sphere of legitimate transactions in land lay between parties who were neither debtors nor creditors. Melvill proposed that no voluntary transfer of land should be permitted in payment of a debt to a creditor, whether alien or of the village brotherhood, the sole exception being a mortgage limited to the life-time of the mortgagor. With this exception, all voluntary transfers of land should be submitted for the Deputy Commissioner's and Commissioner's sanction, that sanction being withheld if the transaction was in any way connected with the payment of a debt. If the money-lender still wanted to acquire land, he could do so only by fair purchase in the open market. As an adjunct to these proposals he suggested the possibility of Government initiating a scheme for redeeming outstanding mortgages held by alien money-lenders.

This was the first project for the wholesale restriction of voluntary alienation to be proposed in the new atmosphere of growing indebtedness and steady change in the ownership of land. Arthur Brandreth may have had something similar in mind a few years earlier, but George Campbell's proposals were shaped in different circumstances, and belonged to an older protective tradition.

The extent to which, and the rate at which, Melvill had moved into a new intellectual stream is made manifest by a comparison of his economic judgements in 1874 with those made by him in earlier years. In 1855 he had been concerned to give a marketable value to land. He did not think, in 1874, that his proposed scheme for the restriction of transfer would seriously depreciate the value of land, and considered that a slight depreciation in its value was not much of a price to pay to render the hereditary owners secure in the possession of their land. In 1869 Melvill had combated further restrictions on compulsory sales by pointing to the harm which would ensue when landowners were no longer able to obtain short-term loans. He did not ignore the problem in 1874, but argued that his scheme for restricting voluntary transfers would not prevent the bankers from continuing to lend to the landholders on whose business they depended. Like Davies in 1873, he expected a cessation of reckless lending; a return, he believed, to the conditions of Sikh rule. He did not think that an increase in the rate of interest would eventuate. Moreover, in 1858 and 1869 he had anticipated that the sale of land to strangers would lead to the improvement of the land, at any rate in some parts of the country. In 1874 he conceded that while this might be true in some instances, hitherto the bankers had not been in the habit of spending money on the land, and confined themselves to squeezing as much as possible out of their cultivators. By 1874 Melvill's practical acquaintance with rural society had gained ascendancy over the doctrinaire *laissez-faire* concepts of the time.

Yet Melvill was aware that there was not much chance of his scheme being adopted. It was a radical one, open to many imposing considerations, and dealt with a subject on which great differences of opinion existed. Accordingly he recommended that if no immediate decisive action was taken, statistics showing agrarian indebtedness and giving full details of alienations of land should be collected each year. He concluded his minute by advocating the abolition of imprisonment for debt, and the restriction of the power of the creditor in regard to attachment and sale of crops in execution of decrees for money.

Melvill did not press his main proposals on Government as strongly as he might have done, partly because he did not take the same view of the significance of what was happening as Arthur Brandreth. To some extent Melvill was offended by the injustice which characterised the loss of land by indebted owners. He did not take the most extreme view of the political danger. Where Brandreth had seen danger in the loss of ownership rights by landholders, Melvill wrote in terms of expropriated owners being ousted altogether from their lands, losing their right to cultivate their ancestral acres, and becoming disaffected and disloyal subjects. Let this process go on for another fifty years, Melvill thought, and Government might find itself face to face with a serious political danger.

Nevertheless, Arthur Brandreth apart, this opinion was already a striking one by contemporary standards. The restrictions which Melvill proposed to impose on the power of alienation were far in advance of the general trend of official opinion. Certainly Melvill did not indicate that other officers had suggested such a remedy with reference to the Chief Court's enquiry. A true estimate of Melvill's position in this respect emerges from a study of the discussion which James Lyall initiated in 1873 with his proposal, already noted, to extend the right of pre-emption to long-term usufructuary mortgages, in order to slow down the transfer of land to the moneyed classes.

The right of pre-emption, it will be recalled, was an important part of the protective policy. Originally confined to permanent dispositions of property, it had been extended to usufructuary mortgages in 1856. By a Chief Court ruling of 1868, however, the right was once more limited to permanent transfers.[130] In this form the right found a place in the Punjab Laws Act of 1872, despite the fact that several officers had urged that, since mortgages could be extended for indefinite periods, the right should apply to them as well.[131] This point was made again on several occasions in 1873 and 1874 by James Lyall, and finally local opinions were sought. These were submitted between April and July 1874 by some forty-one officers, including most of the Commissioners and Deputy Commissioners in the Province, as well as a few officers engaged in settlement work. About two-fifths of those consulted either saw no particular reason for legislation, or simply noted that they were not aware of any attempts to evade the law of pre-emption by means of long-term usufructuary mortgages. Only two officers indicated any strong opposition to the extension of the right of pre-emption, and even they did not question the right as it stood. About three-fifths of the officers who submitted opinions were in favour of legislation; and almost half of these urged the extension of the right of pre-emption to usufructuary mortgages generally, and not merely to such mortgages when made for long periods.[132] The whole debate shows how deeply this aspect of the protective policy had taken root, there being not a single challenge to the existing right, and a majority in favour of its extension. Consider too some of the officers who supported legislation. Not long before, when the Punjab Laws Bill was being discussed, Douglas Forsyth, who had attacked the right of pre-emption in 1867, supported its inclusion in the Bill.[133] In 1874 and 1875 support for some extension of the right of pre-emption came from Gore Ouseley, Robert Egerton and Charles Lindsay, all opponents of any general legislative intervention in regard to land transfer.[134] But if the maintenance of pre-emption was common ground among British officers, the fact that in 1874 and 1875 not one of them took the liberty of suggesting that any more drastic restriction was desirable, does support the view that when Melvill proposed to restrict the general power of alienation, he was not representing any significant section of official opinion. As regards pre-emption the Lieutenant-Governor, Henry Davies, rejected its extension to long-term usufructuary mortgages in August 1875, on the ground that a sufficient case had not been made.[135]

The main issue, however, had been settled long before this happened. The minutes of the Judges of the Chief Court on the general question of land transfer, submitted in April 1874, were followed in July by another note by Charles Boulnois and one by an officiating Judge of the Chief Court. Both notes showed the vague sense of uneasiness which the Judges felt in regard to the transfer of land, stimulated in this instance by a judgement they had given in a case concerning a usufructuary mortgage.[136] In regard to a comparatively minor point in one of the notes, the Lieutenant-Governor approved of an enquiry in August 1874;[137] but he did not take up the main question until the views of Robert Egerton, who had been making a special enquiry, were before him. The revenue report for 1873–4, submitted by Egerton, contained a most carefully prepared defence of a *laissez-faire* policy.[138]

Then in December 1874 Davies argued that the protection of the landowners had been recognised by the Punjab Government from the beginning and had largely influenced its revenue and judicial administration; and that the question now was whether any *additional* safeguards were required. Noting the conflict of opinion among the superior officers of the Province, Melvill and Boulnois on one side and Lindsay and Egerton on the other, he determined to examine the evidence. Those officers, he argued, who believed that the agriculturists were indebted to an alarming extent to the money-lender and that transfer of land was being effected to a serious extent to the money-lending classes, founded their opinions upon their own experience and impressions, or the opinions and impressions of others, rather than upon a comprehensive survey of the facts. Such 'gloomy' views were the result of limited observation, proceeding as they did mostly from judicial officers who were perhaps day after day engaged in the decision of suits against agriculturists. In any case even the judicial officers were not unanimous—and besides Lindsay he instanced McMahon, Gore Ouseley and Blyth as officers whose opposition to legislative interference carried great weight. That opposition seemed to be in accordance with public opinion, as far as that had been ascertained—and here he referred to a meeting of landholders and money-lenders convened in the Jullunder district by the Deputy Commissioner. After expressing his sympathies with the advocates of legislation, he proceeded to found his case squarely on statistics provided by Egerton, arguing that in number and extent transfers of land were insignificant, and that the proportion of extravagance which prosperity and credit naturally produced was, in the Punjab, creditably small. Moreover, there was no reason to assume that all these transfers were made under pressure of debt: some of the sales were doubtless due to the high prices offered, many of the mortgages made to raise capital for agricultural improvements. Again, certain statistics collected in one district of the Province (Hoshiarpur) indicated that the bulk of the transfers of landed property were made not to village bankers but to brother agriculturists. Nor did he base his opinion on statistics alone, for during his annual tours he had found that though there were individual cases of embarrassment, the state of the peasantry was in general eminently prosperous. There was a significant reference to Egerton, also well acquainted with every part of the Province; and Davies concurred in his opinion that the transfers which were taking place did not exceed or nearly equal the number which might safely accompany the natural and healthy development of wealth in a country in backward circumstances. Hence Davies no longer saw any need to deviate from the laws of political economy. Now he could dwell on the probability that restrictions on the transfer of land or further interference with freedom of contract, would do more harm than good, depreciating the value of land as a security, raising still higher the rate of interest, and destroying that self-reliance and industry which characterised many Punjab landholders and which was one great cause of the agricultural prosperity of the

Province. Accordingly all proposals for legislation were rejected. Even measures to save larger landowners no longer appeared to be justified in present circumstances. The only action taken was that the Financial Commissioner was ordered to furnish more complete statistics with the next revenue report.[139]

It had taken Davies several years to reach this position. He had begun, in February 1872, by condemning Arthur Brandreth's remarks on voluntary transfers as unwarranted and irresponsible. In June 1872, however, he had sanctioned Melvill's proposed enquiry. By January 1873 Davies' attitude had become one of alarm tinged with hope. That position had given way in its turn, for by February 1874 Davies had arrived at the conclusion that, apart from large landowners, there was no danger to be apprehended from the voluntary alienation of land. This attitude hardened to the point where almost all reservations disappeared, and Davies was able to prepare an elaborate and confident defence of a *laissez-faire* policy.

In a way Davies had returned to his original standpoint, but with a significant difference: it was once again unwarranted to refer to the voluntary transfer of land as a great political danger, but it was no longer irresponsible. The fact, of course, was that the period from 1869 to 1874 had seen the growth of a conviction among a number of officers that land was passing steadily from the agricultural to the trading classes. This was not something which Davies could ignore or explain away entirely.

The extent to which land was being transferred was quite another matter. Those officers who favoured legislation could rely only on personal impressions; impressions which nearly convinced the Lieutenant-Governor, in January 1873, that some action had to be taken. Ultimately, however, Davies came to rely on the land transfer statistics collected annually for the revenue report, these being the only statistics which purported to give some idea of what was happening in the Province as a whole. Now whatever the accuracy of these figures (and later experience proved them far from accurate), and whatever their omissions, all this apart, these figures could not but reduce all the local variations and complexities in the situation to one dead level. We have seen how conditions which prevailed in the south-west had hardly begun to appear in a central and a north-western district, to say nothing of other variations. The point is appreciated easily in the light of the vast literature of succeeding settlements. To Robert Egerton and Henry Davies, however, in possession only of the scanty information of the time, it was not obvious that they were considering, at best, the average of a multitude of local conditions. Indeed, it is doubtful whether many local officers were aware of the diversified nature of changes in landholding. A few might have appreciated the variations within the limits of their own districts or divisions, past and present. But at a time when reliable accounts of land transfer were not available, when the cumulative effects of the process were only beginning to attract attention, no one man could have had a large experience or understanding of the varied changes in the possession of land which were taking place throughout the Province. Hence those officers who sought legislation could only speak of their local experience as if it had a universal application. The British were still very much in the dark about land transfers, and it was this which gave Egerton and Davies the opportunity to overrule unfavourable local impressions by reference to what appeared to be an objective, Provincial standard, the revenue report statistics, supplemented by their own impressions of various parts of the Province.

This should not obscure the fact that Egerton, Lindsay and Davies were eager to find evidence to disprove the claims of those who urged remedial action. Egerton and Lindsay were consistently sceptical of these claims. On the only occasion that Davies appeared to accept them, he did not cease to hope for counter-indications. Once Davies had made up his mind that a serious problem did not exist, he became increasingly anxious to prove his point. His treatment of the opinions advanced in the Chief Court enquiry bears all the marks of one who was no longer open to argument. Why otherwise an independent enquiry by Robert Egerton, whose approach to the subject was well known? Why otherwise the attempt to reject so completely the 'gloomy' impressions of a number of officers, even admitting that it would have been difficult not to give some weight to the Provincial statistics? Again even if Lindsay's evidence from Hoshiarpur as to alienations to landholders was accepted, and even if these alienations were treated as unobjectionable, why was the contradictory evidence from Gurdaspur ignored?

If it be asked why Egerton and Lindsay, and those who thought like them, were so sceptical of the need for legislation, one answer is that they found it difficult to appreciate that the voluntary transfer of land involved any political danger. At the most they were prepared to concede that it might be politic to do something to maintain large and influential proprietors. The view that a much wider agrarian problem existed was, after all, a new one championed by a few officers like Arthur Brandreth and Philip Sandys Melvill, who would not have taken such a view themselves some years earlier. Though the Lieutenant-Governor temporarily shared their fears, he was supplied, to his relief, with arguments and evidence which appeared to confound the notion of growing political danger.

The idea of a new agrarian problem was greeted with disbelief by many officers because it did not fit accepted notions of what constituted such a problem. The protective policy had been fully incorporated into the administrative system of the Province. The enforcement of pre-emption in permanent transfers, and restrictions on compulsory sales, found the widest support. The attitudes which underlay the protective policy had persisted as well; but far from giving much support to a new protective policy, they played in many respects a negative role. The canons of the protective policy were now not only respectable and unquestionable, but they also provided a ready answer to those who claimed to discern agrarian troubles. Many officers strove to prove that transfers were not due to oppressive assessments; for in the old scheme of things only this, or some other disturbing influence, could constitute a reason for remedial action. To many a mere reference to low assessments, the value of land, the existence of agricultural credit and prosperity, sufficed to render the notion of agrarian difficulties unreal. That, as Melvill saw, it was precisely in such circumstances that the voluntary transfer of land would proceed apace, was not an idea which found ready acceptance. Nor could every officer share the belief that the courts played a sinister role in the whole process. For many it was all too new and unexpected.

Then the accepted economic and social doctrines of the time told against legislation. If the Government provided a suitable framework for society, then nothing further could be done. The extravagant or the improvident could not be saved. Attempt to do so, and matters would only become worse, at any rate they would not improve. So ran the orthodox *laissez-faire* argument (coloured in Lindsay's case by social Darwinist notions), stated in terms adapted to the circumstances of Indian rural society. The fact that the protective policy itself was a departure from political economy did not make much difference. The protective policy had made its mark on Punjab administration, but without invalidating the absolute truths of political economy in British eyes. It is true that the fact that political economy had been set aside once, did provide a precedent, on which Davies might have drawn, indeed which he might have extended, witness the economic arguments which he used in January 1873. Nevertheless, political economy still provided a barrier which every proposal for intervention in society had to surmount. This was so partly and obviously because *laissez-faire* notions appeared to render legislation futile, and partly and less obviously because it was not easy to conceive of voluntary transfers of land as a political danger or an agrarian problem when according to the doctrines of political economy nothing could be amiss. These ideas were so pervasive that many officers could not help but think in these terms, to some extent. To all this there was only one exception: officers like Arthur Brandreth could argue, and Lindsay could to some extent accept, the idea that the Government in India was the chief or real landlord and hence could interfere to protect its tenants (the landowners). This idea, if it was indeed influenced by a theoretical source, being perhaps as much suggested by actual conditions in India,[140] never acquired any more than a shadow of the authority enjoyed by the *laissez-faire* aspects of political economy.

It would be a mistake to assume, however, that all those who opposed legislation were doctrinaire by nature, so to speak; though in Lindsay's case one may have one's doubts. That Henry Davies could speak both for and against the relevance of political economy, depending on his assessment of other elements in the situation, suggests that doctrinaire considerations alone did not dictate the opinions of all opponents of legislation. If one did not believe that an agrarian problem existed, *laissez-faire* political economy provided a convenient source of authoritative arguments against legislation. And while the inability to perceive an agrarian problem was related to popular notions of political economy, it was related to actual conditions in the countryside as well.

When Davies, in 1874, turned against legislation, he laid great stress on the prosperity of the Province; and did not hesitate to represent voluntary transfers, which revealed the rising value of land, as evidence of that prosperity. In part this was no doubt a tactical move; but it was derived from an aspect of change which had been perceived for some time, and which was particularly striking to many who remembered the conditions prevailing under Sikh and early British rule. The improvement in the circumstances of the Province had been a subject of constant remark in the 1860s, so much so that some officers had not hesitated to challenge the continued relevance of the protective policy on these grounds. Nor did this aspect of change disappear simply because Brandreth and Melvill raised their standard. Indeed, it is a question whether in many parts of the Province in the early 1870s increased prosperity was not a more obvious fact of rural life than increased indebtedness. Until 1869 perception of increased prosperity had weakened, if anything, the case for existing restrictions on alienation, while thereafter it remained as a stumbling block to the new legislative proposals, which observation of increased indebtedness had stirred into life. That changes in society did not always exert their influence in one consistent direction is not surprising when it is recalled firstly, that different things were happening in different parts of the Province (or the same things were happening to different degrees or at different rates) and, secondly, that the influence which social change exerted was dependent on the views taken by large numbers of men whose interpretations were bound to vary.

If those who spoke in doctrinaire terms were not always or not necessarily unaffected by developments around them, it is likewise unsafe to assume that those who emphasised the danger of land transfer were unaffected by doctrinaire considerations. In 1874 Melvill had to at least consider, even if he generally rejected, the economic arguments against legislation. Melvill, after all, was attempting to escape from the sort of opinions which he had cherished himself not so many years before.

Any overdrawn contrast between doctrinaire opponents of legislation, on the one hand, and pragmatic advocates, on the other, or indeed any too sharply drawn contrast between all opponents and all advocates, is bound to founder on the rock of individual differences. The working of Lindsay's mind cannot be equated with that of Davies'. Brandreth did not arrive at his conclusions by the same process of reasoning as Melvill.

It has to be borne in mind as well that the years from 1869 to 1874 showed the attitudes of most of those who favoured legislation in a comparatively undeveloped state, the discussion having been launched for the first time in these years. As yet there were perhaps few officers who took such an alarmist view of the political danger as Arthur Brandreth: even Melvill thought it would take half a century for that political danger to be realised. Melvill's scheme for the restriction of alienations would have gained Brandreth's approval no doubt, but that might well have been the limit of its support. At his most alarmed the Lieutenant-Governor contemplated little more than a regulation of the rate of interest allowed by the courts. Most of the officers who thought that there was a problem to be solved, looked to such restrictions on interest, to the extension of the period of limitation for debt, and to better agricultural education.

All this is not to deny the fact that a new rift in official opinion was beginning to make itself felt at a time when the principles and measures of the old protective policy had been widely accepted.

## THE PUNJAB TRADITION

The years from 1869 to 1874 had seen the emergence of a debate which raised, and would increasingly raise, questions of the most fundamental kind in both the intellectual and political spheres. Already in these early years it is apparent that the new issues were more far-reaching than those which had characterised the old protective policy even in its heyday. To restrict compulsory alienations, or to enforce rights of pre-emption, was to admit the unsuitability, often only the temporary unsuitability, of certain aspects of the British system. To propose the restriction of voluntary alienations of land was tantamount to questioning the very principles on which the whole system was based.

Consider, first of all, the intellectual implications. In the early days of British rule the advocates of the protective policy had assumed, like everyone else, that the maintenance of agricultural credit was desirable, and that it was of the greatest importance to stimulate the investment of money in the improvement of land, and to encourage the growth of the marketable value of land. At a time when agricultural credit was comparatively limited, and land of little value, rural circumstances threw no doubt on such assumptions. In the context of the older debate it was only David Simson, and then only in 1869, who went as far as to suggest that some limitation of agricultural credit was desirable. This was the kind of position which Davies assumed in 1873 and Melvill in 1874; one of the chief aims of the latter being the restriction of agricultural credit. In asserting that restrictions on voluntary alienations would not be likely to increase the rates of interest, Melvill was also departing from the logic of political economy in a way which an old advocate of the protective policy like Robert Cust had not been able to do. The point of course is that there were now officers who discerned circumstances in which agricultural credit was being abused, and hence were not convinced, or like Melvill no longer convinced, that the maintenance of existing credit facilities was desirable. As regards the improvement of land Simson in 1869 adverted to the fact that the landowners did not generally improve their land, while Melvill made the same point in 1874 with reference to the money-lenders. The maintenance of the marketable value of land, it is true, was still considered of great importance, even Melvill only going as far as to say that a slight depreciation in its value was not to be weighed against the security of possession of hereditary landowners. And while all these matters touched prevailing notions of political economy, there had been little explicit criticism of the relevance of political economy to rural problems. At his boldest Davies, drawing

## A POLITICAL DILEMMA EMERGES

on the older, ambivalent tradition, was prepared to set political economy aside in certain limited respects. Only one direct and explicit statement of the irrelevance of political economy to village society had been made; and then by a very junior officer in the context of the debate about pre-emption, and in a manner which betrayed its immediate intellectual origins.[141] More generally doubts about the relevance of political economy were implicit and piecemeal, indicating most clearly the role of direct social influence, which did not necessarily lead men to take their views to their logical conclusion. Yet gradual and tentative as the process was, there can be no doubt that officers like Brandreth and Melvill, with their demand for government interference, were questioning current notions of progress and *laissez-faire*. Their views implied that Indian society would not progress, or continue to progress, if left to its own devices, uncontrolled by protective measures.

Of course the problems of *laissez-faire* and government intervention are familiar themes in Victorian history. *Laissez-faire* ideas could be applied to a host of problems otherwise unrelated. To apply them to the transfer of land in the Punjab was to apply them to a problem which had no close parallel in British experience outside India. The rural problems of Britain itself had little specific bearing on this issue. It is not surprising therefore that we find the role of English ideas at this stage to be great only in the sense that they seriously inhibited recognition of a new rural problem in the Punjab. As soon as we look for direct English influences on the side of legislation to combat the problem, there is little that is not of the most miscellaneous or partial description. Brandreth's references to English history, and the possible influence of English ideas on the notion that Government was the supreme landlord, are instances in point. While admitting such influences, it is clear that they pale beside the role of social influence; for while social influence did not always work in one consistent direction, the debate of 1869–74 certainly derived directly from observation of developments within Punjab society itself.

One further point deserves emphasis. If we attribute historical developments to social influences, we must ask whether there were any factors at work which induced men to view social developments from a particular angle or which encouraged them to give these developments a certain weight. The answer in the Punjab in the early 1870s can only be that while orthodox economic assumptions played a negative role, there were certain widely held political presuppositions which were likely to lead officers to look, more or less carefully, at manifestations of rural indebtedness and land transfer. A survey of the British political tradition in the Punjab not only touches on these presuppositions, but shows why the years from 1869 to 1874 marked the opening stages of a new era in the history of that tradition.

VI

When Arthur Brandreth declared in 1864 that the most effective way of keeping the country contented was to secure the goodwill of its leading and aristocratic elements, he made it clear that he had been in earlier days an adherent of light settlements with small holders. A mere five years after presenting his case for an aristocratic land policy, he began to urge the political dangers inherent in the transfer of land from hereditary landholders to the Hindu trading castes. This was primarily a problem relating to small owners of land; and Brandreth did not think that interference on behalf of more substantial landowners alone would be of much avail.[142] Three stages, then, may be discerned in the development of Brandreth's political outlook, involving a commitment, firstly to the favourable treatment of small holders of land, secondly to the favourable treatment of aristocratic elements, and finally to measures to ensure the survival of existing owners of land. An understanding of the wider significance of the third stage depends on an estimation of the degree to which the preceding stages reflected not merely Brandreth's personal opinion, but official opinion in the Province at large.

In his second or aristocratic stage Brandreth saw the years before 1857 as the period in which the British aimed to depress the upper classes, while raising up a peasantry who were to take the British part in all commotions.[143] Now there can be no doubt that the British, under the influence of the village settlement system of the North-Western Provinces, were determined to make their land-revenue settlements with village communities, and as a rule hardly considered leading and aristocratic elements in the light of full proprietors. In some parts of the country, perhaps, they were not even over-generous in adjudging these elements small dues as superior proprietors. Again, though a good deal of research would be required to show precisely how these aristocratic elements fared in the quite different sphere of assignments of land-revenue (Brandreth thought they were harshly treated in this respect as well, certainly in his district of Jhelum), it need not be doubted that the new regime had less need for the aristocracy as a class than the old, and that anti-aristocratic sentiment was rife. But did British policy before 1857 contemplate more than a contented and prospering peasantry to keep the country quiet, did it in fact contemplate an actively loyal peasantry, as Brandreth suggested?

Henry Lawrence made his position clear in 1844, before he ruled the Punjab, when he wrote that 'the time may come when we shall find our best safeguard in the hearts of a grateful people', but added that 'that time has not *yet* come, nor is there a near prospect of its advent'.[144] His later writings do not suggest that his experience in the Punjab led him to change his views on this subject to any great extent.[145] Many years later one of Henry's nominees made much the same remark about not yet being able to trust implicitly the loyalty of the masses of India; for like Henry he championed 'the policy of holding India by the strong hand'.[146] Again the apprehensions which Herbert Edwardes, another of Henry's men, entertained in 1857 of a civilian rising, hardly suggest any faith in the active or sentimental loyalty of the masses.[147]

But whence did the idea of the possibility of such loyalty come? Richard Temple provided a clue in one of his books when he averred that it had been James Thomason's ambition to attach the masses to British rule as one for which it was worth their while to fight. Temple indicated that he had never met a statesman who came closer than Thomason to the belief that the agricultural classes could be induced to render an actively patriotic support to a foreign government.[148] How close did prominent Punjab civilians, committed to Thomason's revenue system, come to such a view? In the late 1840s and early 1850s George Campbell was perhaps not entirely without hope of attaching to British rule the manly and industrious tribes of the Punjab as well as those of Hindustan. The British had more in common with the Jats and Sikhs of the Punjab than with any other Indian race, he wrote in 1849.[149] Temple himself, writing after the close of his Indian career, discounted Thomason's notion, being quite reconciled to the idea that active or sentimental loyalty to an alien Government could not be expected from the peasant proprietors of India. They were loyal but passive.[150] It appears that Temple was echoing the views of his old master, John Lawrence, whose mutiny administration report had this to say about the situation in the Punjab in those critical years:

... so long as we were at all able to assert authority, most agriculturists were quite willing to pay tribute to Cæsar. It were vain from such facts to assume the existence of any active heartfelt loyalty. But, at all events, there existed no feeling against us; there was a kind of passive sentiment in our favour among the masses. The best revenue administration will not secure much more than this; but recent events have shown that, to secure even this much, is great gain . . .[151]

While evidence of this kind is hardly conclusive in regard to British feelings before 1857, it does suggest that it would be unsafe to accept uncritically Brandreth's account of British expectations of active loyalty. As for the situation from 1857, one officer at any rate thought that the events of the mutiny showed that to some extent the Punjab system had succeeded in attaching the people to the Government.[152] More generally it may be said that a strong faith in that passive loyalty of the masses, of which John Lawrence and Richard Temple spoke, was or became the central feature of the early Punjab political tradition. In John Lawrence's case this faith was not created by the events of 1857; for during that crisis he never wavered in his conviction that, apart from the frontier, the people of the Punjab bore the British no ill-will.[153] And after the mutiny even the frontier could be seen as loyal.[154] On the other hand, Herbert Edwardes had feared risings in the Punjab in 1857; and it was their failure to eventuate here or in most of India which made the greatest impression on his political outlook.[155] Whatever the precise antecedents of the tradition in individual instances, its persistence for some years in its original, confident form, is not in doubt. Thus in a farewell speech in 1877 a prominent military civilian suggested that the majority of the people of India had no objection to British rule.[156] And the later writings of a number of officers who had served under Henry and John Lawrence, but who had left the Punjab at a comparatively early stage, contain passages suggesting that British rule in the Punjab or India was based on the tacit consent or well-being of the many.[157] To this may be added the views of Lepel Griffin, who did not join the service till shortly after John Lawrence's departure. In the preface to his book on the Punjab Rajas, Griffin wrote in 1870 that the people had accepted good government with 'a quiet gladness', but with 'no feeling of thankfulness'. It was futile to expect to find in the hearts of the people of India 'any affection for ourselves'. But esteem was 'stronger and better than love'. And for the English Government the people of India had a 'sincere esteem', based on their appreciation of its just character and of the solid material advantages which it conferred.[158]

But if there was such faith in the passive loyalty of the people,

## A POLITICAL DILEMMA EMERGES

what then are we to make of the second stage in the development of Brandreth's political outlook, the commitment to an aristocratic policy? Some historians have argued indeed that the post-mutiny period witnessed an 'aristocratic reaction'[159] or 'an extensive growth of landlord sentiment'[160] in the Punjab as in some other Indian Provinces. The tenancy debate of the 1860s has been cited as evidence, one account suggesting that the views of Edward Prinsep, the Punjab Settlement Commissioner, placed him squarely in the tradition of the aristocratic reaction.[161] As far as the Punjab is concerned, these views are based on a complete misreading of the evidence. It has been assumed that because tenancy debates had certain political implications in some Indian Provinces they must carry the same implications in a Province with quite different tenures. The words 'landlord' and 'tenant' have been interpreted literally, as if the legal relationship which they expressed made it unnecessary to examine the social realities. Prinsep's proposals in the Amritsar division were made on behalf of landlords, and these proposals were adverse to the interests of occupancy tenants. But while the holdings of occupancy tenants in that division were estimated to average four acres, those of the landlords were estimated to average six acres,[162] so that these 'landlords' could be more aptly described as peasant proprietors. In the Punjab context, therefore, it is only in the strictly technical sense that Prinsep can be described as an advocate of the interests of the landlord; and any thesis on the general growth of landlord sentiment in the Province is subject to similar qualifications. To describe Prinsep as an advocate of the rights of small peasant proprietors against those of small peasant cultivators would do more justice to the practical issues at stake. Hence there is nothing strange in the fact that we find Prinsep lamenting at one stage that a particular course of action would 'bring the British Government into disfavour with the rural population who hitherto have been our stand-by':[163] a comment which places him in the normal Punjab tradition of reliance on the agricultural classes. Nor need we be surprised that in 1865 Arthur Brandreth was among Prinsep's strongest critics,[164] for the tenancy debate was primarily one between proprietary and non-proprietary cultivators, and did not bolster the position of the Punjab aristocracy in any particular way.

This does not mean that the possibility of growing aristocratic sentiment in the Punjab can be dismissed out of hand. It will not do to assume, for instance, that events in the Punjab during the mutiny necessarily vindicated John Lawrence's policy in the eyes of all and sundry, or that Punjab policy was not influenced by events outside the Province.[165] Many prominent Punjab officers had served their apprenticeship in northern India, or had been employed there after the mutiny, considerations which underline the distinct possibility of influence from outside. In the Punjab itself the very passivity of the peasantry might be a source of disappointment, as in Arthur Brandreth's case; particularly since his district of Jhelum was one of those in which the superior claims to land had been rather more compelling than in most of the Punjab. Brandreth also provided some suggestive evidence about the views of others. He noted that Edward Thornton, his immediate superior, had expressed his disenchantment with the political consequences of existing policy at the outbreak of the mutiny.[166] And Brandreth asserted that after the mutiny superior claims were treated more favourably in the adjudication of landed rights, a point which the Commissioner of the division confirmed for a neighbouring district.[167] The Punjab response to the Government of India's sirdar scheme also suggests an increased interest in the aristocracy as a political support to Government.[168] And the disposition of some officers in the early 1870s to worry only about the indebtedness of substantial landowners may be part of the same pattern. The full extent of these notions, and the degree to which they qualified earlier political ideas, can be settled only by detailed enquiry. It is clear enough, however, that no abatement of anti-aristocratic feeling, no concern for the promotion of aristocratic interests, could touch the basic tenures of the countryside, already largely determined, in a Province which had stood the strain of the mutiny. Such aristocratic sentiment as existed could only shape policy to the extent that it did not seriously undermine the fruits of earlier political notions. In this sense a concern for the loyalty of the majority could go hand in hand with a desire to strengthen the aristocracy. But the creation of the kind of aristocratic society which Brandreth envisaged in 1864 was out of the question, and Brandreth knew it. His was an impassioned but in many respects a rhetorical protest, and as such a fit comment on the limited development of an aristocratic policy in the Punjab.

The central and persistent feature of the early Punjab political tradition, then, was reliance on the loyalty of the agricultural classes, particularly the peasant proprietors. Generally there is little evidence that more than passive loyalty was expected, though at times some individuals had hopes of better things. The impact of the mutiny on this tradition was complex. It could be favourable, confirming the value of the tradition, or even enhancing it in the

## A POLITICAL DILEMMA EMERGES

eyes of some officers. It could be unfavourable, raising varying degrees of doubt in the minds of other officers. In the sphere of policy such doubts resulted in little or nothing inconsistent with the persistence of the tradition. But we may ask, was the early Punjab tradition ever touched by fears that the passive loyalty of the peasant proprietors might be undermined?

The existence of a protective policy in regard to land transfer would suggest that it was. It must not be forgotten, however, that at every stage the application of or the demand for a protective policy was stimulated by outside influences – by experience in northern India in the early 1850s, by events in the same part of India at the end of that decade, and by recollection of those events at the end of the next decade. It is true that gradually conditions in the Punjab itself came to have more and more to say to the matter. But on the whole the dangers anticipated in the Punjab were only potential and could be seen to be averted from the beginning by the application of a protective policy. The very success of the policy of restricting the compulsory alienation of land for debt ensured that such alienations would not generate political anxiety. The law of pre-emption, of course, did not stop the voluntary transfer of land, and despite some anxiety after the mutiny no further restrictions were imposed on voluntary alienations; but in the 1860s the rising value of land tended to inhibit concern on this score. The protective policy came too early in the history of the Punjab, it was accepted too easily and solved the limited range of problems perceived too completely, for it to be associated with grave and growing fears as to the loyalty of the peasant proprietors.

The point may be illustrated from the writings of several officers connected with a protective policy in the first two decades of British rule. George Campbell and Richard Temple held their last offices in the Punjab in 1857 and 1860 respectively. Temple's pen had often defended the protective policy of his superiors, while Campbell was imbued with notions of a protective policy far in advance of the official version. In later years Temple adhered to a protective policy in certain respects.[169] Campbell remained throughout his Indian career an exponent of his own ideas about restrictions on landed rights in the initial stages of British rule.[170] Campbell also favoured arrangements which would enable courts to go behind contracts, arrangements of a kind sponsored later by Temple with reference to, and as a result of events in, the Deccan.[171] Yet neither Campbell nor Temple gave the impression that they were wrestling with problems which were not primarily administrative and social in character.

While their policies obviously had political implications there was no suggestion that they were answers to great political dilemmas. The loyalty of rural India was not seriously in question. This is not to say that the protective policy was of no political significance. References to the mutiny in the debate of 1869-70, for instance, show that political implications were inherent in problems of this description. Nevertheless, this does not by itself make the problem one of *central* political importance. Lieutenant-Colonel Coxe might urge complete prohibition of compulsory alienations of land for debt in 1869 in the strongest terms, emphasising the one-sided relations between landholders and money-lenders; but he hardly considered rural indebtedness a major political issue.[172] Similarly Lepel Griffin supported restrictions in 1869, while declaring in the following year that popular risings against British rule could be considered impossible as long as the administration of the country was based on just and enlightened principles.[173]

To gauge the true political significance of the protective policy it must be seen against the whole political background of the early years of British rule in the Punjab. In the first decade we see a Province conquered only after hard fought battles, its cohesive military and religious community humbled, its aristocracy reduced to a shadow of its former self, its frontier a perennial source of trouble, its political stability strained to the limit in 1857–8. It was a situation which generated the most overt and pressing political problems; and for many of those who passed through this period it doubtless left a legacy of anxiety and uncertainty. Moreover, the Punjab only presented in a more acute form what was conceived at the time as the predicament of the British in the whole of India. One finds in the contemporary and later writings of many of the earliest Punjab officers a distinct awareness of the fragility of British rule in India. The alien character of British rule; the very limited numbers of the British themselves; the uncertainty as to the changes which the future might bring, whether in the character of the British themselves, or with reference to what Temple called 'volcanoes not wholly extinct and hardly extinguishable within any definite time'[174] —these were some of the elements in the analysis.[175] In such circumstances the well-being and contentment of the village proprietors, the leading element in rural society, might well appear as a solid or at any rate indispensable foundation for British rule. Yet in all this the protective policy was only an adjunct to those far-reaching administrative measures by which the British sought to transform the Punjab, and by means of which they thought they would secure the

## A POLITICAL DILEMMA EMERGES

loyalty of the village proprietors. In a political sense the protective policy was at once important and marginal. Important, because it was intended to prevent the appearance of any distressing side effects to the cure the British were trying to work; marginal, because it was the whole administrative system which was designed to work the cure.

In other words, the tradition of reliance on the loyalty of the peasant proprietor was touched as fleetingly by fear as by hope or disappointment. And this fact clarifies the wider significance of the third stage in the development of Arthur Brandreth's political outlook; for nothing could be plainer than Brandreth's conviction from 1869 that the voluntary transfer of land to Hindu traders constituted an agrarian problem of fundamental political importance. Fear had gained a grip on the tradition at last. Of course Brandreth's opinion taken by itself involved no greater change in the political tradition than had his earlier commitment to an aristocratic policy. Even in the early 1870s, however, Brandreth did not stand alone. In future years his analysis of the political situation came to be shared by ever larger sections of official opinion, so that it is justifiable to date a new period in the political tradition from 1869; a period in which there was little room for hope or disappointment as to the active loyalty of the peasant proprietors, but only steadily increasing concern whether they would remain passive in any new crisis.

The fears of the new period were related to the political beliefs and experiences of the old, though in a rather complex way. There was little direct continuity in the fears expressed in both periods regarding the transfer of land. Arthur Brandreth had shown some concern about indebtedness before 1869; but in the 1850s and 1860s the opinions of Philip Sandys Melvill regarding the transfer of land had been all the other way. No prominent advocate of a protective policy in the 1850s perceived the new problem in the 1860s. Recognition of the new problem was inhibited, in fact, by those widespread assumptions about the nature of rural problems which the protective policy had generated. It is true that those who sought remedies for the new problems appealed to the events of the mutiny in northern India, just as the advocates of a protective policy had done. Yet this establishes the persistence of a state of mind rather than continuity in the perception of agrarian problems. In the early 1870s, it must be recalled, the new fears were expressed by men who had passed through the politically tense years of the 1850s and notably those of 1857–8. Once such men perceived distinct trends in the voluntary transfer of land, it may well be that recollection of earlier events helped to define and sharpen their anxieties. In future years this legacy was likely to diminish somewhat, as the mutiny became an impersonal memory, and outbreaks in other parts of India could serve as examples of the turmoil which could be engendered by rural indebtedness. Quite apart from the protective policy or the state of mind produced by the mutiny, there was one way in which the fears of the new period were firmly embedded in the political convictions of the old. Men could conceive of the voluntary alienation of land as a major political problem only because the political tradition placed such emphasis on rural loyalty, and because that tradition had been embodied in the land tenures of the Province. If the peasant proprietor had not been considered an indispensable foundation for British rule, his indebtedness or disappearance could hardly have been seen as a great political problem.

These considerations help to explain why the manifestation of distinct changes in the possession of land could lead to the kind of political debate which took place between 1869 and 1874. It is, however, one thing to explain the appearance of a new thread in the political tradition. It is quite another to explain why over a period of thirty or more years this new thread grew increasingly impressive, till it finally enveloped the older tradition altogether. It was not as if land transfer constituted an overt political challenge which all men could recognise as such.[176] Complex and varied in itself, the process of land transfer could be considered from any number of points of view and interpreted in any number of different ways. It is of some interest, therefore, to see what made the unprecedented notions of one officer in 1869, the political heritage of a Province.

CHAPTER III

# The Tradition Transformed

I

The deductions which the Lieutenant-Governor had drawn from the revenue report statistics at the end of 1874 settled the approach of superior authority to the problem of land transfer for some six years. This is not surprising, considering that the key executive positions during these years were held by opponents of legislative interference, or by men of very moderate views. Egerton remained Financial Commissioner till 1877 when he succeeded Davies as Lieutenant-Governor. At the Financial Commissioner's office Egerton's place was taken by Gore Ouseley, and after the latter's death in 1879, by James Lyall.

From the annual statistics these men drew the satisfactory conclusions that not much land was alienated in the Province as a whole; that of the land transferred much was acquired by agriculturists; that many of the transfers took place in districts known to be prosperous; that the value of land was increasing and that the Government revenue had nothing to do with the alienations; and generally that indebtedness and land transfer must be set against the large increase of general prosperity which had taken place. Some less satisfactory features were also apparent. It was noticed in the revenue report for 1875–6 that the number of sales was twenty-five per cent and the number of mortgages forty per cent greater by the registration than the revenue returns; but the question was not pursued in succeeding reports. The annual increase in the total area alienated could be explained sometimes, as in the report for 1876–7, by reference to the transactions of former years which only now were being recorded in some districts. In 1877–8 the increase, following widespread distress, seemed more disturbing; but part of it could be explained away. It was also apparent that the distinction between transfers to agriculturists and to non-agriculturists, made since 1875, was not reliable, but not too much stress was laid upon this aspect of the matter. The investigations of these years, however, did dispel the illusion that any significant proportion of the alienations might be effected for agricultural improvements rather than for debt or necessity.[1]

To Arthur Brandreth, and others of his way of thinking, the results of figures and averages were contrary to personal experience. As Commissioner of Multan Brandreth indicated in 1875 that it was not sufficient to point out that agrarian difficulties did not generally prevail, when there were tracts in which such difficulties were undoubtedly common.[2] In the succeeding year, as Commissioner of Jullunder, he quoted with great approval some remarks made by the Deputy Commissioner of the Jullunder district. While the statistics were so incomplete, the Deputy Commissioner noted, too much importance should not be attached to the number of cases in which transfers were made to agriculturists. The fact that landholders had become habitual lenders of money to their neighbours should not be allowed to divert attention from the extent to which other landholders, in some instances large communities, had become hopelessly involved in debt. Again there were numerous other cases in which communities, not yet sunk to this level, were so little above it that unfavourable seasons might at any time reduce them to it, while only the greatest economy and forethought would enable them to rise above their present precarious position.[3] Sharing views of this kind Brandreth did not hesitate to press on Government in 1875, in 1876 and again in 1877 the need for a law which would limit the liability of land for debt to the life of the holder or for some fixed period. This would check agricultural borrowing powers and inhibit reckless borrowing, while protecting the heirs, and thus ensuring that transfers engendered no political troubles.[4] No official notice was taken of these suggestions.

While Brandreth had little time for the statistics and attitudes of the superior authorities, it would be a mistake to conclude that the battle was only one between officers in district or division and those at the centre. True, throughout the second half of the 1870s there were other local officers who spoke ominously of the extent of indebtedness or who thought that land was more encumbered than was generally believed.[5] Yet in 1877 Brandreth was to be found defending his proposals for legislation against a new Deputy Commissioner in Jullunder. That officer saw matters in an entirely different light from his predecessor, arguing that sales, arising chiefly from the minute division of land, were unobjectionable as only merging small properties in large ones. Besides, the purchaser generally kept on the old owner as cultivator, a position which the

Deputy Commissioner appeared to think advantageous for the old owner.[6] Nor was this Deputy Commissioner the only local officer who took an optimistic view of the situation. Charles McMahon, the Commissioner of Hissar, and Alexander Benton, the Deputy Commissioner of Multan, for instance, were not convinced that land was being transferred to professional money-lenders to any serious extent.[7]

Not every officer who took a calmer view of what was happening was necessarily out of touch with rural society. Consider the attitude of William Coldstream, the Deputy Commissioner of Hoshiarpur, one of the districts in Brandreth's Jullunder division. In 1876 Coldstream, in connection with a proposal for the remission of revenue in about sixty riverain villages, had made particular enquiries in regard to indebtedness. Of his sixty villages only two were found to be free from debt. In the others an enormous amount of debt existed, the villages owing on an average nearly half the selling price of their assessed land. It was not that the revenue demand was high or the crops poor. It was just that the owners of these riverain villages, notoriously improvident and extravagant, had succumbed in the last twenty or twenty-five years to the temptation of raising money on the security of their land. Coldstream was not greatly alarmed. He believed that the next generation of landowners might be better able and willing to look after themselves. Yet he admitted that in many cases another generation would not see them in possession of their land. Land had already changed hands to some extent. The professional money-lenders carried away most of the grain from the threshing floor. The landholders continued to live from hand to mouth, hardly anticipating the time which appeared to be drawing near for many of them when their proprietary rights would cease to exist even in name. This state of things, Coldstream thought, while not applicable to the district generally, was not at all uncommon throughout the district.[8] This description was in some respects not unlike that which a Deputy Commissioner of the neighbouring district of Jullunder had given in 1876, and which had gained the approval of Arthur Brandreth. But that did not mean that Coldstream took the same view of the significance of the situation as Brandreth.

Another civilian of moderate opinions, who was taking careful stock of existing conditions, was H. E. Perkins, who had served in the Punjab since 1857, with only a short period of service elsewhere.[9] By 1875 he was not a complete convert to the policy of restricting sales in execution of civil decrees. As Deputy Commissioner of the

Rawalpindi district he remarked in that year that the policy was wise up to a point; for experience showed that money borrowed on the security of land was spent on domestic ceremonies rather than agricultural improvements. Nevertheless, he suggested that the Chief Court might sanction compulsory sales more freely. The landholder could borrow money from the Government for improvements but not, as a rule, for the purchase of cattle. On occasions when cattle died through starvation or murrain the landholder was driven to the moneylender who would lend only on exorbitant terms because, as Perkins thought, the restrictions on compulsory sales depreciated the value of land.[10] These opinions, however, did not blind Perkins to the need for studying changes in the possession of land. Appointed Commissioner of the Amritsar division in 1877, he did refer in his revenue report to the remarks of his district officers as showing that no special harm arose from alienations. But he added that he would make a careful study of the subject when he had time to go among the people, for it was a matter which had interested him deeply for many years.[11]

The special report which Perkins submitted in 1878 was essentially a critique of the line taken in the revenue reports. Among other things Perkins argued that transfers were taking place to a much larger extent than had been admitted. While he noted distinct differences between the districts of his division, he stressed that the revenue report statistics for the Amritsar division as a whole showed that during the last ten years nearly fourteen per cent of the total area had been alienated by sale and mortgage. Taking into account the fact that these revenue returns seemed to be below the registration returns, he thought that the true figure was likely to be nearer eighteen per cent. But he showed no real signs of alarm, and allowed that the evil was materially qualified by the fact that nearly half of the transfers were to agriculturists.[12]

This analysis already went too far for the superior authorities. James Lyall, the Financial Commissioner, and Robert Egerton, the Lieutenant-Governor, indicated in 1879 that fuller statistics were necessary before Perkins' conclusions could be accepted, and they did not think that the amount of land transferred in the Amritsar division need cause alarm. They also repudiated a suggestion in Perkins' report that the assessments in the worst districts were not light.[13]

The example of Perkins, as well as that of Coldstream, shows that there is no reason to suppose that those officers who sought legislation to control the transfer of land were the only ones in close contact with rural society. The point is made abundantly clear by a survey of the opinions of Settlement Officers during the second half of the 1870s, all of them men who had acquired a comprehensive knowledge of particular areas over a period of years. Their accounts and opinions, as well as those of some other local officers, further illustrate the gradual increase in official knowledge of changes in the possession of land.

Most of the Settlement Officers were civilians who had joined the service between 1863 and 1875. With the exception of W. E. Purser, those engaged in the settlement of the south-eastern districts of the Punjab had commenced their service in the later part of the period, between 1870 and 1875. In the south-east, or rather in those parts of it under settlement, where the land was held largely by Hindu Jats, and here and there to a significant extent by other tribes, the Settlement Officers did not find alienations to be extensive or the proportion acquired by money-lenders anything but small. That the Settlement Officers did not always trouble to collect or present complete statistics of alienation suggests that most of them did not pay the most particular attention to the problem.

W. E. Purser, an officer who had gained much of his experience since 1866 in the south-east, was in charge of the Rohtak settlement.[14] The statistics collected for the assessment reports of three tahsils showed six per cent or less of the cultivation alienated by sale and mortgage.[15] Even after the drought of 1877–8 H. C. Fanshawe, also employed in the settlement, was able to write that only a little more than six per cent of the cultivation of the district had been alienated, and that almost everywhere most of it had gone to landholders. The people were well-to-do and free from debt. Such indebtedness as existed occurred largely in the villages of Hindu and Muslim Rajputs, and in some canal estates which had lived beyond their means. The Jats, who held so much of the land of the district, were by no means ruined, even if they had to mortgage their land, for they were certain to redeem it in the end. Though special causes of indebtedness existed, such as marriage expenses, litigation and loss of cattle, the most common cause of indebtedness was a natural one, where a family lost its proper complement of workers; and as a rule the debts which resulted in these instances were paid off.[16]

As far as the situation before the drought of 1877–8 was concerned, Denzil Ibbetson in part of Karnal, Robert Maconachie in Delhi and Francis Channing in Gurgaon did not produce statistics for tracts of any size which did more than suggest that the total extent of alienations occasionally ranged somewhat higher than in Rohtak.

In only one instance, in one of the tahsils of the Delhi district, did it reach as much as twelve-and-a-half per cent of the cultivation.[17] In Karnal, as in Rohtak, most of the alienations were to landholders. Ibbetson's statistics, which he thought to be below the mark, showed only from about a half to one-and-a-half per cent of the cultivation in the hands of professional money-lenders. Ibbetson would play a great role in later years, and even in 1878 he did not like alienations to money-lenders.[18] But several years before, in 1874, when he was Assistant Settlement Officer after about three-and-a-half years' service, he had been one of the very few officers in the Province to oppose the extension of the law of pre-emption to mortgages, on the ground that it would carry interference with the freedom of contract too far.[19] And years later, in his final report on Karnal, he described the village money-lender as a much and wrongly abused person, and stressed the absolutely vital role which he played in the village economy.[20] Robert Maconachie in Delhi apprehended that the money-lender's power over the landholder had increased in the last thirty years. Yet he could not forego the pleasure of quoting as wise and right some remarks made by James Lyall, with regard to the assessment of landowners who were hopelessly bad managers, to the effect that even a light assessment would drive these men out, and that they were only fit to be tenants compelled to work and with no credit to pledge.[21]

The idea that there was little or no hope for notoriously unthrifty tribes was in fact quite common. Perhaps it would not be an unmixed evil, the Deputy Commissioner of Gurgaon observed in 1879, if the Meo landholders of the district, who appeared to be incapable of learning thrift, lapsed into the condition of tenants and labourers. Not only would the ex-proprietors be compelled to exert themselves or starve, but the new landlords, mostly of the trading classes, would pay the revenue more readily. If the Government did not want to see the Meos gradually alienating their proprietary rights, it must be prepared to make large remissions of revenue in every year of drought or scarcity.[22] This was written at a time when the marked effects of the drought of 1877–8 on landholding in Gurgaon had become clear. In 1875 and 1876 when Francis Channing had submitted the assessment reports for the Gurgaon district he had indicated that sales had been few and that in only one tahsil, that of Firozpur, held by Meos, was as much as eight per cent of the area mortgaged[23] (the settlement report which Channing submitted several years later showed that nearly thirteen per cent of the cultivation of this tahsil was under mortgage in June 1877).[24] Then came the drought of 1877–8 and a great rise in alienation throughout the district. By the end of 1878 nineteen per cent of the cultivation of the Firozpur tahsil was burdened with mortgage, and a further two per cent of the cultivation had been sold. Another tahsil largely owned by Meos was not far behind. The three remaining tahsils were held by more thrifty tribes, and their fortunes varied; but even where, as in one of these tahsils, the rate of increase in alienation was very great, the absolute figures were not nearly as large as in the Meo tahsils, in which an appreciable area of land had been under mortgage before the drought.[25] Channing did not like the oppressive and inflexible revenue policy which had been pursued throughout the crisis;[26] but there is no evidence that he was particularly disturbed by the increase in the transfer of land as such. He saw little point in reducing the revenue on behalf of those who had become deeply involved with the money-lender, for in their case the mischief was done. Besides, Channing thought that among the improvident Meos much of the surplus of prosperous years would fall to the share of the money-lender under any circumstances.[27] The Assistant Settlement Officer, James Wilson, who had joined the service as late as 1875, shared the view of the Deputy Commissioner and Settlement Officer as to the character of the Meos; but he thought that their condition called loudly for special consideration, though he found it difficult to see what could be done for them.[28]

In 1878, the year of the drought, the condition of the Umballa district, a south-eastern district not under settlement, caused the Deputy Commissioner of the district and the Commissioner of the division some uneasiness. It had been four years since the Deputy Commissioner, a military officer in civilian employ since 1860, advocated the extension of the right of pre-emption to usufructuary mortgages on the ground of both justice and political expedience.[29] Now he thought the indebtedness of the Umballa district was increasing considerably, a matter of grave importance, which he tried to illustrate by some particulars concerning the indebtedness of various tribes and tahsils.[30] The Commissioner of the Umballa division, J. W. MacNabb, a civilian of twenty-seven years' standing, had occupied this particular post on previous occasions; and since 1870 at least he had become aware of the acquisition of land by professional money-lenders in the Umballa district.[31] He recalled in 1878 that during his tour the previous winter he had not found a village that was clear of debt: most owed the equivalent of three or four years' revenue, and many much more than that. This state of indebtedness, he admitted, he had been prepared to find among the

Rajputs, but not to such a large extent among the Jats. Among other things he thought the matter might receive careful consideration at the impending settlement, when the facts might be arrived at with greater precision.[32]

Years would pass before it would be ascertained that transfers of land, particularly in favour of professional money-lenders, were more extensive in Umballa than in any other south-eastern district. Meanwhile in the 1870s the work of Settlement Officers in other parts of the Province revealed a situation which at times differed widely from that prevailing in most of the south-east; and yet the Settlement Officers were not seriously alarmed.

Take the case of Septimus Thorburn, a civil officer appointed in 1864 and entrusted with the settlement of the frontier district of Bannu in 1872; a district in which he had served since 1867 and which he would not finally leave till 1879.[33] Thorburn published a popular account of his district in 1876, much of the manuscript having been written in 1874 and 1875.[34] This book shows that Thorburn was aware of the problem of indebtedness, but that it had not yet disturbed his peace of mind. The contempt which the Pathan landholders expressed for the Hindus of the district Thorburn did not think without foundation;[35] and this attitude would have much to say to his future political judgement. At the time, however, Thorburn did not look at indebtedness in a political light; or so his remarks on the loyalty of the district would lead one to think. The people of the district, the self-cultivating owners, he thought, believed implicitly in the impartiality, justice and good faith of the British.[36]

> Indeed, were the question of independence or a continuance of British rule put to a plebiscite tomorrow, there would be an overwhelming number of votes in our favour, so fresh is the recollection of the oppression and miseries under which the country groaned up to thirty years ago, and so strong the conviction the people have of their own incapacity for self-government and self-defence.[37]

In a frontier district like Bannu, much of which suffered grievously enough before British rule, the benefits of that rule might well appear to be great to a British officer. Thorburn had hardly begun to question them.

Nevertheless, in an embryonic form a number of Thorburn's later ideas and proposals can be found in this book. The experience which Thorburn had gained in settlement work led him to make an assessment of the capacities of the Pathan landholders which would not be without relevance when the responsibility for increasing rural indebtedness was in question.

> Instead of being the lazy ignorant beings I once thought them, the majority of the agriculturists of the District have proved, on better acquaintance, to be a shrewd, hard-working and intelligent class, who understand thoroughly how to make use of their slender means in extracting full measure from their soil.[38]

Conversely some of the arguments which led Thorburn to insist in later years that the British were responsible for increasing indebtedness were already apparent, though not emphasised or expounded in any coherent way. Thus the book contained the odd reference to the payment of usurious interest which the British courts enforced, and to the rigid exaction of revenue as a cause of indebtedness. While Thorburn knew that alienations of land in Bannu had occurred before as well as during British rule, he remarked in a footnote that it was during the last twenty-five years (that is, since the commencement of British rule) that the Hindus of Bannu had grown wealthy and become large landowners.[39]

But this was as far as Thorburn's view of British responsibility went. His view of landed property was informed by quite conventional notions, as witness his remark that the rude summary settlements of the district had been a great advance on Sikh practice, because these settlements created a valuable property in land which until that time had not existed.[40] This point is also borne out by Thorburn's discussion of the *vesh* tenure, a system of collective property in which the tribal lands were redistributed periodically by lot according to the number of mouths in the tribe. This tenure still survived in some instances in a part of the district known as Marwat. Thorburn admitted that any system of tenure which was not one of permanent severalty was generally condemned. Under a collective system little capital could be laid out on the permanent improvement of the productive qualities of the soil, while the rules regarding trees were subversive of any attempts at arboriculture. No encouragement was given to special thrift and industry, every one remained at a dead level, and a community which laboured under the trammels of *vesh* could not be a progressive one. Yet he could not help noting that in practice some of these objections did not operate fully in Marwat. In most *vesh* communities agricultural conditions were such that any outlay of capital was useless. The rules regarding trees were a dead letter, and it was the rats and the soil which explained the absence of trees. That the system gave no encouragement to extra thrift and labour, and did not increase material prosperity, he did not dispute; but he thought it was more than compensated for by the check which the custom exercised on the community's moral decadence, and by the stimulus it gave to the habit of self-government. It was to this that the Marwats owed their moral superiority over their neighbours.[41]

In addition to these specified advantages, Thorburn knew that the *vesh* tenure, while it permitted mortgages, made the permanent transfer of land impossible.[42] Yet in the final analysis he stood by the concept of individual landed property. His disposition to accept it as the touchstone of progress, in spite of some qualifications, was reinforced by his acquaintance with Henry Maine's *Village Communities in the East and West*, published in 1871. Under Maine's influence Thorburn saw the *vesh* tenure of Marwat as a living example of that collective form of property which everywhere constituted the common germ from which individual rights in land must have sprung.[43] He thought his settlement would extinguish the last remnants of the tenure. Discoursing on the reasons for its decline he pointed, among other things, to the 'civilising and destructive-of-equality' influences of British rule. A feeling of individual rights in land had developed, it had been fostered by British land laws and by the unintentional tendency of the administrators of these laws to sympathise with such a feeling.[44] The reasoning was rather confused and uncertain; but it is clear that there were intellectual influences at work which prevented or would prevent Thorburn from placing the British impact on land tenure in the same category with the civil courts and an inflexible revenue system as causes of indebtedness.

Here, then, we have an officer in close contact with rural society, grappling with the issues raised by indebtedness, but not yet taking the problem as one of the most serious significance. By 1878, the year in which Thorburn submitted his settlement report, there were more signs of uneasiness, though nothing like alarm.

With two exceptions, Thorburn noted in 1878, the self-cultivating landholders of the district were fairly prosperous and in infinitely easier circumstances than before British rule. In most of the district there was no really oppressive burden of debt in fair, average years. The first exception was Marwat; and in this part of the district Thorburn put much of the blame for indebtedness on over-assessment and rigid revenue collection, while admitting that even if no revenue demand existed, some proprietors would still be driven to sell or mortgage their holdings in bad years. As to over-assessment, he had given substantial reductions in his settlement, a partial reparation. Concerning the rigidity of the revenue system he had believed at one time that a cyclic system of revenue collection would be a panacea for Marwat; and he had reported on this subject, as well as on the indebtedness of Marwat, in October 1875. But he now thought that, given changes in district officers, such a system would not be of much use. He confined his recommendation therefore to a liberal working of the rules regarding suspensions and remissions of revenue, at any rate as long as the settlement did not break down. In the other exceptional case, that of the owners of minute holdings in the Bannu valley, he suggested that no action be taken. Here the crop being a certainty, the revenue system was elastic enough; and the root of the problem lay in over-population, for which the State was not called upon to find a remedy. Thorburn revealed, however, that the problem of land transfer had assumed a political dimension for him. For he added that the Bannuchis were such a poor hybrid race as to be of little political account. With them there was no fear of a stalwart hereditary peasantry being expropriated, as there was in Marwat.[45]

Yet even at this stage Thorburn was not certain that this fear was a real one. This in spite of statistics for large parts of the district showing that between twenty and thirty-three per cent of the assessed area had been transferred by sale and mortgage in the preceding twenty years, figures of a kind hardly heard of in the south-eastern districts under settlement. Thorburn believed that transfers in the district, with the exception of a significant proportion of cases in Marwat, had been made under the pressure of necessity. But in his opinion the figures were robbed of much of their gravity by the fact that so much of the land alienated had been acquired by landholders. Thus his statistics showed that only from four to ten per cent of the assessed area had been alienated to Hindus, figures which in absolute terms might have loomed large in much of the south-east, but which did not constitute a large proportion of the total extent of alienation in the district with which Thorburn was concerned. Still, Thorburn added that the major portion of the transfers to landholders had been to men of money, who did not cultivate themselves; and that but for property devolving in equal shares to all sons, large landed proprietors would be springing up, and the bulk of the old peasant proprietors would sink into the position of tenants.[46]

In the other Pathan and semi-Pathan districts of the upper frontier the Settlement Officers did not find that alienations covered a large area. This was the case in the Kohat district, the military civilian who settled that district thinking that the ordinary proprietors were not much indebted.[47] The same officer had reported in 1876 as regards the neighbouring district of Peshawar that the people, though generally better off than under former rulers, were not extricating themselves from debt, a fact which he attributed to increased expenditure on domestic ceremonies, on jewels, food and clothes, as well as to the prevalence of gambling. In five tahsils of the district the land sold and mortgaged ranged between three and eight per cent of the cultivated or total area (with a few tracts with exceptionally high figures). The percentage must have been larger in the sixth tahsil, for alienations for its constituent parts ranged between nine and twenty-six per cent of the cultivation.[48] In the adjoining district of Hazara, partly held by Pathans and partly by tribes of Indian origin, Edward Wace, another military civilian, noted in his settlement report of 1874 that of the transfers made by sale and mortgage since annexation those still in force extended to three-and-a-half per cent of the cultivated area, there being little to choose between one tahsil and another.[49]

Wace, whose civil experience dated from 1860, had been in the Hazara district since 1868.[50] He was even more impressed by the increased prosperity of his district than his fellow Settlement Officers in Bannu and Peshawar, and probably with good reason.[51] The greatly increased value of agricultural and milch produce which had followed the sudden rise in prices in 1860-1, the extension of cultivation, and the reduced proportion of the produce absorbed by the State, had brought about in Wace's opinion a substantial rise in standards of comfort, both as regards food and clothing. Land commanded a higher value than ever before, and the number of transfers which occurred annually was not abnormally large. Wace believed, however, that partly as a result of the sudden increase in prosperity, and partly as the result of the introduction of a limitation law for debt, a material unsettlement of the relations between landholders and money-lenders had eventuated. The restrictions which both parties had observed under Sikh rule had been loosened. The landholder was far more willing to borrow than before, while looking to the limitation law as a means of evading payment in case of difficulty. Indeed, the principal difficulty of the problem lay in the newly-acquired recklessness of the landholders in incurring expenditure in excess of their former standard of living, unaccompanied by any improvement in their intelligence. The money-lenders, looking to agricultural prosperity, were more willing to lend, while in view of the restrictions of the limitation law they had raised their rates of interest, so that less than three years' interest generally equalled the principal. The growth and prevalence of such a high rate of interest called for careful attention, one of the best means of observing it being the annual registers of transfers of land. Nevertheless, for the present Wace considered that while there was more borrowing than before, there was less real indebtedness. As to the future, he was reluctant to believe that the ultimate result of the enormous increase in assets which had occurred in Hazara in the last thirty years would be the impoverishment of the agricultural classes by debt and usury.[52]

After completing the Hazara settlement Wace was entrusted with that of the Jhelum district, in the north-western Punjab. Here he found that though there were distinct local variations in the extent of transfer, the situation in the Jhelum district as a whole was not very different from that in Hazara. About one per cent of the cultivation had been sold between 1871 and 1876, while some two per cent was under mortgage.[53] Despite these very limited transfers of land, Wace was no less conscious in Jhelum than he had been in Hazara of the problems posed by debt and usury. All over India the story was much the same, the money-lenders making extortionate demands on agriculturists in difficulties. It was something that lay deep in the social life of the people, and the cure did not lie in matters of civil procedure. But the problem was aggravated by a civil procedure which told heavily against the landholder; and moderate restrictions on the decree-holder's powers over the debtor's means of subsistence were necessary.[54] In advocating in 1879, as Settlement Commissioner, the adaptation of civil procedure to the circumstances of the agricultural classes, Wace revealed both the depth of his insight into those circumstances and his readiness to consider the views of those classes. His practical knowledge of rural society led him to suggest changes in administrative structure and civil procedure which were in closer accord with the traditions of the people and the practice of the Indian rulers who had preceded the British. He envisaged a more personal system of administration, in which officers uniting civil, revenue and magisterial functions would control smaller areas, and exercise greater care and discretion in the decision of suits between landholders and money-lenders, while protecting the landholder against any undue pressure in execution proceedings.[55]

As Wace discovered, not much land had been transferred in the Jhelum district; but later settlements would show that this was hardly the case in some other north-western districts. Meanwhile in at least one of these districts, that of Gujranwala, where difficulty had been felt even in the early days of British rule, the serious extent of alienation did not escape the attention of the Deputy Commissioner, A. R. Bulman, a civilian with nearly as many years of civil work behind him as Wace.[56] Very considerable quantities of land in the Gujranwala district were passing into the hands of the so-called non-agricultural classes, Bulman remarked in 1879. This did not worry him much. Like his opposite number in the Gurgaon district in the same year he believed, indeed believed much more strongly, that the process was advantageous. For his part of the country Bulman challenged the notion of the Khatri as an avaricious rack-renter, that being only the role he played in the process of acquisition, when he was deliberately trying to ruin the old proprietors. But when the Khatri became a considerable landed proprietor in the neighbourhood of his home, he made a much better landlord than the thriftless squireen or stupid yeoman whom he displaced. The Khatris, far from being the mean-spirited money-grubbers which so many officers thought them to be, had restless energies which must be employed in a worse direction, if they could not find scope in a better. The Khatris had made gallant soldiers of fortune in the past (it must be remembered that Bulman was speaking of a district which was the home of Khatri families who had achieved distinction under Sikh rule);[57] and those who in other circumstances would have adopted such a career, now resorted to the acquisition of estates and the attainment of the dignity and influence of landed proprietorship. The more widely the leaven of men of this character was diffused among the agricultural classes, Bulman concluded, the better.[58]

If any further evidence were required to show that the opinions of officers were not simply a direct reflection of the degree of their local experience, or of the extent of land transfer in the areas with which they were familiar, it is surely furnished by the settlements of the lower frontier and the south-west. Almost every Settlement Officer in these parts of the Province remarked on the striking incidence of indebtedness in part or all of his charge; and by their own admission transactions in land were decidedly brisk in most districts, a point which the far more complete statistics of later settlements would not lead one to doubt.[59] Yet in this part of the country few of the Settlement Officers of the 1870s, mainly civilians who had joined the service between 1863 and 1865, wrote about these matters in anything more than a routine administrative context.

Of the frontier district of Dera Ismail Khan H. St G. Tucker wrote in 1879 that a good deal of land had changed hands, but not to an unwholesome extent. Tucker believed that in certain limited tracts, which were heavily indebted, the small Muslim proprietors would be expropriated in the course of time. But as far as these areas were concerned, he agreed with James Lyall that these men were not fit for the improved status which the British had given them, and that all that could be done was to amend anything in the revenue system which accelerated their decline.[60] The Settlement Officer of Dera Ghazi Khan, F. W. R. Fryer, was aware of the activity displayed in the acquisition of land, by Hindus as well as by others, but nothing in his settlement report of 1875 suggests that he considered this a matter for anxiety.[61]

In connection with the district of Dera Ghazi Khan the views of Lewis Tupper, a civilian whose career began in 1871, deserve some attention. At an early stage in his career Tupper had been appointed Assistant Settlement Officer of the district; and it was during his tenure of this post in 1873 that he expressed an opinion on the law of pre-emption.[62] Only an extract from this opinion is now available, quoted by Tupper himself in an official treatise on Punjab customary law published in 1881. Tupper's note shows how, in the early years of his service, he viewed the transfer of land in a broad historical perspective, keenly appreciative of the fundamental changes which had occurred, and for that very reason committed to innovation as a means of preserving the past.

> ... the *Pax Romana* of the British Government has given a vast strength to the trading classes, and a vast impetus to transfer of every description of property. The formation of the roads and railways, the establishment of liberty and order, have opened every village gate. The armed exclusiveness of the small proprietary bodies of the Punjab is recalled only by the nomenclature of their villages and the shape of the mud fortifications which surround them. The necessity for emphasising and protecting the right of pre-emption arises from the indirect effects of peace and commercial prosperity, and from the deliberate policy of the Government of India, which has determined to preserve in this part of its dominions the village community as the unit of society for the purposes of revenue administration. As the conditions of Native life have changed and are changing, we must create some new rights, if we would preserve particular ancient institutions. Innovation, of which the effect is to weld into our system the portions of the old order which we have determined to use, is as unobjectionable as it is necessary. The question is not, was the

right of pre-emption in mortgage a part of Native customary law, but is it desirable to communicate to village co-proprietors the right of pre-emption in long-term usufructuary mortgages, in order that, under the changed conditions of Native life, the integrity of the village system may be preserved. I think it is desirable. The legal device which has occasioned these remarks is too obvious to escape the sagacity of the growing middle classes, and cannot be frustrated too soon.[63]

It is easy to see that the man who wrote this could come to favour a new protective policy, and ultimately play a prominent role in the imposition of far greater restrictions on the power of alienation. Already in 1881 Tupper observed that since 1875, when the Lieutenant-Governor had decided against the extension of the right of pre-emption, much had happened in other parts of India, which gave weight to the doubt whether transferability of property as a means of securing loans was often beneficial to the peasant proprietor.[64] It is necessary to add, as indicating the official atmosphere of the time, and the limited development at this stage of Tupper's own views, that Tupper reproduced the extract from his 1873 memorandum on pre-emption in case, as he remarked, the subject should ever again be taken into consideration.[65] In terms of remedies Tupper still remained within the fold of the old protective policy.

Nevertheless, the potential for a development of opinion was already there, and it was further aided by Tupper's view of political economy. The position of the old advocates of a protective policy, who had refused to defend the right of pre-emption on economic grounds, Tupper assailed as totally erroneous. Tupper was well acquainted with the ideas of Henry Maine,[66] and his refusal to concede the relevance of political economy was obviously influenced by Maine's views on the subject.[67] Political economy, considered as a science, Tupper declared in 1873, had no bearing on the question of pre-emption. Theorems based on physical laws, such as those which treated of the relation of the population to the land, were of universal application. There were others, deduced from moral phenomena so exceedingly widespread, that they might be taken to be universal: as, for instance, the proposition that the intensity of industry depended on the proportion of the results of the industry enjoyed by the labourer. But the third, and by far the largest class of theorems, was purely hypothetical, depending on the assumption that society had outgrown status and custom and was based on contract and competition. This class of theorems was consequently of very limited application, being by no means wholly true even of mercantile Europe. Within this class fell theorems relating to the supply and demand of the market. The very existence of the village community, with its strong sense of the brotherhood of the proprietary body, and its hereditary servants, was a proof that status was still a living fact. It was absurd therefore to apply to sales or mortgages in the village communities of the Punjab, reasonings which were based on the assumption that society had progressed to the point where village communities would be an anachronism, perhaps an impossibility.[68] Here was an attitude which must have facilitated the development of Tupper's views in future years. Compared to a close contemporary like Denzil Ibbetson, whose initial intellectual premise was the relevance of political economy to Indian society, Tupper's starting point was quite different.

It is difficult to say what, if anything, Tupper's views of 1873 owed to his experience of settlement work in the Dera Ghazi Khan district. The reference to the great increase in the transfer of property might appear to fit the conditions of a district in which land was freely alienated; but the references to village communities, which in the true sense were hardly to be found in Dera Ghazi Khan, suggest the influence of earlier experience or ideas.[69] Again, Tupper's readiness to support the extension of the right of pre-emption was probably less attributable to his acquaintance with any particular variant of the Punjab situation than to his intellectual grasp of the concept of social evolution, of societies at different stages of development. But whether conditions in Dera Ghazi Khan influenced Tupper's judgement or not, the important point for present purposes is that Tupper was the only Settlement Officer connected with any part of the lower frontier or the south-west who showed any signs of concern in regard to land transfer in the 1870s. In terms of remedies there is no evidence that even he went very far at this stage.

Though conditions in the south-western Punjab had played a prominent role in the land transfer debate, the Settlement Officers described these conditions without much ado. In the Montgomery settlement report of 1874 W. E. Purser, speaking apparently of all but the canal tracts, noted that there were very few villages which were not seriously in debt. He thought this was a matter of little importance so long as the money-lender did not try to obtain the land for himself. Such proceedings were rare in the district, because in all but the canal villages the money-lender made a great deal more as the creditor of the owner than as owner himself. Observing that the people were very bitter about the exactions of the money-lenders, Purser conceded that there was much truth in their unpleasant comparisons between the adjudication of debt cases under Sikh and British rule. He qualified this, however, by making the point that if the money-lenders did not rob the people as much under Sikh rule as they did now, this was simply because the Sikh officials left nothing to be robbed.[70]

In the other south-western districts debt was accompanied by the alienation of land. In Multan Charles Roe was even less sympathetic than Purser. Where Purser had conceded a point in regard to British civil procedure, Roe admitted in his final report, probably written around 1880, that some excuse might be made for the landowners owing to the fact that they were totally unprepared for a fixed cash settlement, which was not suited to the agricultural conditions of the district. Nevertheless, Roe emphasised that the bulk of the smaller landowners were ignorant and careless farmers, destitute of energy and forethought, never looking into their accounts as long as the money-lender gave them an advance. When the day of reckoning came at last, and they found themselves hopelessly involved, they attributed their ruin not to their own laziness and extravagance, but to the avarice of the money-lender; and they looked to the district officer to cancel their debts and reduce their assessment. Nor did Roe spare the larger landowners for their extravagance. In some respects Roe tried to play down the significance of the alienations which had occurred. A great part of the land which had changed hands since the previous settlement was due, Roe argued, to the voluntary exchange of land between men of the same family or tribe, or to the more thrifty and energetic members buying up the shares of the weaker. There had been no considerable decrease in the proportion of land held by the Jats, the great mass of the Muslim land-holding tribes of the district. Yet Roe could not but admit that the area of land under mortgage, amounting to nearly ten per cent of the total area of the whole district, represented a very serious amount of debt.[71]

In the neighbouring district of Muzaffargarh, Edward O'Brien considered that indebtedness was greater than in any other district with which he was acquainted (his previous experience extended to one central and several south-eastern districts).[72] O'Brien put some of the blame on the British failure to manage the inundation canals, and on the agricultural calamities which the district had suffered since the end of the 1860s, most of the indebtedness dating from that time. In the Alipur tahsil (the same tahsil in which alienations had attracted attention in the first few years of British rule) he concluded that in the five years from 1872 to 1876 nearly three times as much land had been mortgaged and more than twice as much had been sold as in the previous ten years.[73] Nevertheless O'Brien, like Roe, attributed most of the trouble to the deficiencies of the landowners as farmers and managers. He parted from Roe in laying rather more stress on the change in the administrative system, the British having completely discontinued the minute superintendence of agriculture which the Sikhs had enforced in this area. The people had been placed in a position for which they had not been trained, and it was this which explained the bad farming, the improvidence and extravagance. The money-lender had simply stepped into the position occupied by former Governments. Apart from the trouble with the canals, this was the true origin of indebtedness in Muzaffargarh, in O'Brien's opinion. No more than Roe, however, did O'Brien suggest the possibility or desirability of any remedy for agricultural indebtedness *per se*.[74] The same was true at this stage of his fellow Settlement Officer in Jhang, a more recent recruit to the service than any of the other officers engaged in settlement work in this part of the Province.[75]

It is apparent, then, that the relationship between experience and opinion was a complex one. Though there was an element of conflict between some officers in district and division and those at the centre, the conflict of opinion transcended any such division. Nor is it possible to describe the situation simply in terms of a struggle between those with much and those with little local experience, or even between those familiar with one particular kind of land transfer situation and those familiar with another.

This problem is pointed up by a final example from the south-west and the lower frontier. James Lyall, a civilian who had joined the service in 1858, had gained considerable experience in settlement work. In 1873, in his early days as Settlement Commissioner, he had repeatedly urged the extension of the law of pre-emption to long-term usufructuary mortgages. A little earlier he had advised the introduction of fluctuating assessments in certain tracts. Financial Commissioner from 1879, the Provincial revenue reports, for which he was now responsible, continued to take the familiar official line in regard to land transfer that nothing much was amiss. Yet in the meantime, as Settlement Commissioner Lyall had enjoyed unexampled opportunities for acquainting himself with land transfer and indebtedness, and he had gained a wide experience of the lower frontier and south-west. It would be impossible to reconcile his opinions with any simple, universally applicable explanation of social influence.

The point, of course, which this example illustrates so well, is that different individuals were influenced in different ways, even by the same social phenomenon. Though Lyall saw the communal implications of the expropriation of Muslim landowners by despised Hindu money-lenders, he was not unduly disturbed by the relatively extensive alienations which came to his notice on the lower frontier and in the south-west. For one thing, he knew that alienations had not been uncommon in this part of the Punjab before British rule; so that the phenomenon did not appear to be a revolutionary one. For another, he regarded it as inevitable that only a minority among the weaker tribes would retain their proprietary rights; the majority relapsing into a condition akin to that which they had occupied under indigenous rulers, and one which was more suited to their attainments. This conviction was shared, as we have seen, by several officers in different parts of the Province. It would be unwise to explain it merely in terms of a doctrinaire commitment to the idea of the weak inevitably going to the wall, though that was doubtless an important influence. Much must be attributed to the fact that there were landholding tribes throughout the Province, who in every aspect of agricultural and general character, fell below the standards of their neighbours. Even as regards these tribes Lyall was concerned that the process of expropriation be not too rapid. In particular he sought to amend anything in the revenue system which hastened the inevitable; and under his cautious guidance the 1870s saw the extension of fluctuating assessments to a number of tracts in the south-west and along the frontier. A limited programme in the eyes of some no doubt, but one reflecting clearly the peculiar difficulties to which orthodox British revenue management was subject in these parts of the Province.[76] Not that Lyall's programme was necessarily confined to these parts. When in 1879 the Government of India, in connection with the relief of indebtedness in the Deccan, asked the Punjab Government to consider the possibility of a more elastic system of revenue collection for arid tracts, Lyall, as Financial Commissioner, pressed for cyclical assessments for several tracts in the south-eastern Punjab.[77] Though a number of other officers supported such a scheme, it was negatived by the Lieutenant-Governor, Robert Egerton, who did not consider it practicable, and who argued that only collections in kind could prevent the peasant borrowing cash to pay the revenue, and such collections were only necessary in exceptional tracts.[78]

## THE TRADITION TRANSFORMED

It might appear from this that Robert Egerton at least remained true to form. In earlier years he had helped to convince Davies that the transfer of land posed no serious problems; and this was the attitude he had continued to take when he succeeded Davies as Lieutenant-Governor in 1877. There was at any rate, it would seem, a sharp division between the head of the Province and some of his officers. By 1879, however, even this division was becoming a little blurred. Speaking in the Indian Legislative Council in July 1879, Egerton noted that the circumstances which had led to the introduction of the Deccan Ryots Bill were of such general prevalence throughout India, that the manner in which they were to be treated in the Deccan might possibly form a precedent for their treatment in other parts of the country. There were many proprietors in the Punjab whose condition fitted the description given in regard to the Deccan; there were parts of the country in the Punjab where the rainfall was uncertain and the crops precarious. Egerton's suggestion that in Bombay there was considerable danger in altering the ordinary law of contract in the case of agriculturists, unless the Government made some attempt to alter its revenue system, so as to relieve the peasant from the risks attending a scanty rainfall and a precarious crop, reads strangely enough when it is recalled that a year later Egerton would reject such proposals for arid tracts in the Punjab.[79] But that Egerton was prepared to consider the application of some remedy in the Punjab is apparent from a despatch of September 1880, replying to the Government of India's query whether it would be expedient to invest courts in the Punjab with a summary jurisdiction. This matter, like that of fluctuating assessments, had been referred to the Punjab Government in connection with the Deccan case, and Egerton rejected the one proposal as readily as the other. Nevertheless, despite his conviction that not much land was changing hands and that indebtedness was not great, Egerton informed the Government of India of his own accord that in the Punjab he was favourably disposed to an amendment of the law which would empower courts to go behind the bond; to a gradual extension of rural courts; and (following Wace) to limitations on the attachment of produce in execution of decrees.[80] Here, then, under the influence of the Deccan legislation and the gradual development of Punjab opinion, was the first authoritative hint of a new protective policy.

Robert Egerton was neither the first nor the last officer to alter his position in regard to the alienation of land. But he provides an interesting example of an officer whose strong opposition to any attempt to control the voluntary transfer of land gradually weakened over a period of years. It serves as a reminder that in any attempt to trace social influence on political and intellectual currents the factor of time is of great importance. Under the influence of changes which varied widely in degree, which were cumulative and only rarely dramatic, occasionally assuming prominence but always present, a gradual metamorphosis of official opinion would come to pass. Some officers like Thorburn and Tupper held views in the 1870s which developed considerably in the ensuing decades, though in a fairly direct fashion. The opinions of others, as for instance Wace and Roe, were less subject to change, though few were entirely unaffected by later developments. Many officers, however, would undergo a transformation so distinct, that it could not have been anticipated from their earlier opinions, Denzil Ibbetson being a case in point. Nevertheless, varied as the responses of individual officers were, even with reference to identical circumstances, it is a tribute to the subtle but effective influence of social change, that the development of opinion was very largely in the direction of increasing concern and commitment to legislation.

II

In the revenue report for 1879–80 it was noted that the abnormal increase that year in sales of land in the Derajat division was largely nominal, being due to the disposal of large arrears of mutation cases during the year.[81] This explanation seemed hardly sufficient to the Lieutenant-Governor, Robert Egerton, and in March 1881 he called for further information. He was also disturbed by the remarks of the Inspector-General of Registration to the effect that the registration returns showed more transfers than the revenue returns; and to ensure that these transfers, on which many arguments regarding the condition of the country were founded, should be recorded accurately up to date, he ordered that the registration and revenue returns be compared annually in the revenue report.[82]

As regards the Derajat, an enquiry followed which Egerton's successor, Charles Aitchison, was not prepared to accept as sufficient.[83] Further reports being submitted in 1882 and 1883, the serious deficiencies of the revenue returns in the Derajat became abundantly clear. In some instances the returns included items which were unreal or unimportant; thus exaggerating the area alienated. More generally increases in alienations were related to settlement operations. These probably stimulated the growth of the habit of recording transfers, this accounting for some increase, while causing transfers to be recorded long after they had occurred. As well as the gradual improvement in the working of the record agency, which would explain gradual increases, transfers were more carefully recorded after the completion of settlement than before completion. Finally, the sudden disposal of arrears of mutation cases which had been allowed to accumulate during settlement, explained certain enormous increases and decreases in the annual returns.[84]

The annual comparison of the registration with the revenue returns, soon brought to light the fact that a large number of transfers were not recorded in the revenue records of the Province at all. At times this was due to the neglect of village accountants and tahsil officials in not bringing changes of possession to record. Often the parties themselves were not prepared to get the transaction recorded in view of the expense and trouble it entailed. This was particularly the case with mortgages for short periods or those in which the owner retained possession. Or sometimes the alienee was prepared to trust to the honesty of his debtor, or to consider registration sufficient security.[85]

For these reasons Aitchison set but slight store on the statistics on which his predecessors had founded their opinions. A system was elaborated in 1884, however, to secure a more complete record of transfers.

At the same time as the value of the annual revenue statistics came to be seriously questioned, the growing concern felt by certain officers regarding the transfer of land became apparent.

In his settlement report of the Jhang district, dated May 1881, E. B. Steedman, a civilian in his tenth year of service, wrote that there was nothing to show that the original proprietors were being rapidly expropriated. In this south-western district, he thought, sales to money-lenders pure and simple were rare; the chief purchasers of land being Hindus whose estates had been built up before British rule, and some of whom had given up trade altogether. Nevertheless, Steedman deplored the indebtedness which existed. He attributed it chiefly to the vast increase in credit which had accompanied the grant of full transferable proprietary rights, a mistaken and misplaced gift. The landholders would borrow as long as they had credit; and as long as they borrowed the annual returns of land transfers would slowly but surely and steadily increase. Take away the landholder's transferable property in land, he argued, and the money-lender's only security would be the annual outturn of crops; the landholder's credit would shrink and his indebtedness decrease. There might be many outward signs of improvement in the condition of the landholders, but how was it possible to be satisfied with things when all this was accompanied by a steady increase in debt? If the cultivators had been given only occupancy rights, and all transfers except such as were sanctioned by the State, absolutely prohibited, indebtedness would have been limited and the State would have been able to take a larger increase of land revenue. As things stood now, land transfer and indebtedness impaired the landholder's ability to pay a fair revenue demand to Government.[86] About the same time the Settlement Officer of Ludhiana, who had joined the service only a little later than Steedman, referred to the 'doubtful privilege' which British rule had bestowed when it made possible the command of unlimited credit on the security of land. Unlike Steedman, however, this officer, writing about a part of the country markedly different, notably in its preponderance of thrifty and industrious landholders, considered that those who were likely to sink had already done so, and that the amount of land mortgaged since the regular settlement (five-and-a-half per cent in the tahsil under reference) was not to be taken as the normal rate of progress.[87]

It was in connection with the settlement of another central district, that of Hoshiarpur, where alienations appeared to be more extensive than in Ludhiana, that the Settlement Commissioner, E. G. Wace, began to show concern in the early 1880s. The figures which Wace himself had brought to light in Hazara and Jhelum some years before, were easily exceeded by those for Hoshiarpur, which amounted to about twenty per cent of the cultivated area or of the revenue payable in three out of the four tahsils.[88] Sensitive as ever to agricultural opinion, Wace saw that the growth of mortgages was a source of serious anxiety to the landholders; and he could not refuse assent to the proposition, advanced in conversation by landholders, that the unrestrained liberty to sell and mortgage had modified profoundly the status and prospects of the agricultural classes. At this time, in January 1881, he also anticipated Steedman's point that these transfers must largely discount the hope of increased revenue.[89]

Not, as Wace remarked, in July 1882, that the transfers were any evidence of want of prosperity, for land was not transferred except at its due price. And under existing circumstances a very considerable number of transfers would necessarily occur in a rich and densely populated tract such as Hoshiarpur. Nevertheless, he could not agree with those who thought that the increasing number of land transfers was a matter of no importance. To an increasingly large number of the agricultural population it meant a revival of the heavy cash and grain rents which they had paid before British rule, irrespective of whether the land was acquired by an agriculturist or a capitalist. Any measure, however small, which influenced such a change was of the first political importance, for evil if it accelerated the process, for good if it helped the cultivating owners to hold their own.[90] Later in the year Wace ventured to disagree with one of the Settlement Officers of the district who argued that the total extent of alienations in a particular tahsil, in which only ten per cent of the cultivation had been alienated, was no indication of failing resources or of very general or very rapidly increasing indebtedness among the industrious classes.[91] Wace hesitated to say now what he had said a few months before in regard to another tahsil, namely that alienations were not evidence of any general want of prosperity. It was the rapid growth of the mortgage debt in recent years which he saw as a difficulty (in this as in other tahsils of the district the progressive nature of the increase in alienations was a striking feature of the figures prepared for the assessment reports). But if Wace experienced disquiet in regard to the existing circumstances of the Hoshiarpur district, disquiet of a kind which he had not felt some years before in regard to the Hazara district, he was still disinclined to face up to the question of future consequences. It would be for their successors to judge what the increase in land transfer would lead to during the succeeding twenty years.[92] Indeed, as he remarked a little later, both those who made light of the increasing mortgage debt, and those who took a gloomy view of it, were forejudging the event.[93]

In the final analysis, Wace's increased concern about land transfer, and his practical acquaintance with rural society, did not dispel the influence which the ordinary ideas of the time exerted on his thinking. It is this which explains why the man who in January 1881 acquiesced in the proposition of landholders as to the serious effects of the liberty to sell and mortgage, could not bring himself to agree in September 1882 with Steedman's strictures on the grant of proprietary rights. Missing or ignoring Steedman's point about the actual prohibition of transfers, Wace did not see how any settlement could have been made which would have prevented the holders from borrowing on it; for irrespective of whether the settlement was on ryotwari or proprietary lines, it was good government which made the land valuable and gave the holder an established title to it. Even if it had been possible to devise such a settlement, it would not have been adopted, as it would have been alien to British experience of what was good for any country in the long run. Holding such views Wace could argue, as in 1877, that the root of the trouble lay in the nature of society itself. A society of a rather loose moral and social constitution had been advanced rapidly by the British from a condition of comparative adversity and depression to one in which the landholders had few anxieties and a very considerable command of money. It was the weaker members of the society, and he thought there were many of them, who consequently fell into the bad habits and trouble described by Steedman. Then the faults of the money-lending classes were complementary to those of the landowners. And he added, returning to a favourite theme, much of the trouble had been aggravated by the failure to adapt a civil law and procedure framed on European models to the requirements of the agricultural classes.[94] The extent and progress of land transfer in Hoshiarpur had disturbed Wace, but it had not shaken his fundamental convictions.

In addition to Wace, certain other officers of moderate views and long experience became uneasy. As Commissioner of the Amritsar division, H. E. Perkins, while suspecting that alienations were taking place to a larger extent than had been admitted, had ended his investigation in 1878 on a more or less hopeful note. But in 1882, as Commissioner of the Multan division, he was shocked by the extraordinary number of transfers which careful inspection revealed in the south-western district of Muzaffargarh. Believing that Muzaffargarh was an eminently prosperous district and comparatively free from debt, a view which reflects his limited acquaintance with this part of the country, Perkins shuddered to think of the condition of more depressed tracts. It seemed to him that before very long some of the richest districts in the Punjab would have a Jhansi Encumbered Estates Act—and if this extreme measure was avoided, it would be by depriving the courts of some of their powers at an earlier stage than matters had reached in the Jhansi division.[95] Another example of this kind is provided by C. A. McMahon who, as Commissioner of Hissar, had opposed legislation in regard to land transfer (even the extension of pre-emption to mortgages) in the early 1870s.[96] As late as 1877 McMahon had argued that, while in the south-eastern Punjab the money-lenders might have acquired land to a limited extent, owing to special circumstances in the early days of British rule, even this was not true of the Punjab proper.[97] By the early 1880s, in charge of Amritsar, Perkins' old division, McMahon was asking himself (and others) why agriculturists were getting more and more indebted at a time when the value of land and agricultural produce had risen so much, a fact which he could attribute only to the growing pressure of population and the sub-division of holdings. That the professional money-lenders were getting more and more of the land into their hands he no longer doubted; nor did he fail to note that the friction produced by the transfer of land was increased thereby. 'Everywhere in our villages we see handsome new idol temples rearing their spires aloft, and marking the growing influence, wealth and supremacy of the village baniah.'[98] The increasing indebtedness of the agricultural classes was a matter of considerable political importance in McMahon's opinion.[99]

At the end of 1882 James Wilson, an officer with no more than seven years' service to his credit, launched an attack on the gift of alienable proprietary rights in the soil more forthright even than Steedman's. At an early stage of his career Wilson had witnessed the rather dramatic increase in alienations which accompanied the drought of 1877–8 in the Gurgaon district. For all his sympathy with the Meo proprietors of the district, who were in especially bad straits, Wilson had seen no solution. But when he was posted to Gurgaon again, in November 1882, to revise the settlement which the drought and a succession of poor harvests had rendered unworkable in many cases, he soon submitted proposals to help the Meos. He sought approval for a scheme whereby Government advances would be applied to the redemption of mortgages made by Meo proprietors. Restored to his land, the Meo would repay the advance at six per cent interest by instalments. In the interval he would not be allowed to alienate his land again, it being hypothecated to Government as security for the repayment of the advance. Meanwhile, Wilson hoped, the power of alienating would be withdrawn entirely from improvident communities like the Meos; for he considered that it was the Government which had brought misery and hardship on the Meos, partly by its inelastic revenue system, but chiefly by its ill-advised gift of alienable proprietary rights, which enabled the Meo to convert his land into cash whenever the need arose. Both these features of British administration were unsuited to a people such as the Meos. Wilson deplored the existing situation in terms of the general interests of agriculture and good administration. The money-lender would not improve the land as the Meo had the right of redemption, the Meo would invest no money in it as long as the land was mortgaged to the money-lender. With the examples of Ireland, Bengal and the Deccan in evidence, Wilson saw no need to expatiate upon the evils which resulted from the general transfer of ancestral land from peasants to non-agriculturists. The only advantage which accrued to Government in this respect was greater security for its revenue, a consideration unworthy of a wise Government, and an object which might be more or less attained in any case under a more elastic revenue system. In those circumstances it was only just that the Government should attempt to restore the position of the Meos. In a concluding paragraph Wilson indicated the possibility of extending the scheme for Government advances to the whole of North India; and saw it as paving the way for that 'grand reform', the revocation of the power to alienate ancestral land.[100]

Wilson's remarks on the responsibility which Government had incurred by its mistaken policy of granting proprietary rights were not well received by the Commissioner, Colonel Gordon Young, an officer with nearly a quarter of a century's civil experience.[101] Young considered that this was begging a very difficult question and provocative of a rejoinder from those who held the opposite opinion as to the policy of the past. He saw no merit in Wilson's redemption scheme. If the Meos defaulted frequently in paying their instalments, as seemed almost certain, the Government would be forced to use the power of sale and would itself incur that odium which was now avoided by the interposition of the money-lender. Then there was the unwarranted interference with the ordinary business of the money-lender and the investment of money; and the fact that the peasant would be worse off when his land was hypothecated to Government, as he would not be able to borrow for domestic ceremonies. To these and other *laissez-faire* arguments, designed to show that the scheme was not workable, and if workable harmful, Young added his fear that the scheme would not stop with the Gurgaon district and was likely to take them beyond the bounds of what any Government could reasonably be expected, or safely attempt, to undertake.[102] James Lyall, the Financial Commissioner, did not agree. He proposed a scheme of liquidation based on suggestions made by the Government of India. In order to clear the way for the establishment of agricultural banks, a matter also under discussion, Lyall thought that such an experiment should be tried in the Gurgaon district: both as an experiment and because he thought that under all the circumstances Government should be ready to incur considerable risk in order to relieve the people from debt. The main risk was that Government would have difficulty in collecting the instalments afterwards.[103] He persisted in this opinion, thinking that Young's other objections were not individually formidable, though collectively they had some force.[104] While Lyall was not imbued with out-and-out *laissez-faire* notions, it is doubtful whether he shared Wilson's views in the matter of the grant of proprietary rights. In the past, Lyall had held out little hope in regard to the ultimate fate of weaker tribes. Now, discussing agricultural banks, Lyall noted that they seemed most desirable in the most indebted tracts; yet it was precisely in such tracts that their establishment would not prevent the landholders from continuing their account with the money-lender. In such tracts the system of borrowing appeared to be necessitated by the character of the people, shaped by race and climate, aided by ingrained disposition or prejudices arising from custom or religion. Lyall's attitude, in short, was much the same as that of Wace, like him adding that the difficulty might be aggravated by certain features of British administration, but was not caused by it. It was to these improvident landholders that the better definition and greatly increased value of property in land, accompanied by increased credit, had been a questionable boon.[105]

The Lieutenant-Governor, Charles Aitchison, dismissed Wilson's scheme in April 1883. Ignoring Wilson's references to the restriction of proprietary rights, he conceived that the main defect of the scheme was that it would not prevent the proprietors from again falling into the hands of the money-lenders. Any measure of that nature would have to provide for the supply of the future requirements of the peasantry at reasonable rates. This could be done only by the Government itself lending the money, or by the establishment of agricultural banks. On a permanent basis the former course was out of the question, while the establishment of agricultural banks was beset by difficulties out of which Aitchison saw no safe way. Aitchison pointed out that the notorious recklessness and thriftlessness of the Meos made it unlikely that they would be able to regain their position with the help of Government. Any action taken in the redemption of debts or mortgages was to be exceptional and limited.[106]

Wilson's defeat in this matter did not prevent him from pressing an extended and reasoned account of his general views on Government at the end of 1883, in his report on the distress in the Jhajjar tahsil of the Rohtak district. Agricultural distress here had been of a kind akin to that which the adjoining district of Gurgaon had suffered, but it had been far less severe, and transfers were certainly not on the scale of those in the Meo tahsils of Gurgaon. Nevertheless, Wilson saw alienations to money-lenders in a serious enough light; and he argued his case forcefully, and in a manner which ran entirely counter to *laissez-faire* or social Darwinist notions. Irrespective of the varied degrees of change, or of the admitted defects in the character of the most indebted tribes, Wilson had a passion for justice, and a keen appreciation of the revolutionary impact of British administration on rural society, which gave him his own view of the problem.[107]

Land transfers to money-lenders, Wilson thought, were partly due to rigid exaction of land-revenue in bad seasons, but chiefly to the reduction of the revenue-demand under British rule, which had made land a valuable property, and to the power of land transfer conferred on the landholder, a power which in practice he had not possessed in former days. These measures had enabled the peasant to borrow much more freely and to sacrifice the future for the sake of the present. Nor was it only the less thrifty and the extravagant who were led into debt in this way: density of population and vicissitudes of season often proved too much for the greatest thrift and self-denial. And then the British had established an irresistible system of judicial procedure, and in a way hitherto unknown they enforced the rash promises made by ignorant and unthinking peasants. Cunning and forethought had been given an unfair advantage over ignorance and extravagance. It was easy to say that men must be made to keep their promises, and that the extravagant and thriftless must give way to the thrifty and provident. But Wilson did not think that British theories of political economy were inevitable natural laws, and he clearly distinguished between the operation of natural laws and British administration, thinking that it was the latter and not the former which was at work. The British system of individual transferable rights in land and the inflexible judicial procedure were new to the people, and unsuited to the existing state of society. It was unjust, and bad policy, to leave those who could not quickly adapt themselves to the new system to give place to those who could. Thrift was not the only virtue, and the loss of ancestral land by peasants and their children was too severe and lasting a penalty to impose on carelessness or even extravagance. It was the duty of Government to protect the ignorant against the knowing, as well as the weak against the strong. Rather than requiring the people to adapt themselves to the British system, Government should adapt its system to the state of society. He would be glad to see a system established whereby the power of transfer would be restricted; the revenue taken in kind; and certain judicial reforms effected. The restriction of credit which would follow such a system was exactly what was wanted. Under such a system thrift would still have its reward, and extravagance and want of self-denial would still be their own punishment. But while the penalty would not be so extreme, the development of resources and increase of prosperity would not be affected, for these he attributed not to fixed assessments and transferable rights in land, but to the security of property under British rule, which would remain intact. If such a system could not be introduced at once, or rather restored (for something of the kind had operated under indigenous rule, though accompanied by insecurity of property), the least Government could do was to make its revenue system more elastic by taking revenue in kind or introducing fluctuating assessments in certain cases.

While the Deputy Commissioner of the district thought that Wilson's proposals for the relief of indebtedness deserved great attention,[108] the officiating Commissioner of the Hissar division, L. J. H. Grey, was disinclined to take them up. Grey had served since 1856 in various capacities, military, political and civil, chiefly in the Punjab; and he had been pained in 1874 and even earlier by the intrusion of the money-lender mortgagee into the villages of the Rohtak and Ferozepur districts. Writing in the context of proposals to extend the right of pre-emption to usufructuary mortgages, he had pointed out that it might not be possible to further shackle transfers of property, but if it were possible it would be politically expedient to enforce rigidly the spirit of the pre-emption rules, and to apply them to usufructuary mortgages as well as to sales.[109] As Commissioner of Hissar in later years, Grey regretted the expropriation of less thrifty tribes who exhibited other qualities which were of value to Government. But Grey lacked that sensitivity to human misfortune which led Wilson to mourn the fate of the weakest of tribes, irrespective of their value to Government, and the fate of individuals as well as communities.[110] A confirmed adherent of fixed settlements, Grey could refer to the difficulties of individuals under such a system of settlement in terms of the survival of the fittest, this being a process which must always go on, for it was not only under the British revenue system that the weakest went to the wall. The only issue was whether the revenue system was the best for the general interests of the mass of the people; and he disagreed with Wilson in thinking that the revenue system had played a large part in the development of agricultural prosperity. Otherwise, Grey sympathised with much of what Wilson had written, but he saw no point in recapitulating the arguments which had been advanced against the restriction of the power of transfer or the collection of revenue in kind, subjects which could be dealt with only in a discussion on general principles.[111]

The Financial Commissioner, W. G. Davies, and the Lieutenant-Governor, C. U. Aitchison, also steered clear of the general issues which Wilson had raised. While expressing concurrence with many of Wilson's opinions, the Financial Commissioner thought it unnecessary to embark upon what appeared to be an unprofitable discussion; though he did recommend fluctuating assessments as a means of ensuring that payment of revenue did not drive the landholders into debt.[112] Instead Aitchison took the advice of W. E. Purser, the old Settlement Officer of the district, whose opinion he had requested, and opposed the general introduction of a fluctuating assessment in Jhajjar on the ground that if indebtedness was to be its main justification, it would be required all over the Punjab. Beyond a remark, also inspired by Purser, that nothing could save certain weaker tribes from expropriation unless they adopted a thrifty and honest mode of livelihood, Aitchison made no comment on Wilson's general proposals.[113]

Meanwhile, at the other end of the Province, S. S. Thorburn was becoming impatient. In Bannu, as we have seen, Thorburn had begun to appreciate the political problem posed by the transfer of land. As Deputy Commissioner of Dera Ismail Khan, an adjoining frontier district, he had been one of the officers consulted on the large number of transfers of land in the Derajat division. His report, written in November 1882, had not been very full or startling, as he had been down with fever and other work was pressing; but he had indicated that it was a question in which he took much interest and that he held rather decided views as to the remedial measures which might be tried to prevent land passing from the hands of true peasants to non-agriculturists.[114] The Government reference stirred him into action. By 1883 he was collecting, on his own initiative, statistics of indebtedness; and in his revenue report for 1882-3 he wrote that he had been convinced for a long time that sweeping legislation was necessary to avert future agrarian trouble, and that he would submit his views when required.[115] No call for his opinion eventuating, he nevertheless submitted a paper in June 1884 on the indebtedness of the agriculturists of the Muslim districts of the Punjab.[116] Some twenty years after joining the service, Thorburn had taken the first step in a cause which would become little short of an obsession.

Thorburn's paper was at once more alarmist in tone, and yet less far-reaching in its conclusion, than anything Steedman or Wilson had written. Where Steedman had lamented loss of revenue and Wilson had lingered on the injustice done to the peasantry, Thorburn

## THE TRADITION TRANSFORMED

saw only agrarian discontent, leading to political danger which Government, in its own interests, must avert. He thought that the loyalty of the Muslim landholders, about which he had written so confidently in his work of 1876 on Bannu, would be strained beyond endurance if the process of land transfer was allowed to continue. This political problem, which he had touched lightly in passing in 1878, he now spoke of in the strongest terms; chiefly with reference to the frontier division in which he had served, but also in regard to the south-west, which he tended to visualise in terms of his frontier experience. Without minimising the personal factor, it is possible to see that Thorburn's references to disaffection leading to insurrection were more attuned to existing conditions in his frontier districts, where the Muslim landholder looked on the Hindu trader with supreme contempt, and where in the trans-Indus regions the pride of race and pride of arms of Pathans and Biloches were to the fore, than in Steedman's district of Jhang, unsettled Muslim district though it was. Certainly Thorburn's remarks did not have the extravagant character which they would have assumed in the far more orderly and peaceful districts of the south-east in which Wilson had served. Thoroughly alarmed, Thorburn was not prepared for more than a token discussion of land transfer statistics. Statistics, he argued, did not, and could not, show the full measure of indebtedness. The time was reasonably near when seventy-five per cent of the peasantry would lose their proprietary rights to Hindu moneylenders and to a few favoured Muslim landowners.

But when it came to causes Thorburn spoke a different language. In this matter his paper revealed a mind struggling to reconcile, not altogether successfully, the impressions derived from district experience with the commonplace notions of the time. The man who was trying to find some explanation and remedy for increasing indebtedness was at war with the man who equated British rule with progress and civilisation. Though Thorburn could refer to 'our system' as the cause of indebtedness and land transfer, he could not condemn the system altogether. Some of the causes of indebtedness, Thorburn thought, were indicative of general prosperity and more or less inevitable in the change from weak, unsettled government to strong, settled and good government. As one of these causes he cited the inherent qualities of the Hindu and the Muslim which were allowed unlimited scope under a system which fostered individualism, and which had given the superiority to the Hindu. (Yet, inevitable or not, he also spoke of the advent of unqualified individualism as a grave mistake.) In the category of inevitable causes Thorburn further enumerated the growth of population, which made itself felt in bad seasons when cultivation was confined to protected localities; and the fact that the wages and profits of agriculture had not risen in the same ratio as the cost of living. Coming to preventable causes, Thorburn referred to the introduction of laws and civil procedure which mistakenly assumed that agriculturist and money-lender stood on an equal footing as sharp business men. Here he was able to reconcile his theoretical commitment to these features of civilisation with his practical observation of their effects in the Punjab by speaking in terms of the introduction of laws which were in advance of the state of progress of the masses. As preventable causes Thorburn also instanced the rigidity of the revenue system, which made peasants borrow for revenue when they had no crop, and the diversion of executive officers from administrative to desk duties.

Thorburn further pointed to the expansion of agricultural credit which had taken place since annexation. At one moment he ascribed this to good government in general and regular settlements in particular; an explanation which the tumultuous history of the frontier division with which Thorburn was acquainted doubtless rendered all the more convincing, while fitting in with his view of credit as a product of civilisation. At another moment, looking to practical consequences, he blamed British rule for placing such an instrument of self-destruction in the hands of agriculturists without restriction; for in the western Punjab at any rate the average agriculturist was not to be trusted with the dangerous boon of unrestricted credit. But Thorburn did not join Steedman in his condemnation of the policy of granting transferable proprietary rights. This seems strange enough, for as a general proposition Thorburn was not loath to assert that the British had created and fostered individuality and destroyed the old bond of community of interest. It is necessary to remember, however, that Thorburn's experience was confined very largely to the Derajat division in which (areas of *vesh* tenure apart) individual, transferable rights in land were fully recognised and in some cases at any rate freely exercised under indigenous rule, so that in that respect British rule could not be held responsible. To this must be added the commitment which Thorburn revealed in earlier years to individual rights in land as the civilised norm. For these reasons it may be hazarded, reasons partaking in this instance of both Punjab experience and English ideas, Thorburn did not propose restrictions on the power to transfer land. Instead he concentrated his attack on the unsuitable legal system which had over-facilitated credit and usurious practices. To restrict credit he recommended a number of changes in law and civil procedure which would make the civil courts less of a tool in the hands of the money-lender and more of a protective shield for the peasant. In making these proposals Thorburn was influenced by the Deccan Act of 1879, having acquainted himself with the literature on the Deccan situation. That he could speak of the Deccan Act as a sweeping, heroic, even a revolutionary measure, illustrates something of its significance in the development of an officer whose fear of the political consequences of land transfer led him to assume positions at odds with his intellectual heritage. In addition to reforms in law and procedure, Thorburn advocated the extension of fluctuating assessments to unprotected tracts, and the reduction of reports and returns required from officers.

Not one of the superior officers who reviewed Thorburn's paper was inclined to give much weight to his assertion that the inelasticity of the revenue system was a serious cause of indebtedness, and discussion centred on Thorburn's proposed amendments in law and civil procedure.

E. L. Ommanney, the Commisioner of the Derajat division, a military civilian who had been appointed to the Punjab Commission more than twenty-five years before, was himself conscious of the political danger which the subordination of the Muslim peasant proprietor to the Hindu money-lender and landlord involved.[117] An experience in 1879 in the frontier district of Hazara had made a great impression on him. Here the action of the Hindu money-lenders through the courts had strained the relations between the money-lenders and the agricultural community to the point where a wealthy bazaar in a large village was burnt down. That a simple order, to interpret and work liberally the law regarding exemptions from attachment in execution of decree, had sufficed to restore good relations was something Ommanney had not forgotten.[118] He was favourably disposed to greater flexibility in the working of the civil courts;[119] and several omens in the Derajat division, including the murder of several usurious Hindus, had led him to make suggestions of this kind early in 1884 for the guidance of the civil courts within his jurisdiction.[120] Hence in July 1884, though Ommanney did not entirely share Thorburn's alarm about the expropriation of the Muslim landholders, and thought that the Pathan communities in the Derajat had not transferred their land to money-lenders to any great extent, his fear of the explosive situation which could be created by the civil courts in a Muslim country, led him to support the kind of judicial reforms proposed by Thorburn.[121]

Thorburn's paper was considered by the officiating Financial Commissioner, Colonel McMahon, shortly after his review of Steedman's settlement report of the Jhang district, and this perhaps explains McMahon's belief that Thorburn also favoured some restriction of transferable rights in land. In one sense McMahon, who had joined the Punjab Commission as long ago as 1856,[122] showed himself to be an opponent of legislative interference, as he had been in the 1870s; in another sense his reviews of Steedman's and Thorburn's remarks reflected the uneasiness which he had felt about the transfer of land in the last few years. McMahon was in the uncertain position where his old notions did not allow him to go as far as Thorburn and Steedman, while his new anxieties did not enable him to dismiss their views altogether. In one respect McMahon had advanced a step since 1882 when he had puzzled over the question of why indebtedness was increasing when the value of land and agricultural produce were rising; for he could now agree with Steedman that when the margin of profit was largest, and agricultural credit easiest, the temptation to borrow was greatest. Hence McMahon was able to take some interest in Steedman's comments on the creation of transferable rights in land, and its effect on credit; and, looking to restrictions on the power of transfer in England, he discerned rather more clearly the point of Steedman's discourse than Wace had done in 1882. This did not prevent him from concluding that it was futile to argue about the policy of the past; and, like Wace, preferring to defer questions the outcome of which he could not fully fathom, he added that the time had hardly yet come when it could be considered with profit whether any steps should be taken to arrest the alienation of land by the agricultural community in the future. In the meantime he was gratified to note that Steedman did not think the proprietors were being rapidly expropriated; and took comfort from the social Darwinist notion that even if they were, perhaps no great harm would result, as better men might take their place. In all communities the extravagant and profligate would gradually drop out of the ranks and disappear and legislation could not arrest the action of natural causes.[123] A little later, in his review of Thorburn's paper, he expressed his disagreement with Steedman's views more distinctly and indicated that the policy of teaching the people self-reliance should not be reversed. Nevertheless, when McMahon came to consider the possibility of a Deccan Act, he rejected it on the more practical ground that neither the circumstances of the Derajat, nor those of the Punjab generally, justified such a drastic remedy at present (an implicit admission that he could

THE TRADITION TRANSFORMED

not altogether dismiss the possibility of such legislation in the future). McMahon's decision to oppose legislation along the lines of the Deccan Act was also influenced, despite his new-found appreciation of the practical consequences of agricultural credit, by his old notion of the theoretical consequences of the restriction of credit, such as a rising rate of interest.[124] Having disposed of violent remedies, McMahon was prepared to endorse certain reforms in law and civil procedure as a means of preventing the money-lender from putting severe pressure on the landholder; most of the reforms in question being simply extensions of existing amendments in law and procedure designed to aid landholders. He asked the Lieutenant-Governor's permission to have submitted for the opinion of revenue and judicial officers those of Thorburn's proposals which he considered at present reasonable. These proposals were the abolition of the ordinary imprisonment of agriculturists for debt, the exemption from attachment of some portion of the crop, and the extension of the period of limitation in rural debt suits.[125]

The Lieutenant-Governor, Charles Aitchison, received Thorburn's paper with apparent equanimity. In July 1882, shortly after his appointment as head of a Province in which he had served briefly as a young civilian, Aitchison had ordered a more thorough investigation into the causes of the abnormal increase in alienations in the Derajat division. He had not been clear then whether the increase in transfers was a healthy symptom or not, and whether Government should take any action in the matter.[126] Similarly in March 1883 he had called for reports on the increase in transfers in certain other districts.[127] The reports which were submitted regarding the Derajat districts did not show an entirely satisfactory state of affairs, but as nothing particularly alarming was brought to the fore, Aitchison saw no reason to take any action.[128] The very enquiry which had stimulated Thorburn's concern inspired Aitchison with no dread.

When Aitchison came to review Thorburn's paper in May 1885, therefore, he felt on safe ground, and combined a conventional explanation of land transfer in terms of natural causes with an equally conventional view of the futility of drastic interference. In so far as the trouble was inherent in the character and traditional habits of the people, or in the gradual extension of law and systematic government over a country previously governed more or less irregularly (and this Aitchison feared was at the root of most of the evils) little if anything could be done to improve the position of the agriculturists. There was no hope in usury laws which not only could be evaded but which in the long run brought greater evils in their train, adversely affecting that credit which was so indispensable, in a poor agricultural country like India, to even the smallest agricultural operations. Where, however, the evils arose out of the existing state of British laws and executive arrangements, Aitchison argued, the remedy was no doubt in the hands of Government. The distinction which Aitchison drew between the natural and remedial aspects of British law and government was rather subjective. Thorburn had drawn a somewhat similar distinction; but Aitchison limited the possibility of remedial action to those reforms which McMahon had considered reasonable. The abolition of imprisonment for debt was already under consideration. The proposals to exempt part of the crop from attachment and sale, and to extend the limitation period for debt, were to be discussed by selected officers, it being understood that all these reforms should be of general application and not confined to agriculturists.[129] Aitchison's tolerance of further discussion within this limited framework might seem a small enough concession; but it is significant that a Lieutenant-Governor whose intellectual bent was similar to McMahon's,[130] and who had steadfastly ignored Wilson's larger proposals, was not prepared to dismiss Thorburn's paper out of hand. This suggests that Aitchison, despite his confident tone, was not entirely easy about the matter. At any rate seven months after his review of Thorburn's paper Aitchison recommended detailed village studies of land transfers on the grounds that at present the question was undoubtedly of great importance, that it was not likely to grow less important in the future, and that if at any time action should become necessary, at least mistakes due to ignorance might be avoided.[131] There is no reason to think that Aitchison was inclined to discount the political importance of the 'masses': in his study of John Lawrence, written some years later, the contentment of the masses figured prominently enough.[132] It was just that Aitchison was not convinced, or not fully convinced, that land alienation posed a serious danger in this respect, while he found it difficult to conceive that any legislation could solve the problem.

Between June and August 1885 the local opinions which Aitchison had requested were submitted to the Financial Commissioner's office. Most of the officers consulted were civilians and almost without exception they were men whose civil experience dated from the 1860s or the 1870s. Despite the Lieutenant-Governor's attempt to restrict the discussion, several officers expressed opinions which were more in accord with those of Thorburn (or Wilson) than those of Aitchison. The political danger of land transfer was taken seriously by men who had served in various capacities and in different parts of the Province. J. A. E. Miller, an uncovenanted civilian with more than his fair share of secretarial and strictly bureaucratic experience, did not feel that it was for him to say whether there were political dangers lurking beneath the smooth surface of affairs. He found it difficult to conceive, however, that even the most fervent believers in political economy and in the inherent tendency of events to shape themselves aright, could think that the process described by Thorburn for the western Punjab was of no political consequence. Though he did not doubt that the main cause of indebtedness lay in the shortcomings of the landholders, rather than in those of the courts or the moneylenders, he professed himself a believer in legislation and State action, especially in the Indian context. Legislation along the lines of the Deccan Act, to be applied to such parts of the Punjab as required it, he thought the most hopeful remedy for indebtedness.[133] Robert Clarke, an officer who had been shuttled in and out of many a district north of the Sutlej river, but who had spent most of his service in the Muslim districts of the north-west and upper frontier, thought that Thorburn had understated rather than exaggerated the political danger caused by the existing system in the Upper Punjab. Rather than run this risk, he would cast political economy to the winds, presumably in the reform of the civil courts.[134]

But the most passionate plea for the subordination of political economy to political considerations came from Denzil Ibbetson, who had joined the service in 1870, in the same year as Robert Clarke.[135] In 1874 Ibbetson had opposed the extension of the law of pre-emption to long-term mortgages as carrying interference with the freedom of contract too far. Yet eleven years later he was among the most outspoken critics of the existing system. Like Thorburn, he had served for a long time as Settlement Officer in a single district, but it had been a south-eastern district, that of Karnal, which was not noted for transfers on any great scale.[136] Village communities had flourished and survived here, as in much of the south-east, to an extent hardly known in other parts of the Punjab;[137] so that British concepts of individual landed property assumed a far more revolutionary character in Ibbetson's district than in, say, Thorburn's frontier districts. It was this qualitative change, rather than the extent of transfer, which had impressed Ibbetson. And when he asserted that the way in which the British had encouraged and compelled the substitution of individual for communal rights in land constituted the 'most grievous blunder that we have committed in India',[138] he was much closer to Wilson, who had also served in the south-east, than to Thorburn. The ease with which ancestral interests in land were permanently alienated was, Ibbetson insisted, one of the most pernicious consequences of the shift to individual ownership. He further challenged Aitchison's explanation of the whole process. If the evils in question were inherent in the character and habits of the people why did they date, at least in their aggravated form, from the epoch of British rule? The root of the evil lay not where Aitchison said it lay, but rather in the extension of a sort of law and system of government unsuited in some respects to the people and their circumstances. Continuing in this vein, in the manner of Wilson rather than Thorburn, Ibbetson declared that difficulties had arisen largely because of the insular ignorance of all concepts of rights in land other than those current in England, an ignorance which was disappearing only now as the result of an enquiry first suggested by the landed tenures of India. These difficulties were further due to the obstinate conviction of the British that the principles of equity were necessary truths independent of the circumstances under which they were to be enforced. The landholders were thriftless largely because the British had placed them in new circumstances which did not demand the exercise of thrift. All that he, and those who thought like him, asked for, was that the people should be allowed to manage their affairs in the way in which they, and not the British, understood them; and the revolutions introduced by the British should be undone. It was often said that it was too late to go back. But if the first steps taken by the British had been retrograde, to retrace them would be to advance. And Ibbetson noted several instances, as in Ireland and in the Deccan, in which the British had gone back in this sense. Admitting the difficulties to be enormous, Ibbetson emphasised that they would have to be faced, and the sooner the better; but he did not clearly specify what his larger measures would entail, though some kind of adjustment of individual rights in land was doubtless included. A power to go behind the contract, perhaps combined with a usury law, he also saw as a hopeful experiment. Aitchison's objection to usury laws as ineffectual applied only, he considered, to such laws taken by themselves; while as regards the effect on agricultural credit, he argued that a general decrease in the value of landed security would not raise the rate of interest.[139]

Robert Clarke and Denzil Ibbetson did not venture to express their general opinions without excusing themselves for having spoken on wider issues or in terms contrary to established policy. Circumstances did not encourage detailed proposals for fundamental reforms, if indeed Clarke and Ibbetson were clear in their own minds

## THE TRADITION TRANSFORMED

as to details. Nor did circumstances encourage the impassioned or uncompromising promotion of far-reaching schemes by all who might feel the need of them. Charles Rivaz and Alexander Anderson, civilians who had spent most of their official lives in a number of eastern districts, were afraid that such reforms as limitations on the attachment of crops might only stimulate that demand for land which they deplored. Rivaz had no doubt about where the root of the trouble lay or what ought to have been done about it. The unrestricted power of voluntary alienation had been a fatal gift to the peasantry; and alienations should have been made subject in greater or lesser degree to the sanction of revenue officers. But Rivaz was not the man to knock his head against a stone wall. He was afraid that such an attempt to retrace their steps, even if deemed desirable, would be regarded as impracticable; and that it was probably only possible to protect the agriculturist when brought into court.[140] Anderson also thought that it was too late to arrest the transfer of land from the true agricultural to the trading classes, and that the most that could be done was to try to make the process more gradual, a compulsory exercise of a power to go behind the bond in court cases being recommended by him.[141]

Of the officers consulted in 1885 those who supported drastic measures to any extent were in a distinct minority. Yet few could have been as hostile to the aspirations of this minority as Charles Roe. In his report on the settlement of the Multan district, written some years before, Roe had shown little sympathy for the indebted proprietor, and he now tackled Thorburn's paper in much the same spirit. It was not that Roe lacked practical experience: he had served in a number of south-western and central districts, for instance, and more than half of his twenty years of active service had been spent in settlement work.[142] He was deeply imbued, however, with notions of society and government which made it peculiarly difficult for him to appreciate Thorburn's arguments. He was inclined not merely to dismiss Thorburn's fear of political danger as insubstantial, for the danger might very possibly never arise at all, but he brought political economy and social Darwinism to bear on the matter as well. If the British legislated in favour of a particular class, not because such legislation was right and economically sound, but because that class might possibly become discontented and dangerous, the British would make more enemies than friends, and the result would be disastrous failure. Again, Roe thought that particular tribes held the land not by divine right, but because they possessed qualities superior to the former occupants; and the tribes in possession would lose their land in turn, and justly, if they allowed their qualities to become inferior to the new men now seeking the land. This proposition blithely ignored the fact that the same qualities might well have been superior in the pre-British and inferior in the British setting, a point which illustrates Roe's failure to grasp the revolutionary nature of the British impact on rural society.[143]

Indeed, Roe demurred at once to Thorburn's contention that the British system of government was responsible for the transfer of land, and he tried to absolve the system of any responsibility whatever. In the quest for revenue, he noted, the Sikh rulers had not scrupled to eject cultivators, but under British rule the transfer of land for arrears of revenue was very unusual. The sale of ancestral land in execution of decrees for simple debts was also rare. These particular assertions were hardly controversial, though Roe's argument that the courts favoured the peasant rather than otherwise (by cutting down interest, for instance), while not without its point, was rather one-sided. In any case it was only when Roe appealed to the principles on which the British system was based that he came to the heart of the matter, and revealed most clearly those influences which shaped his attitude. To Roe, British principles of government coincided not only with regular administration but also with the process of social evolution and the advance of civilisation. No doubt the courts treated the peasant as capable of making a valid contract, Roe remarked, for they could hardly treat all landowners as legally infants or idiots, and the courts looked on a contract as an agreement to be enforced—but this was inherent in any regular administration of justice. Then there was the question of the effect of British rule on the nature of land tenure. Eleven years before Roe had noted that it was almost a natural law that landed tenures changed only in one direction, from joint holdings to severalty in shares, and from shares to possession; a process which he saw operating at certain stages under the influence of the law of natural selection.[144] It was Roe's image of individual landed property as the end-product of a universal and natural social process which made it possible for him to assert in 1885 that the British system had not openly enlarged the general power of a proprietor to alienate his land (though Roe's experience in the south-west, where there had been few village communities to inhibit alienation before British rule, may also have made this claim seem reasonable). No doubt the British system had indirectly enlarged the power to alienate; for as Roe explained, drawing evidently on Henry Maine's view of social evolution, it was simply a natural result of civilisation that property should pass

## THE TRADITION TRANSFORMED

from the tribe to the village and from the village to individuals.[145] It was only when property was vested in an individual that he could make a valid contract concerning it. Ignoring the fact that it was not primarily the civil courts which had extended or created the power to alienate land, Roe stressed, quite correctly, that the courts by following customary law had done little to hasten the change to individual ownership. They checked the full control by the individual over his property which, as Roe thought, would grow up ordinarily by a natural social process; but he failed to add that the restrictions of customary law in practice did not seriously check the power to alienate land in all but a tiny fraction of instances.[146]

But if Roe could absolve the British system of all reponsibility by reference to social theory, where then was the blame to be laid? Several years before, in his report on the Multan district, Roe had tried to minimise to some extent the significance of the land transfers which had occurred, while castigating the proprietors for their faulty management. Now, notwithstanding his social Darwinist explanation of land transfer, he pointed out that indebtedness and land transfer were the natural result of a number of men with little or no capital engaging in a business involving almost more risks and fluctuations than any other. And he proceeded to spell out, in a manner reflecting his intimate acquaintance with rural conditions, the misfortunes which were bound to afflict petty proprietors over a period of time, and which were bound to bring a large number of them to insolvency, without extravagance on their part or extortion on the money-lender's part. Roe's account of the difficulties inherent in peasant agriculture would have done credit to Thorburn or Wilson. But lacking the political concern of the one, and the compassion of the other, and committed to theories which equated British principles with evolution and civilisation, and to a political economy which made Government interference positively harmful, Roe found it difficult to see the need and impossible to admit the practicability of legislation.

Roe did not desire to take any measures whatever in regard to indebtedness and land transfer; but in this respect he was in a minority of one. As the Financial Commissioner's Secretary noted, a great majority of the officers consulted was in favour of an exemption from attachment and sale of a portion of the produce, and a majority almost as great was in favour of extending the period of limitation for debt.[147] Among those who supported action on both counts was Gordon Young, the most senior officer and the only Commissioner consulted, and the man who had dismissed Wilson's remarks about the grant of proprietary rights and condemned his scheme for the redemption of mortgages in Gurgaon.[148] In addition to exemptions from attachment and sale and the extension of the period of limitation, some officers recommended other limited remedies, most often relating to the working of the civil courts. They included old Settlement Officers like Fryer and Tucker, whose settlement reports had given no indication of anxiety in regard to the admittedly brisk transfer of land along the lower frontier; Purser, who had served in many districts in which the transfer of land was comparatively limited, and whose attitude was fundamentally in agreement with that of Aitchison; and Machonachie, who had agreed with Lyall in seeing no hope of saving those who persisted in ruining themselves.[149] In short, many officers who were not inclined to worry unduly about land transfer as such, in their toleration for remedies were closer to Aitchison and McMahon than to Roe. Though some of them thought the problem was fundamentally insoluble, they perceived the shortcomings of the |civil courts, and being asked to discuss only limited proposals, they were inclined to be helpful rather than hostile.

In reviewing the opinions submitted Lieutenant-Colonel Wace, the second Financial Commissioner, showed that he had no sympathy with urgent calls for drastic action. Confronted with fundamental criticism of the existing system, Wace clung, as in the early 1880s, to accepted notions of the conditions which facilitated the well-being of society. Adherence to these notions made it impossible for Wace to conceive that any complete solution could be feasible. It was not possible to save people from themselves, he thought; nor was it right to hamper the thrifty and enterprising, constituting the body of the population, by restrictions intended for the protection of the unthrifty. Credit and the power to borrow freely, and freedom to transfer land, were essential to labour, trade and agriculture. They brought misfortune only to the weak, the reckless and the fraudulent. The restriction of credit and of the power of contract and alienation might be necessary under certain adverse conditions of national life, but it was a misfortune to be avoided by every possible means.[150]

Yet in some respects Wace's logic was not that of Aitchison or Roe or McMahon, or not entirely. Wace's grasp of some of the strong points of Sikh administration, manifested on a previous occasion, and his long-standing awareness of the shortcomings of British revenue and judicial arrangements, militated against any simple explanation of indebtedness in terms of the replacement of irregular by systematic government, such as Aitchison endorsed. Like Roe, Wace was concerned at this time to play down the role of changes in government. In his case, however, this was justified not by any reference to evolutionary theory, but by a view of indebtedness which he had adopted long ago, the view that the fundamental cause of debt lay in the nature of Indian society. This was, of course, common ground with Aitchison. And when Wace spoke of the fate of the weak, the reckless and the fraudulent, it is also possible to see some affinity with McMahon and Roe. Indeed, Wace asserted that the content, thrift and stability of each group of landholders was, as a whole, very much the same under British as under Sikh rule. If under the British system the thriftless were crushed, this result came about more slowly than under Sikh rule. But if this came close to a doctrinaire conviction that the weak went to the wall under any and all circumstances, it was influenced by the fragmented constitution of Punjab society. Nothing, Wace noted, was more striking than the juxtaposition and intermixture, especially in agricultural tracts, of villages and races which flourished, and of others which did not. These differences, which were certainly no figment of Wace's imagination, being the subject of comment in many a settlement report, Wace attributed to soil and physical surroundings, at least as much, or more, than to religion, race or history.

> Travelling from the Jamna to the Indus, across the whole breadth of the Punjab Province, I have observed the same, almost unvariable, rule; the races who live on damp soils and on the alluvial lands, adjacent to our rivers, are unthrifty, physically and morally; those who live on dry light soils are the contrary.[151]

How could a man with this experience in mind be convinced that agricultural troubles were due to forms of government and could be overcome by changes in law?

And yet Wace thought that some things could and should be done. Where one part of his experience confirmed or created a conviction that the situation was not remediable, another part of that experience convinced him that the revenue and judicial arrangements of the British ought to be adapted to the circumstances of the Punjab. Well aware that the fixed assessments which were still maintained in parts of the south-western Punjab were unsuited to the conditions of local agriculture, he had no difficulty in proclaiming, in this context, that the existing system operated to crush the weaker members of the agricultural community. Nor did he hesitate to admit that British law had aggravated the problem of indebtedness; and he was as ready as ever to recommend the adaptation of British civil procedure to rural circumstances and the exercise of restraint in execution proceedings. On this last point a notable development of his earlier views was to be seen in the stress he laid on the need to exercise restraint in employing the extreme processes of the law in the recovery of extravagant charges for accumulated interest, as distinct from the recovery of the principal. He recommended this measure while stressing that nothing should be done to weaken the security of contracts; an illustration of the delicate balance he had achieved between the demands of social circumstances and the received truths of his time.

By 1886 Thorburn, who had initiated the whole discussion, had become really impatient. In that year, in another attempt to convince the authorities of the need for action, he published a polemical work entitled *Musalmans and Money-lenders in the Punjab*, which dealt chiefly with the western Punjab. Here, Thorburn thought, the political danger which the transfer of rights in land from landowners to money-lenders involved, was greatest. Drawing on local accounts written by his fellow officers, Thorburn contended that south of the Salt Range these transfers were taking place, except in good years, in an annually increasing ratio; while he stressed that further north the special local circumstances which up till now had kept the peasant proprietors out of serious debt, were ceasing to operate.[152]

As to the causes of indebtedness Thorburn was no more hesitant in noticing the deficiencies of Muslim landholders as managers of their own concerns than he had been in 1884. This was, in a sense, beside the point, however, for to Thorburn, as to Wilson, this was a given factor, which the British should have taken into account in fashioning their administration. Indeed, Thorburn was now less equivocal in his condemnation of the British system of administration than he had been in 1884. In particular, in addition to attacks on fixed land-revenue settlements and British law and procedure, he made much of the British conversion of collective into individual ownership of land, of the British grant of freedom of transfer, and of the careful definition of individual rights in land by regular settlements, for these measures had extended the landowner's credit up to the market value of his holding. Punjab landholders were unfit for the gift of full individual proprietary rights, Thorburn insisted, the vast majority of them being almost as rude, ignorant and imprudent as they were at annexation.[153] There is little to suggest that this new line of Thorburn's was due to any wider experience in the western Punjab. For that matter some of Thorburn's charges regarding the British impact on land tenure were rather nebulous, and it is difficult to see that all of them were fully applicable to the frontier districts in which he had spent most of his official life, or to many other parts of the western Punjab. Hitherto, Thorburn's frontier experience and his attachment to individual rights in land had inhibited, it may be, any unfavourable conclusions regarding the British impact on land tenure. His new conclusions were only an extension, if a rather careless and in some respects unsubstantiated extension, of his earlier and more general theme of the advent of individualism. They were further an extension of his concern with the baneful consequences of the expansion of agricultural credit. And possibly Steedman's comments on the misplaced gift of proprietary right, made with reference to a south-western district, had made its mark on Thorburn. The result was that aspects and consequences of British administration, such as the advent of individualism and the expansion of agricultural credit, were shifted from the category in which they were seen as unavoidable, or almost unavoidable, parts of good and civilised government to the category in which remedial action definitely became possible. Thorburn had not been entirely consistent in these matters in 1884; but now, in the process of giving a prominent place to the British impact on land tenure as an undesirable aspect of British rule, he had resolved the conflict to this extent at least. The officer who sought an answer to growing indebtedness had gained another victory over the officer who equated British ideas and institutions with civilised standards.

Yet that victory was not as complete as it might have been. Thorburn did not advocate a return to collective ownership of land, or even a general withdrawal of the power of alienation. Instead he proposed that anyone deriving profits from a shop or from moneylending be debarred from acquiring interests in arable or pasture land. Influenced by his experience on the frontier, where the gulf between Muslim landholders and Hindu money-lenders was marked, Thorburn sought to do no more than to prevent the intrusion of alien and despised money-lenders into areas dominated by the old landholders. This objective also placed least strain on his continuing commitment to individual ownership of land as the *sine qua non* of material progress. For in spite of his attacks on the advent of individualism, Thorburn could not surrender his intellectual heritage completely. Indeed, he went to special lengths to ensure that the investment of capital in land, devoted to an increase in its productivity, would not suffer under his scheme. He exempted land in the immediate vicinity of a town or large village, manured and irrigated land anywhere, and land irrigated from a well, from his restrictions. In such areas, he contended, the landowners were in any case of a miscellaneous description, and possessed of more worldly intelligence which would enable them to hold their own. Thorburn realised that his scheme was open to the objection that it left credit unshackled in the richest, while destroying it in the most backward tracts, where it was most needed. To this he had no answer, except the rather doubtful argument that peasants in these backward areas were particularly improvident. Hence a restriction of credit would be beneficial in compelling them to live sparingly and work hard, instead of borrowing in times of difficulty. In his own estimation Thorburn had found an answer to the apparently insoluble problem of making credit easy for the thrifty and difficult for the improvident. In addition to local exemptions Thorburn suggested that the advance of seed grain, repayable only at the succeeding harvest, should be permitted; while he was prepared to empower the district officer to sanction sales or mortages to money-lenders who gave security that they would invest a certain minimum capital in the improvement of the productivity of their property.[154]

Having disarmed criticism on economic grounds as far as possible, Thorburn contended that all indigenous governments, ancient and modern, had placed restrictions on alienation, and that no contemporary state countenanced the acquisition of land by its trading and money-lending classes; and he noted the disabilities of the Jews in Russia and eastern Europe in this respect.[155] Yet Thorburn did not place all his hopes on the restriction of the power of alienation; for he went to considerable trouble to elucidate the reforms required in revenue and judicial administration.[156]

It was judicial reform in the direction of the Deccan Act, indeed, which was making steady headway in the Province at large. And one factor which contributed to this trend was the extensive and progressive alienations of land to professional money-lenders, which were brought to light in the course of the settlement of the Umballa district. The Settlement Officers of this south-eastern district, James Douie and Alfred Kensington, gradually became more and more concerned and outspoken, and knowledge of the situation in Umballa spread.

Kensington, a civilian appointed to his first post in 1878, had gained his settlement experience in the Hoshiarpur district.[157] In his assessment report of the Garshankar tahsil of that district, completed by 1882, Kensington had been able to strike a note of guarded

## THE TRADITION TRANSFORMED

optimism.[158] Of course only one-tenth of the cultivation had been alienated in Garshankar, a figure which compared favourably with the rest of Hoshiarpur. But in Umballa, or rather in its four southern tahsils, Kensington found that things were very different. Thus he reported in 1888 that in the Naraingarh tahsil vendees and mortgagees paid nearly one-fourth of the land revenue. In this tahsil more than two-thirds of the land sold since the previous settlement, and more than four-fifths of the land mortgaged, had been acquired by professional money-lenders.[159] It was Kensington's increasing acquaintance with conditions of this kind which had led him to assert some two years earlier that the district was in a thoroughly unsatisfactory condition, and that its prosperity had been much over-estimated.[160] In February 1887 a general enquiry by the Financial Commissioner regarding the spread of mortgages by conditional sale gave Kensington the opportunity to represent that the indebtedness of the district was increasing by leaps and bounds, and that the people were experiencing increasing difficulty in obtaining money on any reasonable terms. He thought that a crisis was rapidly approaching in the Umballa district, and that within the next ten or fifteen years Government would be almost compelled to step in and enforce wholesale measures of relief similar to those adopted in the Deccan. The time for partial remedies, he thought, had passed.[161]

A similar development of opinion may be traced in the case of James Douie, a civilian whose experience dated from 1876.[162] Serving as Settlement Officer of adjoining tahsils in the Karnal and Umballa districts, Douie had been one of the officers consulted in 1885 on the correspondence initiated by Thorburn's paper in the preceding year. To indicate his approach to the subject, Douie had drawn pointed attention to the extent of indebtedness and land transfer in his part of the country; but as regards remedies he had done no more than support the two proposals which the Lieutenant-Governor had suggested might be discussed.[163] In 1887, when Douie submitted his assessment report of the Jagadhri tahsil, the most involved tahsil in the Umballa district, he went further. His report showed that practically one-third of the revenue was paid on land acquired by vendees and mortgagees. Professional money-lenders almost monopolised the market in land in Jagadhri, having acquired three-quarters of the land sold and four-fifths of that mortgaged. It was not surprising, therefore, that a computation of the loss or gain of land by particular tribes showed that the Rajputs, Jats and Gujars, the major landholding tribes of the tahsil, had suffered a net loss by sale and mortgage, since the previous settlement, of land paying thirty, twenty-eight and twenty-five per cent of their revenue respectively. Also unpleasant was the fact that Douie's figures suggested that nearly three-fifths of the transfers of the last thirty-five years had occurred in the last ten years of that period. Douie characterised the mass of the agricultural population as ignorant, unthrifty and unenterprising. He remarked that it might be said that it was a good thing that such weaklings should go to the wall, and he presumed that the fittest of the agriculturists had survived. But this did not prevent him from stressing that the place of expropriated agriculturists was taken by money-lenders who made greedy and unimproving landlords. Nor did it stop him from predicting that the decay would go on, and that the future of the tahsil was dark, unless drastic measures, such as had been adopted in another part of India, were taken.[164]

The situation in the Umballa district also influenced the views of A. R. Bulman, a representative of an earlier generation of officers. As Deputy Commissioner of Gujranwala in 1879, Bulman had seen little but good in the transfer of land to the trading castes of his district. Aware that considerable quantities of land were changing hands in this way, he had still spoken of the diffusion of a 'leaven' of good landlords among the agricultural classes. But in 1883 and 1884, as Deputy Commissioner of Umballa, Bulman could see that in some parts of that district, and notably in the Jagadhri tahsil, the proprietorship of the soil seemed in a fair way of passing altogether from the hands of the agricultural classes into those of the money-lenders, and chiefly of money-lenders resident in the towns.[165] If Bulman was aware of the full extent of transfer in Umballa, as he had probably not been in Gujranwala, there was also the fact that the money-lenders of Umballa could not be described as good landlords by any stretch of the imagination. Both these features of the situation were apparent in Bulman's letter of April 1887, in which, as officiating Commissioner of the Delhi division, he endorsed Kensington's call for a Deccan Relief Act. There was no doubt, he noted, that in the four southern tahsils of Umballa, and most of all in Jagadhri, a condition of things was imminent, which would demand remedial measures of a drastic kind. The State, in its capacity as landlord of the soil, and with its responsibility for the efficient operation of an administrative system based on the solidity of the village community and the independence and influence of the village headmen, could not allow whole tahsils to be parcelled out among usurers, who were frequently non-resident, and almost

## THE TRADITION TRANSFORMED

always aliens in race, while the old proprietors of the soil were reduced to the lowest level of rack-rented tenants-at-will. And there were unmistakable signs that such a situation was now dangerously close in a large part of the Umballa district.[166]

It was in 1887, too, that Colonel Grey, the Commissioner of the Delhi division, definitely ranged himself on the side of the advocates of drastic legislation. In January 1884 Grey had not been prepared to take up the large questions raised incidentally by Wilson, notably the restriction of the power of transfer. But in several articles, apparently published in November 1887, Grey reviewed the correspondence on indebtedness since 1884, this correspondence having just been published in a series of selections from official records. The papers showed, Grey thought, that the condition of things of which Bulman spoke was by no means imminent in Umballa alone. Grey favoured a measure along the lines of the Deccan Relief Act, to clear the peasantry of existing embarrassments, to be followed by the prohibition of alienations to all but agriculturists. In each case a transfer of land should be made only with the sanction of the district officer. This would stop the transfer of land to money-lenders, while ensuring that holdings which had become too small by sub-division could be sold or mortgaged. Believing that legislation to restrict the power of transfer would not eventuate, or at any rate not for a long time, Grey, like so many others, considered legislation similar to the Deccan Act the most hopeful step that could be taken.[167]

Of course not everyone thought that legislation of the kind adopted in the Deccan was required. But there could not have been too many officers like Charles Roe, who insisted that nothing at all need be done. In the 1880s most of those who did not go as far as to ask for a Deccan Relief Act, or who actually opposed such legislation, nevertheless came out in favour of some of the limited judicial reforms of which the Deccan Act consisted. It was a very different story in regard to the restriction of the power of transfer. A few officers no doubt pressed boldly for some action along these lines, a few had definite ideas about the shape such legislation might take, but few indeed considered that such legislation was likely in the foreseeable future. Such schemes as were put forward in the course of official business by Steedman and Wilson were ignored, dismissed, or treated as of academic interest only, by a succession of senior officers ranging in rank from Commissioner to Lieutenant-Governor.

If the restriction of the power of alienation did not appear to be within the realm of practical politics, the very fact that this question was raised at all was of some significance. Together with the growing interest in judicial reform, it attests to the concern about land transfer which manifested itself in the 1880s among a steadily increasing number of officers. This concern was not confined to any particular generation of officers. It is true that with one or two exceptions the most forthright or far-reaching demands for legislation came from civilians below the rank of Commissioner: from Thorburn, Rivaz and Miller, whose experience dated from the 1860s, and from Steedman, Wilson, Clarke, Ibbetson, Anderson, Kensington and Douie, who had joined the service in the 1870s. This fact, however, should not be allowed to obscure the very clear signs of disquiet among officers in more senior positions, generally men whose civil experience went back to the 1850s or early 1860s. Among Commissioners one need only refer to Perkins, Ommanney, Bulman and Grey for evidence of this state of affairs. And to this list must be added McMahon and Wace, who rose as high as the office of Financial Commissioner, even though they were able to keep their fears within bounds. Nor were the Lieutenant-Governors of the period, Egerton and Aitchison, entirely exempt from concern, though they certainly put a bold front on the matter.

This general trend can be attributed to a number of general considerations. The transfer of land still continued, and in many districts probably at a faster rate than in earlier years. Certainly the cumulative nature of the process ensured that awareness of the problem would be more likely to increase than decrease with the passage of time. To the observation of the phenomenon itself, must be added the impression made in certain instances by statistics of alienation collected in the course of revenue settlement. Now compiled more carefully than ever before, itself possibly a sign of unease, the information which these statistics provided about the extent and rate of transfer in certain districts was not likely to set the mind at rest.

Furthermore, it must be recognised that many officers required years of experience, and above all time to assimilate that experience, before they were able to evaluate what they had seen, and in a position to put their ideas in order. Almost all the assumptions of the time were conducive to the notion that nothing could be wrong, so that any evidence to the contrary might take years to assimilate, and any attempt to reconcile this evidence with existing notions could pose distinct intellectual difficulties. Many examples come to mind. Consider, for instance, the various stages which Perkins and Thorburn traversed before they became alarmed. Or consider how slowly and painfully Thorburn's ideas took shape.

## THE TRADITION TRANSFORMED

Note how Ibbetson began as an advocate of the sanctity of contract, and many years later could do nothing with political economy but shunt it aside. Or how McMahon, an early opponent of legislation, came to admit the gravity of the problem and yet, like Wace, could not bring himself to support more than limited reforms.

A fairly long period of gestation being required before experience began to make its mark on the opinions of most officers, the 1880s also provided an atmosphere a little less hostile to the airing of novel opinions than the second half of the 1870s. By the 1880s the authoritative nature of the Lieutenant-Governor's conclusions of 1874 was being eroded by the revelations regarding the inaccuracy of the revenue report statistics, by the passing of the Deccan Relief Act of 1879, which could be seen as a precedent for the Punjab, and by the sheer passage of time, which made the conclusions of 1874 seem less and less relevant as an appraisal of the contemporary situation.

By the time the stage had been set for the emergence of new currents of opinion, a new generation or more of officers had come to the fore. It is true that something of the impetus of the earlier movement remained, despite the decision of 1874, witness the changed views of parties to the earlier debate, such as Egerton and McMahon. Nevertheless, the new movement was sustained by many younger officers: by Thorburn, who in 1874 had not been unduly concerned about land transfer; by Ibbetson, who had been opposed to legislation at that time; and by many an officer who had been among the most junior civilians in 1874, or not in Government employ at all. There were bold spirits in the new generation, as in the old, and officers like Wilson and Thorburn made the question of land transfer a live one. They obliged others to put pen to paper, forced them to think the problem through, and in Thorburn's case elicited a correspondence which could only help to focus official attention on the problem. In short, the process once set in motion again, would tend to gain impetus for some time, as long as no Lieutenant-Governor closed the question for another generation, and as long as the transfer of land continued to exert a steady pressure.

To stress that the 1880s witnessed increased concern about land transfer, is not to discount the persistence of sharp divisions of opinion within the Province. If anything, the growth of official concern at this stage ensured that more officers favoured or demanded legislation of a kind which their fellows considered extreme. For no less than the 1870s do the 1880s provide evidence that the influence which social change exerted on official opinion was exceedingly diverse. The extent and nature of an officer's local experience was certainly likely to influence his opinions. But that a man's opinion was no mere function of his experience of Punjab society, or of any particular local variant, is something which requires no further emphasis here. What the 1880s reveal with greater clarity than ever before, however, is that any attempt to relate experience to opinion cannot be confined simply to a short period, such as the second half of the 1870s, but must take account of longer periods, which reveal the full potential of an officer's experience. Not that this enables us to establish a more consistent relationship between a man's experience and his opinions; for what the longer perspective shows is that different men assimilated change in different ways, approached it from different points of view, and reconciled it in various ways with current notions of government and society.

These points emerge most clearly from the debate about the fundamental causes of land transfer which took place in the 1880s. Though no broad classification can do justice to the opinions of every officer, some differences in approach stand out in bold relief. To one class of officer, it was the Government which was primarily responsible for the evils which had arisen. This approach was expressed in its most comprehensive form by Wilson and Ibbetson. Whether the Government was held responsible for its creation of the power of land transfer, for its expansion of agricultural credit, or for its revenue and judicial system, any reference to society only served to illustrate the unsuitability of British measures to Indian circumstances. This was the position towards which Thorburn was moving in the 1880s, though he never went as far in this respect as a number of other officers. To men such as Wace and Lyall, however, it was the nature of Indian society which lay at the root of the problem. That problem might be aggravated by certain features, on the whole certain limited features, of British administration, which were unsuited to the country; but these features were not among the fundamental causes of the trouble. This idea, that by and large it was Indian society which did not conform to accepted standards, was taken further in a third approach represented by Aitchison. In this approach a stress on the deficiencies of Indian society was combined with the notion that difficulties were also due to the extension of a regular system of government to a country which had not known such a system. Only minor aspects of British administration could be seen as unsuitable from this point of view. Roe's explanation in 1885 was not dissimilar, if more extreme: for in characterising the British system as regular and civilised, Roe was more concerned to play down its role altogether; while as regards the indigenous deficiencies he stressed inevitable agricultural difficulties as well as social shortcomings. Nor was Thorburn entirely unaffected by this sort of approach: in 1884 he could argue that part of the difficulties could be attributed to the extension of regular and settled government to the Punjab. He might have cherished the second part of the argument too, namely the fundamental importance of Indian deficiencies, had he not changed his mind about the 'lazy ignorant beings', the landholders of Bannu, in the course of settlement work many years before.[168]

While all these approaches reflect some elements of reality, the question remains why changes in society were interpreted in such widely different ways. Why, in other words, was the admittedly diverse experience of officers transmuted into such irreconcilable opinions? Two major reasons may be adduced.

In the first place these approaches reflected the varied degrees of concern, or lack of concern, which different officers felt about land transfer. Roe, for instance, could take the line he did, partly because he felt no anxiety whatever and saw no need for legislation of any kind. But those who were convinced that one remedy or another was required to deal with an unsatisfactory or intolerable situation, were likely to make very different assessments of the fundamental causes of land transfer; for obviously the cure for any disease depended largely on the diagnosis. And if one asks why some officers felt more concern than others, one answer must be that some individuals were more sensitive to particular developments than others. It was differences in personality, rather than political philosophy, which were involved, as will become clear later. And perhaps some of those who became concerned at a time when they were already in higher official positions, were less prone to give free rein to their fears, their responsibility being so much greater.

Secondly, basic differences in approach depended on the degree to which particular officers insisted on regarding Western principles and experience as an absolute standard for all times and places. This in itself reflected the variations in the willingness or ability of different officers to shake themselves free from the preconceptions of their youth. While Ibbetson, for instance, had accomplished much in this respect, Thorburn certainly found it difficult, despite acute political fears. And if one takes Wace as an example, one gets the impression that, almost no matter what he saw, and irrespective of the admissions he might make, he could never really concede that British principles were not of the most fundamental relevance to any society. Hence, in spite of his grasp of rural circumstances, he could not help but stress the shortcomings of Indian society.

Why, it may be asked, did some officers find it easier than others to revise their Western-oriented notions of government and society? It appears likely that something may be attributed to individual differences in intellectual commitment. Thus Roe's commitment to certain evolutionist notions appears to have been far stronger than that of the majority of officers, and these notions influenced his way of looking at the question. Similarly in Thorburn's case the tendency to equate British rule with civilised standards was marked, an influence which was only gradually, and probably not completely, overcome. Apart from the special hold which particular doctrines may have had on particular officers, the quality of an officer's mind was not unimportant. James Lyall and Gordon Young might not have been too dissimilar in their opinions on land transfer; but while Young followed current *laissez-faire* notions blindly, Lyall was given to making his own, admittedly cautious assessment of opposing arguments. Or compare Wilson and Thorburn. In the attempt to reconcile Indian experience with Western principles, no one had moved further away from an insistence on the relevance of Western standards than James Wilson. Yet he was able to reconcile a sweeping away of so many apparently fundamental aspects of British administration with a regard for its underlying purpose, that is the development of prosperity and the investment of capital in land. One does not have to agree fully with Wilson's contentions that the revenue system had played no part in the development of prosperity, and that the transfer of land hindered the investment of capital, to see that this kind of intellectual flexibility was denied to Thorburn, who still tended to think to a large extent in terms of an inherent contradiction between the political and the economic objectives of British rule. In addition to differences in intellectual commitment or intellectual capacity, variations in the readiness of officers to alter their Western-oriented intellectual stance, may be attributed to such things as personality, official position or simply age, all considerations which would affect the ability of individuals to revise their view of the world.

In short, any consistent correlation between experience and opinion is unlikely, because the things which officers perceived in particular localities and the concern which their observations aroused, were likely to vary as much as the ways in which they assimilated this experience and reconciled it with prevailing concepts of government and society.

## THE TRADITION TRANSFORMED

As more time elapsed, the channels through which society exerted its influence increased in number and complexity. An officer's experience was not a constant, unchanging element in the situation. Though some officers might spend years in particular localities, the local experience of others was exceedingly diverse, and that of most officers was likely to become increasingly so with prolonged service. New channels of social influence developed, so that a man's experience, in the full sense, could no longer be even loosely equated with his local experience. The appearance of a more accurate and detailed local literature on land transfer, of which we have seen some examples, ensured that some officers would obtain a view of land transfer at once more comprehensive and less impressionistic. As the debate gathered momentum, it became steadily more likely that a man would be influenced by the opinions of others, or obliged to measure his own experience against the facts and ideas of others. Thus it was that at the end of the 1880s Thorburn's book began a process which resulted ultimately in a great stirring of Provincial opinion. And it was James Lyall, whose 'wailing helplessness' Thorburn had deplored in this very book,[169] who emerged as the champion of a new protective policy, and who in his new position as Lieutenant-Governor confirmed and stimulated the trend towards concern and legislation.

III

In May 1887 the Punjab Government received a copy of a brief despatch from the Secretary of State for India, forwarded by the Government of India, calling for a report on the indebtedness of the agriculturists of the western Punjab. It was Thorburn's book which had drawn the Secretary of State's attention to that subject, a subject which experience in other parts of India showed to be of great importance.[170] After some initial skirmishing among the Secretaries to the Punjab Government, James Lyall, who had returned to the Punjab as Lieutenant-Governor, after several years as Resident at Mysore, expressed a typically cautious opinion early in August. As in the past, he was especially concerned with the rate at which indebtedness was increasing. Indebtedness, he thought, was common among peasant proprietors all over the world. It had been increasing in the Punjab because the absence of credit had prevented serious indebtedness at first; but he did not see why the number of indebted should continue to increase much. There was much in Thorburn's book with which he disagreed. With his special experience of parts of the Punjab in which communal interests in land had not existed, it was not surprising that he pointed out that individual transferable rights in land had not been in many parts of the Punjab, and especially the south-west, the gift of the British Government. Thorburn's proposition that Punjab agriculturists were unfit for such a gift was much too strongly put; and in any case it was not possible to go back from the gift for, as his Government later explained to the Government of India, drawing evidently on Maine's notions of the evolution of property, that 'gift' was in reality a necessary outcome of the development of individual rights and the gradual solution of the village communal bond.[171] Nor would the people support such action. To prohibit the acquisition of land by money-lenders was quite impossible. Fluctuating assessments should be extended only slowly and for the most weighty reasons. That the system of civil justice benefited the money-lender at the expense of the peasant was more or less inevitable. It could be fought only by legislation on the lines of the Deccan Act. He doubted whether such legislation was as yet wanted in any part of the Punjab. Nevertheless, the whole question would be re-examined. Those of Thorburn's proposed reforms in law and civil procedure which seemed reasonable would be submitted to the Financial Commissioners and Chief Court for opinion; and the Financial Commissioners should report on the extent of prevailing indebtedness and whether it was rapidly increasing.[172]

Almost a year later, in July 1888, Lyall found that these orders had not been carried out. Lewis Tupper, the Junior Secretary, all for legislation, had delayed the case in September 1887 by deciding that papers about the Deccan Act had better be obtained from Bombay.[173] A note on the Bombay papers was not prepared till April 1888.[174] The officiating Junior Secretary, H. C. Fanshawe, opposed to legislation, did not think the case an urgent one. It was only pressure from the Government of India in June 1888 that led Fanshawe to propose that Lyall's orders of August 1887 be carried out and that a preliminary reply be sent to the Government of India.[175] Lyall agreed to this course of action. By now, however, he inclined to the view that legislation on the lines of the Deccan Act *was* wanted in the Punjab. For Lyall had made a careful re-assessment of his position, the reasons for which can only be surmised. Possibly something may be attributed to the opinions expressed on Thorburn's paper of 1884. Lyall had been away at this time, and the selections from the Financial Commissioner's records, which contained the local opinions, as well as the warnings about Umballa, were not forwarded to the

Punjab Government till October 1887,[176] several months after Lyall had suggested that legislation similar to the Deccan Act was not as yet required in any part of the Punjab. As regards Umballa, the statistics in the assessment reports may have helped to convince Lyall that a serious situation was arising in some parts of the Province.[177] The scope of the legislation contemplated by Lyall is certainly consistent with such a view. The body of the measure, consisting of certain amendments in law and civil procedure, Lyall indicated, would apply to the whole Punjab. There might also be some stronger provisions – such as sections which would empower courts to go behind bonds, and separate interest from principal, and decree only reasonable interest – which should be applicable only to certain tribes or tracts when formally applied by the Local Government with the consent of the Government of India.[178] The preliminary reply to the Government of India, embodying these conclusions, Lyall ordered in July 1888, should be accompanied by a compilation of statistics from the revenue reports,[179] a requirement which led to a discussion of these statistics in August.

Throughout the discussions of July and August Lyall's wide experience and comprehensive knowledge of the Punjab were very much in evidence. Lyall insisted that the passing of land from landowners to money-lenders had been going on in a gradually increasing ratio for years all over the Punjab, except in tracts with a thrifty population; that the evil or political danger though accentuated in the west by communal differences was by no means confined to it; that alienations in the east were more indicative of poverty and distress than those in the west; and that in both east and west there were districts in which alienations to money-lenders were serious and increasing.[180] It was obviously this informed view of local variations in land transfer which had led Lyall to expand the scope of the question from the western Punjab to the whole Province. Thorburn's alarm and impatience had served to bring the problem into view; Lyall's knowledge and intellectual discrimination ensured that if the question was taken up at all, it was taken up as one of Provincial importance.

In November 1888 a despatch embodying Lyall's provisional conclusions was sent to the Government of India; and this despatch was forwarded to the Financial Commissioners and the Chief Court. Revenue officers were to report whether alienations were proceeding in an increasing ratio and whether such increase involved any political danger. They were to consider whether legislation on the lines of the Deccan Act was necessary, and they were to give their opinion on the particular provisions which Lyall thought might be incorporated in such an Act. These provisions touched every aspect of the judicial system: the examination of the parties, compulsory arbitration, the execution of decrees, the summoning of agriculturists at harvest time, the limitation law, the business practices of money-lenders in regard to receipts and accounts, registration, legal practitioners, rural courts and conciliators, and remission of fees.[181] In regard to the more drastic provisions, empowering courts to go behind bonds, separate interest from principal and decree only reasonable interest, officers were asked whether they were necessary in any part of the Punjab. These provisions of course involved the most obvious attack on the sanctity of contract, and it was typical of Lyall's caution that he also requested officers to consider what safeguards should be provided to restrict the application of these provisions to cases of proved necessity. Nor did Lyall fail to leave an opening for altogether less far-reaching proposals: if officers did not think it necessary that their conclusions be embodied in a special Act, they were to note what special proposals of a legislative or executive nature they considered desirable. On the other hand, it was made clear that officers were not prevented from putting forward suggestions which Lyall had rejected. The opinion of the Chief Court was also requested on certain points.[182]

Lyall's reference to the Financial Commissioners and the Chief Court produced a very bulky file indeed, the detailed replies of some seventy-eight officers being submitted in 1888 and 1889. Forty-four of these officers were revenue officers, consulted on the larger questions.[183]

The replies of the revenue officers showed that there was more or less general agreement among them that the transfer of land to money-lenders was increasing.

There were now many officers, far more than in the 1870s, who believed that the process involved a grave political danger or serious evils. They included many who had expressed their opinions already, fully or partially, notably J. Wilson, S. S. Thorburn, D. Ibbetson, C. M. Rivaz, R. Clarke, A. Anderson, A. Kensington, J. M. Douie and L. J. H. Grey. There were nearly as many whose voices were heard for the first time—J. G. Silcock, L. W. Dane and G. M. Ogilvie, to name only those who played some part in later events.

Taken together with some earlier sources the replies of 1888 and 1889 show not only the kind of political danger which officers anticipated, but also the attitudes which underlay their apprehensions.[184]

## THE TRADITION TRANSFORMED

The political danger apprehended seemed especially serious to a foreign rule. As Ibbetson had remarked in 1885, political considerations outweighed almost everything else in India. In England popular discontent meant only a change of Ministers and an alteration of the law; in India it meant disloyalty.[185]

The landowners, various officers pointed out, represented a political force in the country; and they were being displaced by money-lenders, men of no political significance. The landowning tribes were the foundation of British rule; they had a vast superiority in numbers; they supplied the man-power for the native army; they were the hereditary proprietors of the soil; they were, in many cases, war-like with traditions and a history; they were sturdy, courageous and independent; and if discontented and given an opportunity they would fight. They were, as Thorburn put it in 1886, 'the people of India';[186] and two years before, writing about the western Punjab, he had even apprehended that a hostile agrarian movement might take up a cry dear to liberal sentiment, that of 'the land for the people'.[187] On the other hand, the trading castes contributed nothing to the stability of the State and little to its revenues. Their numbers were insignificant and they were feeble in spirit and physique. They were both feared and despised by the landowners whose social inferiors they had often been before British rule. Far from being able to fight, the trading castes required protection, so that they were a source of weakness rather than strength in time of danger. And in any case, their loyalty to Government was only doubtful.

There was, some officers thought, a special danger in the west where the Muslim landowning tribes were bigoted; where the landowner and the money-lender were sharply differentiated by religion as well as by interests; where there were, across the frontier, races of the same stock, not dominated by the money-lender; and where there was an independent Muslim kingdom, Afghanistan, and Russia in the background.

It was feared that the expropriation of landowning tribes by money-lenders would create a discontented agricultural class, ready for violence against the money-lenders, and at the least not averse to political change. Agrarian discontent, many officers believed, could easily turn into hatred of the Government which encouraged expropriation by the great power which its civil courts gave to the money-lender. In some parts of the country officers already perceived various symptoms of agrarian discontent; in other parts they felt that if nothing was done the growth of such discontent was inevitable. It was not suggested that there was anywhere an immediate political danger. Nor were many apprehensions expressed as to the loyalty of the army; though one officer, remembering one of the causes of the mutiny, stressed that events which make the agricultural population dissatisfied also make the army dissatisfied.[188] There was, however, general anxiety lest one day a crisis should come, and the executive be weakened, perhaps through a threat from outside, and the whole fabric of British order and power in the countryside collapse.

Briefly, we may say that this analysis revealed an obsession with the political importance of large numbers, with physical strength and robustness of character, and with periods of crisis. Details apart, this was the kind of political analysis which Arthur Brandreth had made many years earlier. That so many officers subscribed to it now, and in the same context, certainly underlines the role of land transfer in generating political anxieties. No more than in the 1870s, however, could the alienation of land be seen as a political danger, except by reference to certain prevailing assumptions and attitudes. The greater body of evidence in the 1880s enables us to analyse more fully whence these assumptions and attitudes came.

It is clear that the Punjab tradition of reliance on the loyalty of the many had persisted. In the 1880s it was by no means only those who had served in the early days of British rule in the Punjab, but men of an entirely new generation, who attributed political significance to a numerous body of landholders. The persistence of the tradition deserves explanation. It is not sufficient to attribute it to the tendency by which ideas are passed from generation to generation; for it is unreasonable to suppose that ideas would be accepted by a new generation, unless the general situation was such as to render these ideas plausible.

One of the elements in the general situation was the British position in India. The phenomenon of a tiny handful of foreigners ruling a vast empire was as patent as ever. It may be that in the 1880s the Punjab and India appeared, all things considered, a more settled and stable place to a new generation of officers than to their predecessors of earlier years. Given the alien character of British rule, however, any crisis would always bring great danger in its train; and irrespective of internal conditions, a crisis could always arise as a result of an external challenge. In these circumstances a district officer, surveying the vast numbers within his domain, might well rejoice to think that a large majority would not be hostile in the event of any temporary relaxation of the British hold on the country. Conscious of their isolation and their numerical inferiority, the British were induced to think in terms of mass support for their rule.

Yet notions of this kind, while powerful enough, must be related to social realities if they are to acquire political force. In the Punjab, attempts to secure the loyalty of 'the people' or 'the masses', had to take very particular account of the village proprietors, for they alone combined the required numerical strength with influence in village society. There was neither a class above them, which could command their allegiance, nor any class below them, which appeared capable of challenging their control of the village. Hence there was no point in giving undue privileges to an aristocracy which could not keep the landholders quiet, nor any reason for paying particular attention to those subject to the landholders. Besides, the landowners were the only large class of people on whose loyalty the British could make some direct claim. The British administration might be supposed to have secured benefits to many people; but to an administrator none would appear so direct and obvious, so much the tangible result of administrative and political decision, as the landed rights and favourable assessments which had been secured to the peasantry. In all this one can trace the legacy of the old political tradition, acting through the medium of the landed tenures it had created.

But this is not the whole story. British political notions faithfully reflected some of the inherent features of village society as well as institutional arrangements of their own making. It would be difficult to deny that the landholders considered themselves the *élite* in the village, and thought of all other village residents as simply catering to their needs. In large parts of the western Punjab the subordinate social position of the Hindu trader was particularly marked. In the village, political dominance appeared to be assured by superiority of numbers, and by physical strength and boldness. This was something which the British could hardly miss; and it could only be reinforced by memories of disturbances in which the traders and money-lenders had succumbed or been put to flight. The fact that the army was very largely recruited from landholding tribes seemed to be a further assurance that courage and character were agricultural monopolies. It was almost as if Punjab society was village society writ large, it being assumed that the political forces which prevailed within the village must necessarily prevail within the Province.

This view of social influence on British political notions raises the question why British officers were content to ignore other aspects of Punjab society. Something may be attributed to the nature of an administrator's official duties. An administration dependent very largely on the payment of land-revenue by numerous small landed proprietors must take particular care of its revenue-payers, so that much of the time, the thoughts and energies of its servants must be centred on the village rather than the town. British officers were brought into closer contact with the village, and acquired a more intimate knowledge of village society. So much of the rationale of Indian administration being revenue collection, officers were also likely to look askance at non-agriculturists, whether in village or town, who under the Indian revenue system hardly paid their way. There was also more in the village than in the town to attract the sympathy of the British. Victorian notions of the desirability of manliness and activity, induced the British to look with a kindly eye on the agricultural world, where these particular virtues appeared to be more in evidence than in the non-agricultural world. The towns might be more complex, more sophisticated, but for that very reason they were more alien in British eyes. Then the relationship of ruler and subject was accepted with better grace in the village than in the town. It was comparatively easy to satisfy the needs of landholders, wanting little but a tolerable revenue demand. Their loyalty could be assumed in most instances in the absence of grievances; the mood of the towns was not so certain.

Given the host of factors conducive to the survival of the tradition of reliance on the loyalty of the village proprietors, the pervasiveness of that tradition is not surprising. In the 1880s, as in the 1870s, the tradition provided the essential pre-condition for the development of serious anxiety about land transfer. And in the process the old tradition was transformed. For there was a great gap between the old confidence and the new fears, between the old idea that good administration would secure the loyalty of the proprietors, and the new idea that only reform of the administration could prevent their ultimate disaffection. What had been seen as a vital element in the political stability of the Province before 1869, had become a serious political problem in the estimation of many officers.

Nonetheless, there were still quite a few officers who perceived no political danger in the transfer of land to the money-lending classes, or who at least believed that no such danger existed at present or would arise in the near future. While these men had not succumbed to the new anxieties, there is little to suggest that most of them had shaken themselves free from the assumptions associated with the older political tradition. With no alternative political philosophy to offer, they were simply responding in a negative fashion to the notion that a distinct political problem existed, and had to be met. Robert Maconachie and Mackworth Young argued that the benefits conferred by a British administration in the East involved political risks which must be run. Some officers doubted whether a situation would ever arise in which tribes were entirely expropriated and united in discontent, or inclined to the view that expropriated individuals sank into insignificance. To some there was little political danger when the owners were kept on the land as tenants, or the tenants were well-treated; to others when the owners were ejected from the land. One officer doubted whether any political danger was to be expected from men who lost their land through lack of spirit, as in Umballa; or, as an officer with considerable experience of the upper frontier thought, through sheer recklessness. William Coldstream, who had accepted the process of expropriation without undue alarm many years before, doubted whether those who lost their land blamed Government. Only one officer, Edward O'Brien, denied the reality of political danger in a manner which could not be entirely reconciled with the stress of the older political tradition on the village and the masses. Dispossessed owners, O'Brien noted, did not flock to the cities where they might become a discontented and dangerous element; they did not gather around independent rulers or traditional leaders; and they did not take to crime. In O'Brien's opinion it was only when the unemployed of any profession took to these courses that they became a danger to the State. Apart from an odd opinion like this, the whole debate was conducted within the terms set by the old political tradition.[189]

This aspect of the matter is further illustrated by the fact that almost the entire discussion, O'Brien's opinion included, turned on the question of whether the peasant proprietors were likely to become discontented and dangerous. Of all the officers consulted in the enquiry of 1888–9 only one considered the possibility that there might be some direct political danger from the money-lending classes whose influence was growing; a danger which would not arise, that officer thought, until it was combined with organisation among those classes.[190]

While stressing the political side of the question it is desirable not to overlook the fact that distinct administrative considerations were involved in Lyall's legislative suggestions. The enquiry of 1888–9 showed that it was easier to secure more or less general consent to broad administrative proposals than to speculative political propositions. There were, of course, great differences of opinion among officers as to the particular reforms in law and civil procedure which might be worth trying; but these differences were not necessarily determined by any particular view of the political danger involved in the transfer of land. James Lyall was not far wrong when he wrote at a later date that 'even those officers who have least apprehension of political danger, who have least sentiment or repress it most carefully, and who are disposed to expect least advantage from radical alterations of law and procedure, virtually admit the great unsuitability of some parts of our legal system to the condition and circumstances of the agriculturists of the Province'.[191] On the strongest provision referred for opinion – sections empowering courts to go behind bonds, separate interest from principal and decree only reasonable interest – and on the general question of whether an Agricultural Relief Act on the lines of the Deccan Act was required in the Punjab, the vast majority of revenue officers answered in the affirmative. Only a few of the officers who had questioned the existence of any political danger answered either the first or both of these questions in the negative. The most important of these were G. R. Elsmie and W. M. Young, the two Financial Commissioners, who answered both these questions in the negative. On the affirmative side there were some officers who desired that provisions for going behind the bond be introduced with safeguards, or that a Relief Act be limited in its application. In this category were a few of the officers who had denied the existence of any political danger, and some who believed the political danger to be real. A large number of officers, mainly those who anticipated political danger but also a few who did not, either did not comment on the question of safeguards or geographical limitations, or indicated that such safeguards and limitations were undesirable. A majority of the judicial officers who discussed these general questions replied in the affirmative. The Judges of the Chief Court, including old opponents of legislative action like C. A. Roe and A. H. Benton, were unsympathetic.

It was political anxieties which had brought the question of land transfer to the surface; but once that happened, and a large number of officers were consulted, the tide in favour of judicial remedies was swollen, in 1888–9 as in 1885, by those who recognised the desirability of adapting particular features of British administration to Indian circumstances. Social influence worked through administrative as well as political channels.

Taking the replies of 1888–9 as a whole, the enquiry had established a remarkable consensus of opinion, especially among revenue officers, that for political or administrative reasons, some legislative action on the lines of the Deccan Act was required, while there were many officers who were prepared to go further in this direction than Lyall had been.

The enquiry also showed that a fair number of officers, mainly revenue officers, wanted something more than judicial reform. A few wanted to inhibit alienation by changes in the revenue system. Most of them favoured the imposition of some sort of restriction on the power of alienation. Some of these men, like C. M. Rivaz, J. G. Silcock, J. M. Douie and G. M. Ogilvie, indicated that they considered this to be the only real remedy; and others like J. Wilson, S. S. Thorburn (who had ceased to believe that the particular restrictions he had advocated in 1886 were practicable), D. Ibbetson and L. J. H. Grey certainly favoured it strongly. There was, nevertheless, little hope among these officers that any such solution would be adopted.

The replies of the judicial officers were forwarded to the Punjab Government in June, and those of the revenue officers in October, 1889. Despite several reminders from the Government of India it was not till April 1891 that an office note was prepared on these opinions, and not till June 1891 that James Lyall recorded his opinion.[192] A perusal of the papers convinced Lyall that a serious state of affairs existed, either developed or commencing; that transfers were proceeding rapidly and in an increasing ratio; that there had been a marked tendency to a decline of good feeling among the agricultural classes in many, if not all, districts; and that political danger was to be apprehended shortly in very many districts. That political danger, he thought, was greatly increased by the fact that many of the transfers were to the money-lending classes; but even the transfer of land from one agriculturist to another agriculturist, as far as it was due to the unsuitability of law and civil procedure to the condition of the poorer agriculturists, was a reproach and tended to make the Government unpopular. He was now more strongly of the opinion than before that in so far as land transfers were due to the action of British laws and courts, remedial measures were required. He still believed that only a measure on the lines of the Deccan Act would be of much use; but he now favoured the extension of even its stronger provisions to the whole of the Punjab. The measure which he sketched followed the Deccan Act closely.[193]

Lyall knew that these proposals would not be well received by the Government of India. P. P. Hutchins, the Member for the Revenue and Home Departments in the Government of India, had indicated unofficially his hostility to legislation similar to the Deccan

Act.[194] It looked to Lyall as if general legislation might be proposed for several Provinces which would not meet the requirements of the Punjab. Accordingly, in forwarding his proposals to the Government of India in August 1891, Lyall tried to anticipate objections and suggestions. His proposals, he argued, though they might appear drastic, amounted for the most part only to a return to the law and procedure in force in the Punjab within a comparatively recent period. In this, as well as in other respects, the circumstances of the Punjab were peculiar; and an attempt to frame an Act applicable to the Punjab and other Provinces would mean not only delay, but in the end a law not adequate or suited to Punjab requirements. As to objections to the proposed legislation founded on the general principles of political economy. Lyall explained why he did not consider them to carry much weight. In conclusion he asked for an early reply from the Government of India, so that he might appoint a committee of Punjab officers to draft a Bill on the lines he had indicated, before the expiry of his term of office some six months hence.[195]

Lyall's reference to the principles of political economy serves as a reminder that political anxieties and administrative proposals were accompanied by decided intellectual changes. Given the fact that administrative remedies ran foul of political economy, it could hardly be otherwise. In this sense, the weakening of old ideas and the development of new ones may be seen as the direct outcome of the political apprehensions and administrative remedies associated with the question of land transfer. It is possible, however, to look at it in a rather different way as well, and ask whether there were any wider trends which undermined the hold of political economy on the official mind, and thus facilitated the recognition of undesirable tendencies in land transfer, and the search for administrative measures. Several related questions may be considered in this respect. Were the wider trends largely due to social or to intellectual influences? Was Maine's appraisal of political economy a crucial factor? Or, an increasingly pertinent question from the 1880s, was the gradual change in attitude to political economy in England an important influence?

Of course the attitudes of Punjab officers to political economy varied as widely as can be imagined, at the most specific as well as the most general level. The effects which a flouting of economic laws would have on agricultural credit was one of the major specific issues, and this itself took several forms. In 1885 Ibbetson tried to answer that version of the argument which insisted that, credit being indispensable to the agriculturist, any action that reduced the value of his security would only enhance the rate of interest he had to pay, and hence increase his difficulties. This, Ibbetson suggested, might be true in individual instances, where the money-lender was the master; though even this tendency was weak in a country as conservative as India, where tradition was so strong, and where in many respects guild feeling almost overrode competition. The money-lender was powerless against circumstances which permanently affected all borrowers alike; for while the agriculturist had to borrow, it was no less true that the money-lender had to lend. Having shown in effect that the assumptions on which political economy rested were by no means fully justified in the circumstances of rural India, Ibbetson added an historical argument which appeared to him to clinch the matter. High interest rates prevailed under British rule, despite the increase in the value of landed security. These high rates of interest, Ibbetson contended, were survivals from the time when landed security was of much smaller value. They had survived because the rise in the value of landed security had been absolutely general, giving no individual borrower an advantage over his fellow. An equally general decrease in the value of landed security would probably leave current rates of interest unaltered. In any case, he added, the amount of interest which could be taken was limited to the amount which the civil court would compel the debtor to pay.[196] Without entering into the validity of Ibbetson's reasoning, it is clear that he allowed observed facts to influence his economic judgements. Ibbetson was distinctly aware of some of the economic and social circumstances which limited the applicability of rigid economic propositions to rural India. That awareness was sharpened no doubt by his acquaintance with the concept of social evolution; though his general rejection of the relevance of political economy was based on political and not intellectual grounds.

The impact of social circumstances on economic thinking was also apparent in one of L. J. H. Grey's articles of 1887, in which he tackled the argument that protective measures would do harm by depreciating the value of land and making it impossible for agriculturists to borrow. Grey was defending his proposal to debar the transfer of land to others than agriculturists, and in doing so he drew liberally not only on his experience in the Punjab itself, but also on his knowledge of the conditions which prevailed in some of the adjoining States, still administered in more or less indigenous fashion. His scheme, he noted, would bring down the value of land very considerably, at least for some time. But was it necessary for the welfare of the landholder that land should represent the existing high prices of produce? Was he any worse off in the Indian States where it did not; where land not being transferable, it represented no price at all? The last thing which a landholder wanted to do was to sell his land; on the contrary he wanted to buy, and the cheaper he could get it the better. Of course there was a second issue, the landholder's need to raise money on his land. If he wanted to raise it for an agricultural improvement, the State was ready to lend him the money. If he wanted money for bullocks, agricultural implements, or seed, this also could be obtained to some extent from the State; and Government would probably extend this resource at the same time as it restricted alienation. If money was wanted for food or ordinary expenses, the money-lender, who *had* to employ his capital, was always there, as in the Indian States, to afford credit up to the prospective net value of two or three good crops, after deductions for Government revenue and maintenance. If the landholder was foolish enough to want money for a marriage, a law suit, or a bribe, he would certainly find some less foolish landholder to lend it, in the hope of obtaining his debtor's land. Not as much money could be obtained for extravagance in this way, as under existing conditions could be obtained from a money-lender; but this was desirable. Finally there was borrowing to pay the revenue, which should not be necessary if a man had a sufficient holding, given that in the worst seasons the revenue was suspended. If a proprietor's holding was too small to cover his necessary expenses in good years, then it was desirable that he should be driven to sell out to some more prosperous agriculturist.[197]

Grey and Ibbetson were on common ground when they insisted that the money-lender could not help but continue his business, protective measures for the landholder notwithstanding. A number of officers in favour of legislation made the same point in one form or another in the 1888–9 enquiry. It was an argument which derived partly from the knowledge that there were few alternative channels for the investment of the money-lender's capital. More particularly it was an implicit recognition of the fact that money-lending was to many village lenders as much an occupation as a business; and hence depended for its continuance less on the realisation of any particular rate of profit than on its being a means of livelihood.[198] In most cases it was, as the Punjab Government's despatch to the Government of India put it in 1891, a 'hereditary business', which would not cease to operate on the advent of legislation, having been carried on 'when there were no Courts and no laws in the country, as the

Hindu money-lenders still do among the Afghan independent border tribes'.[199] Once more it was Indian circumstances, past and present, which drove the point home.

James Lyall had also taken into account a third version of the argument that the restriction of agricultural credit would produce unfortunate results. This version, which asserted that the money-lenders would continue to lend, but would insist more than ever on landed security, was of special importance, because it impressed not only the opponents of a Deccan Act, but some of its supporters as well. To Charles Rivaz, for instance, this argument led to the conclusion that only direct restrictions on the power of alienation could touch the root of the evil.[200] To another supporter of legislation, a judicial officer, there was some hope that restrictions on interest would prevent loans from growing to such a sum as would necessitate landed security; and that when the money-lender insisted on it, the landholder would stop short and curtail his expenditure.[201] To James Lyall there was no hope that a Deccan Act would save all landowners[202]—though he did not put it quite so bluntly in official correspondence. His general expectations are clear from the Punjab Government despatch, in which it was argued that the ordinary honest and thrifty agriculturist would not find his credit in any way injuriously affected; that the less thrifty and dependable man would get such loans as were necessary and within his means, though he might have to execute a registered bond more often before he received a considerable loan; and that only an embarrassed or dishonest man would have difficulty unless he could mortgage or hypothecate land, or give good personal security.[203]

The same despatch tried to meet objections based on rigid economic principles at the most abstract and general as well as the most specific level. It was the constitution of Indian society, its lack of homogeneity, which was cited in support of the proposition that political economy had little practical bearing on the question. And it was the contrast with a more homogeneous European society which was insisted on; so that any trace of intellectual influence here must be attributed to Maine's critique of political economy in the Indian context rather than to any awareness of changing attitudes to political economy in an English context. Analogies were drawn between the position of the money-lenders in the Punjab and that of the Jews in Russia. The Jews were prohibited from acquiring land, as were the Hindu money-lenders in Russian Turkestan, the latter being also bound by rules as to the rate of interest they could recover. In regard to the general effect of legislation on the country,

Lyall did not share the views of officers like Mackworth Young, who believed that a Deccan Act would retard natural economic and social development. The despatch referred to the almost entire exemption of agricultural land from compulsory sale or transfer in execution of decree or in insolvency proceedings, which had not stopped, as far as Lyall could see, agricultural progress or produced other evil effects.[204] It was the very prosperity of the Province which was now in effect turned against the advocates of political economy; and the success of the old protective policy was cited in support of the new.

There seems little doubt that Lyall's views represented a fair sample of the attitude to political economy which prevailed in certain quarters. It was the relevance of political economy to Indian problems which was in question; and in this context there were a number of officers who did not hesitate to make their own, independent judgements of the likely consequences of legislation. Nor was the trend strictly confined to those who supported legislation for political rather than merely administrative reasons. It was Indian conditions and Indian experience which lay at the roots of this process. The character of rural economic organisation, and social divisions, exerted their influence. So did acquaintance with the specific rather than the theoretical requirements of a prosperous rural society; and knowledge of conditions prevailing in the Punjab before British rule and in adjoining areas not under direct British administration. It was this wider trend, attributable to official experience of rural society generally, which was brought to the surface by the particular phenomenon of land transfer, and acquired an articulate form in that context. Whether intellectual considerations were as powerful as social in undermining the authority of political economy is doubtful. Certainly we have no ground for thinking that there were many officers like Lewis Tupper, devoted champions of Henry Maine's view of political economy. Some, like Ibbetson and Lyall, were probably influenced by Maine's view. For a rather larger number of officers we have no evidence beyond that of social influence. In any case there was no inherent contradiction between social and intellectual influence. To the extent that Maine's view of political economy was influential, it was influential because it related to India, and made sense in a particular social and political context. In so far as Maine's view of political economy related to India, it was the product of his own observation of Indian conditions; or rather of his deductions from the writings of Indian officials. On the other hand, there is little evidence that in the 1880s

## THE TRADITION TRANSFORMED

changing attitudes to political economy in England were making more than a marginal impact; and this can be attributed to the fact that the change in England itself was such a slow, tentative one, related to specific issues which had no particular bearing on rural problems in the Punjab.

The sensitivity to the circumstances of rural society which was fundamental to intellectual change in the Punjab was also reflected in Lyall's view of the advantages to be anticipated from legislation. A Deccan Act, he believed, would reduce the huge number of suits instituted by a certain type of money-lender against agriculturists. It would discourage those money-lenders who deliberately aimed in the conduct of their business at getting possession of their clients' lands and who used the courts to that end; and those who lent recklessly at high interest to improvident and dishonest men, trusting to make their business pay by prompt recourse to the courts. These classes, he predicted, would be forced to resort to the more old-fashioned course of business still followed by many money-lenders—trying to get a good interest on their capital as a whole, but not trying to acquire their clients' lands, and disinclined to resort to the courts.[205]

Lyall's view of what he thought he was doing in recommending legislation is of great interest; for while Lyall had undoubtedly changed his mind between 1887 and 1891 in regard to the desirability of legislation, there are few elements in his later views which cannot be reconciled to some extent with his references to land transfer since the 1870s. Lyall had never been entirely immune to the notion that the alienation of land involved certain evils; it was just that he was now fully convinced of the probability of political danger eventuating in the foreseeable future. Lyall had not been a consistent opponent of all measures to check land transfer. In the early 1870s, for instance, he had pressed the need for the extension of the law of pre-emption on the Local Government. At that time he had been concerned to slow down the process of land transfer. Could it be said that his proposals in 1891 aimed at anything more than that? In the 1870s Lyall had not hesitated to say that the British should amend those aspects of the revenue system which aggravated the problem of rural indebtedness; and he had been a prominent, if cautious, supporter of more flexible systems of revenue collection. When he advocated judicial reform in 1891, was he doing anything more than amending aspects of the British judicial system which aggravated the situation by giving money-lenders very special advantages as against their debtors? At a time, too, when there was the Deccan precedent to draw on? Believing that the fundamental cause of rural indebtedness lay in the shortcomings of the people themselves, he had never considered that the weakest of agricultural tribes could be saved from themselves. And though he did not stress these matters in 1891, it was perfectly clear that he still had no hope of saving the weakest elements in rural society.

In short, Lyall's changing position between 1887 and 1891 represented a development of his earlier views. And this has some bearing on any explanation of the influence which Provincial opinion exerted on his attitude. There were aspects of Lyall's own attitude to land transfer which, under various pressures and influences, could assume a different guise, without any great intellectual or personal concessions. This does not mean that any Lieutenant-Governor imbued with Lyall's attitude to land alienation would have come to support a special Act, given certain pressures. For in Lyall's case there were personal factors which aided the process. He was not an obstinate man, disposed to retain his own first opinions at all costs, and only changing them under severe pressure. Within certain limits he could assess various aspects of a problem, giving due weight to most of these aspects; and hence he could be swayed to a certain extent by circumstances which tended to give weight to one aspect rather than another. His change of mind between 1887 and 1888, therefore, was not out of character. Not that from that point on his support of legislation was certain. A tepid response from the Province at large might well have induced him to change his mind again. He was not, however, looking for excuses to take the easy way out. In 1891, for example, it is arguable that a different man might have rejected special legislation by an appeal to the fact that both the chief revenue and judicial authorities, the Financial Commissioners and the Chief Court, were opposed to special legislation. Lyall preferred to assess the opinions of officers generally; and these confirmed his tentative move towards legislation. Lyall was of course cautious and circumspect, not the man to propagate his own views far and wide. Yet as Lieutenant-Governor his readiness to consider the question for the whole Province, and to propose legislation, undoubtedly helped to produce that distinct manifestation and articulation of Provincial opinion which confirmed his own, changing estimate of the problem. It was Lyall's intellectual integrity, as well as his basic view of land transfer, which facilitated the process by which agricultural indebtedness became the question of the day.

All this suggests comparison with the man who had done more to stimulate that process than any other local officer. In temperament Thorburn was everything that Lyall was not. Thorburn was hasty and careless in his judgements, lacking in finesse, and tactless to a degree. He was not an impressive writer or thinker. But once convinced of the importance of a question, he was not the man to dismiss it from his mind. He possessed the tenacity, and the certainty of conviction, without which gradual changes in official opinion would not have assumed such prominence at the end of the 1880s.

There are certain ironies in all this; for Thorburn and Lyall had more in common in regard to land transfer than their roles and personalities would lead one to think, It had taken both of them many years before they conceived that the transfer of land was of really serious import; though Thorburn travelled further at an earlier stage than Lyall, and under his own steam. Both officers were distinctly aware of the shortcomings of Indian society; though Thorburn managed to subordinate this aspect of his thought rather earlier than Lyall. Both officers had firm commitments to Western principles and experience; and where Thorburn managed to shed some of these commitments rather more quickly, Lyall did so with less intellectual travail. Both officers believed in individual landed property, though Thorburn was able to qualify this belief, something which Lyall did not achieve while in office. Both officers, in short, were subject to the same process of change, variations in their development being attributable to their individual capacities, temperament and position. Thorburn and Lyall may be compared with James Wilson, of whom a colleague wrote that he had never met a man 'animated with a higher sense of justice'.[206] It was Wilson's sense of justice and compassion, combined with an acute intellect, which led him to take up the question of land transfer at such an early stage of his career. More generally, the pace of change was set by men like Thorburn and Lyall, whose overriding concern was the stability of British rule, and who needed plenty of time to decide whether land transfer threatened that stability.

IV

Between 1874, the year in which one Lieutenant-Governor opposed legislation to combat land transfer, and 1891, the year in which another Lieutenant-Governor pressed legislation on the Government of India, some remarkable changes had occurred in Provincial opinion. The idea that voluntary alienations of land involved a grave political danger was no longer confined to a few officers; it had become the creed of a distinct body of official opinion. No longer was recognition of the new agrarian problem seriously hampered by the recollection of the old. Agricultural prosperity was no longer a bar to the recognition of agricultural indebtedness. Explicit criticism of the relevance of *laissez-faire* political economy was more common, while the tendency to by-pass political economy in regard to specific issues had become widespread. Issues were viewed, to a greater degree than ever before, from the standpoint of Indian society and Indian experience. Not only had a far greater range of remedies for land transfer been discussed, but more far-reaching proposals, such as those for the restriction of the power of alienation, found favour among a much larger number of officers. Instead of an appeal to Provincial statistics to prove that all was well, there was now an appeal to Provincial statistics to show that land transfer had reached serious proportions in a number of localities throughout the Province. Of course there remained an opposition in regard to every conceivable aspect of the question; but between 1874 and 1891 there had been a marked and decisive shift in the balance of opinion throughout the Province. The transformation of the political and intellectual tradition of the Punjab, apparent from 1869, was now well under way.

It is the shift in opinion between 1874 and 1891 which requires explanation, just as the first manifestations of a break with an earlier period in the years from 1869 to 1874 required explanation. In terms of men and events an explanation of developments between 1875 and 1891 has been given already; and some of the influences underlying these developments have become clear as well. It remains to draw some of these threads together, and to make a general assessment of the contribution of various underlying influences to the movement of opinion in this period. Such an assessment must be able to reconcile the diverse nature of social influence with steady development in a particular direction.

It was political considerations which provided the major spur to the movement of opinion. The question of land transfer could become of central importance because it acted on a political tradition which emphasised rural loyalties. That tradition, older than the process of land transfer itself, was perpetuated by a variety of considerations, of which simple transmission from one generation to the next was only one. Deriving its rationale from an acute awareness of British isolation and numerical inferiority, the tradition was influenced in the most striking fashion by observation of the inherent as well as the institutional aspects of village society; observation of a kind to which the British were predisposed by both Indian circumstances and the British cultural background.

Given this political tradition, the transfer of land exerted its influence on the British in a number of ways. It was not that transfers were taking place everywhere on a large scale; though in districts where transfers appeared to be extensive, the effect on some officers was considerable. The process of peasant expropriation was not seen as something which could be accomplished within a short space of time; but when a serious amount of transfer was combined with evidence as to a steady increase in the rate of transfer, as in Hoshiarpur and Umballa, the possibility of a consummation of the process in a more immediate future caused concern. Sudden, dramatic increases in alienation were rare, or at any rate not often obvious; but it was one such instance, that of Gurgaon, which led James Wilson to take a stand on the question. It was not that transfers of land were everywhere breaking down coherent village communities of long standing; though where village communities were strong, as in the south-east, the qualitative change, in this case from communal to individual ownership, was particularly striking, quite apart from the actual extent of transfer. Similarly the acquisition of land by Hindu traders was a sufficiently novel phenomenon in most parts of the Province to convince many an officer that Indian society was being subjected to alien forces for which no precedent could be found in India's past. While communal considerations played a distinct role in arousing anxiety about land transfer, notably in Thorburn's case, the question was by no means confined to those parts of the Punjab where the gulf between Muslim landholder and Hindu money-lender yawned. Nor was it a question of rural discontent having assumed alarming proportions throughout the Province; though here and there signs of unrest or of a decline in goodwill did exercise a distinct effect on official opinion. But whether transfer was seen as extensive, rapid, unprecedented, or unpopular, one feature of the situation was plain throughout the Province, namely the fact that transfer was continuous and cumulative. And these aspects of the matter encompassed all the others. Being continuous, land alienation was an issue which could never be disposed of entirely; it was constantly coming up in the course of official business, whether in the shape of statistics in revenue and assessment reports, or in regard to day to day observation of rural conditions. And being cumulative, the process of expropriation led the British to look to the future: for if unpleasant symptoms were to hand now, the passage of time could only magnify the problem, or so it seemed. Unfavourable symptoms assumed an importance which was often out of all proportion to their immediate significance, because they appeared to be a promise of things to come. And the increase in indebtedness and land transfer ensured that unfavourable symptoms would not be lacking.

To the political anxieties raised by land transfer must be added the administrative, financial, economic and moral considerations, which contributed their quota of concern.

Certain aspects of rural indebtedness, as well as certain wider features of village society, facilitated the intellectual changes which were necessary if concern was to find expression in remedial measures. The heterogeneous character of Punjab society, and more particularly the wide gulf which separated the landholder and the money-lender in terms of commercial aptitude, undermined the authority of economic principles which asumed that all men were, or should be, equally capable of looking after their own affairs. An awareness of the interdependence of landholder and money-lender in village India, past and present, helped to dispel the fears of some officers that any measure which restricted agricultural credit would bring greater disasters in its train. Observation of the non-productive uses to which credit was put had a similar effect, suggesting indeed that the restriction of credit might be beneficial.

So much for those social influences which aided the tendency to increased concern and commitment to legislation. But what of those social influences which inhibited this movement of opinion? Why did their role diminish between 1875 and 1891? An answer to this question would help to explain the change in the balance of opinion throughout the Province.

During the 1870s awareness of the increasing prosperity of the Province had minimised the significance of agricultural indebtedness in the eyes of a number of officers. That the influence of agricultural prosperity in this respect decreased in later years was not due to any slackening in the augmentation of agricultural resources. But in the course of time such augmentation was likely to exert a steadily decreasing influence on official opinion, for a number of reasons. It was not calculated to make quite the same impact on a new generation of officers, who were not personally acquainted with the conditions prevailing under Sikh and early British rule, and therefore not subject to the enthusiasm of those who saw the first signs of the advent of prosperity. Apart from personal experience of this kind, there was the simple fact that a steady increase in prosperity exerted a totally different influence than a steady increase in indebtedness:

## THE TRADITION TRANSFORMED

for whereas the latter was likely to draw more and more attention as an unfavourable omen, the former was more apt to be accepted as something which occurred in the natural course of events. Moreover, the increase in rural resources was likely to have a great effect on official opinion only as long as it appeared to be accompanied by the development of the prosperity of the original landholders. And in several parts of the Province that was liable to be less striking in some ways, the more the indebtedness of the original landholders increased. Finally, as more officers came to realise that the augmentation of agricultural resources, measured in terms of the increasing value of land and the expansion of agricultural credit, indicated not only an increase in prosperity, but also provided inducements to the steady increase of indebtedness, the tendency to shrug off indebtedness by reference to prosperity was bound to weaken.

But there was another feature of Punjab society which tended to inhibit anxiety or desire for legislation, and it was one which continued to manifest itself in the 1880s. Whereas the sharp distinctions in character between landholder and money-lender induced doubts regarding the applicability of political economy, the distinctions between skilled and unskilled agricultural tribes, between thrifty and improvident cultivators, appeared to bear out the maxim that the weak must go to the wall. In the context of land transfer this was something which was likely to remain prominent; for settlement statistics of land transfer revealed the special weakness of the less skilled and less thrifty tribes in this sphere ever more clearly. And yet, though the notion that the weak could not be saved, survived the 1880s, this aspect of the matter ceased to be a major barrier to the acceptance of some sort of legislation. The reasons are not far to seek. Distinctions between tribes in the matter of land transfer could not be denied, but they could be interpreted anew or subordinated to other considerations. Officers who developed a view of the origins of indebtedness which held the Government responsible for its failure to adapt its system to the character and circumstances of its subjects, could conceive that legislation was even more warranted in the case of the weaker tribes, because they had been even more sinned against. Some of those who did not go as far as this could yet see that the trouble was not due to indigenous shortcomings alone, or that the weaker tribes were not the only ones affected, so that legislation might provide a desirable and perhaps a sufficient if not a complete remedy.

A third aspect of the situation which inhibited the movement towards legislation was the apparent dependence of many landholders on the money-lender. The fact that the landholder borrowed for various purposes which would brook no delay, for food and seed grain, for the purchase of cattle, for payment of land-revenue, and for domestic expenditure, appeared to indicate that he could not get on without agricultural credit. This was a more immediately obvious and striking aspect of the situation than that of the ultimate interdependence of lender and borrower. It was easier to see that an individual borrower's well-being depended on the goodwill of his money-lender than that the money-lender's livelihood depended on the necessities of the landholders in general. There were always officers who were impressed by the fact of dependence rather than by the fact of an underlying interdependence, by the need for credit to sustain the landholder, to maintain cultivation, and to pay the dues of the State rather than by improvident or extravagant borrowing. This was not an inhibiting influence which would cease to operate in future years; for in addition to the long-term dangers which legislation restricting agricultural credit might appear to involve, there was the question of the immediate, practical and possibly drastic effects which such legislation might have on society and hence on the interests of the State. Yet while this would be a closely fought battle in the coming decade, it was essentially a rear-guard action, in the sense that the need to maintain agricultural credit would be used as an argument against particular legislative proposals rather than against legislation in general.

In short, the social influences which tended to inhibit the movement towards legislation had weakened not so much of their own accord, but rather in response to other pressures. The increase in rural resources, the distinctions between tribe and tribe, and the dependence of the landholder on the money-lender, were as much features of the Punjab situation in 1891 as in 1874. Only in regard to the increase in rural resources is it possible to say that this was a matter which was inherently less likely to impress officers as time went on, and even then an explanation of its diminishing influence rests in part on the increase in indebtedness. As for the other two features of village society their influence decreased because the considerations to which they gave rise could be overcome by, or reconciled to some extent with notions which suggested the need for legislation to deal with indebtedness.

While it is clear that there were elements in Punjab society itself which tended to slow down the movement of opinion, it is also apparent that the influence which these elements exerted cannot be considered apart from the British intellectual background. If a

## THE TRADITION TRANSFORMED

clear distinction was not always made between the general increase in agricultural resources and the prosperity of the original landholders, it can be attributed to that anticipation of progress and improvement which distinguished Victorian thought. If marked distinctions in the skill and thrift of different agricultural tribes suggested that there were weaklings in the agricultural community, weaklings who must go to the wall, that belief could not have been so strongly held if it had not been for that evolutionist trend in Victorian thinking which made life in general a competitive process. If the direst predictions were made as to the effects of legislation on agricultural credit, those predictions reflected a widespread commitment to the clichés of *laissez-faire* political economy. While indebtedness only loomed large when it was considered in the light of the British political tradition, features of Punjab society which tended to discount the importance of indebtedness or suggest that it could not be dealt with, made sense only in the context of the British intellectual tradition. This should not lead one to dismiss the inhibiting social influences as unimportant, any more than one would dismiss the dynamic influences as unimportant. Intellectual considerations had much to say to the feeling against legislation; but a certain kind of mind was required to stress doctrinaire considerations in the face of all social experience. Most officers who stressed doctrinaire considerations were able to do so effectively because Punjab society itself appeared to bear out these considerations. One notes, for example, that many officers were inclined to believe that the weak must go to the wall, while a far smaller number indicated that the weak would be replaced by the strong; for the former conclusion appeared to be warranted in the circumstances of Punjab society, the latter conclusion much less so.

When all is said and done, however, it is apparent that while social influences constituted not only the spur to action but the very basis of the political tradition, social influences were only an aid, though an important one, to the orthodox intellectual tradition. Intellectual influences could and did operate even without any particular warrant from the society to which they were applied. Officers like Mackworth Young and Charles Roe laid the greatest emphasis on the most doctrinaire considerations; and in a sense no one could escape altogether from his intellectual background. But it was not only a matter of whether one individual had a more doctrinaire cast of mind, or a greater commitment to particular theories, than another. It was also a question of the degree to which particular convictions were imbedded in the British consciousness.

*Laissez-faire* political economy and social Darwinism might give way to some extent under the pressure of events; but no one conceived of a society without property. Even the suggestion that the right of property in land might be limited in some respects, by imposing restrictions on its transferability, was received by many, including the most powerful, as a desperate or impossible expedient. It might appear that if one objected to the transfer of landed property from the hands of one man to those of another, the most direct and obvious solution of the problem would be simply to forbid that transfer. But the restriction of the power of alienation appeared to involve not only the dangers to which all protective legislation was subject, and then in their most extreme form; such restriction also conjured up visions of interference with property, the commitment to which constituted the very core and essence of the British intellectual heritage. Yet being an obvious solution, the restriction of the power of alienation was bound to crop up; particularly in view of the fact that the British themselves had done so much to mould the various rights attaching to land. This argument could be met, to a certain extent, by pointing to parts of the Province in which the British had not created individual landed rights and transferability. But if there were features of Punjab society which aided the disinclination to limit the transferability of land, there were overt intellectual trends which performed the same function. Maine's evolutionist view of landed property influenced Thorburn, and probably Roe and Lyall; for Maine's reputation and Indian experience appeared to justify as natural and inevitable in the Indian context the transition from communal to individual property in land. Maine bolstered an inherent and pervasive tendency to look on individual rights in land as one of the hallmarks of progress and civilisation. And in doing so, Maine helped to slow down the tendency to look on the British impact on Indian tenures as an unfortunate aspect of British rule which required the attention of the legislature.

Though the orthodox British intellectual tradition was the most powerful inhibiting influence on the development of opinion, not all typically Victorian ideas and attitudes exercised their influence on the same side of the question. Social Darwinism might come to the aid of those who wanted to do nothing about rural indebtedness; but Victorian appreciation of manliness and vigour was one factor influencing the assumption that only the agricultural tribes were politically significant, and therefore worth saving at all. Ideas regarding the natural evolution of landed property might reinforce the conviction that the right to property should not be meddled with,

## THE TRADITION TRANSFORMED

but the whole concept of social evolution as applied to India helped some men to understand that different institutions might be appropriate to different societies. Maine's interest in the scholarly study of Indian tenures, and more particularly his evolutionist approach to political economy, are specific examples of an influence which aided and abetted trends which derived from the observation of Indian conditions at first hand. Again, *laissez-faire* political economy might be the greatest barrier to legislation, but later years would see *laissez-faire* attitudes to judicial reform playing a distinct role in promoting legislation to restrict the power of alienation.

Maine's influence on the Punjab debate may be considered here at somewhat greater length. That officers were able to put his thought to good use on opposing sides of the question is hardly surprising when the character of Maine's ideas is recalled. There was an inherent tension in Maine's thought between the sensitive appraisal of alien societies, and the notion that contemporary European society was the highest form of society, progressive and civilised. Maine himself could defend the Deccan Act, though not without reservation, as an appropriate measure in certain given circumstances, while he did not hesitate to castigate Irish land legislation as unprogressive.[207] Both measures ran counter to political economy; but Maine could bend his thought in particular directions according to the needs and motives of the moment. If Maine could do this, selective borrowing on the part of others is easily explained.

Since Maine's ideas could be found in opposing camps, his view of social evolution must be held responsible both for stimulating and inhibiting the new trends. As regards the latter influence Maine's ideas amounted to nothing more than an evolutionist's justification for what the British had done to Indian tenures. Maine's intellectual contribution to the development of Punjab opinion, however, cannot be seen apart from an explanation emphasising social influence; for in so far as Maine's Indian writings derived from his and others' Indian experience, his theories were themselves a further channel through which Indian society exerted its influence on British officers in direct contact with that society.

It would be all too easy to simplify and magnify Maine's influence. Something of the kind has been done by a recent historian of western India who has asserted that 'a new vision of society' and 'a new conception of the laws and institutions necessary for the realisation of this vision' were required if interference between landholder and money-lender was to prove acceptable.[208] It is contended that it was the 'conservative principles advocated by Maine' which not only inspired 'the reconsiderations and the reappraisals' which were initiated by Raymond West, a Judge of the Bombay High Court, but which also influenced the Deccan Relief Act itself.[209] West's conservative principles are held to have created a 'climate of opinion' which was most favourable to policies seeking to protect the landholders from the money-lenders.[210] It is certainly true that in his pamphlet of 1872 on *The Land and the Law in India* West applied the concept of social evolution to the problem of rural indebtedness. Yet no claim is made, or could be sustained, that West's major proposals regarding indebtedness were embodied in the Deccan Act; so that we are asked to believe in effect that these proposals were ignored, while the principles which underlay them were of the widest significance. If such a conclusion is to be acceptable, it must be supported by direct evidence that those who shaped the Deccan legislation were in fact influenced by the concept of social evolution. Instead we are given almost nothing beyond the specific proposals of a few individuals, it being assumed throughout that they and British administrators generally were influenced by Maine's and West's approach to the subject.[211] All this is, of course, in the orthodox tradition of British-Indian historiography, in which major changes are attributed to the influence of a few sophisticated thinkers; in which the opinions of the vast majority of British officers in touch with Indian society are ignored or treated as if these opinions responded automatically and immediately to every shift and change in formal thought; and in which changes in Indian society, though not ignored, are not examined with any great regard for local variations either.

The question is of some importance at this juncture because the fact that the Deccan Relief Act was passed had a significant effect on the course of the Punjab debate. It created a double precedent, showing that legislation to combat agricultural indebtedness in India was not altogether out of the question, and suggesting the form which such legislation might take. Until 1891 at least, the effect of the Deccan Act on Punjab opinion was probably greater than that of any other single influence external to the Punjab. In regard to the origins of the Deccan Act itself, however, it would be wiser not to accept uncritically the large claims made on behalf of evolutionary theory, and to wait until detailed study of the situation in the Deccan enables us to strike some kind of balance between social and intellectual influences, and between general trends and particular developments.

The Deccan Act could exercise a distinct influence on Punjab opinion because it appeared to offer a specific answer to a specific problem. Events and conditions in England and Ireland exercised

## THE TRADITION TRANSFORMED

comparatively little influence precisely because they could provide no such specific answers. Very occasionally an officer might make some reference to entail in England as a partial justification for the restriction of the power of alienation;[212] though of course the trend of legislation in England in respect of entail and settlement was running in a contrary direction. Other reforms in England and Ireland were potentially relevant, because they contravened the laws of political economy. But the qualifications which they imposed on *laissez-faire* principles were too hesitant to exercise great intellectual influence on Punjab opinion. This is clear, for instance, when we recall Wace's reference to the fact that the restriction of the power of contract and alienation might be necessary under certain adverse conditions of national life, but that it was a misfortune to be avoided at all costs. This is not to say that we cannot trace some positive influences in this respect; witness occasional references to conditions or legislation in Ireland or to a belief in State action generally. It was not surprising that a few officers, some of them with wide intellectual interests, who were casting about for a solution to internal problems, would note briefly now and then somewhat remote parallels. Neither now nor later did it go beyond this, nor did these references carry any weight in the discussion. In England and Ireland, as in the Punjab, social influences were undermining political economy, in a fairly tentative way; but the evidence for the view that the former process had more than a limited effect on the latter is not impressive.

From this survey of social and intellectual influences on Punjab opinion between 1875 and 1891 it is apparent that the cross-currents are many and varied. On the one hand, we have a political tradition rooted in village society, as a result of British-Indian circumstances and British cultural attachments combined; a tradition which provided the essential basis for the development of political anxieties deriving from an awareness of steady change in rural society, anxieties which in turn strengthened and transformed the tradition; the whole phenomenon stimulating, as well as being assisted by, intellectual changes resulting from observation of the nature and working of village society, observation which was sharpened in some instances by intellectual concepts; much of all this encouraged by the Deccan example, and rather less so by other external events. On the other hand, we have an intellectual tradition looking to the British heritage as the ultimate test of its validity, but adapted to and strengthened by particular social phenomena which appeared to justify it; a tradition which had deep roots in British history as well as in the intellectual trends of the day; a tradition of great, if in some respects, declining authority in its country of origin.

What was it that gave one set of influences the advantage over the other? The first answer lies in the fact that those aspects of social change which generated political anxiety were dynamic, in the sense that their influence increased with the steady manifestation of increased indebtedness; while features of Punjab society which reinforced the orthodox intellectual tradition were static, at least in the sense that taken together they were not likely to make any distinctly greater impression on official opinion in 1891 than in 1874. From this point of view the steady subordination of the latter set of influences to the former is understandable. The second answer hinges on the fact that all officers alike were subject to the old political tradition emphasising rural loyalty. This meant that few indeed could ever be entirely confident that land transfer was not striking at the basis of British rule; while a political argument for legislation could be met only by an argument essentially intellectual in character. In this sense those who pressed legislation on Government had the distinct advantage of all those who take, and continue to take, the initiative, and part of whose appeal is to considerations which all parties concerned accept. A purely intellectual reply to a political question was likely to carry less and less conviction as concern increased. A third answer may be found in the development of an alternative intellectual tradition, so that the orthodox intellectual arguments could be met on intellectual as well as on political grounds. It follows that social influence must be given due emphasis in any explanation of the changing balance of opinion: not merely because it was the major element in all this, but more particularly because it was the only dynamic one. The influence which a society exerts on opinion may, indeed must be, diverse for a variety of reasons; but dynamic social influences, of fundamental appeal and wide ramification, may well prevail over powerful but more or less static social and intellectual influences.

Of course the influences which swung the balance of opinion in the direction of legislation required time to take effect. And it is this question of time which brings the historian back from the general to the particular. Underlying influences can explain only so much; they may make certain tendencies meaningful, but they cannot explain why particular developments took place at particular times. Ultimately, too, particular considerations become of general importance. If instead of James Lyall, for instance, there had been a man with a rather different outlook at the head of affairs in the Province

## THE TRADITION TRANSFORMED

between 1887 and 1892, events might have taken a course rather less favourable to the advocates of legislation. And though time was on their side, in the sense that it was likely to swell their ranks, it was also against them in another sense. For in due course the generation which had taken up the question of land transfer would pass from the scene; and if they had not made a definite mark by that time, the development of opinion among a new generation of officers would have taken time again no doubt, with unforeseeable consequences.

As it was, opinion had been given its head, and by 1891 it appeared to have reached the point of take-off among those who had served in the Punjab since the 1860s and 1870s. Yet this by itself does not suffice to explain what followed; namely the fact that the question of restricting the power of alienation came to the fore, and legislation in this regard became the mainstay of the new political tradition. In 1891 legislation to restrict the power of transfer throughout the Province seemed unlikely: it was the most far-reaching solution, involving both the greatest doctrinaire and the greatest practical difficulties. It could be justified only on political and not on mere administrative grounds. There was no such precedent as that in the Deccan to lend a hand. There was much opposition to legislation to restrict the power of transfer throughout the Province, and even the advocates of such legislation saw no way of bringing this issue to a head. Besides, any legislative proposals would require the approval of several Governments. To appreciate the course of events, therefore, it is necessary to take account not only of underlying influences and general trends, without as well as within the Punjab, but also of unforeseen contingencies and complicated manoeuvres.

## CHAPTER IV

# Extending the Conflict

I

James Lyall's proposals of August 1891 reached the Government of India at a time when that Government was almost paralysed by the divisions of opinion within its ranks.

Lyall's tentative proposals of November 1888 had served practically no purpose. Their consideration had been deferred until the submission of his final report. Meanwhile the Government of India had to consider reports on agricultural indebtedness from the Central Provinces and Bombay. The Chief Commissioner of the Central Provinces, A. Mackenzie, wanted a Deccan Act.[1] The Bombay Government could not agree as to whether the Deccan Act had worked well or not.[2] The Punjab and Central Provinces reports were the responsibility of the Revenue and Agriculture Department, the Bombay report that of the Home Department.

One of the most influential of the Government of India officials who had to deal with these questions was E. C. Buck, the Secretary of the Revenue and Agriculture Department. Buck had been Secretary for years, having reorganised the Department, and having a special interest in agricultural improvement and revenue matters generally. The weight attached to his opinions was entirely out of keeping with his formal official position. Buck's opinions had been formed in earlier days when he had been a revenue officer in the North-Western Provinces. To Buck the great mistakes of British policy had been, firstly, the grant of transferable rights in land, which promoted its encumberment and transfer to money-lenders; secondly, the replacement of an elastic system of revenue collection by a rigid one which forced peasants into debt in bad seasons; and, thirdly, arising out of this, the gradual lowering of the revenue demand under British rule, which further promoted the transfer of land. Buck was especially worried by the consequent financial losses of Government. A Deccan Act, he thought, only improved the position of an existing generation of proprietors; future generations would have to pay more for their loans and further difficulties and financial losses would result. In his view the only real solution of the problem was to restrict the right of transfer. Fluctuating assessments were likewise highly desirable.[3]

Buck's superior, P. P. Hutchins, the Member for the Home as well as the Revenue Department, was an old judicial officer with a predilection for general laws extending to the whole of India; for regular courts guided by the ordinary rules of procedure; and for the sanctity of contracts. The Deccan Act offended these cardinal principles. Hutchins, who had gained his experience in the Madras Presidency, had little appreciation of the problems posed by the transfer of land. Anything out of the ordinary, like the restriction of the power of alienation, struck him as simply impossible.[4]

Buck and Hutchins thus agreed about nothing, except that a Deccan Act was not desirable; and that would ensure inaction.

The Viceroy, Lord Lansdowne, was not in a position to initiate any definite policies. While on a tour of the Punjab Lansdowne had heard uneasy references in several quarters to the transfers of land in that Province. He had gone on the consult some of the Punjab registration and administration reports, as also Thorburn's *Musalmans and Money-lenders in the Punjab*; and by January 1890 he was convinced that a serious agrarian problem existed. Lansdowne was favourably disposed to some sort of effective action being taken; but he had no experience of Indian conditions to guide him as to what that action might be.[5]

In December 1890 Hutchins recorded his opinion on the Bombay and Central Provinces reports. He opposed the appointment of a Commission to examine the working of the Deccan Act, a suggestion which had been made at an earlier stage. Hutchins thought that the problem of agricultural indebtedness could be adequately met by certain amendments of the general law, the most important of which were designed to give the courts greater powers to grant relief against unconscionable bargains.[6] Lansdowne wanted Buck's advice on the matter. He was perplexed by the great divergencies of opinion in the Bombay papers and favoured the appointment of a Commission.[7] As several Council members were opposed to a Commission, it was agreed at the Council meeting of February 6, 1891 to drop the idea.[8]

Three days later Buck wrote the note for which Lansdowne had asked. Buck suggested that the time was coming when the Government of India would have to face the general question of agricultural indebtedness; and in particular the desirability of imposing restrictions on alienation and of introducing fluctuating assessments. He believed that a practicable method of restricting transfers might be that proposed by C. Crosthwaite, another old North-Western Provinces officer, during discussions in 1882–4, viz. that Government take power to buy up encumbered estates and re-settle them on enhanced terms with absolute restrictions as to transfer. It was in the investigation of the possibility of such action, and not in regard to the working of the Deccan Act, that a Commission might prove of real advantage.[9]

Buck's note convinced Lansdowne that the question of a Commission should be reconsidered.[10] Hutchins was annoyed and clung to his own proposals; though adding that he preferred a law which would enable proprietors who had been sold up to become occupancy tenants of a reasonable portion of their former estates without power of transfer, to any ambitious scheme for buying up encumbered estates.[11] Lansdowne thought that the examination of the palliatives proposed by Hutchins, the amendments of the general law, should not affect the main question as laid down in Buck's note.[12] The opposition on the Council was still too strong for Lansdowne. At the Council meeting of February 20th the idea of a Commission was once more dismissed, for the time being at least; and the only definite decision made was to refer Hutchins' proposals to the Legislative Department.[13] Buck's first attempt to bring matters to a head had failed.

When Lyall's despatch of August 1891 arrived, Buck pressed once more for a general Commission; and later, when that was not accepted, for the association of an Imperial Officer (himself or Crosthwaite) with a Commission which would examine the working of the Deccan Act.[14] Hutchins was still opposed to a Deccan Act and he had found a kindred spirit in A. E. Miller, the new Legal Member.[15] Lansdowne alone was influenced by Lyall's communication. He now felt even more strongly that a Commission to enquire into the working of the Deccan Act was necessary.[16] Hutchins and Miller gave way reluctantly in deference to Lansdowne.[17] Buck's proposals, however, were not accepted. The Commission, which was appointed in November 1891, was to report on the local working of the Deccan Act and on the possibility of extending the Act to other parts of India. It was to consider the proposed amendments of the general law. If the Commission believed that the Deccan Act afforded no lasting solution it was to indicate what other measures, if any, it thought advisable.[18] The possibility of allowing the Commission to collect evidence in the Punjab, after it had finished in the Deccan, was considered but ultimately rejected.[19]

The Commission dispelled such hopes as Buck might still have had. It reported in favour of the Deccan Act and its extension to other parts of India. It approved of the proposed amendments of the general law. The restriction of the right of transfer was discussed, but not recommended for the Deccan; and for the rest of India no suggestion was made. The Commission's discussion of the restriction of the power of transfer, it was decided, would be dealt with by the Revenue Department.[20] In September 1892 that Department also asked the Governments of the Central Provinces and the Punjab to comment on the Commission's report. Anthony MacDonnell, Chief Commissioner of the Central Provinces, immediately replied that the true remedy lay in the restriction of the right of transfer; but D. Fitzpatrick, the new Lieutenant-Governor of the Punjab, was in no hurry to answer.[21] It was decided in the Revenue Department to await Fitzpatrick's reply before considering the restriction of the power of transfer.[22] Buck had failed once more to get things moving.

Meanwhile the discussion of the Commission's Report in the Home Department focused attention on the question of restricting the transfer of land. Charles Crosthwaite, in a note of November 1892, argued that more than a Deccan Act was needed. The political danger, he thought, was not so great as to now justify a withdrawal of the right of transfer; but ex-proprietors might be maintained as occupancy tenants in part of their land at a favourable rent and without the power of transfer. He also revived his old proposal for the buying up of encumbered estates.[23] In 1893 these proposals were endorsed to a greater or lesser extent by several other Members of Council, including Hutchins.[24]

In August 1893 Buck made a third attempt to force the pace. Instead of a general Commission he proposed that Provincial Committees be formed in each Province to consider the restriction of the power of transfer; and that an Imperial officer, who would also draw up a statement of the case from the records of the Secretariat, be associated with the Provincial Committees. In any case, he thought, it was necessary to put an officer on special duty in the Revenue Secretariat to prepare the case, and his duties could be extended to include attendance at Provincial Conferences.[25] This time it looked as if Buck might succeed. His first proposal was accepted by Hutchins, whose opposition to the restriction of the power of transfer had abated, and somewhat doubtfully by Miller.[26] Lansdowne, now determined to have the transfer question threshed out, supported it strongly.[27] The Punjab Government was accordingly told in answer to a demi-official enquiry that it need not reply to the letter of September 1892, as the question was before the Imperial Council. That Council finally approved Buck's appointment in October 1893; only to have it disallowed by the Secretary of State in December 1893.[28]

Now, on the eve of his departure, Lansdowne was fully convinced that the Government of India was faced with a serious political problem which could be solved only by restrictions on the power of land-transfer, political economy notwithstanding.[29] His opinion to that effect was sent to the Revenue Department for consideration, in January 1894. The Department had a clearer mandate than ever; but it was in no better position to tackle the problem than before.

A few months later, after Lansdowne's replacement by Elgin, the question was revived by the new Member in the Home and Revenue Departments, Anthony MacDonnell who, as Chief Commissioner of the Central Provinces, had advocated the restriction of the power of transfer. MacDonnell secured the assent of Council to a proposal to institute enquiries, the collection of information from the Secretariat records being contemplated in the first instance. The Secretary of State was informed that the matter of restricting the power of transfer had been taken up.[30]

In the Home Department it had been determined to proceed with the amendments of the general law; a circular to the Local Governments being issued in June 1894. In the following month MacDonnell decided that the question of extending a Deccan Act to other parts of India would be postponed till the enquiries relating to the amendment of the general law and the restriction of transfer had been completed.[31]

James Lyall's proposals for legislation on the lines of the Deccan Act had receded into the background. There had been insufficient support for such a measure within the Government of India, while Lyall's successor as Lieutenant-Governor had allowed the question to lapse. Hutchins' amendments of the general law were still under discussion; but Lansdowne, with his eye on the proposals of various Local Governments, and increasingly influenced by Buck, had not allowed them to stand as the final solution to the problem. Buck had played the major role in bringing the question of the restriction of the power of transfer to the fore. His efforts in this respect, despite repeated failures, are sufficient confirmation of his own statement that it had been his ambition to be personally and closely associated with a question which he considered more important than anything else that had to be done in India.[32] With the advent of MacDonnell, Buck's efforts seemed about to bear fruit. Agricultural indebtedness, in MacDonnell's estimation, was the great question of the day in the Revenue Department.[33] And the general trend of opinion, within and without the Government of India, was not lost on the new Viceroy. Everyone agreed, Elgin noted, that growing indebtedness was of the greatest importance, and probably involved more political danger than things more immediately apparent.[34] In appointing a Secretary to act for Buck, who was going on furlough, special attention was paid to finding a man who could deal with this question. The choice fell on Denzil Ibbetson, who appeared to have all the requisite qualities and experience. His intellectual capacity and initiative were admitted on all hands. He had a large revenue and settlement experience, and a particular acquaintance with the indebtedness question, having served as a member of the latest Deccan Commission. Being a Punjab officer, it was thought that he would be able to give invaluable help in regard to indebtedness in that Province, where the question appeared to present some serious political aspects.[35] It was thus the growing concern within the Government of India, itself the reflection of developments within several Provinces, which brought a Punjab man with strong views on land transfer into a position where he might well exercise unusual influence.

II

It was with reference to the introduction of reforms in the revenue system that the problem of land transfer was kept alive in the Punjab in the early 1890s.

Thorburn was now Commissioner of the Rawalpindi division; and as several of the districts of the division were under settlement, he had to review the various assessment reports submitted. Thorburn used the opportunity to re-open the question of fluctuating assessments, which Lyall had more or less excluded from the scope of the 1888–9 enquiry. Several of the assessment reports showed that extensive alienations of land to money-lenders had taken place. This process of peasant expropriation, Thorburn argued, would be accelerated now that such large enhancements of revenue were being taken. In future the landowners would have to borrow still more to pay their revenue in bad seasons than they had done in the past. The enhancements could be safely taken only if fluctuating assessments were introduced.[36] James Wilson, Settlement Officer of one of the districts of the division, hardly shared Thorburn's fears in regard to the enhancement of revenue. He was nevertheless an old adherent of fluctuating assessments; and he made various suggestions in this respect for the Shahpur district.[37]

The general extension of fluctuating assessments was opposed by senior officers whose views on the question of agricultural indebtedness were otherwise incompatible. It was opposed at one time or another by Charles Rivaz and Mackworth Young, the Financial Commissioners; and by the Lieutenant-Governors, James Lyall and Dennis Fitzpatrick. To all these men fixed assessments were the norm; fluctuating assessments, which involved special difficulties of management, the deviation. Lyall was perhaps more in favour of cautious extension than most of the others. Neither he nor Charles Rivaz shared Thorburn's belief that borrowing to pay land-revenue was a serious cause of indebtedness or that fluctuating assessments would provide any real answer.[38]

One of the most confirmed opponents of fluctuating assessments was L. J. H. Grey, who had his own special view of the causes of agricultural indebtedness, and of the reform required in revenue administration. As Commissioner of the Delhi division in the late 1880s and early 1890s, Grey urged his views on Government on several occasions. Light assessments, he argued, did not lead to the accumulation of capital and the improvement of the soil. The low assessments and long periods of settlement introduced by the British, and the rise in the value of produce, had left the peasant with a margin which only encouraged him to live largely and to spend his surplus on extravagance and litigation. At the same time the lowness of the assessment and its fixity for a long term of years increased the value of the peasant's land, and with it his credit, and made the land more attractive to money-lenders seeking an investment for their capital. In the process the British lost a considerable amount of revenue, for when a settlement was revised after thirty years or more the style of life of the peasants had developed to such an extent that it was no longer possible to take the enhancement of revenue which was indicated by the increase in material resources. The revenue thus lost had to be made up by the tax-paying community in general. In so far as this revenue was used to extend communications and irrigation works, it only served to further increase the value of the peasant's land and thus offer him still greater facilities for running into debt and losing his land.[39]

Compare this situation, Grey continued, with that prevailing in the Punjab Native States. These States realised a much greater revenue from their peasants than the British in similar and adjoining territory. Their revenue system was much less considerate than that of the British, no end being spared in realising the revenue, while suspensions and remissions in bad seasons were unknown. Yet cultivation had been extended there as well as in British districts. Standards of material comfort differed little from those in British districts. Above all, the peasants of the Native States were more contented than those under British administration, for adequate assessment coupled with restrictions on alienation had maintained the land in their hands.

In view of these considerations Grey urged a return to heavy assessments and short periods of settlement, or progressive increases in revenue during the term of settlement, as a means of increasing revenue, curtailing the peasant's extravagance and credit, and making him work, decreasing the attractiveness of land as an investment to the money-lender, and in these ways inhibiting transfers of land.

It is doubtful whether these proposals commanded support among any section of officers. Financial Commissioners like Gordon Young and Mackworth Young opposed them as a matter of course. Officers as different in outlook as Gordon Young and Alfred Kensington shared the fear that very large enhancements of revenue might break down the village communities completely. Many were well aware that there was a connection between indebtedness and light assessment. Men like Wilson and Lyall were for that reason not prepared to forego a fair enhancement of revenue on account of existing indebtedness. As to a policy of heavy settlements, Lyall thought that it would undermine the political support of the agricultural classes on which British rule depended. Lyall's successor, Fitzpatrick, was no more inclined to favour such a policy.[40]

While Grey's proposals for heavy assessments were not taken up, a proposal to assess alienated lands at specially high rates in order to check transfers gained favour with some officers after 1889. As first mooted by Louis Dane, Settlement Officer of Gurdaspur, in that year, it rested on a view of agricultural indebtedness which was similar to Grey's. It was the lightness of the revenue demand, Dane asserted, which made the land such an attractive investment to money-lenders. Increase the assessment on lands alienated to money-lenders up to the full half net assets standard, and the money-lender's profits would be reduced, his desire for the land would decrease, and his capital might be diverted to more productive ends. If the agriculturist's credit was affected by such a differential assessment this would not be undesirable, as it would prevent him from borrowing for extravagant purposes. Moreover, the Government would secure an initial increase in revenue and, if alienations continued, a further increase plus valuable proof of the liberality of its assessments.[41]

In his reply to the 1888–9 enquiry Charles Rivaz, Commissioner of the Lahore division, supported the proposal as one which might well be put into practice if it was considered impracticable to impose restrictions on the power of alienation.[42] He referred favourably to the matter again somewhat later in his review of the Batala assessment report.[43] The Financial Commissioners, G. R. Elsmie and W. M. Young, had no hesitation in rejecting what they considered to be an extraordinary measure.[44] Lyall dismissed the scheme as impracticable but thought it might be worth considering whether a heavy entry fee should not be imposed on alienations and whether the revenue of a village should not be redistributed when an outsider acquired the most lightly assessed lands.[45] Ultimately Lyall, in a hesitant mood, dropped the former suggestion;[46] while the latter was forgotten. In any case the idea of imposing a heavy entry fee on alienations did not satisfy Rivaz and Dane; for, as they later pointed out, the alienee would probably be able to shift the burden of such a fee on to the alienor, as it was not a recurring charge.[47]

Despite the rejection of Dane's and Rivaz's suggestions in 1890, the question of a differential assessment was taken up by Thorburn and Wilson. From 1890 to 1893 Thorburn made the fullest use of his position as Commissioner by repeatedly referring to the question in his reviews of assessment reports. These opinions were, as Thorburn later put it, 'forlorn hopes... against a position which the assaulters knew would not be carried at that time'.[48] Dane also continued to refer to the matter in his reports. Rivaz, the second Financial Commissioner, was rather more circumspect; but after Fitzpatrick succeeded Lyall as Lieutenant-Governor, Rivaz also began to press the matter. Finally in February 1894 Fitzpatrick, in response to one of Rivaz's representations, reluctantly promised to take up the question.[49]

The advocates of a differential assessment disagreed on certain points. Dane, Thorburn and Wilson wanted to impose the heavier assessment on lands alienated in the past as well as the future, while Rivaz, at least at first, did not.[50]

The second point of disagreement reflected fundamental differences in outlook. Thorburn and Dane agreed in limiting the measure to lands alienated to money-lenders, while Wilson wanted to apply it to all alienated lands. Rivaz at first agreed with Dane, but later changed his mind.

Thorburn approached this question from a political point of view.

He believed that transfers to hereditary agriculturists and even those to self-cultivating proprietors of low status were inevitable and did not signify future agrarian trouble. It did not matter who the actual cultivating proprietary was, as long as money-lending middlemen did not intercept the profits of cultivation. Once this object was attained, Thorburn was quite ready to apply social Darwinist notions. Even if one class of agriculturists should gradually expropriate another that would only mean that the vigour of the latter, which gave them political importance, had passed to the former.[51]

Wilson was preoccupied with securing for the State the full amount of revenue to which it was entitled wherever that amount could be safely taken. It could be safely taken, he thought, wherever outsiders, whether agriculturists or money-lenders, had acquired land. It was only just that those who had voluntarily acquired land as a mere pecuniary speculation should pay the full half net assets assessment. Their ability to buy or lend showed they had some command of capital and could well afford to pay. In this way it would also be made clear that the measure was not directed against money-lenders as a class.[52]

Rivaz looked at the issue from an economic standpoint. He had at first taken the view that it would not be desirable to inhibit transfers to agriculturists as it was obviously expedient for land to pass from the hands of a man who could not make use of it to one who could.[53] On reconsideration he advised the imposition of the heavier revenue on land alienated to agriculturists as well as to money-lenders, on the ground that while such a measure would not be severe enough to check the acquisition of land by those who wanted to cultivate it themselves, it would inhibit the acquisition of land as a commercial speculation.[54] Rivaz's change of mind shows his ability to adapt economic propositions, supposedly universal in their application, to the requirements of a particular rural society.

Dennis Fitzpatrick was not inclined to look favourably on these proposals for differential assessment. As Secretary to the Government of India he had been associated with the framing of the Deccan Act. He had since occupied high offices in several Indian Provinces and had formed views on the subject of agricultural indebtedness of the most decided kind. He readily admitted that the steady expropriation of the agricultural classes could lead to serious political danger.[55] His economic views were more unorthodox and yet more inflexible than those of his predecessor; for he reinforced his appreciation of the fact that only the direct restriction of the power of transfer could put a stop to alienations with the most rigid application of *laissez-faire* political economy to most other remedies. At the same time he was, as a practical administrator, cautious in the extreme. The proposals for differential assessment offended both his economic views and his practical caution; and it was in a critical spirit that he took up the matter in August 1894.[56]

Fitzpatrick undermined the fiscal argument for a differential assessment by his insistence that it could not be applied to past transfers or to transfers to agriculturists. It would be harsh to give retrospective effect to the measure. In regard to transfers to agriculturists Fitzpatrick was inclined to contradict Wilson's view of the matter. Transfers to agriculturists, he thought, were not so much acquisitions by men of some capital, as small transfers to agriculturists of small means who wanted a little extra land to work and who would find it difficult to bear the extra assessment. Such transfers, Fitzpatrick continued, were not open to such strong objections as those to money-lenders; and in support of this assertion he quoted Rivaz's earlier view. If land had to be transferred it was better to favour transfer to an agriculturist by not raising the revenue demand in his case. As to the objection that the application of the scheme to non-agriculturists alone would be class legislation, Fitzpatrick felt no difficulty whatever.

In regard to the political effects of the measure Fitzpatrick indicated that it would not check transfers to money-lenders, for even a full half net assets assessment left a considerable margin for investment; and the only result of the measure in this respect would be that the money-lender would advance less money for the same amount of land and thus secure the same rate of profit on his investment. Nor would the unthrifty peasant be inhibited to any significant degree from transferring his land by the knowledge that he would get something less for it. Before long both money-lender and landowner would probably devise means to avoid imposition of the extra assessment. As a method of checking alienations, Fitzpatrick concluded, the scheme was useless.

Besides, Fitzpatrick pointed out, a differential assessment was not likely to be harmless; it might set up a good deal of disturbance in the revenue system; and there were practical difficulties in applying it to a village revenue system.

When Fitzpatrick's letter was circulated to selected officers it was found that few of those consulted for the first time favoured applying the scheme to past transfers or to transfers to agriculturists. With two exceptions there was general agreement among all shades of otherwise divergent opinion that transfers to agriculturists need not be deplored or checked. Most of the officers who favoured the scheme limited in this way did not consider the objections against class legislation to be of serious import. A few touched on the difficulty of defining the agriculturist. There was very little discussion of how the money-lending classes would receive such a measure. An opponent of differential assessments mentioned it incidentally; one lukewarm supporter only doubted whether the political discontent among the money-lending classes would be worth the fiscal gain.[57]

There was strong opposition to the whole scheme from a number of officers who were not inclined to attach too much importance to the question of land transfer generally. Among them was J. B. Hutchinson, a military civilian with twenty-six years' civil experience, who had spent some time in the Multan district, and had been deeply impressed by the improvement of the land which resulted from its transfer to a Hindu trader in that particular part of the country. Hutchinson's attitude to differential assessments was shared by senior officers like W. M. Young and C. F. Massy, and by a rather younger officer, F. A. Robertson; all of them men who took, if anything, an even dimmer view of the need for legislation than Hutchinson. Generally speaking, Hutchinson, Massy and Robertson were not prepared to believe that the improvident and extravagant could be saved by legislation. They were not willing to go further than legislation similar to the Deccan Act, which would ensure that the peasant received fair treatment in court.[58] W. M. Young, now first Financial Commissioner, would not even go this far. He opposed a differential assessment as he had opposed almost all measures to check the transfer of land. At the centre of Young's thoughts lay a conviction which overruled all other considerations—the conviction that the British system of administration was based on incontrovertible principles. British administration, Young believed, conferred great benefits on Indian society. The constant rise in the value of land was of incalculable importance to a poor country like India. The gradual growth of thrift, self-reliance and prosperity might not attract much attention, but it was none the less real. The transfer of land was a necessary concomitant of these benefits. Young accordingly deprecated any administrative or legislative departure that was not fully justified by precedent and experience, or any interference with the transfer of land, lest the natural development of society be checked.[59] Young's viewpoint was a perfectly logical one, insisting on the total relevance, without exception, of the doctrines of natural law and *laissez-faire* political economy, and fitting all social manifestations into this framework.

These officers – Hutchinson, Massy, Robertson and Young – agreed broadly with Fitzpatrick's analysis of what was likely to happen if a differential assessment were introduced. Robertson indeed thought that there might be an initial shaking of credit – both the peasants' and the Government's – which would check alienations for a time; but that when confidence returned expropriation would proceed much faster because the value of land would be lower. Massy agreed that under a differential assessment the peasant would come more quickly to the end of his tether; and both he and Young predicted that the restriction of credit would lead to serious peasant discontent. Young also stressed the practical difficulties and the fact that the measure would strike at the root of the village revenue system.[60]

L. J. H. Grey likewise opposed a differential assessment; he still adhered to his policy of general enhancements of revenue.[61]

In addition a number of other officers felt that a differential assessment would not check transfers to any degree; but they were nevertheless willing to try it.[62]

There were, apart from Dane and Thorburn, only two officers, J. A. L. Montgomery and A. Anderson, who strongly favoured a differential assessment. Montgomery and Dane thought that the imposition of an extra assessment on non-agriculturists would give agriculturists an advantage in the acquisition of land; and this competition, Dane pointed out, would prevent the serious depreciation in the value of land which Fitzpatrick feared. Thorburn believed that the money-lender's desire for land would be slightly decreased because his annual income from the land would be less under a differential assessment. Together with Dane, Anderson and Steedman he conceived that the restriction of peasant credit would be beneficial.[63]

Thorburn further criticised Fitzpatrick for approaching the issue from the standpoint of an outmoded assessment policy, the system of village assessments. Increasingly the situation was becoming one in which villages were held in part by peasant proprietors and in part by non-agricultural alienees. Yet the Settlement Officer had very limited powers of distribution of revenue within the village. If he assessed the whole village at rates payable by non-agricultural alienees he might well precipitate the ruin of the remaining peasant proprietors. In consequence the whole village was usually assessed leniently to benefit the peasant proprietors; and this meant a loss of revenue from the alienees who were well able to pay. Moreover, Thorburn asserted, under the existing system of village distribution the best lands were often the most lightly assessed, and it was precisely these lands which money-lenders ordinarily acquired.[64]

Charles Rivaz, the second Financial Commissioner, had been an advocate of differential assessment; but by March 1895 he thought that too many settlements had been concluded to make the adoption of a differential system worthwhile. He nevertheless took the opportunity to express a decided opinion on a point upon which the large majority of officers consulted disagreed with him. To apply a differential assessment to money-lenders alone, Rivaz charged, would be a piece of class legislation which would hardly be justifiable; and, as some officers had noted, it would be difficult to discriminate between money-lender and agriculturist. There were, in many parts of the Punjab, members of the agricultural classes who combined money-lending with agriculture or who were men of some little capital which they wished to invest in land. There was no reason why such men should not pay a proper assessment on their acquired lands. As before, Rivaz believed that in such cases the imposition of a higher assessment would not deter acquisitions by those who wanted to cultivate the land, but would place an appreciable check on the acquisition of land as a mere commercial speculation.[65] In later discussions relating to the restriction of the power of alienation, this aspect of Rivaz's outlook was to be of considerable importance.

The proposals regarding differential assessment were forwarded to the Punjab Government in April and May 1895; but it would be some time before Fitzpatrick bothered to dismiss them. It was a question which he had tackled only in response to repeated and insistent requests from below; and given Fitzpatrick's firm opinions, the issue was probably never in doubt. Nevertheless, this debate, as well as other proposals for revenue reform, throw some light on official opinion in the Province in the early 1890s. The question of land transfer was not a dead one by any means; but there were obvious limitations on the representations which restive local officers could make when the problem was being considered by the higher authorities. The question of revenue reform could be pressed on the Local Government, because this question had not been taken up directly, and because the assessment reports and associated correspondence provided a formal, official channel for representations of this kind. Besides, there were officers who felt strongly about these matters. Thorburn with his insistence on fluctuating assessments, Grey with his policy of general enhancements of revenue, Dane with his proposals for differential assessment—each of these officers believed he held the key, or one of the keys, to the problem of agricultural indebtedness. Yet Thorburn's proposals regarding fluctuating assessments did not lead anywhere because they involved serious departures in the revenue system, while they were not likely to have more than a marginal effect on indebtedness. Grey's proposals for a heavier revenue demand were even less likely to gain support; for whatever effects such a measure might have on indebtedness, no one apart from Grey himself believed that it would not be accompanied by greater evils. Only Dane's scheme for differential assessments was not obviously futile or objectionable to all sections of official opinion. The proposals for differential assessment had a financial as well as a political rationale; and they gained the strong support of some officers, and the temporary or milder approbation of a number of others. Yet it is clear that there was, on the whole, less support in the Province for differential assessments, and stronger opposition to such assessments, than was the case in regard to judicial reform.

There were indications in the opinions submitted on differential assessment that a number of officers favoured some strong remedy to check land transfer. Grey again suggested that the power to alienate be restricted. Anderson, as well as a younger officer, thought such restriction desirable, but doubted whether it would ever be done. Massy considered that such restriction was now impossible. Steedman, Cunningham and Leigh referred vaguely to the necessity for schemes to save the landowner. In Steedman's case this was nothing new; but Cunningham and Leigh certainly wrote in stronger terms than they had done in 1889. At that time Cunningham had been a moderate supporter of a Deccan Act, and Leigh speaking from his experience of the frontier district of Kohat, had more or less opposed it.[66] Thorburn, in an opinion which was not written till March 1895, referred to differential assessments as one of several peasant measures which he hoped to see adopted. Earlier that month he had had discussions with Fitzpatrick which seemed to hold some promise of a decisive turn in events. Before considering developments in that and later months it is worth examining a debate which took place about the same time as that relating to differential assessments; a debate which casts further light on trends in official opinion.

III

In July 1894, shortly before he took up the question of differential assessment, Fitzpatrick referred the Government of India's Home Department circular of June 1894 to the Financial Commissioner and Chief Court for opinion. The circular, the ultimate outcome of P. P. Hutchins' suggestions, proposed certain amendments of the law regarding usury, and of the Contract and Evidence Acts.[67] Fitzpatrick dealt chiefly with the proposed addition to the Contract Act that a contract should be voidable on account of a creditor having taken undue advantage of a debtor's simplicity or necessities; for he feared that provision would be interpreted in widely different ways by the courts and would introduce a large element of uncertainty into the law. He was convinced that every fresh element of chance, everything that made it more difficult for a creditor to forecast the result of suing his debtor, would lead the moneylender to ensure against the risk by devising new methods of doing business and exacting severer terms—something which he thought had happened already to a considerable extent in the Deccan. There might be something to be said in favour of destroying the peasant proprietor's credit altogether, and thus preventing him from borrowing money; but the introduction of a further element of uncertainty only impaired credit so that the debtor would have to submit to harder terms. Fitzpatrick hoped that someone might be able to suggest a way of making the proposed rule more definite.[68]

Of the officers consulted a number, chiefly judicial officers, agreed with Fitzpatrick's view of the danger of introducing uncertainties into the law; and, as some of them added, the peasant was more willing to borrow and to submit to harsher terms the greater the uncertainty whether a particular contract would be enforced or not.[69]

A few of these officers did not endorse Fitzpatrick's standpoint entirely; for they drew a distinction between provisions of law vague in themselves, to which they believed Fitzpatrick's objection applied more or less strongly, and precisely formulated provisions of law, such as, for instance, one which would limit the amount of interest recoverable in court, to which they considered Fitzpatrick's objection applied with diminished force or not at all. All tinkering with existing Acts of general application in the interests of special classes of the population, G. M. Ogilvie, the Financial Commissioner, explained, was open to Fitzpatrick's objection; but not so distinct enactments with sufficiently precise provisions.[70]

Several revenue and a few judicial officers did not even believe that the proposed amendment of the Contract Act would have the far-reaching effects which Fitzpatrick predicted. Many believed that it was not possible to make the amendment more definite, but that uniformity of interpretation would be attained in time through the appellate courts. One judicial officer reasoned that the law could be changed from time to time if money-lenders invented new methods of business. Some thought that the proposed amendment of the Contract Act would introduce no further uncertainty, as many Punjab courts were in practice already in the habit of cutting down interest and so on.[71]

Among those who did not share, or at least not entirely, Fitzpatrick's fear of the introduction of uncertainties into the law there was yet serious disagreement on the related issue of the restriction of credit. Officers like Hutchinson, Massy and Maconachie disagreed entirely with Fitzpatrick; for they feared that the destruction of credit would prevent the agriculturist from being able to borrow for his necessary requirements. On the other hand, Massy and Maconachie favoured certain measures, among them the limitation of interest recoverable in court, and they were prepared to risk the impairment of credit which Fitzpatrick believed would only make things worse in the end.[72] There were officers like A. Anderson and E. B. Steedman who thought that the impairment of credit would be advantageous. Anderson's views stood in direct contrast to those of Massy and Maconachie. The peasant, Anderson believed, did not borrow money to improve his land or to better his circumstances, but only to spend it extravagantly. There was no real loss to him if his credit was reduced and he could borrow and spend less. The custom of excessive expenditure would gradually cease; and the provident members of the community would benefit, for they would have to spend less and incur debt less often on ceremonial occasions.[73] Steedman's argument was something of an answer to Fitzpatrick's. If agricultural credit was impaired, and the creditor had difficulty in recovering unsecured cash loans he would try to obtain a mortgage; but the proprietor would hold out to the last against a mortgage and his position would be strengthened by the knowledge that resort to the courts might not be as successful as usual.[74] All these officers, whether they feared the destruction of credit, or were prepared to risk or welcome its impairment, differed from Fitzpatrick in that they looked to the existing relations between debtor and creditor, and did not simply apply certain rigid rules in a social vacuum.

Officers might disagree as to whether the proposed amendments of the general law were desirable or useful, but no one suggested that they were in any sense an answer to the problem of agricultural indebtedness. In discussing stronger measures a number of judicial officers were prepared to go as far as to suggest or recommend the restriction of the power of alienation. Among them were three of the four Judges of the Chief Court, Channing, Stogdon and Chatterji.[75] As a revenue officer Channing had accepted the increase in land transfers in Gurgaon at the end of the 1870s without much alarm. And while he as well as Stogdon had expressed their opinion on agricultural indebtedness in the 1880s, neither of them had taken the opportunity to recommend the restriction of the power of transfer.[76] Among revenue officers it was not surprising that Grey and Ogilvie pressed for the restriction of the power of alienation; but it was notable that Maconachie, who had been firmly opposed to such restriction in 1889, now thought that some cautious action in that direction might be advisable.[77]

In January 1895 Fitzpatrick accepted the amendments proposed in the law regarding usury and, with certain additions, those proposed for the Evidence Act. He adhered to his view that the proposed amendment of the Contract Act would be dangerous, and instead suggested an alternative and limited amendment by which protection would be given to persons by nature simple or feeble-minded. Fitzpatrick indicated that on this occasion he would not discuss the various proposals made by officers in regard to agricultural indebtedness. He did note, incidentally, that as it would not be advisable to enact usury laws, which would lead to borrowers having to pay more dearly for accommodation in the long run, no amendments of the kind under discussion could touch a large proportion of the cases in which agriculturists ruined themselves by borrowing money. Unless it was decided to impose restrictions on the alienation of land, those agriculturists would be left to their fate. Though the question of imposing such restrictions was one of very great difficulty, he thought that before long it might have to be considered in some parts of the country.[78]

In the next few months Fitzpatrick was moved to consider the restriction of the power of alienation rather more carefully. Early in March Fitzpatrick asked Thorburn to make a detailed local enquiry regarding indebtedness.[79] The reasons for this decision were not explained till May, in a letter from the Punjab Government to the Financial Commissioner. By this time, and perhaps rather earlier, it seems likely that Fitzpatrick had some inkling of what was happening within the Government of India.[80] At any rate in May it was pointed out that, while touring the Jhelum district, Fitzpatrick had received constant complaints, verbal and written, from landowners against money-lenders, and occasional counter-complaints from money-lenders. The Lieutenant-Governor had also had many conversations with Thorburn, the Commissioner of the division, and Silcock, the

Deputy Commissioner of the Jhelum district, as well as others, on the subject of agricultural indebtedness. Thorburn of course took a very serious, and as Fitzpatrick thought, perhaps somewhat exaggerated view, of the rapidity with which alienations to non-agriculturists were proceeding in the Rawalpindi division. As for Silcock, he had remarked only the other day that given even a temporary suspension of British control over the country, there would not be a money-lender left alive in the Jhelum district in a week. The upshot of his discussions with Thorburn, Fitzpatrick explained, was that he had asked him to investigate the worst tracts in his division and show the worst that could be said about them. Fitzpatrick was influenced by the feeling that if there was a real danger of alienations to non-agriculturists going *very* far, and the amount of land in their hands increasing very largely and rapidly, the only effectual remedy would be the restriction of the power of alienation. He thought that before such strong and extraordinary legislation was justified it would have to be shown that in some places the evil was attaining formidable dimensions. Vague clamour by agriculturists and vague expressions of opinion by officers would not suffice for this purpose, but only detailed information as to the history and present state of certain tracts. Unless an irresistible case were made out, Fitzpatrick insisted, there would not be the least hope of obtaining sanction to legislation restricting alienation. If Thorburn's enquiry showed good ground for thinking that there was a case for such legislation, a more exhaustive enquiry into the selected tracts would probably have to be carried out.[81] When the enquiry was finally sanctioned in July 1895, however, it turned out to be rather more searching than had been anticipated at first.[82]

Meanwhile in March 1895 there came a letter from the Government of India requesting opinion on a private Bill designed to prevent courts from decreeing in suits for simple money-debts and mortgage-debts interest exceeding in amount the original principal or, where there had been payment in reduction of principal, exceeding in amount the reduced principal.[83] It was not clear whether the term 'original principal' was intended to include a power to 'go behind the bond' to the very beginning of the transactions between the parties, or not.

A few of the revenue and judicial officers consulted simply accepted the measure as desirable. Many pointed out that if the term 'original principal' did not include a power to 'go behind the bond' the measure could be very easily evaded by the renewal of bonds as well as in other ways. Some officers though favouring stronger restrictions on the award of interest, thought that even a limited measure of this kind might do some good and would be worth having as a first small step in the right direction. Others rejected such a limited measure as useless or even harmful. They wanted either full power to 'go behind the bond' or restrictions on the rate of interest. The replies as a whole showed that there was a general feeling among both revenue and judicial officers that some regulation of the award of interest was desirable to combat agricultural indebtedness.[84]

One judicial officer, about to retire, recorded a strong opinion that the power of alienation should be restricted, though he had no hope whatever that his proposal would be adopted.[85]

The replies of officers to a Government of India circular of May 1895, concerning reforms, in the Court of Wards system, designed to save large proprietors, further showed the way the wind was blowing. In addition to old advocates of legislation like J. M. Douie and S. S. Thorburn, there were several officers who hitherto had said little on the general question but who were now showing signs of restiveness at the apparent failure of the Government of India to deal with the indebtedness of peasant proprietors.[86]

The opinions of revenue officers on the interest Bill and on the Court of Wards system were reviewed by Charles Rivaz, the second Financial Commisioner. Rivaz had long since favoured the restriction of the power of transfer, but he had not pressed a measure which he knew would not be considered practicable. Now that Fitzpatrick had shown some indication of moving in that direction, Rivaz came out strongly in favour of some general scheme for the restriction of the power of alienation.[87]

The views expressed by revenue and judicial officers between July 1894 and August 1895 on differential assessments, on the proposed amendments of the general law, on the interest Bill and on the Court of Wards system indicate that official opinion favouring drastic legislation to combat agricultural indebtedness was stronger than in 1888–9. At that time proposals for judicial reform had won general assent; now they appeared to be overdue. Proposals for differential assessment had caught on to some extent, and were the subject of official consideration despite the Lieutenant-Governor's scepticism. The desirability of imposing restrictions on the power of alienation was more widely accepted in 1894–5 than before, and this change was especially notable among judicial officers. The majority of the Judges of the Chief Court approved such restrictions. The effects of legislation on agricultural credit were debated by many officers with a keen eye on practical rather than theoretical considerations. In the wake of the enquiry of 1888-9 concern had spread to a wider circle of officers; so that those who had said little on the larger questions in earlier years did not hesitate to speak out of turn now. While differences of opinion remained, they hinged on the nature of the remedy considered permissible, rather than on any question whether the situation was sufficiently serious to warrant Government intervention. In this respect it was of the greatest importance that there was now a Lieutenant-Governor who, unlike his predecessor, was disposed to reject all remedies short of the restriction of the power of alienation; and who was about to consider, however cautiously, the imposition of such restrictions. It was at this juncture – long before Thorburn could finish his enquiry and Fitzpatrick could formulate definite conclusions – that there arrived a circular from the Government of India, dated October 1895, indicating that the Governor-General in Council was '. . . as at present advised, distinctly of opinion that some action in the direction of restriction upon the alienability of land is generally advisable, and even necessary . . .'[88] The debate between Ibbetson and Fitzpatrick had begun.

IV

It was to E. D. Maclagan, the Under-Secretary in the Government of India's Revenue Department, that the task of preparing a statement of the land transfer problem from the Secretariat records had been entrusted. Maclagan, a Punjab civilian whose experience dated from 1886, completed his lengthy note in March 1895. In this note he summarised such factual information on the subject of land transfer as was available for the various Provinces; he dwelt on the economic, administrative and political evils of land transfer; and he discussed the remedies which had been proposed from time to time. Special attention was given to the various schemes for restricting the power of land transfer which had been devised in the past, and an attempt was made to answer the objections raised against them. Beyond indicating that absolute prohibition of alienations was impracticable, Maclagan did not suggest the particular restrictions which it might be advisable to adopt.[89]

The initiative was now taken by a Punjab man of decided views, Denzil Ibbetson, the officiating Secretary in the Revenue Department. In a long argumentative memorandum Ibbetson pointed out that the transfer of land was, or would become, everywhere in India a political danger of the first magnitude. And though Ibbetson was not unaware of a new political challenge, he tended to see it as a subordinate part of the problem of rural stability; as long as the masses were contented, he noted, professional agitators would be powerless; but agricultural discontent would open the ears of the people to the various forms of political organisation which were coming into existence.[90]

Amendments of the civil law, Ibbetson thought, were not sufficient to meet the danger. They might diminish transfer but they would not prevent it; and even if the British did not produce the evils they would reap the odium for not preventing them. Heavy assessments were not desirable for the prevention of transfers; for one did not keep a man contented by absorbing his profits. Moderate enhancements of revenue would be no more than a palliative. Differential assessments were desirable as a revenue measure; but Ibbetson agreed with Fitzpatrick that they would not check transfers. The imposition of a crushing, as distinct from a merely enhanced, assessment on alienated land was the only revenue measure which deserved serious consideration as a means of checking alienations. It was the restriction of the power of transfer, however, which Ibbetson conceived as striking at the root of the evil.

Ibbetson did not consider that the limitation of credit which would follow the restriction of the power of transfer was a serious objection; for Indian experience and Indian conditions did not give weight to such an objection. The reduction of agricultural borrowing powers was, as experience in the Deccan had shown, beneficial and not injurious. That the agriculturist would still be able to borrow sufficiently to carry on his agricultural operations was abundantly proved by the state of affairs existing prior to British rule, by the example of the Native States, and by the existence in certain parts of British India of agricultural classes which did not possess the power of transfer and which were more prosperous and less involved than the small proprietors among whom they lived. It was admitted that by diminishing the facilities for the recovery of debt an element of uncertainty was introduced which would probably raise the rate of interest; but the result was not likely to follow a limitation of landed security. Here Ibbetson argued on much the same lines as in his 1885 paper, with certain additions. A general decrease in the value of landed security would leave the condition of competition between individual borrowers unaltered. If borrowing decreased, capital would be diverted but not to an extent which would materially affect rates of interest, the field for investment of capital in India being too limited. Custom was all-powerful and would probably prevent any increase in traditional rates. The rate of interest upon unsecured debt in the Punjab, Ibbetson noted, was believed to be no higher than in the adjoining districts of the North-Western Provinces; yet in the former land was practically exempt from sale in execution of a money-decree, in the latter it was not.

The real objection to the restriction of the power of alienation, Ibbetson continued, was its unpopularity and the consequent political danger. To ensure that the restriction would not be regarded as a breach of faith it was necessary to make it clear that it did not profit Government except by promoting the prosperity of the people. The argument that the measure would be regarded as a confiscation involved some confusion of thought; for it was only as a negotiable article that the value of land would be depreciated, and it was precisely the negotiable nature of land that it was intended to destroy. The landowners would approve of the measure in this respect, at least until the individual experienced inconvenience; and those who had purchased land as a negotiable article were by comparison few, and their interests would have to be deliberately subordinated to those of the landowners wherever they were in conflict. The danger which Ibbetson, with his early and extensive experience of parts of the south-eastern Punjab, deemed as of the greatest moment, was that the landowners would regard any measure as an attack upon their status as proprietors. This danger, Ibbetson believed, existed in North-Western India where the proprietary status had existed from time immemorial and where membership of the proprietary community was regarded as a sign of superior social rank. Yet here where the danger of restriction was greatest, the need for restriction was also greatest; for it was these people who clung most firmly to their land, who felt its loss most keenly and whose manly pride and independence made them the sturdiest of friends and the most dangerous of foes.

A choice, Ibbetson argued, had to be made between the danger of action and inaction. Entire prohibition of alienations was impracticable. No scheme for the restriction of permanent alienations could be applied to the whole of India. The precise restrictions imposed upon the power of alienation must be carefully adjusted to local conditions, lest the remedy be more dangerous than the disease. It would be advisable to confine restrictions on the power of transfer to small owners; the great landlords could be more easily saved by means of the Court of Wards, the buying up of encumbered estates, and so on.

Restrictions on temporary alienation, Ibbetson believed, would probably not arouse discontent among small proprietors. Most forms of mortgage were objectionable because the landowner entered into them with the rarely-fulfilled hope of being able to redeem. Outright sale, to which the peasant would be driven only by the greatest necessity, was safer than a mortgage which must end in sale. Consequently in the case of small proprietors all forms of mortgage should be absolutely and everywhere prohibited except that form of usufructuary mortgage in which the mortgagee took the land into his proprietary possession and enjoyed its profits for a term limited by law, on the expiry of which the land passed back into the hands of the mortgagor free from all encumbrance, both capital and interest having been liquidated. In some parts of India the further condition might be added that the mortgagor would retain an occupancy right in the whole or portion of the alienated area at a rent not exceeding double the revenue. The duration of the mortgage might be limited to the life of the alienor, the current term of settlement or, as Ibbetson thought was perhaps best, to a term of years. It would have to be provided that no further alienation could be entered into during the currency of the original alienation, and this disability might well extend to two or three years after the expiry of the term. Leases would have to be treated in the same way as mortgages. It was not possible to protect a man completely against himself by these measures. They would ensure nevertheless that whatever a man did, he would do in full knowledge of the ultimate results of his action. The consequences of a single act would be confined to a limited term, at the end of which the alienor would be as far as possible in the same position as before the act. He would not have been able to repeat the act until he was relieved from the pressure of the unfavourable circumstances in which the original act had placed him.

To Ibbetson's way of thinking the restriction of permanent alienations involved greater political danger and greater problems. Alienations to the money-lending castes were a great evil. Those made to agriculturist money-lenders were not always so objectionable; but there was often little to choose between the agriculturist money-lender and the regular money-lender. Permanent alienation to these classes, Ibbetson was certain, ought to be restricted. He was more doubtful about permanent alienations to self-cultivating agriculturists. Even these alienations often had evil consequences; yet they were not infrequently beneficial. There were, however, two weighty practical reasons which inclined Ibbetson to the view that even permanent transfers to self-cultivating agriculturists ought to be restricted. In the first place it did not seem possible to give a legal definition of agriculturist or non-agriculturist which would effectively exclude both the regular and the agriculturist money-lender from the permanent acquisition of land. The second difficulty was that if alienations were prohibited to one large class and permitted to another, members of the latter class would set up as agents for the former. If the scope for such operations was only sufficiently large, it would be worth the agents' while to be honest; but if the field of operations was limited, such professional purchasers would not be able to make a living, and almost each transaction would require a new agent, whom it would not be possible to trust. Given the necessity for a narrow restriction of permanent alienations, Ibbetson considered the possibility of confining such alienations to the village community, to co-sharers in the village or, and this he thought the most hopeful suggestion, to the near agnates of the alienor. Thus restricted permanent alienations would assume their most unobjectionable and least unpopular form, and the freedom left would usually be sufficient to permit alienations of a beneficial character. It might be hoped that the partial freedom of alienation remaining would suffice to show the landowners that their proprietary status continued intact.

Together with this limitation, Ibbetson thought, there might be a prohibition of alienation except with the sanction of the revenue authorities. This would ensure that the regular money-lender who owned land, the agriculturist who had taken to money-lending, and the professional purchaser could be prevented from acquiring land in individual instances by executive decision. At the same time all beneficial alienations would be allowed. There might be many applications for sanction at first, but soon it would become known what sort of alienations were likely to receive sanction and applications would dwindle.

As an alternative to the above proposals for restricting permanent alienations Ibbetson discussed the suggestion that an ex-owner be allowed to retain an inalienable occupancy right in his alienated land at a rent limited by law. This was one of the proposals which had found favour with several Council members in the early 1890s. Ibbetson characterised it as an easy proposal – the proprietors were not likely to object – but an incomplete one, for it would not prevent the loss of proprietary status.

A number of subsidiary questions were also discussed by Ibbetson; among them the restriction of the mortgage of crops, the extent to which retrospective effect should be given to any legislation, the manner in which the prohibition against transfers should be enforced, the reasons for and against confining measures to selected areas in the first instance, and the amendment of the law of pre-emption.

In August 1895 Ibbetson proposed that Maclagan's note, his own memorandum, a selection of papers and a resolution be submitted for consideration to Local Governments. He further suggested that the resolution be published together with his memorandum to ascertain educated Indian opinion.[91] Ibbetson was firmly supported by the new Member for the Home and Revenue Departments, A. Mackenzie, who, as Chief Commissioner of the Central Provinces in the late 1880s had called for legislation to combat agricultural indebtedness, though he had thought it too late to restrict the power of transfer.[92] The Viceroy, Lord Elgin, thought highly of Ibbetson and he was favourable to the consideration of a question, the importance of which had been impressed upon him by Lansdowne and by men whom Elgin thought knew India best. No doubt there would be points on which differences of opinion would arise, Elgin noted; but the memorandum dealt with Indian problems, and it was in the light of the customs that had prevailed, the circumstances which existed, and the danger which threatened *in India* that he thought the memorandum had to be read and criticised. He demurred only to publication, thinking that public criticism would be more valuable at a later stage; and instead of publishing a resolution he proposed that the papers be circulated confidentially to Local Governments. There was a gentle hint that Council Members should not object.[93] Nor was there much disposition among Council Members to do so; only one Member, A. C. Trevor, an old Bombay officer, was really obstructive, insisting that the question of the restriction of voluntary alienations need not be considered at all, at least for the present.[94] At a time when the Government of India had gone so far in this direction, this view was not likely to gain favour.[95] Most Council Members confined themselves to the question of the precise way in which the Local Governments should be approached. Lesser criticisms on this head were met by certain verbal amendments in the resolution, now transformed into a circular.[96] One Member's preference for a more colourless memorandum does not appear to have been pressed.[97] The circular which was issued in October 1895 indicated that the Government of India considered some restriction on the power of alienation advisable, but was not committed to the views stated in the memorandum.[98] Ibbetson could have hardly expected more.

Meanwhile the question of framing a Deccan Bill which could be applied to any part of India had been revived in the Home Department; and a circular to Local Governments on this matter was issued shortly after that relating to the restriction of transfer.[99] Local Governments would be obliged to consider the two major remedies for agricultural indebtedness at the same time.

V

In the Punjab there was little doubt about the line Fitzpatrick would take. As we have seen, he had seriously considered the restriction of the power of alienation. The Government of India circular merely induced him to state his views at greater length, in December 1895. He had not changed his mind about the futility of differential assessments; and he had just rejected all proposals on this head.[100] Legislation on the lines of the Deccan Act, which his predecessor had pursued in vain, and which was now within the sphere of practical politics, he considered to be at best palliative and at worst dangerous on economic grounds. He agreed with Ibbetson that the creation of inalienable occupancy rights would fail to prevent the all-important loss of status by the ex-proprietor. If political danger threatened anywhere, the restriction of the power of transfer was the only solution.[101]

Fitzpatrick did not agree with Ibbetson that political danger necessarily existed either in the present or the future. In Fitzpatrick's eyes political danger could be assumed to arise only in tracts where the amount of land alienated and the number of proprietors dispossessed was about to reach formidable proportions. It was only in these tracts that restrictions on alienation could be applied, and then only after detailed enquiry. This was not merely a matter of their own sense of responsibility; the opposition of the proprietors, of the moneyed classes and those who held with them, and of outsiders in India and England, who could look at the question only from the economic point of view, had to be taken into account.

To lessen the opposition of the proprietors Fitzpatrick contemplated giving the Local Government power to apply the restrictions on alienation only to land which would after a certain date come into the possession of individuals by purchase, inheritance or otherwise. To overcome the difficulty that in this way the restrictions might come into effect only after the mischief had been done, Fitzpatrick proposed to confer a special power to apply the restrictions to land vested in possession in the case of tracts in which an

## EXTENDING THE CONFLICT

overwhelming case had been established by special enquiry. The Local Government would not be able to exercise this special power at will; for if alienations were increasing in any tract, and the special power could be applied at any time, the money-lenders might be induced to put severe pressure on their debtors. Accordingly the tracts subject to the special power would be specified in the Act; and the special power could be applied to other tracts only by an amendment of the Act.

As regards the classes to whom the restrictions would be applied Fitzpatrick was equally cautious. Unlike Ibbetson, he was not prepared to sacrifice the interests of the money-lenders who had acquired land. The money-lending classes, he thought, were likely to be most vehement in their opposition to the measure; and it was neither necessary nor politic to restrict their right of alienation. Nor did Fitzpatrick think that there was any need to prevent alienations to hereditary landowners. There was no doubt, as Ibbetson had noted, a difficulty in distinguishing between agriculturist and moneylender; but Fitzpatrick thought it could be overcome by the suggestion, made to him by James Douie, that those classes whose right of alienation it was considered desirable to restrict should be specified by their tribal name.

In regard to the actual restrictions on the right of alienation Fitzpatrick also departed from Ibbetson's scheme. He proposed to allow proprietors to alienate for life; for any attempt to prevent them from dealing with their land during their own life-time would lead to inextricable difficulties. Proprietors would be allowed to alienate for a term of ten years as well, to obviate the difficulty that the life-term afforded too precarious a security. After ten years or life the land would return to the owner or his heirs, but the debt would not necessarily be discharged.

As a safety-valve in the whole scheme Fitzpatrick suggested that the Deputy Commissioner be allowed to sanction any transfer under special circumstances and for strong reasons.

Ibbetson and Fitzpatrick were thus poles apart. Both asserted that political danger could be met only by restrictions on the power of transfer; but while Ibbetson was more impressed with the risks of inaction, and sought to impose the maximum restrictions feasible, Fitzpatrick was preoccupied with the risks of action, and aimed to reduce restrictions to a minimum.

Fitzpatrick's note accompanied the Government of India papers which were forwarded to selected revenue and judicial officers in January 1896.

It was a remarkable feature of the discussion which followed that the old opponents of drastic legislation failed to offer effective resistance to the proposals for restricting the power of alienation.

Robert Maconachie's views had been changing slowly since the late 1880s. He had begun to think that a restriction on the power of transfer might be advisable; but he was by no means certain. Forced to re-examine his position by the proposals of the Government of India and the Lieutenant-Governor, he completely reversed some of his old opinions. The political danger, which he had minimised in the 1880s, he now thought serious enough. He adhered to his belief that the weaker classes could not be saved by any law; but set himself to devise restrictions on the power of alienation which would save the more worthy men among the landowners.[102]

Hutchinson was not yet convinced that a serious political danger existed; and he hoped that legislation on the lines of the Deccan Act would prove sufficient. To restrict the power of alienation, he thought, an overwhelming case would have to be established by minute enquiry. If such a case was made out and restrictions were imposed they had better be effective; for the delays involved in the application of Fitzpatrick's measures to various tracts would only promote alienation.[103]

The outright opposition of certain other officers was disarmed by the limited application which Fitzpatrick proposed to give to restrictive measures. Not long before C. F. Massy had asserted that the restriction of the power of alienation was impossible; now he agreed to the very sparing introduction of such restrictions into special tracts requiring strong remedies.[104] E. B. Francis did not think that in Ferozepur, the only district with which he was intimately acquainted, there were political or economic grounds to justify the new legislation; a not altogether surprising conclusion when one remembers that most of Ferozepur was held by Sikh Jats, probably the most prosperous and least indebted peasantry in the Punjab.[105] But Francis took it on the authority of officers with better opportunities of observation that things in the western Punjab were different.[106] The experience of W. R. H. Merk, the Commissioner of the Peshawar division, had been confined almost entirely to that part of the Province, where the acquisitions of Hindu money-lenders had not been marked. He was quite certain that no measures were required in his division; but with his limited experience he could not altogether oppose the application of Fitzpatrick's proposals to tracts in other parts of the Province.[107]

Charles Roe, the Chief Judge of the Chief Court, was now prepared to admit, as he had not been in the 1880s, that the agriculturists were being supplanted by the money-lenders to a serious degree, and that this constituted a political danger. He still doubted the wisdom of maintaining large bodies of insolvent men as owners; and only proposed amendments of the pre-emption law to give solvent communities a better chance to exclude outsiders. If further measures were to be taken they should be on the lines of Fitzpatrick's proposals; but this would be very undesirable, at least until his own remedy had been tried and found inadequate.[108]

There was only one officer of weight, F. A. Robertson, who strained every nerve to prove that restrictions on the power of alienation were politically unnecessary and economically unsound.[109]

That there were not more officers like Robertson, taking a bold stand against the most drastic remedy yet proposed, was due partly to the fact that a few officers had succumbed since the late 1880s to the notion that a serious political danger existed. More generally it was due to the fact that the Government of India and the Lieutenant-Governor of the Province had set new terms of reference for the debate by declaring their support for proposals to restrict the power of alienation. The question of the day was no longer whether the power of alienation should be restricted, but to what extent and in what manner it should be restricted. And finally it was Fitzpatrick's *limited* support of the Government of India proposals which in several instances prevented that strong opposition from certain officers which might well have eventuated had they been asked to adjudicate directly on Ibbetson's memorandum. Fitzpatrick's ultra-cautious application of the most sweeping proposals lulled several officers into thinking that legislation would be kept within bounds or would not be applied to those parts of the Province with which they were acquainted. Ultimately this turn of events was to prove of advantage not to Fitzpatrick, but to Ibbetson.

Several officers who up till now had said little or nothing in regard to agricultural indebtedness also assented to enabling legislation.[110]

Many of the foregoing officers differed among themselves and with Fitzpatrick as to the degree to which the power of alienation should be restricted in the local areas to which the legislation was to be applied. Among officers who had pressed strongly for remedies, and who were now given an opportunity to indicate in detail the sort of restrictions they would impose on the power of alienation, great differences of opinion were also apparent.

Robert Clarke had served in many a Punjab district; but for the last nine years he had been stationed at Delhi, as Deputy Commissioner of the district or Commissioner of the division. Apart from certain tracts and tahsils the division was held largely by thrifty and industrious Hindu Jats, not prone to alienate on any scale except perhaps at those times when a failure of rainfall brought acute agricultural distress. Clarke had examined the alienation statistics of the division for the preceding decade, a period of, on the whole, favourable rainfall. From these statistics he drew the conclusions that almost everywhere in the division the mortgaging process had come to a standstill; that agriculturists were supplanting money-lenders as mortgagees; and that agriculturists managed to secure most of the land sold. As he did not think that alienations to agriculturists were objectionable on the whole, though they might be so in individual instances, he suggested amendments of the pre-emption law which would give agriculturists a larger share of the land that came into the market. He also approved of the abolition of the mortgage by conditional sale, and of Ibbetson's suggestion that the self-redeeming usufructuary mortgage should be the only legal mortgage. Prevention, he concluded, was better than cure and these provisions should be extended to the whole Province.[111]

Thorburn had long since taken an alarmist view of the political danger attending alienations from Muslim landowners to Hindu money-lenders in the western Punjab. He had just completed a detailed enquiry into certain tracts in the north-western Punjab which might well justify the gloomiest forebodings. No longer was Thorburn satisfied with legislation on the lines of the Deccan Act, as he had been to some extent even in the late 1880s. Such legislation by itself, he claimed, would promote rather than restrict the passing of land to money-lenders. Thorburn had never been able to conceive that alienations to agriculturists involved any political danger. His experience had been confined largely to parts of the country where the gulf between Muslim landholder and Hindu money-lender yawned widest, and where the acquisitiveness of the ordinary peasant proprietor was not particularly marked. Thorburn indicated that it was too late to maintain the village community and to restrict alienations to the hereditary proprietors of the village. No law would keep the land in the hands of the weaker agriculturists. All that was possible was to preserve the land to self-cultivating proprietors of any kind, and failing them to landlords whose hereditary occupation was agriculture. That would be sufficient to secure the contentment of the peasantry. The main way to achieve that object was to make permanent alienations of land to non-agriculturists illegal without official sanction. Only one or two forms of time-limited mortgages should be legalised. As an afterthought he added that perhaps even agriculturists should be confined to these forms of mortgage; but he was not certain.[112]

A number of advocates of strong remedies were in closer agreement with Ibbetson than with Clarke or Thorburn.

Less than a year before Alexander Anderson had doubted whether the British would ever restrict the power of transfer. Now he tried to get the most out of Fitzpatrick's proposals. In one respect he foresaw serious difficulties. If those, whose right of alienation was to be restricted, were to be specified by their tribal name it would be difficult to deal with tribes like the Kangra Brahmins, which contained both agriculturists and money-lenders. Leave the Brahmins unnotified and the agriculturists among them would become the special prey of professional money-lenders unable to acquire land permanently from other tribes. Notify the Brahmins and the money-lenders among them would have special facilities for the acquisition of land. To avoid these difficulties Anderson suggested that lists be made of land which was subject to the restrictions on alienation. In concrete instances it would be easy to determine the true agriculturists whose land should be listed; and the land of money-lenders of every description would be excluded from these lists. The owners of listed land would be allowed to alienate freely only to owners and tenants holding listed land. Alienations to others would hold good only for life or ten years. The circle within which unrestricted transfers of listed land were allowed might be further narrowed by permitting such transfers only within certain local limits or to men of the same tribe within those limits; and otherwise only by official sanction. This plan, Anderson added, had the further advantage that wherever restrictions were not applied or only to a future generation of proprietors, the present owners might be given the option of putting their land on the list. The knowledge that a debtor might at the last moment put his land on the list would go far to discourage money-lenders from exerting special pressure.[113]

One of the earliest advocates of the restriction of the power of alienation, James Wilson, had felt keenly the injustice suffered by the individual peasant from the changes wrought by British rule. In the early 1880s, serving in the south-eastern Punjab and on the fringes of the central Punjab, he had not taken this so far as to deprecate unduly transfers to self-cultivating peasants. The transfer of land from the poorer to the richer members of the brotherhood, so common in parts of the south-east, he had not thought a great evil;

and even where the land passed out of the tribe or the village, there was still some advantage in the replacement of a poor cultivator by a thrifty one.[114] Since 1886, however, Wilson had been employed almost entirely in a north-western district, that of Shahpur, where alienations to landholders were not so much alienations to self-cultivating peasants as to rich and prominent men of landowning stock. In these circumstances Wilson's compassion had free play. Unlike Thorburn, Wilson insisted that legislation should be based on the principle that the land belonged to the heirs. Alienations should be allowed only for life; and members of the notified tribes should not be able to alienate otherwise even to other members of those tribes. A far-reaching change of this nature, Wilson believed, could not be introduced at once all over the Punjab. It should be introduced gradually and experimentally and its consequences estimated. Wilson had another reason for preferring enabling legislation. His experience had brought him into contact not only with indebted communities in both the eastern and the western Punjab; but also with the Sikh Jats, who, as a whole, were able to take care of themselves. In the case of communities like the Sikh Jats, Wilson considered the withdrawal of the power of transfer to be unnecessary. Yet Wilson felt the evils of the situation to be so great, that rather than wait twenty years to see all his views accepted, and thereby share the responsibility for the ruin of millions more of the Indian peasantry, he was prepared to accept any restriction on the power of transfer immediately.[115]

As Deputy Commissioner of the Jhelum district, J. G. Silcock had watched the growth of the pronounced discontent of the agricultural classes of that district since the late 1880s. He assumed that the situation was more or less the same in other parts of the Punjab; and proposed an almost complete withdrawal of the power of transfer all over the Province. He was influenced to a smaller degree by the consideration that such an enactment would put a stop to the endless litigation about the rights of proprietors to dispose of their land by gift or will.[116]

As far as Stogdon and Chatterji, Judges of the Chief Court, were concerned, the reduction of litigation was a major consideration. They were willing to take it on trust that political danger existed; but they were personally acquainted with the ruinous litigation which the customary restrictions on alienation promoted. It was chiefly as a means of clearly defining the powers of the proprietor over his ancestral land that they supported legislation. Chatterji suggested that the new restrictions should replace those imposed by customary law. The arguments of Stogdon and Chatterji implied a preference for an enactment extending to at least large parts of the Province. They argued that to stifle litigation the restrictions on alienation would have to apply irrespective of the classes to which alienations were made. Besides they feared that if unrestricted alienations to agriculturists were allowed professional purchasers would spring up and agriculturists would soon become money-lenders.[117]

Most of these officers thus favoured general legislation of some sort. There was a broad distinction between those like Clarke and Thorburn, who wanted to restrict alienations to professional money-lenders, and the others, who sought, like Ibbetson, to restrict alienations as such.

The most important scheme for checking alienations, as it turned out, was that put forward by the Financial Commissioners, Charles Rivaz and Lewis Tupper. They took the line that general legislation was required to combat a political problem which varied only in degree from one part of the Province to the other. Rivaz characterised Fitzpatrick's proposals as an attempt to shut the stable door after the steed had been stolen. As with the question of differential assessment, Rivaz was not prepared for class policies. He accepted Ibbetson's proposal that the self-redeeming usufructuary mortgage should be the only legal mortgage. With reference to permanent alienations he thought there was a convenient basis for action in the customary law of the Province, which was in accordance with popular feeling. The basic principle which he proposed was that all permanent alienations of ancestral land should be prohibited except by official sanction. In many instances such transfers would be allowed freely, perhaps even to money-lenders when no other purchasers were forthcoming. Tupper elaborated certain aspects of these proposals, and explained why he had assented to fastening restrictions on ancestral land instead of preventing agriculturists from alienating to professional money-lenders. In this way the activities of the agriculturist turned money-lender and those of the professional purchaser could be curbed; and it was also possible to check the acquisition of the lands of one tribe by another. The proposal further avoided the difficulty of defining either the money-lender or the landowner; but raised the difficulty of defining the land to which the restrictions would apply. Anderson's scheme for listing such land Tupper rejected on the ground that the labour involved would be enormous. Instead he proposed a definition of ancestral land which could be applied in individual instances by reference to the land records and which in the majority of cases would impose the restrictions only on the land of the hereditary proprietors of a village. Tupper also indicated the flexibility of these proposals. In districts or parts of districts where there was little necessity for restricting permanent alienations sanction could be given freely. The legislation was to be general; but its application would be adjusted to local circumstances.[118]

Some of the underlying differences between the officers consulted only emerged incidentally.

There was a marked difference in estimates of the probable economic consequences of restrictions on alienation. Nearly all the less strongly committed officers feared what both Ibbetson and Fitzpatrick had treated lightly, namely, that restrictions on alienation would undermine the credit of the agricultural classes to a dangerous degree. Many predicted difficulty in the revenue collections; and thought that Government would have to step in to supply loans for necessary purposes. Other officers relied generally on the old argument that the money-lender had to lend to live and that he would adjust himself to the new conditions.

As regards the political aspect, few officers thought in Ibbetson's terms. Most of the more doubtful supporters predicted that restrictions on alienation would be unpopular among the agricultural classes; but this was a secondary argument deriving from the postulate that credit would be injuriously affected. The committed advocates of legislation varied in their assessments from thinking that the measure would be well-received by small, if not by a few large, proprietors, to thinking that the proprietors would soon acquiesce in the situation. Only Maconachie, who, like Ibbetson, had spent many years in the south-eastern Punjab, shared Ibbetson's fear that the restriction of the power of alienation would be considered by landowners as an attack on their proprietary status. He inclined to the view that this feeling could be allayed by careful management.

There were few echoes of Fitzpatrick's fears in regard to the opposition of the trading castes. Robertson it is true thought their opposition could be far more effective than was generally supposed. Maconachie, Wilson and Silcock expected strong opposition from the trading castes, but they did not consider this an argument against legislation. Anderson and Thorburn considered the opposition of these castes to be of little or no account. Rivaz and Tupper, among others, did not even refer to this matter.

Silcock argued that enabling legislation alone would bring about the dislocation of credit (by the flight of capital from the affected tracts); and that enabling and class legislation would create political danger (by creating invidious distinctions between proprietors and between them and the money-lenders). Rivaz adopted this argument in so far as it applied to enabling legislation.

In January 1897 Fitzpatrick attempted to defend his views. He claimed that there was a strong case for legislation in at least the worst of the four tracts examined by Thorburn. The arguments against enabling legislation did not impress him. Believing that political danger could arise only at a fixed and determinable point, he drew a rather precarious distinction between closing the stable door after the steed had been stolen and closing it just before the steed was about to be stolen. The view that partial measures would humiliate those to whom they were applied he met with the contention that opposition was to be expected from the landowners and from others and that this opposition would be the more formidable the more widely the measure was applied.[119]

On one point he did give way. He now thought it would be better to give the executive a free hand in applying not only the ordinary power of imposing restrictions on land which would after a certain date come into possession, but also the special power of imposing restrictions on land vested in possession. He saw that if the tracts to which the special power could be applied were specified in the Act, the application of the special power to other tracts would mean delays and the promotion of alienation in the tracts concerned. He had another characteristic reason. If the executive had only the ordinary power it would be inclined to use it freely; if it had the special power as well, it could afford to wait in regard to any particular tract until it was quite certain that the steed was about to be stolen.

Fitzpatrick still maintained that restrictions on the power of alienation should not apply to landowners of the trading castes and that no restrictions should be imposed on transfers to agricultural tribes. He did not fully grasp the difficulties which Anderson foresaw in any attempt to notify agricultural tribes; and agreed with Tupper that it was not feasible to prepare lists of land, as suggested by Anderson. Tupper's definition of ancestral land Fitzpatrick also rejected, partly because he misunderstood it.

There was no necessity for imposing restrictions, Fitzpatrick thought, on acquired land. Land acquired after the passing of the Act, however, could not be exempted from the restrictions, as otherwise any landowner could buy land from another landowner and immediately transfer it to the trader as acquired land.

As to the actual restrictions to be imposed on the power of alienation, Fitzpatrick modified some of his earlier conclusions. He now thought it might be best to allow alienations only for a fixed term and not for life. Ibbetson's suggestion that the time-limited usufructuary mortgage should necessarily discharge the debt for which the alienation was made might be further considered. It would prevent the proprietor from alienating his land repeatedly for a fixed term; but it might restrict credit too much.

Schemes like those of Tupper and Rivaz, which depended to a very large degree on the grant of official sanction, Fitzpatrick charged, were unworkable. The applications would be so great that they could be dealt with only haphazardly. Subordinate officials could not be entrusted with the power to grant sanction. The Deputy Commissioner alone should have that power, and it should be a mere safety-valve in the scheme.

In January 1897 Fitzpatrick's proposals were forwarded to the Government of India. In a note sent to that Government in the following March, at the end of his term of office, Fitzpatrick opposed legislation similar to the Deccan Act, though there was still considerable support for such legislation within the Province.[120] Fitzpatrick was not the man to change his mind in regard to the essentials; but ultimately the Government of India would be dealing not with him but with his successor.

VI

Meanwhile the Government of India had been setting its house in order. In September 1896, after some discussion, it was decided to deal first with the replies from the Punjab, Central Provinces and North-Western Provinces. These were available or were expected in November, while it was anticipated that the replies of other Local Governments would be delayed.[121]

Consideration of the restriction of the power of transfer in North-Western India was unexpectedly delayed, however, by the famine of 1896–7, which posed more pressing problems for the Local Governments and the Government of India.[122]

In the Punjab the impetus given to land transfers by the famine of 1896–7 led to renewed pressure for legislation: first in June 1897 by Thorburn, as Commissioner of the Rawalpindi division; then in November 1897 by his successor, James Wilson, supported by Thorburn from his new vantage point as Financial Commissioner. Mackworth Young, the new Lieutenant-Governor, agreed readily with his Secretaries that there was no point in stirring up the Government of India and that it was impossible to initiate legislation in the Provincial Council before that Government declared its policy.[123] The next move was still the Government of India's.

The delay caused by the famine strengthened Ibbetson's position, for in October 1897 Charles Rivaz entered the Government of India as Member for the Home Department. Nevertheless, the prospects for legislation in North-Western India were unfavourable. Official opinion in the Central Provinces and North-Western Provinces was opposed to substantive restrictions on the right of permanent alienation. Fitzpatrick's proposals were anathema to Ibbetson; and it seemed unlikely that much could be expected from the new Lieutenant-Governor in the Punjab.

In January 1898 Ibbetson finished his note on the replies received from the Punjab, the Central Provinces and the North-Western Provinces. It was a more moderate statement of views than that given in his 1895 memorandum. Then he had been concerned to make restrictions on the power of transfer as complete as possible; now, after reading the correspondence, there was a subtle change in emphasis: a greater concern with making legislation safe and workable.[124]

The prohibition of all forms of mortgage except the self-redeeming usufructuary mortgage had found wide support, save that some strongly favoured the retention of the collateral mortgage as well. To Ibbetson the collateral mortgage was open to the same objections as other forms of mortgage, though perhaps to a lesser degree. It induced the borrower to accept conditions which led eventually to the loss of the usufruct; whereas he would have borrowed less, or not at all, if faced with the immediate prospect of losing the usufruct. Reluctantly Ibbetson agreed to retain the collateral mortgage, which would be enforceable only by conversion to the self-redeeming usufructuary mortgage. If the collateral mortgage was to be permitted, Ibbetson thought, his previous suggestion of giving the mortgagor an occupancy right at a fixed maximum rent had probably better be dropped. The collateral mortgage gave the creditor the security of the land without possession. If he required something more, and possession could not be given, then the value of the security would be enormously reduced; the man who otherwise would mortgage half his land, under the additional restriction would have to mortgage the whole. The position of the agricultural mortgagee, who wanted the land to cultivate, had also to be borne in mind. Ibbetson favoured fifteen years as the term of the self-redeeming usufructuary mortgage. He repeated his suggestion that no lease or mortgage should be valid while a lease or mortgage already existed; but he was inclined to abandon the idea of enforcing an interval between two successive temporary alienations.

The sale conditions in existing mortgages by conditional sale, Ibbetson declared, should be cancelled and these mortgages only enforced as ordinary mortgages with possession. Relief from other existing mortgages, Ibbetson decided reluctantly, could be more safely given by legislation similar to the Deccan Act and confined to the areas in which such measures were most required.

Ibbetson failed to agree with those, like Fitzpatrick, who wanted to prohibit permanent alienations to non-agriculturists alone. That, Ibbetson thought, would probably be as far as it would be wise to go (he now minimised the objections to transfers to agricultural creditors) except that such a restriction could not be enforced, the scope for professional purchasers being too great.

Yet the restriction of permanent alienations, Ibbetson thought, could hardly be absolute, without the possibility of relaxation. Not a single officer advocated such a course. Ibbetson revived his idea of allowing freedom of sale among the original stock of the village or among the near relations of the alienor; and was very much inclined to favour a combination of these two proposals. In the Punjab at least, where the settlement records included genealogical trees, such a scheme would not give rise to too much uncertainty or litigation. An objection was that in the worst villages, where transfer was most common, it would be impossible to find purchasers; but transfers were not confined to such villages. In Ibbetson's eyes the great advantage of the scheme was that the partial freedom of alienation which remained might avert the greatest danger involved in legislation, the growth of the feeling among landowners that their proprietary status had been destroyed. The proposed limitation of the restriction would be in accordance with customary law, which recognised the prior rights of the agnatic group and of the village community; and this was the only general exemption of which this could be said. Freedom of alienation within a limited circle would also place a limit upon sub-division by inheritance which would otherwise lead to the virtual disappearance of an inalienable estate.

Ibbetson was prepared to attach some importance, as he had not done before, to a point stressed by Fitzpatrick. It might be wise to give a general exemption from the restriction on permanent alienation to non-agricultural landowners, whose alienations would be exempted by revenue officers in individual instances almost as a matter of course. Not that this would save much work, for these people were more concerned to acquire than to sell land; but their opposition would be noisiest (though Ibbetson hardly thought such opposition of much significance) and a general exemption from the restriction on the power of sale, while not touching the real reason for their hostility, would leave them little justification for overt opposition.

This raised the old problem of defining either the agriculturist or the money-lender. In practice Ibbetson considered it impossible to specify, as Fitzpatrick had proposed, all the tribes of true agriculturists to whom alone the restrictions would apply. It would be easier to enumerate the non-agricultural tribes, and therefore to specify those to whom the restrictions would not apply. To this there were other objections. There were tribes like the Khatris, Aroras and Brahmins who would be difficult to put on such a list because the tribe contained hereditary agriculturists and landowners; and unwise to exclude from such a list because the tribe was largely or partly composed of money-lenders. Besides, the agricultural tribes might resent the fact that they were deprived of one of the main attributes of proprietorship, while it was left to non-agricultural intruders. This could be overcome by specifying the non-agricultural tribes as those who would not be permitted to purchase from others; but as certain officers had remarked, it would be invidious to stigmatise any class as unfit to acquire land, and any distinction based upon caste would be opposed in England and even in India on theoretical grounds.

An alternative to defining the agriculturist or the money-lender, Ibbetson noted, was to specify the land to which the restrictions would or would not apply. Many had suggested that restrictions on permanent alienations should be confined to ancestral land, but though in harmony with customary law, Ibbetson rejected the suggestion, for it would open the door to evasion and introduce too many complications and uncertainties. Tupper's definition of ancestral land, Ibbetson thought, did not really succeed in applying a different order of restriction to land held by the old village stock and other land; and it would only stimulate litigation. Ibbetson much preferred Anderson's scheme of scheduling the holdings to which the restrictions would apply, thus giving general sanction once and for all to those whose alienations would always be sanctioned as a matter of course. This plan had the enormous advantage over Tupper's that it could be ascertained quickly and with certainty whether a particular piece of land was or was not subject to the restrictions.

Anderson's plan was also much less likely to create jealousy and discontent than a distinction based upon caste or tribe; though the question of whether a particular holding should or should not be scheduled might not always be easy to determine and the distinction would give rise to much heartburning in the case of individuals. In answer to Tupper's and Fitzpatrick's objection that the preparation of the schedules would be an enormous task, Ibbetson modified Anderson's plan by suggesting that schedules be compiled for the small area of land to which restrictions would not apply. This could be done as each district came under settlement. Meanwhile the restrictions would apply to all land not scheduled; and until schedules for a district were ready sanction would have to be obtained by individuals who would not require it after the schedules had been prepared.

In the final analysis Ibbetson was not prepared to make general exemptions in favour of non-agricultural landowners either by specifying the people or the land to which the restrictions would or would not apply. He reverted to his idea of prohibiting permanent alienation except with the sanction of the revenue authorities. Previously, preoccupied with the desire to make legislation as effective as possible, he had stressed the checks which this would impose on attempted evasions, while also indicating that it would allow beneficial alienations. Now he was more impressed by the necessity to remove restrictions in cases in which they were unnecessary. A transfer from one agriculturist to another was less objectionable than from an agriculturist to a money-lender; a transfer from one money-lender to another was not objectionable at all. There were tribes mentioned in the Punjab correspondence, such as the Jat Sikhs of Ferozepur mentioned by Francis or the Pathans described by Merk, in the case of which it might be politically or economically unwise to interfere. There were always individual cases in which the circumstances were exceptional, and which had to be provided for in any scheme lest it cause infinite harm and discontent. The work involved in giving sanction, Ibbetson thought, would not be overwhelming; and the discretion which Rivaz proposed to give to subordinate officials, in large classes of cases in which transfer was ordinarily unobjectionable, would reduce the pressure on their superiors. With proper rules and periodical returns, subordinate officials might be entrusted with the power of sanction, Fitzpatrick's objection notwithstanding. Nor would the discretion allowed result in much uncertainty. As the policy of Government became defined and understood, uncertainty would rapidly diminish. Besides, un-

## EXTENDING THE CONFLICT

certainty antecedent to transfer, though undesirable, did little harm. The great advantage of the proposal was that it treated all alike, so that there was no room for jealousy and heartburning. The people would readily appreciate the distinction by which an agriculturist wanting to sell to a money-lender had to obtain the sanction of the district officer, while a subordinate official could allow a money-lender to sell to an agriculturist.

Ibbetson was not content to re-state his own views. He had to bear in mind the sort of legislation that was likely to be considered acceptable. In the Central Provinces and in the North-Western Provinces, Ibbetson did not consider it possible to override the opposition of the Chief Commissioner and Lieutenant-Governor to restrictions on the power of sale. They had arrived at conclusions based upon a deliberate and reasonable weighing of the benefits and admitted dangers of restriction. They were supported, in the Central Provinces by an almost unanimous, and in the North-Western Provinces by a weighty body of official opinion. The Secretary of State would never permit their views to be overridden. It was better to accept such restrictions and such legislation as the Lieutenant-Governor and Chief Commissioner were ready to impose. In the Punjab, however, official opinion in favour of restrictions on permanent alienation appeared to be very strong; and Fitzpatrick had not opposed such restrictions outright, but had sought merely to limit them in ways which, it could be easily demonstrated, verged on the absurd.

There could be little objection, Ibbetson thought, to excluding, say the Delhi division, from the more severe restrictions, if that was considered desirable; but to pick out isolated tracts, as Fitzpatrick proposed, would be fatal. Ibbetson agreed with Rivaz that it was tantamount to shutting the stable door after the steed had been stolen. Besides, how long would it take to examine the whole Punjab? Would successive Lieutenant-Governors decide on the results for tract after tract? What facts would be strong enough to justify legislation if Thorburn's were not? What would happen to the landowners in a tract in which an enquiry was started? This was not the worst. There were the dangers anticipated by Silcock and Rivaz. The greatest danger in the Punjab – the feeling among the people that they were being deprived of their status as landowners – was not likely to be entirely absent under any circumstances; but if restrictions were to apply only to isolated tracts, the resentment among those subject to them would be intense. General measures, while they would restrict credit to a healthy degree, would not raise the rate of interest; local measures would certainly do so by weakening the competitive position of individuals subject to the restrictions. In tracts unaffected by the restrictions the effect upon credit would be hardly less injurious, for it would be known that at any time restrictions might be, and at some time which was wholly uncertain probably would be extended. Capital would tend to leave a tract in which restrictions existed. It would flow into tracts unaffected by legislation and there increase the competition for land, which might be good for a while for these tracts, but certainly not in the long run. Fitzpatrick's scheme would bring many of the disadvantages and none of the advantages of legislation.

To circumvent Fitzpatrick's proposals, Ibbetson suggested that the scheme proposed by the Financial Commissioners, Rivaz and Tupper, was suitable. Ibbetson proposed, following Chatterji's suggestion, that the new restrictions be substituted for the existing restrictions imposed by customary law. Permanent alienations would be prohibited except by official sanction. Since this prohibition was based on the ground that popular feeling only recognised the proprietor's interest as a life interest it seemed difficult to ignore the life-term in fixing the maximum term for the self-redeeming usufructuary mortgage. Besides, as Fitzpatrick and others had pointed out, it was difficult to prevent a man from doing what he wished with his land during his lifetime. To overcome the difficulty that the life-term was so uncertain a security, the mortgagor would also be able to alienate, with the consent of the heirs, for a fixed term not exceeding fifteen years.

To thus set aside the Lieutenant-Governor's scheme in favour of that of his Financial Commissioners was a desperate move, considering that Mackworth Young was now Lieutenant-Governor of the Punjab; and Ibbetson did not expect much result. He proposed that Young be asked whether he was prepared to accept these proposals and, if not, what other measures he would adopt. Rather than call for further opinions, he should be advised to discuss the matter verbally with a few selected officers.

Rivaz, the Home Member, agreed with Ibbetson that it would be impossible to impose restrictions on permanent alienations in the North-Western Provinces and Central Provinces. For the Punjab Rivaz accepted Ibbetson's modifications of his own scheme and strongly supported Ibbetson's proposal to address the Punjab Government.[125] John Woodburn, the Revenue Member, was in charge of the question; and his whole approach was superficial. He was not opposed to the restriction of the power of transfer where political danger threatened; but he was ready to seize on any indication that the situation was improving or that action was not required. He had served in the North-Western Provinces and Central Provinces, thought nothing serious was required there, and agreed that the Local Governments of these Provinces could not be coerced. Woodburn had no Punjab experience; his careless examination of the Punjab correspondence did not bring to light too much evidence of a tolerable situation; there were authorities like Ibbetson and Rivaz in the Government of India to support strong measures; and the easiest way out of a difficult question seemed to be to accept Ibbetson's final proposals. Woodburn had taken little trouble to understand Ibbetson's views; he was opposed to schemes involving the grant of official sanction, and concluded that Ibbetson had rejected the Financial Commissioners' scheme and accepted a scheme proposed by Chatterji! Woodburn adopted only that part of Ibbetson's final proposal which related to temporary transfers. All alienations, he explained, would be forbidden except alienations for life, or, with the consent of the heirs, for a maximum of fifteen years.[126] Elgin accepted Woodburn's conclusions as a matter of course; and Council approved the reference to the Punjab Government.[127] In March 1898 that Government was addressed as Ibbetson had suggested; but it was Woodburn's proposals for general legislation which were submitted for further consideration.[128]

Ibbetson, who had been away on leave, returned after Woodburn had left the Government of India. Ibbetson feared that the objectionable scheme proposed by Woodburn would strengthen Mackworth Young's hand in refusing to take action; and in May 1898 he prevailed on Rivaz and Elgin to send a telegram to the Punjab Government suspending consideration of the question until the arrival of an amended letter indicating that it was proposed to allow permanent alienations with official sanction.[129] It was in this rather undignified, one might almost say comic fashion, that the conflict between Ibbetson and Fitzpatrick came to an end.

VII

The struggle which Ibbetson and Fitzpatrick had waged had deep roots in trends of very general extent. In the Punjab, Fitzpatrick had assumed office at a time when the signs of a rising tide of opinion were unmistakable. Lyall had opened the flood gates by his enquiry of 1888–9. That enquiry had filled the advocates of legislation with hope and anticipation; it had committed officers who had not sought legislation themselves to judicial reform; and it had stimulated the development of opinion among a larger number of officers. Fitzpatrick's move towards legislation can be understood only with reference to this legacy; for Fitzpatrick was not prone to act on sudden impulse, and not inclined to pay much attention to the views of others. Provincial opinion wore him down; though he may have had some inkling of developments within the Government of India as well.

Given a restive Province, Fitzpatrick's particular contribution to the debate was of considerable moment. Local officers could do little more than hound the Lieutenant-Governor; they could not set the machinery moving in any direction in which Fitzpatrick did not want it to go. In 1894–5 a Lieutenant-Governor still had considerable room for manoeuvre. With the Government of India's intervention, it is true, it would have become difficult to deny or ignore the existence of any problem. Even then, however, a Lieutenant-Governor's potential choice in regard to remedies was a wide one. The question of differential assessments was very much to the fore. Legislation along the lines of the Deccan Act was not only favoured by many sections of Provincial opinion, it was also one of the questions which the Government of India had asked the Lieutenant-Governor to consider. If Fitzpatrick had been prepared to support either judicial or revenue reform, the question of restricting the power of alienation could have been deprived of its importance. With a Lieutenant-Governor deprecating such restriction, far more opposition to such a measure could have been anticipated from one wing of official opinion. Ibbetson's position would have been rendered infinitely more difficult.

But if Fitzpatrick was to move at all, he could move only in the direction of legislation to restrict the power of alienation. And if he did move, he could move only a very little way. This attitude, it is arguable, did more to advance the interests of those who wanted a general restriction of the power of alienation than even simple support of such general legislation would have done. For if it had become clear that such legislation was contemplated, it would have resulted, in all probability, in a polarisation of opinion, with a number of officers strongly denying the necessity for any such action in the Province or in the parts with which they were acquainted. Instead Fitzpatrick, by supporting the principle of legislation but denying the substance, not only helped to silence this wing of official opinion, but did much to ruin the case for enabling legislation from the very outset.

Fitzpatrick's failure was due in no small measure to personal factors. His mind functioned essentially at an abstract level, taking little account of facts or opinions which did not fit in with his own inflexible views. While accepting the possibility of political danger, he insisted that such danger be demonstrated in the most precise and rigorous fashion. This led him to take a view of the political question which made sense to himself, but to no one else. It had never been claimed that land transfer posed an *immediate* political problem to the British in any part of the Punjab, let alone in very small, scattered tracts. Yet in effect this is the problem Fitzpatrick proposed to solve. That he was not only out of touch with official but also with social realities is apparent when it is recalled that he took up the general question as a result of agricultural unrest in the Jhelum district; a district in which alienations were so limited by Provincial standards that Fitzpatrick could not possibly have admitted that any political danger existed there.

The same tendency to abstract and logical thought which induced Fitzpatrick to formulate his own version of the political problem led him to champion the restriction of the power of alienation. He saw that if one was determined to stop altogether the transfer of land from the hands of one party to those of another, only a direct order to that effect would be of any use. And this conclusion was reinforced by a commitment to certain *laissez-faire* arguments which made all indirect legislation not merely useless but dangerous. In itself this was an attitude which was common enough; and its importance is apparent from the fact that not only a number of Punjab officers, but also Edward Buck, had argued in this fashion. The orthodox intellectual tradition was so pervasive that not even the advocates of the restriction of the power of alienation could always escape its influence; some of them probably taking up *laissez-faire* arguments regarding indirect legislation precisely because it appeared to strengthen the case for direct legislation (just as some used arguments regarding the danger to agricultural credit to combat enabling legislation). As far as Fitzpatrick was concerned, the stress on *laissez-faire* principles revealed a doctrinaire approach to affairs, a conclusion which may not seem to fit in with Fitzpatrick's readiness to restrict the power of alienation. But in effect Fitzpatrick gave great weight to doctrinaire opposition to the restriction of the power of transfer; for when he applied his abstract conclusions to the world of affairs, his excessive prudence took over. His was the mentality of the brilliant secretary, whose ability to cut down other men's proposals was second to none, but who could not formulate effective proposals of his own. From this point of view Fitzpatrick had been horribly miscast.

Fitzpatrick did not appreciate, of course, the role which he was designed to play; for he had his own vision of his role. It was that of the bold and practical statesman, prepared to set doctrinaire considerations aside in the event of great danger, but sound all the same, and in touch with political realities. That this turned out to be the wildest of political miscalculations was due not only to Fitzpatrick's limitations, but also to the changes which had brought Ibbetson into the Government of India. Fitzpatrick might well have emerged as a courageous statesman, had it not been for the change which had come over the Government of India.

Developments within the Government of India were themselves a reflection of movements of opinion in a number of Indian Provinces. These movements were manifested in the representations received from a number of Local Governments, most notably Bombay, the Central Provinces and the Punjab. Within the Government of India these movements found spokesmen in such influential figures as Buck, Crosthwaite, MacDonnell, Mackenzie, Ibbetson, and Rivaz; representing experience and opinion in the North-Western Provinces, Central Provinces and the Punjab. Successive Viceroys, Lansdowne, Elgin, and later Curzon, were carried along by these trends, and did not a little to ensure their success. The doubtful elements in the Government of India were won over or put on the defensive. It was these general trends which now exerted a decisive influence on the debate in the Punjab. In a sense that debate had always been part of a much larger story; but with the Government of India suggesting legislation, and the Lieutenant-Governor a confirmed opponent of the Deccan Act, outside influences were at work with a vengeance.

With the Government of India involved, it is desirable to consider the degree to which new intellectual and legislative tendencies in Britain were influencing the course of events in India in the 1890s. Clearly, in so far as that matter relates to the development of opinion in Provinces other than the Punjab, it is not possible to appraise it here. That is a subject for separate studies, and will involve detailed analysis of opinion over long periods of time. As regards the Government of India and Punjab opinion, however, some comments are in order. The informative note on land transfer and indebtedness which was prepared in the Revenue Department in 1895 by a Punjab officer consisted of some two hundred and forty pages, of which less than two full pages were devoted to the question of similar problems in foreign countries, only part of that relating to Britain.[130] As an example of the amount of attention devoted to British parallels, this was fairly typical of Punjab opinion; that is, in those instances where Punjab officers were aware of these parallels at all.[131] Fitzpatrick could see only opposition on economic grounds emanating from outsiders in England; though this attitude may be due as much to a desire to take all possible opposition into account as to ignorance. If British parallels were ignored or not considered highly relevant by Punjab officers, it is arguable that the Viceroys could have hardly escaped the influence of new intellectual trends at home. This may be so, and it may help to explain their readiness to go along with trends running counter to political economy. Nevertheless, all the evidence indicates that Lansdowne and Elgin were not only swept along by Indian trends, but that they themselves were duly impressed by the political danger which appeared to threaten in India, and that they saw the whole question purely in terms of Indian policy. The influence of Indian society on the Viceroys might be only indirect, but its importance should not be underrated.

A stress on the general influences which set the Government of India moving must be balanced by due appreciation of the contributions of individuals. Here we are concerned more especially with Denzil Ibbetson, who was certainly no mere creature of circumstance. To the question of land transfer he brought the passion of personal conviction, a sense of dedication and sheer hard work. His memorandum of 1895 revealed perhaps the most painstaking and the most coherent philosophy ever devised regarding restrictions on alienation. Ibbetson's intellect was both powerful and deliberative; weighing one consideration against another, seeing all the advantages and disadvantages of various proposals, but in the end not uncertain as to where the balance of the argument lay. Distinctly in favour of the most far-reaching restrictions on the power of alienation, he appreciated the great practical difficulties which such proposals involved, and the need for care and discrimination in the application of restrictions to particular areas. Ibbetson had been chosen to play a role which he could play to perfection.

The results which flowed from Ibbetson's efforts were not slight. That he won the confidence of the Viceroy and of successive superiors in the Revenue Department was of some importance; for they swung the Council in Ibbetson's favour. In consequence Ibbetson's voice became the voice of the Government of India in this matter of land alienation; Woodburn's departure from Ibbetson's scheme being something of an anomaly reflecting the inescapable, formal ladder of authority. Ibbetson transformed the whole question of the restriction of the power of alienation. He gave it shape and substance; and the boldest proposals of earlier years did not cut much of a figure when set against Ibbetson's proposals. MacDonnell was no doubt responsible; but a lesser man than Ibbetson, one less energetic, committed or flexible, would not have made the same use of his opportunities.

Ibbetson obtained the backing of the Government of India; but that did not mean Ibbetson's wishes would prevail. It has been suggested in a recent and rather incomplete account of the Government of India background to the Punjab Alienation of Land Bill, that a number of individuals within that Government and 'especially Ibbetson' not only made most of the decisions concerning the scope of legislation, but 'dictated revenue practice for all of British India'.[132] As a conclusion to an impressionistic sketch which is, unfortunately, often inaccurate in its account of the facts, this may have some merit in reducing the somewhat disproportionate roles which Viceroys and Secretaries of State for India have played in accounts of British policy. But it goes altogether too far; as do the statements that in the alienation discussion 'the opinion of the Viceroy counted for little', and that the Council and the Secretaries 'often ruled India'.[133] This is simply to transfer absolute importance from one element in British administration to another; what is required in the study of policy is examination of the whole official hierarchy, from the district officer to the Secretary of State for India. It is also unwise to generalise so widely on the basis of the alienation discussion; for Ibbetson's role in that discussion derived not so much from his position as Secretary, as from his personal qualities and his absolute and unchallenged mastery of a particular question. Ibbetson was obviously a rather exceptional Secretary; it does not seem likely that men of his calibre were to be found in that position as a rule. And besides, the Secretary's position was at best one of influence, not power. Ibbetson's predecessor, Edward Buck, also a remarkable figure, had been frustrated for years before his views on rural indebtedness made headway within the Government of India. Ibbetson was influential enough; but far from being able to dictate to British India, he realised full well that while the Government of India might exert great influence, it could not impose novel and drastic schemes on unwilling Provinces.

Ibbetson had failed to achieve even simultaneous consideration of the question in all the Provinces, as Buck had wished. Such a procedure might have strengthened the hands of the Government of India in dealing with particular Local Governments. But the disintegration of the all-India question into its Provincial components was not the main reason for Ibbetson's inability to bring particular Provinces round. General trends favouring some action to deal with rural indebtedness had enabled Ibbetson to make his mark; and if those trends did not prove to be sufficiently strong to favour the most drastic legislation, as they were not, apparently, in the North-Western Provinces and Central Provinces, then Ibbetson could not carry the day. In regard to the Punjab, however, both general and particular considerations provided Ibbetson with an opening. Fitzpatrick had played completely into Ibbetson's hands by committing himself and many of the more doubtful elements in the Punjab to legislation to restrict the power of transfer. With another Punjab officer in the Government of India to support legislation, and with Fitzpatrick no longer Lieutenant-Governor, Ibbetson saw his opportunity to press for general measures entirely unacceptable to Fitzpatrick.

To recognise that it was by this rather narrow margin that the basis was laid for legislation which would become the core and symbol of the new political tradition in the Punjab, is not to disparage the role of underlying social influences in that Province. The dynamic character of those influences, and the trends to which they gave rise, were maintained after as well as before 1891; and without them there would have been no question of legislation at all. In one respect, too, the analysis of general tendencies can be carried a step further with reference to the 1890s. It has been suggested that the old political tradition was not only a starting point for the development of the new, but that the well-nigh universal attachment to the old tradition prevented the opponents of legislation from framing an effective reply in political terms. In similar fashion in the 1890s it was the old as well as the new political tradition which prevented official opinion from appreciating anywhere near fully one of the most potent political arguments against legislation. Much of the debate about the political risks involved in legislation turned on the question of the possibly hostile reactions of the landowners. In regard to a measure which was designed to restrict seriously the rights and privileges of non-agriculturists, the reactions that might be expected from them received less attention than anything else. Fitzpatrick took the opposition of the money-lenders into account, it is true; but only as one more argument against any schemes other than his own. Most of the officers who discussed the probable reaction of the money-lending classes were committed to general legislation. Ibbetson was among those prone to dismiss the opposition of non-agriculturists as of no account; for in spite of the fact that Ibbetson foresaw political problems of a new kind, he proposed to meet them by securing the loyalty of the countryside. One senses here the Achilles' heel of the Punjab political tradition.

Early in 1898 the development of that tradition was still in the balance. With the Government of India recommending legislation to the Lieutenant-Governor, the scales had tipped heavily in favour of the new political tradition; but no one could foresee the outcome. In particular the form which any legislation to restrict the power of voluntary transfer would take was by no means predictable. On paper Ibbetson had defeated Fitzpatrick by securing the Government of India's assent to two major and controversial propositions, namely that legislation should be general and not enabling, and that legislation should restrict the power of alienation rather than the power to alienate to non-agriculturists. But this was to put the inherent possibilities at their highest. The Punjab Government was hostile, and Punjab opinion divided in many respects. Punjab officers in favour of restrictions on alienation approached this question from several points of view; schemes for such restrictions were various, based on different principles and stressing different expedients; and the bearing of legislation on agricultural credit was one which caused much concern. Then there was the attitude of the India Office to consider. The roles of Ibbetson and Fitzpatrick had not been played out completely. But Charles Rivaz and Mackworth Young were to be the protagonists in what followed.

CHAPTER V

# The Shape of Legislation

I

Mackworth Young had not changed his views, and the despatch of March 1898 placed him in a difficult position. In April he nominated a mixed committee of British and Indian officers and non-officials; but soon decided that it would be necessary to get written replies to some leading questions before meeting in committee.[1] In May he resisted most of the suggestions of his Secretary, W. R. H. Merk, to establish a case against legislation.[2] Though there was some indication in mid-June that Young might not assemble a committee after all,[3] his behaviour suggested an unwillingness to take a completely obstructive line to the Government of India proposals.

Finally on June 22, 1898, Young nominated a small committee of British revenue officers.[4] He later explained that he had not packed his jury, but had chosen the best officers available.[5] Nonetheless, the composition of the committee gave some indication of Young's attitude. None of the confirmed opponents of drastic legislation was included; though apparently Young had intended to include Charles Roe, who had just retired.[6] With the exception of L. W. Dane, the officers chosen had expressed their opinion already on the questions circulated. Out of eight officers three, J. M. Douie, J. A. L. Montgomery and G. C. Walker, favoured the tentative extension of severe restrictions on the power of alienation to a limited number of districts; while S. S. Thorburn, R. Clarke, J. R. Dunlop-Smith and C. L. Tupper could be expected to press for general legislation, though in most cases not for more than restrictions on alienations to non-agriculturists.[7]

The committee met on 1st and 2nd July 1898. The first question on Young's agenda was whether there was a case for general treatment all over the Province or for special measures in certain localities. Tupper explained the scheme which he and Rivaz had put forward in 1896 by which alienations all over the Province would require official sanction; sanction being made easy in districts where no

247

restrictions were required. The committee rejected the scheme. It was recognised that Tupper's scheme, while nominally one for general legislation, was practically an enabling scheme; and it was probably thought that it involved all the risks of the former while only conferring the benefits of the latter. The committee also thought, in common with Fitzpatrick, that there were grave objections to investing subordinate revenue officers with power to refuse sanction; a disadvantage which Tupper admitted and which his scheme could not avoid.

After further discussion the committee agreed that there was a case for general measures; and they proposed to explore the possibilities of agreement on such measures before considering whether there was a case for special measures in certain localities. Thorburn proposed that the law of pre-emption be amended in certain respects; a proposal which the committee accepted. It was resolved to declare all mortgages by conditional sale illegal for the future. Tupper, Dunlop-Smith, Douie and Montgomery had been opposed to legislation curtailing the term of existing mortgages; and this probably explains why no such proposals were made. Only Tupper and Dunlop-Smith had been opposed to declaring conditions of sale in existing mortgages null and void; and this proposal was carried, with their dissent. The discussion of the forms of temporary transfer to be permitted roused considerable controversy; and a sub-committee consisting of Thorburn, Tupper, Douie and Walker was constituted to consider the matter.

The committee resolved that it would not put the question of differential assessment before the Government of India on the present occasion. Thorburn and Montgomery were advocates of such assessments, and Thorburn had been itching to revive the question on its own merits.[8] Not long before Louis Dane had expressed his preference for differential assessments, which he thought were less likely to rouse discontent among the leading agriculturists than the prohibition of alienation save with the sanction of Government. In the case of the most indebted tracts in the Province, he had pointed out, even the latter policy would be better than nothing.[9] It was doubtless in this spirit that he submerged his personal views.

Douie, Walker and Montgomery had political, economic and administrative objections to general legislation. Douie thought that restrictions on alienation might cause discontent among the peasantry if legislation were made general at once. Walker admitted that general legislation would inhibit litigation and would be less invidious and rouse less discontent among the peasantry; but still preferred enabling legislation, thinking that the restrictions on alienation would become increasingly unpopular among landowners as the effect on credit and the value of land became evident. Like Douie he feared to offend the Sikh and Hindu Jats of the central districts, who were politically influential, and who might object to the imposition of restrictions on their power to acquire land. He also anticipated serious opposition from the trading classes. Political difficulties, he thought, would probably make it impossible to maintain a general measure. Montgomery, Douie and Walker expected a great unsettlement of credit wherever the restrictions were imposed, and consequent strain on the administration, which would find it more difficult to collect revenue and essential to advance money. They thought the risks of general legislation too great; and preferred experimental measures which could be extended as experience was gained.

The advocates of general legislation were less impressed by the risks. Clarke saw no political danger. Thorburn believed that the peasant masses would approve of restrictions. Dunlop-Smith and Tupper did not share Thorburn's optimism; but they did not expect strong opposition from the peasantry. Like Thorburn they expected more opposition from the trading classes than from the landowners; but such opposition they did not rate highly. The advocates of general legislation expected the restriction of credit to be beneficial rather than the reverse; and Tupper had stressed the old argument that general, as opposed to enabling, legislation would not destroy agricultural borrowing powers to any injurious degree. Dunlop-Smith and Tupper expected increased work for the administration; but not on the same scale as did those who favoured enabling legislation.

There were certain considerations which narrowed the gap between the advocates of general and enabling legislation. As Financial Commissioner Thorburn had gained personal experience, for almost the first time, of the south-eastern and central Punjab; and he had been surprised to find Hindu and Sikh Jats holding their own against non-agriculturists. Where this was the case Thorburn was probably prepared to exempt whole districts or tracts from the restrictions.[10] Tupper had been prepared to make the grant of sanction easy in parts of the Province where restrictions were not really required and where injudicious application of the restrictions might cause discontent among the landowners. Once the committee rejected his own scheme Tupper may not have been opposed to the exemption of such areas from the law. Dunlop-Smith had conceded that the frontier might be exempted, as he had no experience of that part of the Province. Clarke had favoured no geographical exemptions.

At some stage in the discussion which cannot be pinpointed, a compromise was reached which was distinctly favourable to the supporters of general legislation. It was resolved that whatever enactment was drafted should contain a provision empowering the Local Government to exempt any district or any part of a district from the operation of any of the provisions of the Act.

There was a serious difference of opinion on whether restrictions on mortgages should apply universally or only when made to non-agriculturists. Douie and Montgomery had advocated the former course; and Walker probably agreed. Tupper's position is difficult to gauge.[11] Thorburn, Clarke, Dunlop-Smith and Dane were disposed to permit the free circulation of land among agriculturists. Thorburn may not have been strongly opposed to making mortgage restrictions universal. In 1896 he had considered that possibility without arriving at any final conclusion.[12]

The result of the discussion was a compromise favourable to those who had given way on the question of enabling legislation. The restrictions on temporary alienation which the committee accepted were of universal application, save that the Local Government was empowered to relax them in any district or part of a district or between any persons or classes of persons. The committee accepted the self-redeeming usufructuary mortgage originally proposed by Ibbetson as one permissible form of mortgage. At least five members of the committee were opposed to the suggestion that the validity of such transfers should depend on the consent of the heirs; among them Thorburn who had pointed to the delays, uncertainties and litigation to which such a provision would lead. This provision was accordingly cut out. The committee also dispensed with the life-term for the self-redeeming usufructuary mortgage proposed by Ibbetson; and extended the maximum term for such mortgages from fifteen to twenty years, a suggestion which probably originated with Tupper. The addition of a provision rendering null and void conditions in such mortgages which imposed special obligations on the mortgagor, or restricted the right of redemption during the currency of the alienation, may probably be attributed to Thorburn, who had made a special study of such mortgage conditions in his 1896 enquiry. The only other form of mortgage accepted by the committee as permissible was the collateral mortgage which could be enforced against the land only by conversion into the self-redeeming usufructuary mortgage. Certain conditions were added designed to ensure that on

## THE SHAPE OF LEGISLATION

such conversion the mortgagee obtained possession only for such part of the maximum twenty years as appeared equitable. Leases were permitted for the life of the lessor or for twenty years, whichever was less.

While the restrictions on mortgage proposed by the committee were more or less in accordance with the spirit of Ibbetson's proposals, the restrictions that the committee resolved to impose on permanent alienation were more in accord with Fitzpatrick's views. The committee decided that permanent alienation of land to a non-agriculturist without the sanction of the Collector should be void.

The decision was hardly surprising. Thorburn, Clarke, Dunlop-Smith and Dane were not in favour of restricting transfers to agriculturists. To Tupper, the chief, though not the only threat, to political stability lay in acquisitions by the trading classes. Before the conference Walker, Douie and Montgomery had committed themselves to a scheme similar to that favoured by Ibbetson by which permanent alienations without official sanction would be confined to the agnatic relatives of the alienor and to co-sharers of agricultural stock in the village. Their adherence to this scheme, perhaps influenced by a desire not to depart too far from the Government of India's proposal to impose absolute restrictions on the power of permanent alienation, was probably soon broken. In discussing differential assessment in 1894 Montgomery had not hesitated to recommend measures which would stimulate transfers to agriculturists.[13] Douie had opposed Ibbetson's scheme in 1895 on the ground that it would arouse the discontent of the politically significant Sikh and Hindu Jats who wanted to buy land; that it would interfere with the economically beneficial acquisitions of thrifty tribes (of which Douie had experience as Settlement Officer of Umballa); and that it might unduly depreciate the value of land.[14] The committee can hardly have missed the point that by permitting transfers to agriculturists the dangers of agricultural dissatisfaction and unsettlement of credit would be minimised;[15] and these were the dangers which had led Walker, Douie, and Montgomery to propose enabling measures. Once these officers accepted general legislation, they might well be ready to minimise the dangers involved by permitting permanent transfers to agriculturists.

The decision to prohibit permanent alienations to non-agriculturists alone, raised the old problem of defining either the landowner or the money-lender. The committee resolved that the Local Government would have the power to declare for any district or part of a district what classes of persons were non-agriculturists. Until such a declaration was made all 'new agriculturists' as defined in the Land Revenue Act (those who were neither in their own names nor in those of their agnate ancestors recorded as owners of land or as hereditary tenants in any estate at the first regular settlement) would be deemed to be non-agriculturists. This latter definition was of course imperfect; for in some districts traders owned considerable areas of land at regular settlement, and permanent alienation to them, therefore, would be permissible. The alternative proposal, originating with Douie and accepted by Fitzpatrick, to specify the agricultural tribes which would not be able to alienate permanently to others, had been approved before the meeting of the committee by several of its members; but found no place in the resolutions of the committee.

The decision to make the restrictions on temporary transfers of universal application, and the decision to define the non-agriculturists instead of specifying the landowners, meant that all the restrictions would apply to landowners of the trading class. Before the committee met at least six of its members had agreed that restrictions should be imposed only on agricultural landowners; and no doubt it was thought that the Local Government's power to exempt classes of persons from the restrictions, added to the Collector's power to sanction sales in individual instances, was sufficient. In this respect the committee's scheme represented a half-way house between the views of Ibbetson and Fitzpatrick.

Before the committee met, most of its members had expressed their opinion that restrictions should apply only to ancestral land or to that and land acquired after the passing of the Act. They were soon driven to the same conclusion as Ibbetson, namely, that such distinctions could lead only to confusion; and they resolved that restrictions should apply to all agricultural and pastoral land.

To prevent evasion of their restrictions, the committee decided that the hypothecation of a share of the produce of land should be prohibited for any term exceeding a year, and that the person in whose favour the hypothecation was made was legally responsible for the payment of a proportional share of the land-revenue.

The committee resolved, Tupper dissenting, that no alteration was required in the law and rules under which land was sold in execution of decree.

There can be little doubt that the findings of the committee influenced Young's policy. The unanimous decision of its members to support general legislation, tempered by the power of exemption, after the Government of India had rejected Fitzpatrick's enabling legislation, made it very difficult for Young to frame enabling proposals. Instead Young seized on the committee's proposals as a more limited restriction on the power of alienation than that proposed by the Government of India; and one which would work less economic harm and consequently cause less discontent. After the committee had concluded its deliberations Young obtained the assent of its members to the proposition that it was not desirable or safe to adopt any more stringent measures. In his note on the committee's proposals Young made it clear that he was personally opposed to legislation; but that if the Government of India were determined to adopt general and stringent measures he supported the committee's proposals as the maximum restrictions on alienation permissible.[16]

In the meantime the Government of India, with Rivaz as Member for the Home and Revenue Departments, had been clearing the ground. On the basis of certain statistics for western India, which seemed to show that the Deccan Act had not checked alienations, it was decided to abandon the extension of such legislation to other parts of India. Rivaz was influenced by the consideration that certain proposed amendments of the Indian Contract Act (the outcome of the proposals initiated by Hutchins in the early 1890s) would enable courts to go behind bonds in cases where undue influence had been exercised; that some exemption of land from attachment and sale in execution of decree was contemplated; and that the imposition of some restrictions on voluntary alienations in Northern India at least seemed probable. Rivaz was primarily concerned to restrict the power of transfer in the Punjab; and he postponed consideration of such action in other Provinces until the matter had been settled in the Punjab.[17]

The Punjab committee's proposals, though only half-heartedly supported by Young, gave Rivaz the opportunity to press for restrictions on voluntary alienation which were more in accord with his own ideas.[18]

The committee's decision in favour of general legislation suited Rivaz well enough, and he took care to add that the power of exemption given to the Local Government should be subject to the sanction of the Government of India, as otherwise a Lieutenant-Governor like Young might nullify the whole measure.

Since August 1889 Rivaz had taken a stand against class legislation, favouring measures which would check the transfer of land to all who acquired it merely as a commercial speculation.

From this point of view the committee's proposed restrictions on temporary alienation were satisfactory; and Rivaz accepted them, save that he reduced the maximum period for such alienations to fifteen years. He added the provision that no fresh temporary alienation could be entered into during the currency of the original alienation; but he saw no safe way of preventing successive temporary transfers.

Rivaz accepted the committee's proposal that, apart from striking out the conditional sale clause in mortgages by conditional sale, existing mortgages should be left untouched. Nevertheless, he may have contemplated further interference with existing mortgages by conditional sale.

The committee's proposal to prohibit permanent alienations to non-agriculturists found no favour with Rivaz. He reverted to the proposal which he had made as Financial Commissioner in 1896; a proposal which the committee had rejected, at least in the form given to it by Tupper. All permanent alienations of land, Rivaz explained, would be subject to official sanction. There was only one exemption which he now urged, perhaps at the instance of Ibbetson, now Chief Commissioner of the Central Provinces, with whom Rivaz had been in touch.[19] At any rate, Rivaz adopted a modified form of the suggestion which Ibbetson had made in 1898 for allowing freedom of sale to the near relations of the alienor and to the original stock of the village. Permanent alienations would be permitted without official sanction, subject only to the law of pre-emption, when made to any descendant in the male line from the common ancestor of the alienor and the alienee; and to any agriculturist who held land as an owner or hereditary tenant in the village where the land permanently alienated was situated. In defence of his scheme Rivaz not only repeated Ibbetson's argument about the scope which would be given to professional purchasers under the committee's proposal, but indicated that it was desirable to prevent the agriculturist, often as much a Shylock as the professional moneylender, from buying up land in a village where he constituted a foreign element in the village community.

Under Rivaz's scheme the necessity for defining the non-agriculturist disappeared, but it became necessary to define the agriculturist, so as to exclude from this category those who did not belong to the original stock of the village. Rivaz simply reversed the committee's proposal. The agriculturist would be the 'old agriculturist' of the Land Revenue Act, i.e. any person who either in his own name, or in the names of his agnate ancestors, was recorded as an owner of land or as a hereditary tenant in any estate at the first regular settlement. As before, the Local Government could alter the definition for any locality, but only with the consent of the Government of India. Rivaz must have realised that in some places his definition of agriculturist would include some traders.

Rivaz agreed with the committee that restrictions should be applied to all agricultural and pastoral land; that the hypothecation of crops should be limited; and the law of pre-emption amended. The sale of land in execution of decree he proposed to abolish entirely, instead of continuing the existing Punjab system.

Elgin could hardly grasp the differences between the various proposals for restricting the power of transfer; he placed the same trust in Rivaz as he had placed in Ibbetson; and now that legislation in his time was out of the question, his main concern was that his Viceroyalty should be marked by an important despatch on land reform. Accordingly, Elgin accepted Rivaz's proposals and made it clear that he hoped Council Members would agree.[20]

The Members of Council showed no inclination to oppose Rivaz's views. Indeed, two of them were very favourable to legislation. Only one Member preferred an enabling Act; but he did not press the matter. Three Members looked on the measure as a means of checking transfers to money-lenders; but they did not challenge the restriction of transfers to agriculturists. A. C. Trevor still held much the same views on the question as in 1895, when he had tried to postpone consideration of Ibbetson's proposals. This time he did not allow his personal views to affect the general action proposed. On one point he was insistent. It would be much better, he thought, if all permanent transfers were subject to official sanction; as otherwise much confusion and litigation might result.[21]

This suggestion undermined one of the main advantages which Ibbetson had seen in permitting unrestricted permanent alienation within a limited circle, viz. that it would show the landowners that their proprietary status had not been destroyed. Rivaz, on the other hand, had always thought of official sanction as the key to any scheme for restricting alienation, and he did not object to Trevor's suggestion. In the despatch to the Secretary of State of November 1898, in which Rivaz's proposals were outlined for approval, a paragraph was inserted by the Revenue Secretary to meet Trevor's views. All permanent alienations made without official sanction would be void; no document purporting to transfer land permanently would be submitted to registration without a certificate of sanction; when the transferee was an 'agriculturist' holding land in the village or descended in the male line from the same ancestor as the alienor, sanction would be given as a matter of right; in other cases sanction would be at the discretion of the revenue officer, guided by executive instructions. It was indicated, however, that it had not been finally decided to accept the proposal.[22]

In London Rivaz's proposals were the subject of considerable controversy among the Members of the India Council. Fitzpatrick led the attack demanding that the measure be an enabling one, as he had originally proposed, and for the reasons which he had given. Apart from other objections he thought that opposition to general legislation would be much greater than opposition to enabling legislation. In particular he predicted that a general law would give a great opportunity to agitators, money-lenders, pleaders and so on and that these people would try to convince the landowners that the real object of Government was to destroy their proprietary rights. The hands of the agitators would be immensely strengthened if the law was general and not merely applied to tracts where there was some intelligible justification for legislation.[23]

Three other Members supported Fitzpatrick;[24] among them Charles Crosthwaite, who a few years before had indicated that it was too late to withdraw the power of transfer; and P. P. Hutchins, who, with his judicial outlook, had a dread of interference with existing rights. Crosthwaite and Hutchins anticipated a great or unforeseeable unsettlement of credit, followed by various difficulties, and accompanied by the discontent of all classes; and they wanted to make legislation as limited and tentative as possible.[25] To the Viceroy's Private Secretary Crosthwaite admitted later that he had been hoping for years that something might be done to prevent the land passing away from the hereditary owners and occupiers; and that rather than see nothing done, he would prefer to accept the Government of India's proposals for the Punjab.[26] Another Member of the India Council, Alfred Lyall, feared that the restriction of proprietary rights would check the investment of capital in land. He only acquiesced in general legislation because he appreciated the peculiar difficulties involved in special and partial legislation. He and John Edge, an ex-Chief Justice of the High Court of the North-Western Provinces, who was strongly in favour of general legislation, stressed that limited and gradual extension would lead to more opposition and discontent than would a general enactment.[27] The only other Member in favour of general legislation, James Peile, an old Bombay revenue officer, conceived of the law as little more than a pre-emption system, in which sanction would be readily given if no purchasers were forthcoming from the agriculturists of the village

## THE SHAPE OF LEGISLATION

or the agnates.[28] It was probably at Peile's instance that it was decided to ask the Government of India to indicate the nature of the executive instructions by which revenue officers would be guided in giving sanction.

By demanding enabling instead of general measures, Fitzpatrick diverted the attention of the India Council to some extent from other aspects of Rivaz's scheme. It is true that Fitzpatrick criticised the restrictions on transfers to agriculturists, and argued that the land of money-lenders should be exempted from the start, so as to remove at least one motive for their opposition.[29] Nevertheless, these had become subordinate points; and only one other Member, Hutchins, referred to them in the final minutes on the subject.

Fitzpatrick might well have succeeded in his demand for enabling legislation. While the Secretary of State for India, Lord Hamilton, was not likely to dispute the political importance of the agricultural classes,[30] he had as much difficulty in deciding Indian administrative questions on their merits as Elgin; and the majority of 'experts' were opposed to general legislation. Besides, the argument of the political danger involved in legislation appealed strongly to one who had seen so much agrarian agitation in Ireland. Hamilton preferred an enabling measure, opposition to which, he thought, would be less formidable than to a general measure.[31]

An essential factor in the situation was the new Viceroy, Lord Curzon, and his relationship with Hamilton. By March 1899 the Government of India had heard indirectly that their proposals were not faring well at the India Office. Curzon looked into the matter and, being hardly the sort of man who did anything by half-measures, decided that enabling legislation would be of little practical use. He was influenced by Rivaz, whose arguments for general legislation he pressed on the Secretary of State.[32] Given Curzon's support of Rivaz's proposals Hamilton was not likely to resist; for even in stating his preference for an enabling measure Hamilton indicated his willingness to subordinate his personal views if Curzon saw serious political drawbacks to an enabling measure.[33]

Even so it was not possible to carry the Government of India's proposals immediately. A despatch, accompanied by minutes of Members of the India Council, was issued in April 1899. It summarised the arguments on both sides of the case; and requested the Government of India to consider whether they saw any reasons for modifying their course of action. Privately Curzon was assured that whatever they decided would be accepted by the India Office.[34]

In much the same way as Fitzpatrick had played into Ibbetson's hands, he had now played into Rivaz's. Under Fitzpatrick's influence Members of the India Council, some of whom might have been persuaded that no restrictions on alienation were required,[35] assented to enabling legislation or even to general legislation. Fitzpatrick's presence helped to ensure that the issue would not be whether restrictions were required at all, but whether they were required in one form or another. And by insisting on an enabling instead of a general measure Fitzpatrick concentrated his attack on a point on which Curzon was least likely to budge as long as Hamilton did not actually overrule him. Hamilton's subservience to Curzon ensured Fitzpatrick's defeat at the hands of Rivaz.

There was still a chance that general measures might not be adopted. In commenting on the Secretary of State's despatch in May 1899, Rivaz argued that if general legislation was not enacted the restrictions should be given a trial in a compact territory like the Rawalpindi division. If general legislation was accepted, Rivaz proposed that the power of exemption be used very sparingly, at least at first; an interpretation of the power of exemption which diverged not only materially from Fitzpatrick's, but probably also from the intentions of the Punjab committee of 1898.[36]

Rivaz reiterated his old arguments that only enabling legislation would materially impair credit and rouse the hostility of the landowners. In regard to general legislation he shared neither Fitzpatrick's views of the significance of the opposition of the trading classes, nor Ibbetson's fears that the landowners would feel that they were losing their proprietary status. There might be quite a bit of writing in the vernacular newspapers against the measure, Rivaz thought, for they were controlled mostly by those on the side of the money-lenders; but the agricultural community would not be affected by such writings and would accept the scheme, at least with tacit satisfaction, as a measure for their protection.

Far from trying to lessen the opposition of the trading classes by exempting their land in the first instance, as Fitzpatrick proposed, Rivaz was not prepared to use the power to exempt classes which the Punjab committee had provided; indeed, he was not even ready to sanction freely individual alienations by the trading classes as Ibbetson had been. Rivaz proposed to impose restrictions on the land of non-agriculturists; so that whenever a non-agriculturist wanted to sell his land, its reversion to some agriculturist in the same village would be facilitated, instead of merely passing to another non-agriculturist.

The proposed restrictions on transfers to agriculturists, Rivaz defended on the same grounds as in 1898.

By now Rivaz had accepted Trevor's suggestion that all permanent alienations should require official sanction. As requested by the Secretary of State, Rivaz outlined the executive instructions by which he proposed to regulate the grant of sanction. There would be three classes of cases. When an agriculturist or non-agriculturist proprietor proposed to transfer land to an agriculturist in the same village or to an agnate, the Tahsildar would sanction the transaction as a matter of course if he was satisfied that the purchaser was really buying for himself. When a non-agriculturist proprietor wanted to transfer land to a person outside these limits, enquiry would be made whether any agriculturist in the village was willing to purchase at a fair full price. If so, the proposed alienation to the outsider would be disallowed; if not, the transfer would ordinarily be permitted, even if the alienee was a non-agriculturist. Power of sanction in this class of cases would rest with the Deputy Commissioner. In the most important class of cases, those in which an agriculturist wanted to transfer land to a person outside the original stock of the village or the agnates, the same procedure would be followed, sanction being refused if an agriculturist of the village was prepared to buy. If not, and the proposed transfer was to an agriculturist of the same tribe as the alienor, sanction would ordinarily be given. If the proposed transfer was to an agriculturist of some other tribe, enquiry should be made whether an agriculturist of the same tribe as the alienor was willing to buy. If such a man was found, permission to the proposed transfer would be refused; if not, permission would be given, unless it looked as if the proposed alienee might become a mischievous element in the village community. If the proposed transfer was to a non-agriculturist permission would be refused, save only in very exceptional cases of real necessity where no agricultural purchaser of any sort was forthcoming. In the third class of cases the power of sanction would be exercised by the Deputy Commissioner, except where the transfer was to a non-agriculturist in which case the Commissioner's sanction would be required.

In June 1899 Curzon committed himself officially to general legislation. He thought that the danger of taking action had been exaggerated by the advocates of enabling legislation; and he echoed Rivaz's argument that if it had not, and if the landowners were really hostile, it would be possible to withdraw the Bill.[37] Most of the Members of Council were new to the question; but all preferred general to enabling legislation.[38]

Two members of Council, R. Gardiner and T. Raleigh, opposed

the imposition of restrictions on non-agriculturist proprietors; and the former also questioned the restrictions placed on transfers to agriculturists. The less interference with the power of transfer, Gardiner argued, the less the danger of harmful economic consequences. Raleigh was impressed by the political danger involved in legislation.

At the Council meeting of July 7, 1899, Rivaz's proposals were approved, with two exceptions.[39] The proposal to impose restrictions on permanent alienations by non-agriculturist proprietors was defeated, presumably at the instance of Gardiner and Raleigh. It was an aspect of the scheme which Rivaz had seen as proper and desirable, but not of the most material importance.[40] Mackworth Young, who attended the meeting at Curzon's invitation, had finally abandoned the idea of enabling legislation; and stated his preference for general legislation which would not place too severe a restriction on the power of transfer. After a long argument Curzon asked Young whether there was not any area wider than the village and yet smaller than the Province, which could be adopted as the unit of exemption. Rivaz suggested that any person should be permitted to alienate permanently to any member of the same tribe with nominal sanction (not too great a concession when it is recalled that Rivaz had proposed to sanction such alienations freely when no agriculturist purchaser was forthcoming in the village). Young immediately accepted the compromise.[41]

In this way the Punjab Land Alienation Bill came to contain not one but two definitions of landowner: the 'agriculturist' and the 'member of an agricultural tribe'. Douie's proposal to specify the landowners by their tribal names had come in by the back door.

Rivaz's scheme for restricting permanent transfers was modified therefore so that sanction would be given as a matter of right to anyone who was not a member of an agricultural tribe; to an alienation by a member of an agricultural tribe to an 'agriculturist' holding land in the village; and to an alienation by a member of an agricultural tribe to another member of the same tribe residing in the same district, the meaning of district being variable. In all other cases the revenue officer was to be guided by the sort of executive instructions which Rivaz had sketched.

The Bill, which was now drafted, was thus the work of many. Its general provisions, tempered by the power of exemption, reflected the decisions of the Punjab committee of 1898, upheld by Young, Rivaz and Curzon. The acceptance of Rivaz's proposal to make the exercise of the power of exemption dependent on the sanction of the

## THE SHAPE OF LEGISLATION

Government of India and later, to make little use of the power of exemption, strengthened the general character of the measure. The restrictions which the Bill imposed on temporary transfers were those advocated by the Punjab committee, as added to and modified by Rivaz in August 1898. The essence of these restrictions was the acceptance of the self-redeeming usufructuary mortgage, which had been advocated by Ibbetson. The restrictions placed on permanent alienations were based on Rivaz's principle that all such alienations should be subject to the revenue officer's discretion; a principle modified in the direction of Ibbetson's views by the concession to the original stock of the village and the agnates; further modified under the influence of Trevor by the provision for nominal sanction; and finally modified to placate Young by the concession to the tribe.[42]

Certain subordinate provisions of the Bill went beyond the recommendations of the Punjab committee of 1898, though this was apparently not intentional. Instead of merely declaring the conditional sale clause in existing mortgages null and void, the Bill provided that existing mortgages by conditional sale would be null and void, save only that the revenue officer was empowered to substitute a self-redeeming usufructuary mortgage of no more than fifteen years' duration. Similarly all hypothecations of produce were declared void, instead of hypothecations for more than one year.

The sale of land in execution of any decree, whether passed before or after the Act, was forbidden, as Rivaz had proposed.

Provisions to ensure the enforcement of the restrictions were included in the Bill.[43]

In July 1899 a despatch, accompanied by the Bill, explained the proposed legislation to the Secretary of State. As anticipated, there was no opposition from the India Office.[44] Fitzpatrick saw that he had lost the game; but he felt his defeat in the matter of general as opposed to enabling legislation so strongly, that he dissented from the decision to sanction the introduction of the Bill into the Legislative Council.[45]

The general application of restrictions on the power of alienation would not be seriously challenged again; but the stringency of Rivaz's restrictions had been whittled down already to some extent. Rivaz had triumphed over Fitzpatrick; but Young had secured the first of a number of vital concessions.

II

On September 27, 1899, Rivaz introduced the Bill into the Governor-General's Legislative Council at Simla. It was not proposed to proceed with the measure until the next Simla session, when the assistance of the Punjab Government and its officers would be available. In the interim, Curzon thought, it would be possible to gauge public opinion. The Bill was forwarded to the Punjab Government for its opinion and that of selected officers and other persons.[46]

Even before the introduction of the Bill into the Legislative Council, rumours of impending legislation against the moneylenders (prompted no doubt by Thorburn's 1896 enquiry and by an attempt inspired by Merk to ascertain the opinions of non-officials and bankers in 1898) had spread in some of the rural areas.[47] Among ordinary peasant proprietors the publication of the Bill gave currency to the notion that existing mortgages would be cancelled or their duration limited. Wherever such views prevailed, the mass of the peasant proprietors were well-disposed towards the measure. In other places the rumour, fostered by non-agriculturist Hindus, that the Bill was a scheme for Government confiscation of the land, gained ground, with resulting discontent among the landowners.[48]

District officers who explained the provisions of the Bill to Hindu and Muslim landowners found that they received it with various degrees of favour and disfavour. There was a tendency to press for retrospective provisions in regard to mortgages. To some landowners the fact that the restrictions on alienation would stop expropriation outweighed their objections to the Bill. Others could see only the objections. The major objection was not, as Ibbetson had expected, the interference with the status of proprietor, but the restriction of credit which it was feared would follow legislation. Some of the proprietors saw this for themselves; others were influenced by the money-lenders who explained the Bill to them. At the time this was a particularly pertinent point. Several parts of the Province were suffering from famine, the need for loans was great, and the famine, as well as the publication of the Bill, had restricted credit. The fear of the restriction of credit weighed most heavily with the smaller or less thrifty proprietors, who were more dependent on the moneylender. Criticism was also directed at the necessity of obtaining sanction to all permanent alienations, which would involve inconvenience and opportunities for exaction by subordinate officials.

The acquisitive elements in the agrarian community, like some of the Sikh Jats of Ludhiana or the agrarian capitalists of Dera Ismail Khan, were torn between opposition to and support of the Bill. Many saw the advantages of a measure which would exclude the professional money-lender from the competition for land. At the same time many wanted greater freedom of alienation between agriculturists than the Bill gave, and the removal of the provisions requiring official sanction to every permanent alienation, as otherwise their own acquisition of land might be hampered. There was also general opposition to the retrospective provisions concerning mortgages by conditional sale which would interfere with their vested interests.

In a few places the Bill, brought to notice by meetings organised by the trading classes, may have been responsible to some extent for the sudden outbreak of violent crime. In Jhelum, for instance, the money-lenders, resenting the Bill, restricted credit with the coming of scarcity. Discontent had been running high among the landowners of this district for some years; and dacoities against money-lenders resulted.

Apart from such outbreaks, connected perhaps as much with the famine as the Bill, the landowners were entirely passive. The petitions actually sent by landowners for or against the Bill could be counted on the fingers of one hand.

Among the Hindu trading classes the Bill created great unrest. Dissatisfaction was apparent among Hindu money-lenders, large and small, among Hindu officials and professional men, and among avowed loyalists as well as among the disaffected. To all, the Bill represented a threat to their liberty to invest in land. The legal profession, which took the lead in opposing the Bill, was probably influenced as well by the consideration that the Bill would diminish litigation.

The unrest was stimulated by the retrospective abolition of the mortgage by conditional sale. Many of the ordinary money-lenders believed that all existing mortgages would be converted into self-redeeming mortgages. Even those who were better informed were excited and apprehensive in regard to a provision which not only affected their existing investments in conditional sales but which, it was feared, would establish the principle of retrospective legislation and render all their acquisitions insecure.

The fears of the professional money-lenders were reflected in the restriction of credit, though here the famine was also responsible; in the decrease in area mortgaged; in the increase in area sold, money-lenders taking pains to convert existing mortgages into sales; and in a large increase in suits to obtain foreclosure of mortgages by conditional sale.[49]

The newspapers gave vent to the strong opposition of educated Hindus to the Bill. The political significance of these writings may be gauged from the fact that the measure was attacked not so much as an interference with the rights of non-agriculturists to acquire land, but as an imposition on the peasantry. This attitude was partly inspired no doubt by tactical considerations; but it nevertheless reflected a claim to speak for society as a whole. The arguments propounded against the Bill, albeit often exaggerated, were couched in the language of *laissez-faire* political economy and showed the confidence of the educated in their ability to meet the British on their own intellectual ground. If the Bill was passed, it was contended, agricultural credit would be restricted; the rates of interest would be higher; the value of land would fall. More land would have to be mortgaged to obtain the same amount of money; mortgagors would be ejected from their land; sales would increase; the concentration of land in the hands of agriculturist money-lenders would be facilitated. The peasantry would be impoverished and rural crime would increase; the Government would find it difficult to collect its revenue or enlist its soldiers.

The claim of educated Hindus to leadership was not a passive one. As Fitzpatrick had predicted, widespread attempts were made to convince the landowners that the Bill was a measure of confiscation. Its effects on the value of land and credit were emphasised. That these attempts to influence the thinking of a passive peasantry met with some degree of success, even among Muslim proprietors, showed the potential resources on which educated Hindus might draw. Nor was organisation lacking. After a few months, Land Alienation Bill committees were formed in various districts. An elaborate petition was drawn up, and the legal profession together with a few wealthy money-lenders played the leading role in obtaining large numbers of signatures from peasants and money-lenders to copies of this petition.

If educated Hindus were united, educated Muslims were more or less divided. The support given to the Bill by a number of Muslim officials and professional men may be attributed to the fact that many educated Muslims were hereditary landowners, whose social connections were with the borrowing rather than the lending classes, and who were inclined to sympathise with the peasant rather than the money-lender. The opposition of other Muslim officials and professional men is understandable, since even landowning Muslims would find an appreciable check placed on their powers of acquisition, while those of trading background would be placed in the same position as their Hindu counterparts. In several instances landowning Muslims of the official and professional classes urged that transfers to agriculturists should not be restricted and that sanction to such alienations should not be required. This, of course, would discriminate against the Hindu money-lender, while leaving all Muslims of landowning stock free to acquire land.

Muslim newspapers seemed to take little interest in the Bill at first. Only the editor of the *Rafiq-i-Hind*, Muharram Ali Chishti, a non-agriculturist, supported the Bill in a determined way. There was little Muslim agitation or organisation. Ata Muhammad, a clerk of court, and a friend of Muharram Ali Chishti, secured the signatures of landowners in a few central districts to a petition which urged the Government to include retrospective provisions against mortgages in the Bill. Muharram Ali Chishti made some attempt to influence some leading landowners of the Lahore district in favour of the Bill. Apart from this, contributions to Muslim newspapers showed only growing irritation at Hindu attempts to organise rural opposition to the Bill.

It is against this background that the opinions of Punjab officers on the Bill must be considered. They were forwarded to the Government of India early in June 1900, together with the opinion of Mackworth Young. A considerable majority of the revenue and judicial officers consulted were in favour of the Bill generally. They included a very large number of officers whose experience of the Punjab dated from the 1880s and 1890s, most of them being consulted on this question for the first time. It was clear that land alienation legislation, and by implication the political analysis on which it rested, would not lack supporters among the new generation. Some officers, like W. S. Talbot, impressed by agrarian discontent in the Jhelum district, thought that retrospective provisions against mortgages were required. A number of officers, like Wilson, still preferred enabling legislation; or, like Douie, thought that the general law would be subject to considerable exemptions of tracts and classes. Only a small minority of officers voiced their complete opposition to the Bill, generally on economic grounds.[50]

There was, of course, much detailed criticism of the Bill. Many officers thought that the restrictions imposed by the Bill were too stringent. It was urged that sanction should not be required where it could not be refused; that the restrictions should not apply to the land of the trading castes; and that restrictions on transfers to landowners were not desirable. The fifteen years self-redeeming usufructuary mortgage, many believed, would restrict credit too much, and might lead to greater areas being mortgaged or to forced sales, especially in the case of insecure lands. Twenty, or even twenty-five, years was considered a safer period. An additional form of permissible mortgage, which would be without a time limit, redeemable on repayment of principal, and subject to the retention of an inalienable occupancy right by the mortgagor, was suggested by a few officers, notably Douie, as a means of maintaining agricultural credit.

The retrospective provisions regarding mortgages by conditional sale were generally criticised as unfair, it being considered sufficient to render the condition of sale invalid in existing mortgages. The entire prohibition of hypothecation of crops was not favoured.

Exception was taken to the definition of 'agriculturist', which would enable many traders in some western districts to buy freely in any village in which they owned land; which was imperfect in other ways as well and which, a number of officers thought, could best be omitted from the Bill.

A host of other suggestions were made on minor points on which the Bill was obviously objectionable, its drafting imperfect or additions necessary to guard against evasions of the law.

Young was still concerned to weaken the restrictions imposed by the Bill. Asked to nominate two Punjab officers to the Legislative Council, he chose Tupper and Fanshawe.[51] Tupper was influenced by the general opinion among revenue officers that the Bill would diminish credit to an undesirable degree, and he thought that less severe restrictions would suffice for the political object in view.[52] Fanshawe had never favoured legislation to check land transfers, and he was doubtful about the expediency of the Bill.[53]

At the Legislative Council meeting of June 22, 1900 the Bill was referred to a Select Committee. The composition of this Committee favoured Young rather than Rivaz. Punjab experience on the Committee was represented by Rivaz, Tupper and Fanshawe. Apart from Rivaz there were three Members of the Government of India on the Committee, Trevor, Raleigh and Law, the last two fresh from England. Of these Trevor, though only a recent convert to the policy of restricting the power of transfer, was perhaps closest in outlook to Rivaz; Raleigh had doubts and misgivings about the whole policy; Law was sympathetic but had not the experience to form his own opinions on the questions at issue.[54] There was one Indian Member on the Committee, Harnam Singh, an Ahluwalia by caste and a Christian by religion. It was indicative of the strength of non-agriculturist Hindu opposition to the Bill that Harnam Singh, a relative of the Kapurthala royal family in the Punjab and a Talukdar in the North-Western Provinces, took the lead in denouncing the Bill.[55] His request for the appointment of another Indian Member to the Council only weakened his hand, while strengthening Young's. Young pressed Muhammad Hayat Khan, an official and an avowed loyalist, on Curzon. As a large landowner in the Rawalpindi district, who had increased his landed possessions at the expense of smaller Muslim proprietors, it was not surprising that Muhammad Hayat Khan had doubts about the Bill and, more particularly, that he was inclined to favour restrictions on transfers to traders while opposed to restrictions on transfers to landowners.[56]

To understand the amendments of the Bill proposed by the Select Committee in their report of August 6, 1900 three factors have to be borne in mind: firstly, the general trend of the opinions expressed by Punjab officers, itself reflecting in some respects public discussion of the measure; secondly, the views of the members of the Select Committee; and, finally, the views of Mackworth Young, who kept in touch with the Committee's discussions.

In deference to widespread criticism, the provision which necessitated the request for official sanction to permanent alienation in cases in which the grant of such sanction was obligatory, was removed. Sanction would now be necessary only where the grant of such sanction was at the revenue officer's discretion; and it was provided that such sanction could be given after as well as before the completion of the alienation. The removal of the provision for formal sanction accorded with the views of Tupper, Fanshawe, Muhammad Hayat Khan and Young.[57] Rivaz was probably not seriously opposed to this amendment.[58] It was Trevor who had pressed for provision for formal sanction as a means of preventing fraud.

The 'agriculturist' was not omitted from the amended Bill despite the complexities and misunderstandings which the retention of this category generated and despite the adverse opinions of several Punjab officers and the opposition of Rivaz and Tupper. It was at the instance of Mackworth Young that the 'agriculturist' was maintained. It is ironic that a definition which Rivaz put forward in 1898 as part of a scheme to keep transfers within the narrowest possible limits was upheld by Young because that definition was imperfect and allowed some traders in certain districts the privilege of buying land in certain circumstances.[59] An attempt was made, however, to keep the position and privileges of the money-lender 'agriculturist' within bounds, despite Harnam Singh's attempt to widen the definition. If the regular settlement of a district had been made in or since 1870 (in which case a large number of money-lenders would qualify as 'agriculturists') the Local Government was empowered to choose an earlier settlement on the basis of which the status of 'agriculturist' could be claimed for that district. The Local Government was also given a general power to exclude any persons from the definition. In the Bill, probably through an oversight in drafting, the 'agriculturist' had been allowed to buy land in any village in which he owned land at the time of the passing of the Act. It was now made clear that the 'agriculturist' would be able to buy land only in the village from which he actually derived his status as 'agriculturist'. These amendments seem to have been made with Young's concurrence. Certain less important amendments of the definition were also made.

The Select Committee removed most of the restrictions which the Bill still imposed upon the power of transfer of the trading castes. This had been advocated by several Punjab officers and was in accord with the views of Tupper, Fanshawe and Raleigh.[60] Rivaz probably had little objection; the restrictions which the Bill had retained on the power of alienation of the trading castes could not possibly secure the reversion of land held by them to the agricultural tribes. The provision for nominal sanction to permanent alienations being excised altogether, alienors who did not belong to notified agricultural tribes could now make permanent alienations without any restrictions. There was only one exception, namely the restriction on the power of transfer of the 'agriculturist' which was now introduced. A loophole had been discovered in the Bill. A moneylender who fell within the definition of 'agriculturist' could acquire land from agricultural tribes in the village; there being no restrictions on his powers of disposal, he could re-sell this land, and thus become an intermediary for the transfer of land from agricultural tribes to traders. To overcome this difficulty the Select Committee accepted an amendment supported by Rivaz by which any land which an 'agriculturist' acquired under the Act by reason of his status as 'agriculturist' could not be sold again without sanction, except to a member of an agricultural tribe or to a person holding land as an 'agriculturist' in the village. Trevor had wanted to go even further in restricting the power of transfer of the 'agriculturist'.[61] All restrictions on the power of temporary alienation and on the sale of land in execution of decree, previously absolute, were now confined to members of agricultural tribes. The restriction on the power of hypothecation, previously applied to the 'agriculturist' (probably through careless drafting), was now applied only to members of agricultural tribes. Mortgages by conditional sale were

## THE SHAPE OF LEGISLATION

likewise subject to the retrospective provisions of the Bill only where they had been entered into by members of agricultural tribes. In future mortgages, however, all conditions of sale were to be invalid, irrespective of the alienors. There was thus almost a complete return to Fitzpatrick's proposal that restrictions should be imposed only on notified agricultural tribes.

The most serious clash in opinion arose over the restrictions which should be imposed on transfers to members of agricultural tribes. Young, emboldened by opinion in the Province which supported his view, was no longer satisfied with the compromise reached in 1899 by which permanent alienations within the tribe would be unfettered. He now pressed for complete freedom of permanent, and even temporary alienation, between all agricultural tribes. His argument was that the restrictions which the Bill imposed would press too hard on the small proprietors of small tribes. Their credit would fall much more than that of proprietors of the larger tribes, and the depreciation in the value of their land would hasten their expropriation by the richer members of their own tribe.[62] Tupper, also fearing the effects of the Bill on agricultural credit, wanted complete liberty of permanent alienation between agricultural tribes.[63] Muhammad Hayat Khan no doubt had reasons of his own for opposing all restrictions on transfers to members of agricultural tribes.[64] Rivaz offered a concession, apparently to the effect that not only permanent but also temporary alienation should be left unfettered within the tribe. Young would not accept this as sufficient.[65] Finally a compromise was reached by which permanent alienations made to a member of the same tribe or to a member of a tribe in the same group, would be permitted; while, apart from mortgages by conditional sale, there would be no restrictions on the mortgages made to a member of the same tribe or to a member of a tribe in the same group. It was explained in Council, but not indicated in the Bill, that grouping was intended to meet only the case of small and cognate tribes.[66] Instead of making the meaning of district variable, power was taken to group districts.

Considering the opposition, Rivaz had maintained his position fairly well. He could not foresee that Young would get an opportunity to nullify the latest compromise.

Rivaz also had to give way to his colleagues in regard to the forms of mortgages which should be permitted. Young, Tupper and Fanshawe, in common with much Punjab opinion, wanted a twenty-year instead of a fifteen-year term for the self-redeeming usufructuary mortgage. This was accepted. Tupper and Young wanted the new form of mortgage proposed by Douie as a further safeguard for agricultural credit. Rivaz gave way. The new form of mortgage was a written usufructuary mortgage in which the mortgagor retained an inalienable occupancy right in the land subject to the payment of rent at a customary rate, or if there was no customary rate, at such rate as a revenue court determined to be equitable. The mortgagor could be ejected if he used the land in an improper manner, failed to cultivate it or did not pay his rent. He could redeem at any time on repayment of principal, even if he had been ejected. The Local Government was also empowered to permit any form of mortgage it thought suitable. This was probably added at Tupper's instance, the aim being to permit local kinds of mortgage which were unobjectionable.[67]

A number of other changes were made in the provisions relating to temporary transfers. Certain objectionable features of these provisions were removed, and certain defects in drafting remedied. Existing provisions designed to safeguard the mortgagor's power of redemption, and to prevent the introduction of special conditions unfavourable to the mortgagor, were expanded and clarified. New provisions were introduced to guard against evasions of the restrictions.

Hypothecations of produce were permitted for one year, and otherwise with official sanction, instead of being prohibited altogether.

The retrospective provisions relating to mortgages by conditional sale were opposed by Tupper at first on the ground that there was no political necessity for such action. He was won over apparently by Rivaz, who stressed economic considerations.[68] The provisions, which had been criticised by many Punjab officers, were made somewhat less severe. The mortgagee now had the choice of having the sale condition struck out, leaving the other conditions of the mortgage to be enforced, or he could accept a self-redeeming usufructuary mortgage or collateral mortgage as defined by the Bill, the terms of which would be fixed by the Deputy Commissioner.

A number of other expansions, clarifications and improvements were made in the Bill, in accordance with the suggestions of Punjab officers.

The Preliminary Report of the Select Committee, which proposed the above amendments in the Bill, was presented on August 6, 1900, with a long minute of dissent from Harnam Singh.[69] Curzon claimed that this minute, as indeed Harnam Singh's speeches in Council, were written for him by some interested pleader or pleaders at Lahore.[70]

## THE SHAPE OF LEGISLATION

Whatever the truth of this allegation, it seems likely that there was some central direction of the educated Hindu opposition to the Bill. Throughout September a number of similarly worded telegrams protesting against the Bill and supporting Harnam Singh's views were sent to the Viceroy from Land Alienation Bill Committees and public meetings. A number of these telegrams laid special stress on the objections to retrospective legislation.[71]

It may be doubted whether the British members of the Select Committee took any notice of this agitation. It had come to their notice that many proceedings were being instituted to enforce the sale condition in existing mortgages; and the possibility of bringing the provisions relating to these mortgages into force as soon as the Act was passed was discussed.[72] In its report of October 2nd the Select Committee extended the retrospective provisions against conditional sales to proceedings pending in the courts at the commencement of the Act.[73] Shortly afterwards an unsuccessful attempt was made to persuade the Chief Court to defer decrees in these pending cases.[74]

On the other hand, notice was taken of the opposition of educated Muslims to the new form of mortgage. It was pointed out by such Muslims that the Hindu money-lenders would take only the new form of mortgage; that the principal and interest for which the land would be mortgaged would exceed the market value, so that redemption would not be feasible; that pretexts would be found to eject the mortgagor; and that the result would be permanent alienations to money-lenders in fact if not in name. The India Office voiced the fear that collusive abandonment might be resorted to in respect of the third form of mortgage; and suggested that this form of mortgage should also be limited as to time. Similar and additional suggestions had been made by a Muslim judicial officer and by Muhammad Shafi, a prominent legal practitioner, and conveyed to Muhammad Hayat Khan, Rivaz and Tupper.[75] The Select Committee adopted amendments along these lines, providing that in case of ejectment or abandonment, the third form of mortgage would be converted into a self-redeeming usufructuary mortgage, as defined by the Bill, the conditions of the mortgage to be fixed by the Deputy Commissioner. The customary rate of rent and the jurisdiction of the revenue court which the Bill provided for the third form of mortgage were excised, and a maximum rent fixed for all such mortgages.

These amendments more or less destroyed the utility of the third form of mortgage.[76] In the end the mortgage restrictions imposed by the Bill were still close to the spirit of Ibbetson's proposals.

Apart from the above, the Select Committee, in its Report of October 2nd, proposed no fundamental changes.[77]

The Bill was finally passed at the Legislative Council meeting of October 19th, various amendments proposed by Harnam Singh being defeated. In his speech Young made it clear that he was not reconciled to the restrictions which the Bill imposed on transfers to agricultural tribes. The final stage of the struggle between Young and Rivaz had begun.

III

In mid-August 1900 Tupper, the Financial Commissioner, anxious that existing conditional sales should not be enforced and that the excitement and misapprehension created by the Bill be allayed, proposed that lists and groups of agricultural tribes be prepared, so that the Act could be brought into force immediately after it was passed.[78] His proposals being accepted by Young, such lists and groups were prepared by several officers. At a conference held on September 10th, a number of conclusions were reached concerning the principles which should determine the selection of agricultural tribes. Village menials and artisans should not be included, though it would be provided that where such men practised agriculture, transfers to them would be sanctioned freely. Tribes of low status should be included, if warranted by their numbers and the amount of land owned. The inclusion of Brahmins, Kalals and Kakezai Shekhs, who were sometimes agricultural, sometimes non-agricultural, would be decided with reference to the circumstances of each district. It was not considered necessary by most members of the conference to include tribes which, though elsewhere notified as agricultural, were represented in particular districts by insignificant numbers or held little land. Differences of religion were to be disregarded in enumeration, though it was considered permissible to use them as a test for including or excluding particular tribes, if this was for some special reason convenient. No definite conclusions were reached regarding the grouping of tribes; but at least four out of nine officers were in favour of placing all agricultural tribes in the same group, so that there would be no restrictions on transfers between them.[79] On October 5, 1900, it was decided that the opinion of local officers should be invited in regard to grouping;[80] but nothing was done immediately.

It seems likely that Young was influenced by these discussions. At any rate in his speech in the Legislative Council on October 19th he

## THE SHAPE OF LEGISLATION

explained his long-standing opposition to the Bill and made a special point of criticising the restrictions on permanent alienations to members of agricultural tribes, which neither the Punjab committee of 1898, nor most of the Punjab officers consulted in 1899, had recommended. Young hoped that the proposal to group only cognate tribes, which was not contained in the provisions of the Bill, would be ignored; that the Government of India would give full effect to the view of the Punjab Government and its officers in considering the Local Government's recommendations on grouping; and that grouping be freely utilised to meet the case of small, scattered tribes.

Rivaz did not let this challenge pass. Earlier in the debate he had stressed that the Bill was designed to secure the preservation of the small proprietor by restricting his credit and thus decreasing his opportunities for reckless extravagance; and he had predicted that the Bill would be followed by a decrease in sales and mortgages. In those cases in which an agriculturist was forced to sell, through the subdivision of the holding, extreme thriftlessness or poverty, the Bill would ensure that his land would pass to another agriculturist, preferably one of the same tribe, instead of to a money-lender. To group all tribes together, Rivaz charged in his later speech, would result in a depreciation of the value of land which would not be sufficient to discourage the small proprietor from selling needlessly. The small proprietor would then disappear even more rapidly than before; for he would have to sell more to raise the same amount of money.

As Rivaz and Young were unable to agree about the grouping of tribes, this question was to be referred to Deputy Commissioners.[81]

In a Punjab Government letter of November 1900, addressed to all Deputy Commissioners, the principles which should be followed in enumerating agricultural tribes were specified. These were more or less in accordance with the conclusions of the conference of September 10th. Officers were requested to revise the lists of tribes which had been prepared.[82]

The letter explained that Young was disposed to think that, as far as the grouping of districts went, it would be sufficient to issue one notification for the Province declaring that each district and all districts which adjoined it should form one group of districts.

Young did not treat the grouping of tribes as he had treated it in his speech in the Legislative Council, as an open question. The Punjab Government letter indicated that grouping was intended only for small tribes, who should be given a fair market for their land, though the market should not be unnecessarily wide; that the tribes grouped should be cognate; that grouping should take advantage, where feasible, of local contiguity, a distant market being useless; and that the grouping should not expose small tribes to agricultural money-lenders and land-grabbers of other tribes, for this might be dangerous.

Commissioners were asked to hold divisional conferences to discuss the enumeration and grouping of tribes.

Rivaz approved of Young's letter;[83] but it would soon become clear that Young had played his cards well.

Almost all the officers consulted proposed to exclude village menials and artisans from the agricultural tribes. Tribes of low status, like the Tarkhans and Labanas, and tribes which contained both agricultural and non-agricultural elements, like the Brahmins, Kalals, Kakezais and Shekhs, were sometimes included and sometimes excluded. The Muslim religious tribes, like the Sayads, and other high status Muslim tribes, like the Pathans and Mughals, were generally, though not invariably, included. The market-gardening tribes, and tribes like the Jats, Rajputs, Gujars and others, whose pursuits were distinctly agricultural or pastoral, were generally enumerated as agricultural tribes.[84]

The method of grouping districts proposed by Young was accepted by most officers.

The only divisional conference which stongly endorsed Rivaz's proposal for the formation of small groups was that of Jullunder, presided over by Alexander Anderson. Anderson had always supported proposals which were likely to decrease agricultural credit and thus inhibit extravagant expenditure. If it was found that the system of small groups did not answer, Anderson argued, it would always be possible to combine groups. Most of the officers of his division agreed with him; partly because in several of their districts the acquisitive tendencies of the Sikh Jats were marked.

In other divisions the fear was expressed that Rivaz's proposals would restrict credit too much, and would depreciate the value of land unduly, especially in the case of weaker tribes like the Rajputs, who might find themselves forced to sell at a very low price to the one or two capitalists in their tribe. The increase in the Deputy Commissioner's work would also be great. These were the arguments not only of men like Merk, Commissioner of the Derajat division, who had opposed legislation, and was concerned to whittle it down as far as possible, but also of men like Clarke, Commissioner of the Lahore division, who had never been prepared to do more than stop the transfer of land to the professional money-lender. Both these Commissioners wanted all tribes in each district to be placed into one group; and Clarke bullied into submission those officers in his division who had attempted to form separate groups. The Delhi divisional conference, comprising such experienced officers as H. C. Fanshawe, G. C. Walker and A. Kensington, only wanted one group of agricultural tribes. The feeling that tribes could always be put into smaller groups, while the combination of groups would be to some extent an admission of failure, influenced the judgement of some of these officers.

Other circumstances favoured the formation of single or large groups of agricultural tribes. In the western districts it seemed pointless that tribes should be formed into separate groups when there were few money-lenders and land-grabbers in these tribes; though the existence of the powerful individual agrarian capitalist in a few of the western districts caused some difficulty. Two practical considerations made themselves felt in the west. Many of the tribes were so scattered that, if grouped singly, they would have little or no market. Then many tribes were so difficult to distinguish from one another that separate grouping would lead to serious ethnological difficulties. These considerations increased the support for single groups at the Derajat and Lahore divisional conferences. They also influenced the decision of the Rawalpindi divisional conference, headed by Montgomery, and the Peshawar divisional conference, headed by Cunningham, to form no more than two groups in any of their districts.

The trend towards single groups was endorsed by James Wilson, now Settlement Commissioner. Hitherto, Wilson had been a determined advocate of a severe restriction of the power of alienation; but also of enabling legislation which would ensure that this remedy was applied with care and discrimination. With a law applying all over the Punjab, Wilson thought it safer to limit the restrictions on the power of alienation in the first instance. He also thought that the power of alienation of agricultural tribes should not be too restricted as long as the money-lender 'agriculturist' was given a free hand in the villages from which he derived his status.

In his review of these opinions in February 1901, Lewis Tupper, the Financial Commissioner, suggested that the local proposals for the enumeration of agricultural tribes be accepted; subject to the entire exclusion of village menials and artisans, Shekhs (except genuine Koreshis and Ansaris) and, for the present, Brahmins. The Shekhs, Tupper pointed out, were a heterogeneous collection, and agricultural tribes should be protected from their acquisitive tendencies. Likewise it was more important to save the agricultural tribes from the money-lending Brahmin than to protect the agricultural Brahmin. The Muslim religious tribes, Tupper retained, for, as Wilson had noted, they were more often mortgagors and vendors than mortgagees and vendees.

Tupper dissented from the conclusion of the majority of officers that all agricultural tribes should be placed in the same group, despite his personal conviction that it would be better to place no restrictions on permanent alienations to members of agricultural tribes. Local officers, Tupper thought, had stressed the importance of the field for sale, but they had overlooked the field for mortgage, which was still more important. Ordinarily peasants did not want to sell their land; but they did want to raise as much money as possible on it. If all tribes were placed in the same group, not only would the field for sale be great, but the agricultural tribes would lose the protection of the mortgage provisions of the Act when mortgaging to men of other agricultural tribes. Tupper accordingly framed groups which would protect the weaker from the stronger agricultural tribes.

Young accepted most of Tupper's proposals relating to the enumeration of agricultural tribes; but the trend among local officers to large and single groups, even though he had given no lead in this respect, gave him the opportunity to press his views on the Government of India. That Government was asked to group each district with adjoining districts and to put all agricultural tribes in each district into a single group.[85]

In his letter to the Government of India, Young stressed, among other things, the artificiality of the groupings proposed. This was something which Tupper felt keenly; and he proposed in April that, if the Government of India rejected Young's proposals, district officers be asked whether it would not be preferable to commence the Act with each tribe notified separately, leaving grouping to be suggested by practical necessities. Tupper did not now think that the restriction of credit, or the increase in work, which this proposal involved, would be very great.[86]

It was too late. Rivaz, influenced by the weight of opinion in favour of single groups and by the idea that separate groups could be formed in future, had accepted Young's proposals already. Curzon, also thinking that separate groups could be formed later, accepted them shortly afterwards. Rivaz and Curzon did disallow the grouping of districts proposed by Young, as this would give too many opportunities for fraud.[87] But this was of little significance beside the decision which allowed all notified tribes in each district to sell and mortgage freely amongst themselves, save only in the form of a mortgage by conditional sale.

Tupper, seeing more clearly than Rivaz, thought it improbable that after this decision narrower grouping would ever be adopted.[88] Young's efforts had not gone to waste. Rivaz's attempt to impose restrictions on alienations to landowners as well as to moneylenders had been effectively scotched.

IV

It is a remarkable fact that the Punjab Alienation of Land Act, which constituted such a landmark in the Punjab political tradition, was formulated, enacted and applied at a time when the two main contending figures were men whose vision was essentially non-political. Rivaz did not deny the political danger involved in land transfer by any means; but it was not a consideration which determined his whole attitude to the question. As regards the political risks involved in legislation he took the most sanguine view possible. Mackworth Young had not succumbed at all to the notion that land transfer involved any great political danger. And as far as the political risks of legislation were concerned, Young's objections derived purely from his view of the economic evils which legislation involved. Where Ibbetson and Fitzpatrick had argued about the best way to meet a political danger without incurring serious political hazards, Rivaz and Young thought primarily in terms of the economic well-being of society. To Young restrictions on the power of transfer were a social and economic evil; to Rivaz they were a desirable feature of a rural society in which the transfer of land served no economic purpose. Young clung to abstract and universal commercial principles; Rivaz's vision was that of a particular rural society in which the hereditary possession of land constituted a way of life and a means of livelihood threatened by the negotiable character of land.

Mackworth Young ought to have been the last person to have been asked to consider the restriction of the power of alienation. Yet the pressure on him was greater than on any previous Lieutenant-Governor. With the Government of India pressing a drastic scheme for the restriction of the power of transfer on him, and with Punjab opinion apparently committed more strongly than ever before to some such restriction, Young's options were limited. It was too late to deny that any action was required at all, for that view would have come close to isolating the Lieutenant-Governor from his own Province. It was also too late to fall back on a Deccan Relief Act; for while this might have been a lesser evil to Young, it would not have enabled him to avoid the question of the restriction of the power of alienation at this stage. Nor could Young very well refuse to discuss the question with selected officers. And if that was the case, he could hardly have failed to include at least a number of those who favoured legislation. In short, Young could not have emerged from the situation with an unimpaired reputation without going into the question of the restriction of the power of transfer. If he had then opposed the implementation of the Punjab committee's proposals, he would have run the risk of losing his standing in the question. As it was, he emerged from the situation with a certain credit, and in a position to exert his influence so as to limit the restrictions on alienation as much as possible.

The decision of the Punjab committee in favour of general legislation, subject to local exemptions, was of vital importance. That decision had not been an easy one for the committee as a whole to make. Once made, however, it became the focal point of the discussion. Young would have liked to oppose it, but dared not; Fitzpatrick did oppose it, but to no avail, partly because he had lost his most valuable ally in Young. And Rivaz made the most of the situation by decreasing the potential importance of the power to exempt given areas from the restrictions. That was something which Rivaz was able to do without the slightest qualms partly because his approach to the subject was economic rather than political: in economic terms general legislation alone made sense, while the political objections to such legislation were considered negligible. Ultimately, however, apart from Rivaz's own views, his achievement in regard to general legislation owed much to political considerations; for while some politically-minded officers feared the political consequences of legislation, general legislation nevertheless made sense to many who feared the political consequences of land transfer. In this respect Rivaz was moving with a current of Provincial opinion which was now in the ascendant, while Young had little in the way of overt Provincial opinion to fall back on; and this was one reason why on this point Rivaz's counsels prevailed throughout the debate.

Another reason lay in the fact that Rivaz was able to gain the support of Curzon who, in his turn, ensured Hamilton's support of general legislation. Indeed, it is on this question of general versus

## THE SHAPE OF LEGISLATION

enabling legislation that the Viceroy and the Secretary of State exerted a distinct influence on the discussion; and in this respect the possible influence of a changing intellectual climate in England demands attention once more. That is an aspect of the question which historians have not hesitated to stress. The Punjab Alienation of Land Act went so far, according to one historian, who has rather exaggerated its provisions, partly because 'the decline of *laissez-faire* removed the major obstacles in its path'. By 1900, it is pointed out, 'political economy was no longer a binding orthodoxy in England' and 'hence deviation from it in India had ceased to be heresy'.[89] Again the same historian has written with partial reference to restrictions upon land transfer that 'the principles of Victorian liberalism were an insurmountable obstacle so long as they remained in the ascendant'.[90] And another historian, writing in a similar context, has gone even further. 'At bottom', he has suggested, 'Indian policy was undergoing the sea-change which accompanied the withering of Victorian liberalism in all its facets.'[91] It would not be worth challenging these conclusions but for the fact that they are part of a general approach to British-Indian history stressing English influences on Indian policy; an approach which tends to assume that instances of parallel development demonstrate the influence of England on India, and that no direct evidence is necessarily required to substantiate this point. Examination of the evidence shows that Hamilton's Irish experience was more likely to have turned the scales against general legislation rather than the reverse; another illustration of the fact that particular developments, even those manifested in England, did not always exert their influence in one particular direction. Moreover, Curzon himself was apprehensive about the consequences of legislation, thinking that Harnam Singh's case was 'in itself a good one';[92] an indication that in this respect orthodox political economy retained a far greater hold on Curzon than on Rivaz. Notwithstanding these facts, however, it is still possible to visualise the possibility of English intellectual influences on the Punjab Alienation of Land Act; for it could be argued that but for the decline of *laissez-faire* political economy in England, Curzon and Hamilton might not have tolerated restrictions on the power of alienation at all.

This suggests that it would be wiser to speak in terms of the removal of obstacles rather than in terms of Indian policy moving in step with English developments. Even so a stress on the removal of 'major obstacles' with reference to English developments is to some extent misleading; for everything shows that some of the most significant obstacles to legislation lay in the minds of British-Indian officers themselves and that it required a more or less autonomous intellectual revolution as well as political anxieties to overcome these obstacles, and that even then they were not overcome without the most intense and protracted debate and struggle. The origins of the Punjab Alienation of Land Act may be traced more particularly to developments in the Punjab and in India than to parallel and no doubt not altogether irrelevant developments in England.

Then it must not be forgotten that India itself influenced English statesmen. Rivaz's influence on Curzon is as undoubted as that of other Indian civilians on Curzon's predecessors. In this sense Curzon was just one more link in a very long chain; just one more important individual who stimulated certain general trends in opinion rather than repressing them. And Indian influences on English statesmen may be traced at the India Office as well as in the Government of India. Hamilton not only shared the general opinion regarding the political importance of the landholders, but also in the particular matter of the restriction of the power of alienation he could not help but be influenced by the India Council. He might try to by-pass the majority of the Council; but he could hardly have met Curzon's wishes if the Council had been opposed to all restrictions on the power of alienation. That they were not was due to general trends in British-Indian opinion which had now reached the India Office; a conclusion which is easily substantiated, for instance, by reference to the views of Fitzpatrick, Hutchins and Crosthwaite, all members of the India Council, and all influenced at an earlier stage by the development of British-Indian opinion.

One aspect of the question on which the Viceroy and the Secretary of State exerted little or no influence was that of the actual restrictions which were to be imposed on the power of alienation. On this point the views of Young and Rivaz were as diametrically opposed as they could well be, for the former wanted to minimise, the latter to maximise the interference with commercial principles. The Punjab committee had imposed general restrictions on the power of mortgage, while only restricting permanent alienations when made to money-lenders. Yet in the end not only did Rivaz fail to bend these decisions further in the direction of his own ideas, but he failed even to maintain fully the restrictions which the Punjab committee had accepted. As applied in practice the Punjab Alienation of Land Act was directed almost entirely against the professional money-lenders, the only exception being provisions regarding mortgages by condi-

## THE SHAPE OF LEGISLATION

tional sale. The reasons for this turn of events must be sought in the character of Rivaz's adversary and in the weapons which that adversary had at his disposal. Young was determined to use every possible means to limit the restrictions imposed on the power of alienation; and in his desire to confine restrictions to alienations to professional money-lenders he stood closer to the bulk of Provincial opinion than Rivaz. Given a different Lieutenant-Governor in the Punjab, Rivaz might have succeeded in maintaining his position; but with Young accentuating those aspects of Provincial opinion which were opposed to Rivaz's schemes, and making certain that men of that opinion were on the Select Committee, Rivaz was forced to give way on a number of points. His desire to impose restrictions on non-agricultural landholders had been defeated very early in the piece, apparently without any particularly important contribution by Young. But Rivaz's aim of restricting the transfer of land to landholders was not likely to have been defeated by any less determined an opponent than Young. It must be remembered that Young had not achieved his ends at once: he had secured the concession to the tribe, then the concession to the group of tribes, and finally the decision to place all tribes in the same group. A more tarnished trophy, but one equally the outcome of Young's tenacious convictions, was the retention of the 'agriculturist' in the Act, a provision which had been introduced into an earlier version of Rivaz's proposals, for a purpose which differed from that of Young's, and which did not a little to render legislation unnecessarily complex and obscure. Here Young was working against rather than with the grain; and it is not surprising to see that within the first decade of the new century Young's victory in this respect was set at nought by an amendment of the Act.

Throughout these struggles between Rivaz and Young one consideration was overlooked by both; and that was the attitudes of the urban and educated sections of Punjab society. It was not merely that the British were trying to shore up the rural foundations of British rule at a time when the trading castes were showing their capacity for organisation and agitation, and the landholders their passivity; or that retrospective provisions regarding mortgages by conditional sale which formed no essential part of the legislation were maintained despite the special rumours and anxieties to which such provisions gave rise among those most critically affected by legislation. It was also a question of the communal implications of legislation. Those implications were revealed most clearly perhaps when educated Muslims showed their concern that the third form of mortgage should not be allowed to undermine the Act. The inherent communal implications of the measure were distinctly heightened, however, by the concessions which Young extracted from Rivaz; for the attempt to discriminate against the money-lender alone, ensured that educated Muslims would not be placed on the same level as educated Hindus. The privilege of acquiring land permanently would be denied to the educated Hindu because his membership of a trading caste ensured that he would be ranked with the money-lender; but it would not be denied to most educated Muslims for their appellations ensured, quite apart from their occupations, that they would be placed among the agricultural tribes and hence free to acquire land. Yet no one touched on this point at all. Ironically enough a legislative measure which became something of a communal issue in the Punjab, acquired much of its character in that respect from a debate about the economic feasibility of restricting the power of alienation.

## CHAPTER VI

# Triumph of the New Tradition

I

In June 1901 the Punjab Alienation of Land Act came into force all over the Province, only land within municipal and cantonment limits, the Simla district, and the areas incorporated in the new North-West Frontier Province being exempted.[1] The advocates of legislation had won the day; but their victory would not be complete or even ensured unless legislation achieved the objects for which it had been designed. For some eight years the Act was the subject of special official attention; and its working during that period confirmed the trends which had led to its formulation.[2]

The Act was undoubtedly effective in preventing the permanent acquisition of land by the trading castes. In a few western districts the numbers of those who could claim the status of 'agriculturist' were limited by fixing a settlement earlier than the regular settlement as the one from which the status derived. The privileges of the 'agriculturist' were not understood at first; and in 1907 these privileges were abolished by an amendment of the Act. Contrary to expectation, applications for sanction to sell land to non-agriculturists were not numerous; but they gradually increased over the years. These applications were sanctioned only in exceptional circumstances: where the land was required for building sites, for instance, or where the mortgagor could redeem his land by selling part of it. Professional money-lenders were very shy of the new forms of mortgage; and it was only after the first few years that they gradually began to accept the self-redeeming usufructuary mortgage. The third form of mortgage, which provided for the retention of occupancy rights by the mortgagor, remained a dead letter. Many expedients were devised to evade the provisions of the Act; but Ibbetson's fears that a measure which prohibited transfers to non-agriculturists alone, would be constantly evaded, did not materialise. The legal position of the alienee was usually too insecure for evasion to be widespread and common.

The decrease in the area of land sold and mortgaged each year appeared to be directly traceable to the Act. At first the area of land redeemed also decreased; not surprisingly, as often land had been redeemed only to be re-mortgaged. After a few years, with rising agricultural prices, redemptions increased. In each year from 1905 to 1908 the agricultural tribes redeemed more land than they mortgaged; and the Provincial percentage of cultivated area under mortgage began to fall.

The less provident tribes, Rajputs and others, continued to lose land, though perhaps not as quickly as before; and acquisitive tribes like the Hindu and Sikh Jats and the market-gardeners continued to acquire it. It was only in the central Punjab that the acquisitive spirit was marked and widespread among agricultural tribes. The Act probably strengthened the position of all those notified as agricultural tribes, the acquisitive, the thrifty and the improvident.

The serious depreciation in the value of land, which many had anticipated, did not eventuate. There was a temporary depreciation in the selling and mortgaging value of land; but after a few years it began to rise again and by 1908 it certainly stood at a higher level than ever before. Agricultural credit was restricted to some extent; but the Act stood the test of scarcity in 1905–6 and 1907–8. There was no great difficulty in collecting the revenue. A significant, though no doubt temporary, decrease in extravagant expenditure and litigation was apparent. It may be too that the professional money-lenders began to show greater care in lending, lest the borrower be unable to repay principal with interest; and that some of the capital which previously would have been advanced to landowners now sought an outlet in wholesale and retail trade and industry.

The Act did not greatly increase the work of the revenue authorities; and in some respects there was a counter-balancing decrease in work.

Among the agricultural tribes the introduction of the Act occasioned no excitement. Rumours about legislation curtailing existing mortgages or about Government confiscation of the land gave place to an idea much closer to the truth, namely, that Government had forbidden landowners to alienate to money-lenders. There was no sign of any feeling that the proprietary status had been destroyed. On the contrary, those notified as agricultural tribes thought that a social distinction had been conferred on them; and they looked down on those who had not been notified. It was social considerations, as well as the protection from the money-lender which the Act afforded, which made it distinctly popular among the agricultural tribes of the Province.[3]

## TRIUMPH OF THE NEW TRADITION

The landowners who had not been notified felt their exclusion keenly. There were petitions for notification from ordinary landowning tribes, whose numbers had not been considered sufficient to warrant notification. There were petitions from the tribes of low status: from the Ramgarhia Sikhs (Tarkhans), presented by an educated member of their community; from the Sikh Labanas in the army supported by the military authorities; and from Kalals and Kakezais. Petitions from Brahmins came from several parts of the Province. The few communities of Sayads, Kureshis, Mughals and the like, who had not been notified, and Shekhs of all descriptions, sought notification. Nor did such petitions cease after the first few years; they became a regular feature of the administration of the Act.[4]

Various motives appear to have inspired these petitions. There were some who sought the protection of the Act. More often those who petitioned desired the power of acquisition. Some wanted to obtain grants of land in the colonies, these grants now being confined to members of notified agricultural tribes. The military Brahmins of Rawalpindi sought notification in order that they might still be eligible for military service, their chances in this respect having been severely prejudiced apparently by their exclusion from the agricultural tribes. Very often petitions for notification were entirely or partially inspired by the desire to escape the social degradation which exclusion from the agricultural tribes involved.

These petitions led to much enquiry and debate among British officers. Generally those tribes which had been excluded merely because they had been overlooked were notified. There was not much support for the claims of Kalals, Kakezais, Shekhs and others, who were too often non-agricultural. There was more support for the Labanas and Brahmins. Rivaz, who had succeeded Young as Lieutenant-Governor, had been obliged to accede to a grouping of tribes which exposed the weaker to the stronger; and he was determined not to give the privilege of acquisition to any tribes not already notified whose antecedents were to any degree non-agricultural or commercial. He finally consented to the inclusion of Labanas, because they had been notified already in one district. He refused to notify the Brahmins; but his successors were more liberal in this respect.

To the discontent of those whose petitions were rejected must be added that of the thrifty village menials and artisans whose acquisition of land was hampered if not altogether checked.[5]

Among the Hindu trading castes, money-lenders, officials, business and professional men, the Land Alienation Act created serious discontent. All found their investment in land checked; and the pleaders suffered a serious diminution in income from the decline in litigation. Agitation and organisation had disappeared with the passage of the Bill into law; but there was a widespread and deep-seated feeling among educated Hindus that they had been unjustly dealt with and that the British did not govern in their interests.[6]

The Muslim newspapers and most educated Muslims, on the other hand, were strongly in favour of an Act which prevented the acquisition of land by non-agricultural Hindus, while placing no restrictions on acquisitions by the vast majority of educated Muslims. There was, nonetheless, discontent among educated Muslims of commercial background, like the Shekhs and Kakezais, whose power of acquisition was limited just as much as that of the Hindu traders.[7]

The Act, in short, had accomplished the main ends of its advocates. It had done so without marked administrative inconvenience or economic dislocation. The Act had gained not the obloquy but the support of the agricultural tribes; and their appreciation of the measure had been more distinct than anyone had dared to predict, owing to the social advantages attaching to notification. The most serious opposition had come from a quarter from which it had been more or less expected and discounted in advance. Not only had the opponents of legislation been defeated, but it also appeared that they had been proved wrong.

This was not a judgement which Mackworth Young, in retirement, was prepared to accept. In a paper on the progress of the Punjab, read to a meeting of the East India Association in December 1904, he adhered to his personal view that the Act had not been required and that it would diminish the agricultural prosperity of the Province in the long run.[8] Dennis Fitzpatrick attended the meeting but did not speak. It was remarkable, however, that a third ex-Lieutenant-Governor, James Lyall, defended the Alienation Act against Young. There had been a great danger which had called for immediate legislation, Lyall thought, and it was better on the whole that that legislation should be strong, as it could be relaxed if necessary. Under the influence of apparent success, Lyall could assent to legislation of a kind which he had opposed in no uncertain terms while in office. It was the last prominent example of that gradual development of official opinion which had done so much to advance the cause of legislation and which would sustain that legislation when passed. Lyall was supported by Thorburn who had every reason to be satisfied with the course of events, but who still looked forward to revenue and judicial reform.[9]

These were the views of men no longer in direct touch with events. In India itself the working of the Act in both its economic and political aspects had silenced the old opponents of legislation. Its advocates at every level – Ibbetson, Council Member in the Government of India, Rivaz and Dane, Lieutenant-Governors, Tupper and Wilson, Financial Commissioners, and other senior Punjab officers – were convinced that their policy had been more than justified. Alexander Anderson still wanted to create smaller groups of agricultural tribes; but Tupper and Rivaz himself took the line that this should not be done until the alienation statistics showed that this was necessary.[10]

The agitation of the trading classes had not been entirely without effect on the minds of the British. There was a feeling, shared by Ibbetson, Rivaz, Tupper, Douie, Montgomery and others, that for some time to come there should be no more class legislation in the Punjab. The attitude of the trading castes to future legislation was taken a little more seriously. No hesitation was shown, however, in abolishing the privileges of the money-lender 'agriculturist' in 1907, even though little use had been made so far of these privileges.

As for a new generation of officers, those who had come to the Punjab since the 1880s, they accepted the Land Alienation Act as an integral part of the administrative system of the Province.[11] Just as aspects of the old protective policy had come to be widely accepted because they worked more or less well, so the Land Alienation Act became an accepted feature of British rule in the Punjab. The economic objections to legislation had been misplaced, or so it seemed; the true political objections to legislation most British officers were hardly able to appreciate.

It may be that it is even more difficult to assign an end than a beginning to a movement of opinion. But when we read in the concluding paragraph of the last special report on the Land Alienation Act, dated 1909, that the hereditary proprietors looked on the Act as 'the charter of their rights' and as 'evidence that the Government sympathises with them in their dearest interests'[12] it is difficult not to feel that the new opinions had become the orthodox and established ones.

II

It is further testimony to the varied effects which social phenomena exerted on official opinion that the Punjab Alienation of Land Act, so closely bound up with the new political tradition, should prove to be in one instance the catalyst for the development of a political vision altogether without precedent.

John Maynard may not have been opposed to legislation to restrict the power of alienation from the very beginning. As Junior Secretary to the Punjab Government he referred incidentally in September 1898 to the prohibition of alienation as the real remedy for agrarian troubles. This, however, was in the context of opposition to 'benevolent tinkerings' with the general law of contract; opposition of a kind which found favour with Mackworth Young.[13] And the distaste which John Maynard showed in 1899 for the Alienation of Land Bill certainly derived from a commitment to the most orthodox version of the intellectual tradition. All Maynard's sympathies were with the lender, the businessman and the natural economic and social process. Yet given this particular slant on affairs, it would not do to underrate Maynard's powers of observation. His defence of the freedom to alienate might be inspired by intellectual considerations, but that defence was intimately related to particular circumstances prevailing in the district in his charge.[14]

By the same token the charges which Maynard levelled at the Punjab Alienation of Land Act in the years which followed, while not without their economic content, took particular account of all the practical weaknesses and anomalies which characterised that legislation. What others deemed to be unavoidable concomitants of a worthwhile endeavour, Maynard singled out for special condemnation. First and foremost in this respect stood what he referred to in December 1901 (with reference to attempts to discriminate between agriculturists and others in the matter of a limitation law for debt) as the 'vicious principle of legislation in favour of a particular class'.[15] That was a principle which had become all the stronger by the decision to put all agricultural tribes in the same group, a decision to which Maynard himself had contributed in his efforts to minimise the restrictions imposed on natural economic and social processes.[16] Maynard objected, however, to the extension of the principle of class legislation; a principle which he thought was not really applicable to the conditions which prevailed in Punjab society.

> The original justification for according special treatment to the cultivating classes was their assumed unfitness for holding their own with men of business. This was reinforced by the consideration that discontent among the peasantry which is the backbone of the population is politically dangerous. The Punjab has been ruled

## TRIUMPH OF THE NEW TRADITION

for fifty years on the old-fashioned principle of equal laws, and the people have learned something in that period. The simple zamindar who will agree to anything because he knows no better, is no longer a normal type. He has given place to an astuter being who knows how to play upon the benevolent sentiments of his governors, who not infrequently makes money and lends it, and is sometimes harder on his debtor than the most stony-hearted of Banias.

I have before me the case of a Saiyad who, having lost heavily by speculation over canal contracts, has for years resisted the just claims of his creditors by fair means and by foul, and is now on the eve of a final triumph over them because he is a member of an agricultural tribe and therefore the land which is his only tangible property cannot be sold in execution of decree. Such 'simple zamindars' are by no means uncommon. The argument based on a supposed 'political' danger is harder to meet. But it is permissible to point out that the sturdiest of the Punjab peasantry are not, as a rule, incapable of defending their own interests. The Jat, at all events, needs no nursing.[17]

And Maynard went on to argue that, if the landholders were by no means always simpletons, the money-lenders were not as black as they had been painted. As a 'widespread type' the 'cruel money-lender' was another creation of the 'philanthropic imagination'. There were whole colonies of Banias who never thought of taking cases before the courts and regarded their money as already lost as soon as there was a rupture of amicable relations with the borrower. But these lenders were not sufficiently attractive figures to enlist sentiment, as the rival class had succeeded in doing. Examination of the figures for the execution of decrees, Maynard added, should suffice to convince the 'most ardent poor man's friend' how weak the lender really was.[18]

Quite unable to appreciate the logic which lay behind the Punjab Alienation of Land Act, Maynard had more than an inkling of the dangers of class legislation.

It is possible, by the authoritative demonstration of sympathy, to encourage dangerous delusions. The cultivator is led to believe that he has the support of the authorities in resisting pressure; and a claim to special treatment once admitted, is not without hopes of a coming jubilee when debts will be extinguished and lands restored.

> I do not say this without tangible reason. From petitions, oral and written, which have come before me, I find that the people have no idea at what point Government draws the line between justice and repudiation.
>
> Something had been done to uproot the oriental notion that law is the caprice of the ruler. This is being undone; and both order and credit will suffer.[19]

This was as far as Maynard went at the end of 1901.

In 1904 in criticising discrimination between classes in regard to pre-emption Maynard went rather further. His attacks on class legislation had now assumed the character of a crusade.

> There remains for consideration the proposal to exclude from the right of pre-emption in agricultural land those classes which are not privileged under the Punjab Land Alienation Act. This, I understand, to be the kernel of the Bill, and the policy involved in it is not discussed by the Select Committee because the matter is regarded as res judicata. I shall venture to offer some remarks on the point, because those evils, which I apprehend from the introduction of class distinctions into the law, do not arise so much from the enactment of a particular statute, as from the establishment of a precedent, out of which further legislation of a similar character is likely to grow: so that each successive stage at which the principle of discrimination is applied becomes a suitable occasion for the delivery of such protests as can without impropriety be put on record. Government has entered upon a course which is, in my opinion, to be deprecated: but the extent to which it has already committed itself is not so great that no useful purpose would be served by now calling a halt.[20]

The favourable response of the landholders to the Punjab Alienation of Land Act had done anything but convince Maynard of the desirability of that piece of legislation. The working of the Act provided him with further material for his critique of class legislation.

> To be classed among the privileged tribes is undoubtedly regarded as a mark of favour, to be omitted a mark of disfavour. The spirit of rivalry is very easily aroused in this country, and probably most of us have seen, in the course of district administration, the untoward results of any actual or apparent inclination to one party or another on the part of authority. In ordinary course the

European officer escapes the suspicion of bias, because, Gallio like, he cares for none of these things: but occasionally his zeal, or his sympathy, appears to engage him personally in the controversy: and, when that happens, faction always tends to assume a more serious aspect, because the party which thinks itself disfavoured has ceased to feel the existence of an impartial referee standing outside the sphere of controversy, and because the opposite party is encouraged to press the supposed advantage. It seems to me that, in discriminating between classes, Government has done, on a large scale, that which a District Officer, inexperienced or off his guard, occasionally does on a small scale. It has conveyed the impression that it regards itself as the patron of the zamindar, and that it identifies political advantage with his contentment and well-being, not with the contentment and well-being of the whole mass of its subjects. In doing this it has set the various classes by the ears, and called into existence jealousies and rivalries which should have remained dormant. It is impossible to converse widely with natives, without observing how large a part in their thoughts is now played by the establishment of their own tribal status, as against that of rivals. The Sheikhs, who cannot be classed with the agricultural tribes because his caste includes so many who are obviously not entitled, burns with eagerness to prove the descent of his own particular section from Arabian immigrants. The Kalal, self-named an Ahluwalia, points to the number of his tribe who are in the Army, and claims to be as good a Kshatriya as any Rajput. The Brahman bitterly hints that he is, among Hindus, precisely what the Syad is among Muhammedans, and that he is only excluded from the privilege allowed to the latter, because of some mysterious preference in high quarters for the other religion. The Jat or Rajput, who has the desired privilege, wants to know why Government made the strange mistake of putting such mere tenants, 'raiyat log', as Malis and Rains, on the same footing as real zamindars. As for the Khatri, Arora and Mahajan, they say nothing, because there is obviously nothing to say: but they unquestionably feel that they are not in favour; their temper both towards the privileged tribes and towards Government is not improved by this feeling; and the relations of confidence which, despite the dominant opinion to the contrary, did exist between many money-lenders and their clients, have received a serious blow. Now these are the classes which supply the bulk of the professional men, as well as the leading traders and capitalists: and it is a very narrow conception of political advantage which assumes that their attitude can be ignored.[21]

Maynard had begun to question rather more seriously not merely the economic but the political advantages of legislation.

At the end of 1901 Maynard had not been certain about how to combat the argument that land transfer involved political danger. He was at that time still under the spell of the old though not the new political tradition. A year later his remark with reference to 'the preservation of existing aristocracies, as a potential source of light and leading' that 'no one who has realised the hopelessness of influencing the masses of men otherwise than through their natural leaders, or of creating such leaders where the material does not exist, can doubt the justification for the attempt' shows an awareness of the role of influential minorities which fitted but ill with either old or new political tradition.[22] That awareness stood him in good stead in 1904 when his observation of various social manifestations led him to take a view of British rule which cut right across both the old and the new political tradition.

> We appear to stand at the commencement of a new phase of development. The country is ceasing to be exclusively agricultural, and the beginnings of industrial activity are discernible. In the course of the present century it is probable that town populations will grow, and, should this happen, they will tend to have an increasing influence on the rural tracts. I have observed (principally in connection with measures of plague prevention) that the zamindar takes his opinions mainly from the place where he does his marketing, and the larger the town, the more notably does it affect the ideas of the neighbourhood. Now it is immeasurably harder for an official to win confidence among the sophisticated, yet ignorant, crowd of a city than among a rustic population; and the British Government, which has done so much to enlist the sympathies of the latter, has before it an infinitely more difficult task in establishing the loyalty of growing industrial centres. In the long run, I believe, we must stand or fall, not by our solution of the simple and attractive problems of rural India, but by the faculty which we shall develop of dealing with the educated man, the trader, and the townsman generally, classes for whom we have no instinctive sympathy, and who are everywhere apt to be captious and unappreciative. If this be a correct forecast of what lies before us, how bad a beginning are we

making, by establishing privileges from which the classes which will dominate the towns are deliberately excluded, under the delusion that political advantage consists in establishing the landed rights of the peasantry only.[23]

Nor was Maynard content to stress the political role of the town alone. In tackling the argument that British laws had from the beginning given special privileges to particular classes, he pointed to social change at levels below that of the peasant proprietor, levels which the Punjab tradition had assumed to be of very subordinate or no political significance.

> It will be urged, no doubt, that our law, as it stood, practically created a privileged class, because of the advantage which it gave to the astute and business-like. It favoured brains, no doubt: but the brains might belong to a man of any tribe or race, and if they were largely monopolised by particular classes, this was in some measure a temporary condition. At all events it was felt that our system established no fixed status, opposed no impassable barrier to development and advancement: and anyone who has conversed with the more eager spirits among the backward classes must realise how greatly this feature of our rule was, and is, appreciated. It is impossible to do more than hint at all the issues which are involved in the free opening of every door to every class: but I feel bound to point out that ... we are witnessing ... the rise of the outcaste, the non-Hindu or aboriginal, in the social scale: and that, by including him among the non-privileged classes in regard to land, we shut one of the doors upon a legitimate aspiration. Our truest and greatest political advantage consists in the establishment of the unassailable belief that our rule offers equal opportunities to all, though it cannot redress the inequalities which nature has created: that we keep the ring clear, and see fair play, without allowing foul blows or savagery in the struggle.[24]

Maynard ended his protest against the introduction of class differentiation into the law of pre-emption with a historical reference. 'I find it impossible to forget that the greatest of the predecessors of the British in the dominion of India began to lose control over her heterogeneous populations when they ceased to hold the balance even between them.'[25]

Maynard continued to press these ideas on Government, missing no opportunity of castigating class legislation in general or the

Alienation Act in particular. Despite the apparently favourable economic results of the Act, he still insisted at the end of 1904 that the 'economic evil consists in the frightening of the capitalist and the impairing of credit', though it is significant that his arguments in this respect were now more or less confined to the 'deplorable decision to make a portion of the recent legislation retrospective in its character'.[26] But if Maynard's economic arguments were becoming less forceful, he was beginning to find social arguments against legislation. One of the most serious changes which he apprehended from the operation of the Land Alienation Act, he noted in July 1906, was the artificial arrest of those natural and beneficial processes of social change which prevented society from becoming stereotyped in an outgrown form; namely the process by which the names and status of particular castes were adjusted to changes of material wealth and condition.[27] This aspect of his outlook was also apparent in the opposition which he expressed at the end of the year to the abolition of the 'agriculturist' of the Alienation Act. The statutory agriculturist was something of an anomaly in the Act, but Maynard defended the retention of that category as a check on other anomalies in the Act, namely the supposed division of a changing society into water-tight compartments.

> The essential rigidity of our law, by necessitating the treatment of all classes as equally capable of understanding and defending their own interests, gave rise to the conditions which were considered to justify legislation in restraint of alienation. The same rigidity, changed in form, but unchanged in essence, has divided classes into agricultural and non-agricultural, according to the labels of their caste names, assigning the Shekh or Ahluwalia Native Officer, the Arora or Brahman Zamindar, the Bedi or Sodhi with his inheritance of dull-wittedness and sanctity, to the category of the astute and predatory, and leaving the close-fisted and ruthless Jat Sahukar among the innocents who are unfit to take care of themselves. This is doubtless inevitable, but every element of elasticity should be fostered by way of palliative to the evil. The legal status of the agriculturist was the recognition of facts of daily experience: that the 'structure of rural society' is not a thing fixed from time immemorial, and immune for ever from change and development: and that sections and individuals have attained a position to which the label of their caste-name does not . . . entitle them.[28]

Maynard also continued to urge the political significance of non-agriculturists on the Government. 'It is an error to suppose', he wrote in December 1904, 'that the so-called non-agricultural classes are of no importance politically.' History showed that they had often produced leaders; and, he added, he had observed that the 'intelligence, as well as the wealth', of one of the non-agricultural groups gave it occasionally 'a dominating influence over rural opinion'.[29] The historical point was driven home in November 1906 in conjunction with a social point. Maynard, arguing for the retention of the statutory agriculturist in the Land Alienation Act, noted that stress had often been laid on the danger of subordinating the hereditary owners of land to their social inferiors.

> It will be found that the person who can establish agriculturist status is rarely of inferior social standing. At least, it would have been startling to the Bedi or Sodhi, or the Khatri General or Administrator, of a couple of generations back (to General Hari Singh Nalwa, let us say, or Diwan Sawan Mal) to learn that the humble Arain or Mali tenant, whom he valued for the same reasons that he valued a good cow or bullock, would one day be held *on social grounds* to have superior claims to the ownership of the land.[30]

In criticising the Punjab Alienation of Land Act Maynard took no account of the fact that the more overt elements of class discrimination in that legislation, and the anomalies which characterised its working, were to be attributed not only to the new political tradition, but also to the old intellectual tradition, which insisted on reducing economic evils by cutting down the severity of the restrictions imposed on the power of alienation. Approaching legislation from the standpoint of the old intellectual tradition, however, Maynard could perhaps hardly be expected to realise the responsibility which officers like himself bore for the particular form which legislation took. It was that same standpoint as well as other considerations, which helped Maynard in drawing a novel political lesson from the response to the Land Alienation Act. It was not a lesson which the majority of officers could appreciate, or which they would find it easy to learn. The new political tradition had been long in the making; and John Maynard's protests testify only to its hour of triumph.

III

'We appear to stand at the commencement of a new phase of development.' So John Maynard had written in 1904. But the dead weight of the new political tradition would exert its influence well into the twentieth century. The considerations to which John Maynard pointed were not likely to receive much attention because there was so little in the Punjab tradition to which they could appeal. The new political tradition had been able to appeal to the old; but John Maynard had few foundations on which to build. Yet the political awakening among urban and educated Indians was increasingly becoming an overt and immediate political problem, in a way that the question of land transfer had never done. And whatever the merits of the British political tradition in the Punjab, the Province could not escape the influences which were beginning to shake the Indian Empire as a whole. It seems doubtful whether even John Maynard had more than an inkling of what was to come. The man who sought to protect British rule against urban disaffection in 1904 was apparently a strong supporter of the Montagu-Chelmsford reforms after the war,[31] and in retirement in later years played a role in preparing the Labour party in England for greater concessions to Indian nationalism.[32]

It was in this period of rapid change that the legacy of the nineteenth century worked itself out. A glance at the Lieutenant-Governors who succeeded Mackworth Young serves to tell the tale. Little need be said about his immediate successor, Charles Rivaz; but that individual never declared his opinion more clearly perhaps, than when, towards the end of his term of office, being asked in a social gathering what he thought of the fact that the Indian National Congress had declared its aim to be self-government, he replied with characteristic brevity, 'bunkum'.[33] About Ibbetson likewise little more need be said; but it is interesting that in writing of the agitation of 1907, 'essentially addressed to the townsfolk', he should add that the movement had also assumed 'a far more dangerous form', in that 'a definite anti-English propaganda' had been started 'among the villagers'.[34] To Rivaz and Ibbetson must be added L. W. Dane, T. G. Walker, and J. M. Douie, the last two having officiated as Lieutenant-Governor. All these men without exception had played some fairly prominent role in furthering the cause of restrictions on the power of alienation. Walker's position is perhaps sufficiently clear from his comment as Financial Commissioner in 1906 that John Maynard was prejudiced against the Land Alienation Act.[35] James Douie, who held the office of Lieutenant-Governor for a few months in 1911, could write after his retirement, in a work published in 1916, that in 'a country owned so largely by small farmers, the first task of the Government must be to secure their welfare and contentment'.[36] Nor were views of this kind confined to Lieutenant-Governors whose service in India dated from the 1860s or the 1870s. M. F. O'Dwyer, who assumed office in 1913, held exactly those views which were current in the 1880s, when his period of service began. 'Throughout my term of office', O'Dwyer wrote in a work published in 1926, 'I did what I could to further the interests of the rural masses whom I regarded as the basis of the stability and prosperity of the Province.'[37] To O'Dwyer 'the races that count' were still 'the races that can fight'.[38] And when the Reforms scheme was under discussion in 1918–19, he objected to 'the transfer of such wide powers to a small class of politicians, mainly urban, who were not in any sense either representative of the rural masses or sympathetic to their needs and interests'.[39] O'Dwyer's successor, E. D. Maclagan, did not hesitate to recall in later years the role he had played 'behind the scenes' in the discussions which led to the enactment of the Punjab Land Alienation Act.[40]

And what of future generations of officers? Consider H. K. Trevaskis, who served in the Punjab from 1905, and whose economic history of the Province, published in 1928, made no secret of his admiration for Thorburn's campaign for rural legislation.[41] But against Trevaskis there must doubtless be set Punjab officers like the one who wrote in 1924 that 'in the future there is not much prospect for British officials except such as are willing to be fellow-workers with Indians in the realisation of ideals the last word on which is to lie with Indians.'[42] Many years before another officer, Malcolm Darling, who appears to have made John Maynard's acquaintance,[43] had commented with reference to Rivaz's dismissal of Congress aspirations that 'when you see a spark near gunpowder, it is better to take the thing seriously'.[44] It is fitting, indeed, to end with a reference to Malcolm Darling; for in him we still find many of the elements which had gone to the making of the Punjab tradition. While accepting the Land Alienation Act, he shared those doubts about the ultimate results of protective legislation which had been so influential in the nineteenth century. And with his interest in urban and educated India he combined that involvement with rural India (in his case shorn of much of its political implications) which had done so much to shape the Punjab tradition,[45] and which had rendered its adherents so unprepared to meet the political problems of the twentieth century.

# CHAPTER VII

# Conclusion

To recall that in 1869 Arthur Brandreth emerged as the first representative of a point of view which by 1909 found an outspoken opponent only in John Maynard is to realise that these forty years encompass a distinct period in the British political and intellectual tradition in the Punjab. A period, that is, not in any sense of the persistence of given opinions, but in the sense of an overt movement of opinion. That view is not rendered any weaker by recognition of the fact that from different standpoints it might be quite possible to discern different periods in the history of the Punjab tradition. Nor is the sense of period invalidated by any admissions to the effect that faint signs of its tendencies may be detected in earlier years or that views which do not come into their own until later already find some limited expression in the closing stages of the period. Considerations of this kind are inseparable from any attempt to detect a pattern in the thoughts and impulses of many men.

The attempt to detect such a pattern raises a fundamental problem of historical explanation. Once it is admitted that men differ one from the other, and respond in different ways even to similar stimuli, it is easy enough to see that no historical period can ever be visualised in absolute terms, that individual exceptions to general rules must always remain. It is more difficult, however, to see why there should be any periods at all. How does one explain general trends in spite of individual differences? It is this question which leads to the search for major influences on the minds of men.

In the present context it is social influences which are to the fore. Changes in the possession of agricultural land were themselves immensely varied, and their influence was exerted in a number of ways, but common to all these changes was their steady and progressive character which provides a focal point for any explanation of the movement of opinion over the years. The opening stages of the period saw a gradual acceptance of the notion that distinct changes in the possession of land were taking place; the continuation of these changes stimulated opinion throughout the period; and attempts to control these changes marked the closing stages of the period. The beginnings, development and alleviation of political anxiety on the score of land transfer distinguish a complete cycle in the British political tradition in the Punjab.

The new political tradition could not have developed without the old. It is inconceivable that so many officers could have taken such a serious view of land transfer but for their belief that British rule was based on rural loyalty. It is exceedingly difficult to believe that the views of such men could have made much headway had they not been able to appeal to a political tradition which was generally accepted. And towards the end of the period it seems more than likely that the desire for drastic legislation would have been less apparent, and opposition to such legislation stronger and more effective, had it not been for a political tradition which discounted the political importance of the town, the trader and the educated Indian. Yet to confer such importance on the old political tradition is to stress the role of social influence once more; for the old tradition modelled itself on Punjab village society, looking primarily to the stability and welfare of those who appeared to dominate the village by virtue of indigenous social circumstances as well as by virtue of British land and revenue policy.

Of course this particular social manifestation cannot be considered in isolation, apart from other factors, any more than the process of land transfer itself. A variety of considerations, some internal, some external, combined to induce the British to look to the village. Indian administrative circumstances served to rivet their attention firmly on the village. It was here too that a handful of alien rulers could find some semblance of mass support, some tokens of acquiescence or good-will, and some cultural traits which struck a responsive chord in Victorian hearts. By contrast the British were administratively less concerned with the towns. The urban areas did not appear to provide a mass base, or an easily satisfied class ready to extend loyalty. And culturally the towns were entirely alien, striking no spark in the British imagination, and perhaps arousing considerable offence at times. But to take account of these larger considerations is not to deny the role of social influence; for acting within these conditions it was social influences which shaped that particular version of the British political tradition which came to prevail in the Punjab.

A desire to emphasise positive factors should not lead us to discount the importance of negative factors. Intellectual considerations of the orthodox type played a very considerable role in the whole story. In the opening years of the period such considerations inhibited recognition of the new agrarian problem; throughout the period these considerations seriously affected the action considered feasible or permissible; and in the end these considerations had much to say to the final shape which legislation took. Without *laissez-faire* and evolutionist trends in British thinking, without the strong British commitment to individual property, there would have been no rising tide of anxiety at all; for without these ideas the problem could have been tackled at once. It was the orthodox British intellectual tradition which ensured that the new political tradition would not triumph easily, that it would not triumph for many years, and hence when it did triumph, that its victory would be considered of immense importance. In this sense the ordinary intellectual tradition was ultimately of great political significance.

It would not do to see this intellectual tradition purely in terms of outside influences on British officers. That is no doubt an element which requires very distinct emphasis. But just as social influences did not operate independently of other factors, so it is clear that in some respects intellectual influences cannot be considered apart from the society to which they were applied. It may be that some officers were only stressing particular elements in Punjab society which fitted in with *laissez-faire* or evolutionist ideas; but it is also true that other officers were induced to give particular importance to such ideas because they appeared to be peculiarly appropriate in the circumstances of Punjab society.

It is with reference to the development of an alternative intellectual tradition, however, that social influence comes into its own. Practically all the ideas which suggested that legislation was feasible or desirable were drawn from Punjab and Indian experience. Here too social influences cannot always be separated from intellectual; or, to put it rather more precisely, the influences exerted by Indian society cannot always be separated from those intellectual influences which originated in Britain. But the intellectual revolution which rendered the Punjab Alienation of Land Act possible, owed far more to Indian experience than to new intellectual trends in Britain.

Without giving due emphasis to social influence it is not possible to make sense of the period between 1869 and 1909 at all. Yet that is not the same thing as saying that a complete explanation can be given in terms of social influences acting within certain conditions; for these influences worked through the minds and personalities of men. And since different individuals were influenced in different

## CONCLUSION

ways, and some individuals were more powerful or influential than others, any explanation must take account of the actions of particular individuals at particular times. It is tempting of course to see in those influences which radiated from Punjab and Indian society an irresistible force before which all must bend and give way. But that is to ignore the fact that at every stage general trends might be inhibited or stimulated by particular individuals. At any particular point in time it was not just general trends but the response of individuals to those trends which determined the outcome. All that can be said is that general opinion favouring legislation became steadily stronger, as a result of a combination of general and particular factors, and that it set ever more specific terms of reference for those who sought to control the course of events.

Ultimately the period from 1869 to 1909 witnessed a new political as well as a new intellectual tradition; and this is important in its own right. But there were also implications for the future. The new intellectual tradition was not likely to lose its hold on the official mind once the Punjab Alienation of Land Act had proved to be so successful; and indeed it was not the last example of official intervention in the relations between debtor and creditor. It could be argued that once the Act had set British anxieties at rest, the new political tradition was only the old political tradition writ large. But that conclusion is not without importance. The political tradition had not been submerged, it had been revised and emphasised, and given institutional recognition at a time when quite new political problems loomed on the horizon. It is interesting to reflect that a political tradition which looked on the peasant proprietor as a political force, albeit a passive one, in times of crisis, developed in such a fashion that it came to dominate British thinking at a time when it was not so much isolated crises as a state of crisis which demanded attention.

# Notes

CHAPTER I

1 Only specific references, and matters not discussed in greater detail in succeeding chapters, are documented in this chapter.
2 *Punjab Quarterly Civil List*, January 1882, pp. 2–3.
3 For the early history of land-revenue settlement, discussed in this and the succeeding paragraph, see the administration reports of the 1850s, and the settlement reports of the first regular settlements. Later settlement and assessment reports provide supplementary information.
4 The first regular settlement of most Punjab districts was completed in the 1850s or, more rarely, in the 1860s. In a few frontier districts regular settlements were not introduced till the 1870s. The districts of the Delhi territory, which did not become part of the Punjab Province till 1858, had come under regular settlement from the 1830s.
5 A. Brandreth, *SR Jhelum*, 1864, paras 98, 157–60, 186–210, 212, 222–36, 263, 271–2.
6 The long-term effects of British policy, referred to in this and the succeeding paragraph, are discussed in many settlement and assessment reports written in the last two decades of the nineteenth and the first decade of the twentieth century.
7 Remarks of Forsyth, CR Lahore, quoting Brandreth on Gujranwala district, *ERR*, 1861–2, p. 48; A. Brandreth, *SR Jhelum*, 1864, paras 190, 214, 289, 299–300.
8 Abstract of A. Brandreth, CR Multan's No. 196, 28 August 1869, PP, Judicial, November 1869, 17A.
9 The brief conspectus of the working of the judicial system, given in this paragraph and the next, is based on a number of sources. For the last two or three decades of the nineteenth century there are a considerable number of Proceedings of the Punjab Government and of the Government of India which deal with the working of specific aspects of the system. Scattered references are to be found in settlement and assessment reports and in most official correspondence on agricultural indebtedness. As an example of a particularly rich file see IP, Revenue (R), December 1891, 10–11A. The evidence for the working of the early Punjab judicial system is widely dispersed and less detailed.
10 *History of Services*, 1911, p. 81.
11 Social and agricultural variations are depicted in the most minute detail in the settlement and assessment reports, particularly the latter.

NOTES

D. Ibbetson, *Panjab Castes*, 1883, is useful on the social side. An impression of the complexity of Punjab society may be obtained from the author's 'Changes in Status and Occupation in Nineteenth-Century Panjab', in D. A. Low (ed.), *Soundings in Modern South Asian History* (London 1968).

12 The single most important source for the study of variations in land transfer is the large collection of assessment reports. These reports, usually prepared for every sub-division of a district, contain land transfer statistics drawn from the revenue records, as well as other information about land transfer. Though each set of statistics has to be considered on its merits, those given in the assessment reports of the 1880s and later are by and large quite reliable for certain purposes. Additional information, of varying worth, is to be found in other official sources dealing with agricultural indebtedness.

13 H. J. Maynard, DC Umballa's No. 19/92 R, 18 January 1900, Punjab correspondence 1899–1900, Legislative Papers.

14 H. J. Maynard, Commissioner of Excise, Punjab, No. 23, 24 March 1904, para. 17, FF, 441/104 A.

15 Cf. also H. J. Maynard, DC Umballa's No. 437–2200 R, 24 December 1902, para. 3, FF, 441/6 D.

16 For Brandreth's interest in history see generally *SR Jhelum*, 1864, and references given in note 17. Note also his reference to the British having made the same mistake in India as Austria had in Hungary, and Russia in Poland, i.e. attempting to put down upper classes by helping peasantry, *SR Jhelum*, 1864, para. 271. Maynard studied history at St John's College, Oxford. See E. Barker's Foreword to J. Maynard, *The Russian Peasant and Other Studies*, Book one (London 1942). Maynard's interest in Russia dates from at least 1894, when he spent eight months in that country, *History of Services*, 1911, p. 81.

17 A. Brandreth, CR Multan's No. 181–478, 11 March 1875, PP, Revenue, May 1875, 6A. Note also remarks by A. Brandreth, CR Jullunder, *ERR*, 1870–1, p. 44, for a reference to English experience up to 1648.

CHAPTER II

1 Extract from Govt of India's No. 418, 31 March 1849, para. 7, in C. L. Tupper (ed.), *Punjab Customary Law* (Calcutta 1881), Vol. 1, p. 49.

2 C. E. Buckland, *Dictionary of Indian Biography* (London 1906), pp. 246, 274, 297–8.

3 *PAR*, 1849–50 and 1850–1, para. 99, Parl. Papers, 1854, LXIX, p. 497; P. Woodruff, *The Men Who Ruled India* (London 1957), Vol. 1, p. 334.

4 Extract from Govt of India's No. 418, 31 March 1849, paras 10, 12, in C. L. Tupper (ed.), *Punjab Customary Law* (Calcutta 1881), Vol. 1,

pp. 49–50; *PAR*, 1849–50 and 1850–1, paras 92, 93, 221–3, Parl. Papers, 1854, LXIX, pp. 496–7, 526–7; extract from letter by H. Lawrence, written *circa* 1852, quoted in J. W. Kaye, *Lives of Indian Officers* (London 1867), Vol. 2, pp. 304–5.

5  R. N. Cust, DC Umballa's No. 76, 26 February 1850, *Circular Orders*, Vol. 1, p. 60; R. N. Cust, *Memoirs of Past Years of a Septuagenarian* (Hertford 1899), pp. 25–34.

6  Sec. to Board of Administration's No. 1546, 9 August 1850, *Circular Orders*, Vol. 1, pp. 67–70.

7  Circular No. 28, 3 May 1852, *Circular Orders*, Vol. 1, pp. 178–9.

8  *PAR*, 1849–50 and 1850–1, para. 227, Parl. Papers, 1854, LXIX, p. 528.

9  On Campbell's early career see his *Memoirs of my Indian Career* (London 1893), Vol. 1.

10  G. Campbell, *Modern India: A Sketch of the System of Civil Government* (London 1852), pp. 322, 324–6, 330–1, 337, 342, 347.

11  *Ibid.*, pp. 324–6, 345–6.

12  G. Campbell, *India as it may be; an outline of a proposed Government and Policy* (London 1853), pp. 178, 181–2, 186. The quotations are from page 181.

13  G. Campbell, *Modern India* (London 1852), pp. 53–4, 65, 68, 89–90, 323, 331–2, 360; G. Campbell, *India as it may be* (London 1853), pp. 175–6, 179, 182, 372.

14  *Abstract Principles of Law circulated for the Guidance of Officers employed in the Administration of Civil Justice in the Punjab* (London 1865), Part 1, section 9, and commentary on principles, section 9, pp. 16–17, 70.

15  *Ibid.*, Part 1, section 13, and commentary on principles, section 13, pp. 23, 73–4.

16  Note by S. M. Robinson, Sec., Legislative Council, forwarded by his No. 183 L.C., 22 November 1904, FF, 441/104B, p. 139. Robinson suggests that the courts took little or no action on these orders.

17  This incident is related in E. O'Brien, *AR Alipur*, 1877, para. 39.

18  G. Campbell, *Memoirs of my Indian Career* (London 1893), Vol. 1, pp. 179, 189.

19  On the exceptional state of affairs in the frontier district of Bannu before British rule, for instance, see: Political diary of H. B. Edwardes, 22 January 1848, *Punjab Government Records: Lahore Political Diaries 1847–1849* (Allahabad 1911), Vol. 5, p. 224 and H. B. Edwardes, *A Year on the Punjab Frontier in 1848–49* (London 1851), Vol. 1, pp. 221–2.

20  R. H. Davies, *SR Gurdaspur*, 1854, General report, para. 12; R. H. Davies, *SR Amritsar*, 1854, General report, paras 8, 19.

21  For a general impression of indebtedness and land transfer before or during the early years of British rule, and for the views of local

NOTES

officers, see: R. Temple, *SR Jullunder*, 1851, paras 79, 195–200, 262–9 (this report is printed in Parl. Papers, 1854, LXIX, p. 455); P. S. Melvill, *SR Hoshiarpur*, 1852, paras 100, 111, 117; G. C. Barnes, *SR Kangra*, 1852, paras 126–8; H. B. Lumsden, Report on the Yoozoofzaee district, forwarded by Commissioner in 1853, *Public Selections* (Lahore 1853), Vol. 1, No. 5, Art. 15, pp. 364, 375; W. Wynyard, *SR South Umballa*, 1853, para. 379, and supplement pp. xiv, xvii, xxv, xxviii, xxxv; H. R. James, Report on the Revised Settlement of the Momunds, 1853, and Commissioner's remarks, 1853, *Public Selections* (Lahore 1854), Vol. 2, No. 7, Art. 18, pp. 20, 27; J. Clarke, Some account of the agricultural condition and operations of perguna Goojranwala, *Public Selections* (Lahore 1854), Vol. 2, No. 8, Art. 21, pp. 135–8; R. H. Davies, *SR Gurdaspur*, 1854, General report, para. 12; R. H. Davies, *SR Amritsar*, 1854, General report paras 8, 19, and report on Turun Tarun (by W. E. Blyth), paras 93, 138; P. S. Melvill, *SR North Umballa*, 1855, paras 98, 111, 195, 223, 259, 296; E. L. Brandreth, *SR Ferozepore*, 1855, para. 82; J. H. Morris, *SR Gujranwala*, 1856, paras 15, 84, appendix 2, para. 5, appendix 4, paras 6, 12, appendix 7, para. 10; N. W. Elphinstone, *SR Googaira*, 1858, paras 47–9, 120; H. Mackenzie, *SR Gujrat*, 1859, paras 113, 139, 178; J. Morris, *SR Multan*, 1859, para. 21, appendix C, paras 10, 28, 43, appendix D, para. 8; H. Monckton, *SR Jhung*, 1859, paras 37, 39, 46, 57; memo. on re-assessment of Narowal by Blyth, paras 8–10, 13, 29, forwarded by Commissioner in 1859, *SR Amritsar*, 1854.

22 R. Temple, *Men and Events of My Time in India* (London 1882), p. 89.

23 M. P. Edgeworth CR Multan's letter, 10 April 1851, para. 40, and E. Thornton, CR Jhelum's letter 25 September 1851, para. 108, together with *PAR*, 1849–50 and 1850–1, para. 227, Parl. Papers, 1854, LXIX, pp. 710, 703, 528; *Abstract Principles of Law* (London 1865), circulated in 1854, Part I, section 19, Part II, section 1, section 5, Commentary on Principles, section 19, Commentary on Procedure, section 1, pp. 34, 43, 51, 54, 81, 85. In N. G. Barrier, *The Punjab Alienation of Land Bill of 1900* (Durham, N.C., 1966), p. 14, a few sentences are quoted from the remarks of Edgeworth and Thornton in such a manner as to lend colour to the supposition that John Lawrence acted on these 'warnings', and placed controls on moneylenders' account books. This rather distorts matters. The brief remarks of both officers, regarding the need for reform of certain limited aspects of civil procedure to protect the agricultural debtor, were made in the course of long reports, and they are certainly not evidence of any great alarm among the British regarding existing indebtedness. The measure regarding account books (to which these officers did not refer) does not appear to have been undertaken till eight years later, after the revolt of 1857. See article cited in note 32.

24 *PAR*, 1856–7 to 1857–8, para. 8, Parl. Papers, 1859, XVIII, p. 459.

25 Sec. to CC's No. 642, 3 September 1858, paras 12–13, PP, Judicial, 4 September 1858, Nos 46–56.
26 E. Thornton's No. 461, 28 September 1858 is summarised in minute by Boulnois, JC, 29 March 1869, PP, Judicial, May 1869, 13A.
27 *PAR*, 1856–7 to 1857–8, para. 8, Parl. Papers, 1859, XVIII, p. 459.
28 Extract para. 6 of Sec. to CC's No. 335, 22 October 1858, *Book Circular Orders*, Vol. 3, pp. 134–5.
29 Judicial Commissioner's circular No. 103, 30 October 1858, PP, Judicial, 13 November 1858, Nos 40–1.
30 Extract para. 5 of Under-Secretary to Govt of India's No. 585, 20 January 1859, *Book Circular Orders*, Vol. 3, p. 135.
31 According to the minute by Boulnois, JC, 29 March 1869, PP, Judicial, May 1869, 13A, the Govt of India ordered on 4 November 1859 that the principles declared in Code of Civil Procedure, Act VIII of 1859, should be followed as an authoritative guide wherever law of procedure in Punjab was silent.
32 *PAR*, 1856–7 to 1857–8, para. 8, Parl. Papers, 1859, XVIII, p. 459; E. Thornton, Judicial Commissioner's No. 530, 3 November 1858, paras 1–11, PP, Judicial, 1 January 1859, Nos 4–6; Judicial Commissioner's circular No. 29 of 1859, quoted in note by Hamilton, 23 April 1900, FF, 441/100B; Y. B. Mathur, 'Judicial Administration in the Punjab, 1849–75', *Journal of Indian History*, Vol. XLIV, part 3, December 1966, p. 717.
33 These events are related in R. Temple, CR Lahore's No. 15, 23 January 1860, para. 20, *SR Gujranwala*, 1856. See also: J. H. Morris, *SR Gujranwala*, 1856, paras 65, 99. R. Cust, CR Amritsar's No. 276, 6 August 1859, para. 24, *SR Amritsar*, 1854, and R. Cust, *Manual for the Guidance of Revenue Officers in the Punjab* (Lahore 1866), pp. 70, 78, 86, 125, 185–6, suggest that sales at the instance of the Settlement Officer occurred to some extent in other districts besides Gujranwala. M. F. O'Dwyer, *AR Gujranwala*, 1890, para. 8, M. F. O'Dwyer, *AR Wazirabad*, 1892, para. 10, and M. F. O'Dwyer, *AR Hafizabad*, 1893, para. 72, give details of the transfers made in Gujranwala. It is also noted that in 1890 in the Gujranwala tahsil the transferees or their descendants were still in proprietary possession in all but four of the transferred villages, despite the fact that these transfers were supposed to have been set aside in 1858.
34 Extract from letter of Cust, CR Lahore, 7 May 1858, paras 4–5, 8, *Book Circular Orders*, Vol. 3, p. 55. See R. N. Cust, *Memoirs of Past Years of a Septuagenarian* (Hertford 1899), p. 388, for outline of his Indian career.
35 Circular No. 64, 7 September 1858, *Book Circular Orders*, Vol. 3, p. 53.
36 *PAR*, 1856–7 to 1857–8, para. 42, Parl. Papers, 1859, XVIII, p. 469.
37 Note, however, that these influential views were not necessarily confined to the senior officers mentioned in this section. For similar

views see also: H. Davidson, *SR Ludhiana*, 1853, paras 47, 58–9, 66; N. W. Elphinstone, *SR Googaira*, 1858, paras 46–7.

38 G. F. Edmonstone, Offg CR Cis-Sutlej States' No. 126, 2 March 1850; W. Wynyard, SO Cis-Sutlej States' No. 461, 23 May 1850; Offg CR Cis-Sutlej States' No. 309, 1 June 1850, all in *Circular Orders*, Vol. 1, pp. 57–9, 62–5; C. E. Buckland, *Dictionary of Indian Biography* (London 1906), pp. 131–2 for Edmonstone's career. Note that in 1860 Edmonstone, as Lieutenant-Governor of the North-Western Provinces, opposed the imposition of restrictions on the compulsory sale of land by the civil courts, despite considerable support within the Province for such a measure. See T. R. Metcalf, *The Aftermath of Revolt: India, 1857–1870* (Princeton 1964), pp. 210–11.

39 R. Temple, *SR Jullunder*, 1851, para. 79 (printed in Parl. Papers, 1854, LXIX, p. 455).

40 R. H. Davies, *SR Gurdaspur*, 1854, General report, para. 12, report on Batala, para. 11; C. E. Buckland, *Dictionary of Indian Biography* (London 1906), p. 112 for Davies' career.

41 E. L. Brandreth, *SR Ferozepore*, 1855, para. 226.

42 P. S. Melvill, *SR Hoshiarpur*, 1852, paras 100, 111, 117; P. S. Melvill, *SR North Umballa*, 1855, paras 98, 111, 195, 223, 259, 296, 366.

43 An account of Melvill's enquiry, and of its outcome, is given in A. Kensington, *AR Kharar*, 1887, paras 23–4. C. E. Buckland, *Dictionary of Indian Biography* (London 1906), p. 285, for Melvill's career.

44 H. Mackenzie, *SR Gujrat*, 1859, para. 178.

45 E. Lake, CR Jullunder's No. 81, 5 April 1859, quoted in minute by Boulnois, JC, 29 March 1869, PP, Judicial, May 1869, 13A.

46 E. Thornton, Judicial Commissioner's No. 2953, 27 June 1859, quoted in minute by Boulnois cited in note 45.

47 This account of the controversy between Cust and Edwardes is taken from a letter of 25 July [1862] (the correspondent's name is not decipherable) in which reference is made to para. 3 of Cust, Judicial Commissioner's No. 2583, 29 May 1862. See PP, Judicial, 21 June 1862, Nos 5–6. For Edwardes' career see C. E. Buckland, *Dictionary of Indian Biography* (London 1906), p. 132.

48 Notes by A. H. W. and R. Montgomery, n.d. and Sec. to Govt's No. 472, 16 June [1862], PP, Judicial, 21 June 1862, Nos 5–6.

49 R. Cust, *Manual for the Guidance of Revenue Officers in the Punjab* (Lahore 1866), introductory remarks p. 3 and main text pp. 30–1, 200–1.

50 Remarks by H. Edwardes, CR Umballa, referring to Tighe's remarks, *ERR*, 1863–4, p. 17.

51 Remarks by J. Naesmyth, CR Hissar, *ERR*, 1860–1, p. 19 and *ERR*, 1861–2, p. 20. See also his remarks in 1862–3, quoted in Extracts from

THE PUNJAB TRADITION

Annual Revenue Reports bearing on Agricultural Indebtedness, IP, Revenue (R), December 1891, 10–11A.
52 Remarks by E. Brandreth, Offg CR Cis-Sutlej, *ERR*, 1860–1, p. 34. It is stated in Extracts from Annual Revenue Reports (cited in note 51) that Deputy Commissioner of Thanesur was apparently Lord F. Hay.
53 Remarks by H. Edwardes, CR Cis-Sutlej, referring to remarks by Capt. Busk, *ERR*, 1861–2, p. 29.
54 See references in note 19.
55 Sec. to Govt's No. 1,292, 9 August 1861, para. 31, *RR*, 1860–1.
56 *RR*, 1860–1, para. 659; *RR*, 1861–2, para. 166.
57 Minute by D. F. McLeod, LG, 27 August 1867, paras 8, 10, *SR Shahpur*, 1866.
58 *RR*, 1859–60, para. 591.
59 Circular No. 96, 13 October 1860, *Book Circular Orders*, Vol. 3, pp. 396–400.
60 R. Cust, *Manual for the Guidance of Revenue Officers in the Punjab* (Lahore 1866), main text pp. 29, 186–91.
61 *Ibid.*, introductory remarks p. 3, main text pp. 27–31, 38, 47, 114. The quotation is from p. 29.
62 Remarks by T. D. Forsyth, CR Jullunder, *ERR*, 1866–7, pp. 47–8. For Forsyth's career see E. Forsyth (ed.), *Autobiography and Reminiscences of Sir Douglas Forsyth* (London 1887).
63 Remarks by R. Taylor, CR Umballa, referring to and quoting remarks of Tighe, *ERR*, 1868–9, p. 30.
64 The extracts from local revenue reports, bound with the annual revenue reports of the 1860s, do not as a rule refer to the reasons for official interest in the market price of land. This was too obvious to discuss; an assessment of reasons depends on reading these extracts in the light of the general economic and administrative concepts of the time.
65 Remarks of Forsyth, CR Lahore, quoting Brandreth, *ERR*, 1861–2, p. 48; E. A. Prinsep, *SR Sialkot*, 1863, para. 367; A. Brandreth, *SR Jhelum*, 1864, paras 190, 214, 289, 299–300; Munshi Amin Chand, *SR Hissar*, 1864, para. 105; J. E. Cracroft, *SR Rawalpindi*, 1864, paras 175, 196, 208, 297; W. G. Davies, *SR Shahpur*, 1866, paras 98, 244, 300.
66 On this point see: G. Campbell, *Modern India* (London 1852), pp. 6, 148, 215, 406, 417; G. Campbell, *India as it may be* (London 1853), pp. xii, xvi, xxv, 4–5, 75, 85, 91, 132, 172, 206, 231, 371, 400, 411, 420, 424; R. N. Cust, *Pictures of Indian Life* (London 1881), pp. 5, 100, 106, 107 (these references are to papers composed between 1849 and 1859); R. N. Cust, *Memoirs of Past Years of a Septuagenarian* (Hertford 1899), pp. 89–90, 92–3 (this refers to a reprint of a document composed in 1857); E. Edwardes, *Memorials of the Life and Letters*

*of Major-General Sir Herbert B. Edwardes* (London 1886), Vol. 1, pp. 187, 280, 294–5, 303, Vol. 2, pp. 126, 232–4, 286–7, 392, 397, 401.

67 It is a matter for investigation whether Mackenzie and Tighe, both military civilians, had any experience of the North-Western Provinces. In any case, as the next paragraph suggests, the question is not of decisive importance.

68 The details of the transition are described in: minute by Boulnois, JC, 29 March 1869, PP, Judicial, May 1869, 13A. See also *RR*, 1866–7, para. 285.

69 Registrar ChC's No. 1550, 10 May 1869, minute by Boulnois, JC, 29 March 1869, and minute by Simson, JC, n.d., PP, Judicial, May 1869, 13A. For C. Boulnois' career see: *Punjab Quarterly Civil List*, 1 October 1877, pp. 20–1.

70 Sec. to Govt's No. 678, 22 May 1869, PP, Judicial, May 1869, 13A.

71 Sec. to FC's No. 874, 4 November 1869, PP, Judicial, November 1869, 17A.

72 Abstract of A. H. Benton, DC Gurgaon's No. 249, 20 July 1869, PP, Judicial, November 1869, 17A; *History of Services*, 1894, pp. 10–11.

73 Abstract of Lt-Col. Coxe, CR Jullunder's No. 200, 29 June 1869, PP, Judicial, November 1869, 17A; *Punjab Quarterly Civil List*, October 1874, pp. 2–3.

74 Abstract of Col. Cracroft, CR Lahore's No. 278, 17 August 1869, PP, Judicial, November 1869, 17A. For Cracroft's attitude to indebtedness some years before see J. E. Cracroft, *SR Rawalpindi*, 1864, paras 175, 196, 208, 297.

75 Abstract of A. Brandreth, CR Multan's No. 196, 28 August 1869, PP, Judicial, November 1869, 17A.

76 Abstract of L. Griffin, DC Lahore's No. 429, 3 August 1869, PP, Judicial, November 1869, 17A.

77 Abstract of Major McMahon, DC Delhi's No. 243, 2 July 1869, PP, Judicial, November 1869, 17A.

78 Abstracts of A. H. Benton, DC Gurgaon's No. 249, 20 July 1869; Capt. Parsons, DC Karnal's No. 140, 5 August 1869; memo. by R. T. Burney, Offg DC Multan, n.d.; Col. Elliott, CR Hissar's No. 195, 25 June 1869; Lt-Col. R. Young, CR Amritsar's No. 154, 29 June 1869; Lt-Col. Graham, CR Derajat's No. 117, 7 July 1869. Together with opinion of Offg FC (P. S. Melvill), n.d., PP, Judicial, November 1869, 17A.

79 See opinions of Benton and Elliott, cited in note 78.

80 Sec. to Govt's No. 1652, 26 November 1869, PP, Judicial, November 1869, 17A.

81 Note by C. R. Lindsay, JC, n.d., PP, Judicial, February 1870, 4A.

82 Registrar ChC's No. 292, 31 January 1870, minute by Boulnois and Simson, n.d., opinion of Edwards, n.d., PP, Judicial, February 1870, 4A. Edwards' opinion appears to have been taken from W. Edwards,

*Reminiscences of a Bengal Civilian* (London 1866), pp. 152–3, or possibly from an earlier published version of this part of the work.
83 Sec. to Govt's No. 227, 18 February 1870, PP, Judicial, February 1870, 4A.
84 The Government of India discussion is in IP, Home (J), 24 September 1870, 37–41A, which also reproduces the Punjab correspondence. T. R. Metcalf, *The Aftermath of Revolt: India, 1857–1870* (Princeton 1964), pp. 214–15, outlines part of the discussion, and indicates that the Punjab Government was ordered to rely upon Sect. 244 of the Code of Civil Procedure as affording an adequate remedy. Metcalf does not cite any despatch in support of this statement, nor was it traceable in the file.
85 Offg Registrar ChC's No. 1065, 7 May 1870, PP, Judicial, May 1870, 7A.
86 There is much scattered evidence on the working of the rules regarding the transfer of land in execution of civil decrees after 1870. See particularly: 1873 correspondence, PP, Revenue, January 1874, 13A; 1889 correspondence, PP, Revenue (R), March 1891, 3–36A; 1895–6 correspondence, IP, Revenue (LR), December 1896, 22–47A.
87 Remarks by A. Brandreth, CR Multan, *ERR*, 1868–9, p. 53.
88 Remarks by A. Brandreth, CR Multan, in *ERR*, 1868–9, p. 53, and *ERR*, 1869–70, pp. 73–4, and as CR Jullunder *ERR*, 1870–1, p. 44.
89 Remarks by A. Brandreth, CR Multan, quoting Fendall, *ERR*, 1868–9, p. 53.
90 Remarks by A. A. Munro, CR Multan, *ERR*, 1870–1, p. 59.
91 W. G. Waterfield, *SR Gujrat*, 1870, paras 60, 121, 156, 163–5, 278–92, 309, 475–6, 479; L. S. Saunders, *SR Lahore*, 1870, paras 70–1, 224–6, 351.
92 Remarks by Naesmyth, CR Hissar, *ERR*, 1869–70, p. 8.
93 This judgement is based on various sources. For the Hissar division itself these included settlement or assessment reports of its districts (Rohtak, Hissar, Sirsa), as well as the provincial revenue reports, especially those compiled towards the end of the nineteenth century.
94 Remarks by J. W. MacNabb, Offg CR Umballa, quoting Tighe, DC Umballa, *ERR*, 1869–70, p. 20.
95 *RR*, 1870–1, pp. 42–3.
96 Proceedings of LG, No. 162, 3 February 1872, para. 16, PP, Revenue, February 1872, 6A.
97 Memo by P. S. Melvill, Offg JC, 11 June 1872, PP, Home, June 1872, 26A.
98 Offg Registrar ChC's No. 1593, 15 June 1872, PP, Home, June 1872, 26A.
99 Offg Under-Sec. to Govt's No. 2271, 28 June 1872, PP, Home, June 1872, 26A.
100 Remarks by Gore Ouseley, CR Umballa, *ERR*, 1871–2, p. 33.
101 Remarks by J. W. Smyth, CR Lahore, *ERR*, 1871–2, p. 64. Accounts

of conditions in Gujranwala in the early days of British rule, and statistics of land transfer in later years, are given in M. F. O'Dwyer's assessment reports, cited in note 33.
102 *RR*, 1871–2, para. 169 gives a brief account of Fendall's enquiry.
103 Remarks by R. Taylor, CR Amritsar, *ERR*, 1871–2, p. 44.
104 *RR*, 1871–2, para. 169.
105 Translation of petition of Fazil Shah and Sayad Mahmud, Lambardars of Mouza Khai, and eleven others, PP, Revenue, December 1872, 3A.
106 Memorandum by G. Wakefield, 3 December 1872, PP, Revenue, May 1875, 6A.
107 Offg Sec. to Govt's No. 4C–1657½, 23 November 1872, PP, Revenue, November 1872, 19½A; Offg Sec. to Govt's No. 1694, 2 December 1872, PP, Revenue, December 1872, 3A; Sec. to Govt's No. 2, 2 January 1873, PP, Revenue, May 1875, 6A.
108 Marginal note by J. B. Lyall, SC, on note by F. C. Channing, 15 August 1879, para. 4, *Selections* (Lahore 1887), p. 859.
109 Proceedings of LG No. 107, 22 January 1873, para. 62, *RR*, 1871–2.
110 Proceedings of LG No. 107, 22 January 1873, paras 54–63, *RR*, 1871–2.
111 Remarks by C. A. McMahon, CR Hissar, H. W. H. Coxe, CR Jullunder, R. Taylor, CR Amritsar, *ERR*, 1872–3, pp. 3, 9, 13.
112 Remarks by H. W. H. Coxe, cited in note 111.
113 J. B. Lyall, SC's No. 67, 2 July 1873, Govt's No. 1148, 1 September 1873, and J. B. Lyall, SC's No. 127, 22 October 1873, are summarised in Sec. to FC's No. 428–2087, 15 April 1875, PP, Revenue, May 1875, 2A.
114 G. Wakefield, DC Jhang's No. 307, 23 August 1873, PP, Revenue, January 1874, 13A.
115 R. Young, Offg CR Multan's No. 662–1782, 28 August 1873, PP, Revenue, January 1874, 13A. For Young's opinion on Boulnois' suggestion see Abstract of R. Young, CR Amritsar's No. 154, 29 June 1869, PP, Judicial, November 1869, 17A.
116 Sec. to FC's No. 983, 5 September 1873, PP, Revenue, January 1874, 13A.
117 Abstract of T. W. Smyth, Offg DC Montgomery's No. 629, 16 June 1873, submitted to Punjab Govt by Offg Registrar ChC's No. 2344, 4 September 1873, PP, Revenue, January 1874, 13A.
118 Petition of Wilayat Shah and others, Montgomery tahsil, 10 November 1873 and Sec. to Govt's No. 1666, 14 November 1873, PP, Revenue, May 1875, 6A; H. W. H. Coxe, CR Multan's No. 810–2218, 18 November 1873, PP, Revenue, January 1874, 13A.
119 F. M. Birch, Offg DC Montgomery's No. 367, 5 December 1873, PP, Revenue, May 1875, 6A.
120 Sec. to Govt's No. 160, 24 January 1874, PP, Revenue, January 1874, 13A.

121 Sec. to FC's No. 983, 5 September 1873, PP, Revenue, January 1874, 13A.
122 *RR*, 1872–3, paras 210–11.
123 Proceedings of LG No. 273, 9 February 1874, para. 21, *RR*, 1872–3.
124 Offg Registrar ChC's No. 278, 6 February 1874, PP, Revenue, March 1874, 20A.
125 Note by C. R. Lindsay, JC, n.d., PP, Home, August 1874, 12A.
126 Note by C. Boulnois, JC, 13 March 1874, PP, Home, August 1874, 12A.
127 Lindsay's note is cited in note 125.
128 Minute by P. S. Melvill, Offg JC, 1 April 1874, PP, Home, August 1874, 12A.
129 The circular referred to by Melvill was Book Circular No. 3–153, 18 January 1873, PP, Home, December 1874, 18A.
130 Remarks by W. G. Davies, CR Lahore, *ERR*, 1869–70, p. 43.
131 Note by S. M. Robinson, Sec. Legislative Council, forwarded by his No. 183 L.C., 22 November 1904, FF, 441/104B, p. 139.
132 The local opinions are in PP, Revenue, May 1875, 2A.
133 Note by S. M. Robinson, cited in note 131, FF, 441/104B, p. 141.
134 Offg Sec. to FC's No. 312, 21 March 1874 (Gore Ouseley's opinion), Gore Ouseley, CR Umballa's No. 151, 4 July 1874, and Sec. to FC's No. 428–2087, 15 April 1875 (Egerton's opinion), PP, Revenue, May 1875, 2A; minute by C. R. Lindsay, JC, 27 June 1875, PP, Revenue, August 1875, 13A.
135 Sec. to Govt's No. 1257, 31 August 1875, PP, Revenue, August 1875, 13A.
136 Note by T. H. Thornton, Offg JC, 24 June 1874 and by C. Boulnois, JC, 29 June 1874, PP, Home, August 1874, 12A.
137 Offg Sec. to Govt's No. 3109, 22 August 1874, PP, Home, August 1874, 12A.
138 Extract paras 149–50 from annual revenue report for 1873–4, PP, Home, December 1874, 18A.
139 Proceedings of LG in Home Dept. No. 4609, 23 December 1874, PP, Home, December 1874, 18A.
140 G. Wakefield wrote in 1872 that the principle of Government being the real landlord looking after the affairs of large landholders was thoroughly understood and admitted to be equitable in the East, while in the West it formed only the theories and dreams of a minority headed by such men as J. S. Mill. See memorandum by G. Wakefield, 3 December 1872, PP, Revenue, May 1875, 6A.
141 The statement had been made by C. L. Tupper, whose views are discussed in Chapter 3, Section 1.
142 A. Brandreth, CR Multan's No. 181–478, 11 March 1875, PP, Revenue, May 1875, 6A.
143 A. Brandreth, *SR Jhelum*, 1864, paras 98, 263, 271.
144 H. M. Lawrence, *Essays Military and Political* (London 1859), p. 5.

145 *Ibid.*, pp. 369, 373.
146 L. Bowring, *Eastern Experiences* (London 1872), p. 303.
147 E. Edwardes, *Memorials of the Life and Letters of Major-General Sir Herbert B. Edwardes* (London 1886), Vol. 1, pp. 370, 379, 398; Vol. 2, pp. 12–13.
148 R. Temple, *Men and Events of My Time in India* (London 1882), p. 47.
149 G. Campbell, *Memoirs of My Indian Career* (London 1893), Vol. 1, pp. 112–13 (quoting article written in 1849). See also G. Campbell, *Modern India* (London 1852), p. 254 (but cf. p. 108); G. Campbell, *India as it may be* (London 1853), pp. 64, 108, 122.
150 R. Temple, *Men and Events of My Time in India* (London 1882), pp. 14, 47, 504–5, 508, and R. Temple, *The Story of My Life* (London 1896), Vol. 2, pp. 65–6, 67.
151 *PAR*, 1856–7 to 1857–8, para. 39, Parl. Papers, 1859, XVIII, p. 468.
152 F. Cooper, *The Crisis in the Punjab* (London 1858), pp. 242–3.
153 R. Bosworth Smith, *Life of Lord Lawrence* (London 1883), Vol. 2, pp. 29, 31, 33, 55, 58, 77, 116, 139, 149–50.
154 *Ibid.*, p. 349.
155 E. Edwardes, *Memorials of the Life and Letters of Major-General Sir Herbert B. Edwardes* (London 1886), Vol. 2, pp. 154, 265–6, 302–3 (but cf. p. 306).
156 E. Gambier Parry, *Reynell Taylor* (London 1888), p. 339.
157 L. Bowring, *Eastern Experiences* (London 1872), p. 304; R. N. Cust, *Pictures of Indian Life* (London 1881), pp. viii, 139–40; R. Temple, *Men and Events of My Time in India* (London 1882), pp. 111, 505; G. Campbell, *Memoirs of My Indian Career* (London 1893), Vol. 1, p. 236.
158 L. H. Griffin, *The Rajas of the Punjab* (London 1873), pp. xi–xii (Preface dated 9 November 1870).
159 G. R. G. Hambly, 'Richard Temple and the Punjab Tenancy Act of 1868', *The English Historical Review*, Vol. XXIX, No. CCCX, January 1964, pp. 53–4.
160 T. R. Metcalf, *The Aftermath of Revolt India 1857–1870* (Princeton 1964), p. 202, and also T. R. Metcalf, 'The Struggle over Land Tenure in India, 1860–1868', *The Journal of Asian Studies*, Vol. XXI, No. 3, May 1962, p. 307.
161 See note 159.
162 Memorandum by A. A. Roberts, FC, 6 March 1868, Parl. Papers, 1870, LIII, p. 636.
163 Memorandum by E. A. Prinsep, SC, 18 April 1868, Parl. Papers, 1870, LIII, p. 648.
164 See A. Brandreth's views as cited in report of L. Griffin, 31 March 1865, Parl. Papers, 1870, LIII, pp. 448, 450, 452–4.
165 This appears to be R. J. Moore's view. See R. J. Moore, *Sir Charles Wood's Indian Policy 1853–66* (Manchester 1966), pp. 198–9.
166 A. Brandreth, *SR Jhelum*, 1864, para. 271.

167 *Ibid.*, paras 98, 263 and E. L. Brandreth, CR Rawalpindi's No. 168, 28 June 1864, paras 36–7, *SR Jhelum*, 1864.
168 T. R. Metcalf, *The Aftermath of Revolt India 1857–1870* (Princeton 1964), pp. 164–5.
169 Minute by R. Temple, 24 August 1870, IP, Home (J), 24 September 1870, 37–41A; and speech by R. Temple in Legislative Council, 26 March 1872, C. L. Tupper (ed.), *Punjab Customary Law* (Calcutta 1881), Vol. 1, p. 135.
170 G. Campbell, *Memoirs of My Indian Career* (London 1893), Vol. 1, pp. 149–50, 188–9; Vol. 2, pp. 119–20, 179, 270, 341.
171 *Ibid.*, Vol. 2, pp. 269–70; R. Temple, *Men and Events of My Time in India* (London 1882), pp. 465–7, and *The Story of My Life* (London 1896), Vol. 2, p. 11.
172 This may be deduced from: An old Punjaubee, *The Punjaub and North-West Frontier Province* (London 1878). This work, attributed to Coxe, refers repeatedly to a great variety of serious political problems confronting India, internally and externally. While Coxe insisted on the absolute necessity of having a contented people (p. 173) his references to indebtedness (pp. 7–8), or indeed the general tenor of the book, do not suggest political anxiety on this score.
173 L. H. Griffin, *The Rajas of the Punjab* (London 1873), p. xii (Preface dated 9 November 1870).
174 R. Temple, *The Story of My Life* (London 1896), Vol. 2, p. 71 and see also Vol. 1, p. 68.
175 H. M. Lawrence, *Essays Military and Political* (London 1859), pp. 13, 378; L. Bowring, *Eastern Experiences* (London 1872), p. 304; H. B. Edwardes and H. Merivale, *Life of Sir Henry Lawrence* (London 1873), pp. 175–6, 194, 259, 310–11; An old Punjaubee, *The Punjaub and North-West Frontier Province* (London 1878), passim; R. N. Cust, *Pictures of Indian Life* (London 1881), pp. viii, 63, 107; R. Temple, *Men and Events of My Time in India* (London 1882), pp. 13–15, 504–9; R. Bosworth Smith, *Life of Lord Lawrence* (London 1883), p. 417; E. Edwardes, *Memorials of the Life and Letters of Major-General Sir Herbert B. Edwardes* (London 1886), Vol. 1, p. 390, Vol. 2, pp. 236–9, 266. Among the officers who served in the Punjab in the 1850s George Campbell had least apprehension of political danger. The books he wrote in the early years of the decade show an unusual degree of confidence in the strength and stability of British rule.
176 In the 1870s at any rate even a political alarmist like Coxe could ignore the political significance of land transfer. See note 172.

CHAPTER III

1 See revenue reports and LG's reviews bound with these reports for the years 1874–5 to 1878–9. See also: *Punjab Report* (Lahore 1878–9),

## NOTES

pp. 679–83, and Sec. to Govt's No. 459S, 17 September 1880, para. 6 (Egerton's opinion), *Selections* (Lahore 1887), p. 868.

2  A. Brandreth, CR Multan's No. 181–478, 11 March 1875, PP, Revenue, May 1875, 6A.

3  Remarks by A. Brandreth, CR Jullunder, quoting remarks by D. G. Barkley, DC Jullunder, *ERR*, 1875–6, pp. 14–15.

4  A. Brandreth's letter of 1875 and remarks of 1876, cited in notes 2 and 3 respectively; remarks by A. Brandreth, CR Jullunder, *ERR*, 1876–7, p. 16.

5  Remarks by J. E. Cracroft, CR Rawalpindi, *ERR*, 1875–6, pp. 32–3; remarks by W. G. Davies, CR Delhi, *ERR*, 1876–7, p. 3. Other examples are cited later in this chapter.

6  Remarks by A. Brandreth, CR Jullunder, referring to remarks of Major Beadon, DC Jullunder, *ERR*, 1876–7, p. 16.

7  Remarks by C. A. McMahon, CR Hissar and A. H. Benton, DC Multan, *ERR*, 1876–7, pp. 5–6, 32. Cf. also remarks by M. Macauliffe, DC Montgomery, *ERR*, 1876–7, p. 34. Some other examples of optimistic attitudes are cited later in this chapter.

8  Remarks by W. Coldstream, DC Hoshiarpur, *Punjab Report* (Lahore 1878–9), pp. 433–4. Cf. also Coldstream's remarks on pp. 432–3.

9  *History of Services*, 1886, pp. 37–8.

10  H. E. Perkins, DC Rawalpindi's No. 1894, 28 July 1875, paras 3–4, *Selections From the Records of the Government of the Punjab*, New Series No. 12, Current Rates of Interest on Loan Transactions in the Punjab (Lahore 1876), pp. 19–20.

11  Remarks by H. E. Perkins, CR Amritsar, *ERR*, 1876–7, p. 21.

12  H. E. Perkins, CR Amritsar's No. 2899, 4 September 1878, PP, Revenue, June 1879, 6A.

13  Sec. to FC's No. 636, 26 May 1879 (Lyall's opinion) and Sec. to Govt's No. 746, 16 June 1879 (Egerton's opinion), PP, Revenue, June 1879, 6A.

14  *History of Services*, 1890, p. 39.

15  W. E. Purser, *AR Jhajjar*, 1878, para. 25 and *AR Sampla*, 1878, para. 24; H. C. Fanshawe, *AR Rohtak*, 1878, para. 29.

16  H. C. Fanshawe, *SR Rohtak*, 1879, paras 55, 94.

17  R. Maconachie, *SR Delhi*, 1880, appendices 12 and 13. These figures cover only the period from 1861 to 1874. It should be noted that, adding the percentages of cultivation sold and mortgaged which are cited for each tahsil, they amount in round figures to twelve-and-a-half, twelve-and-a-half, and eighteen per cent, with a district figure of seven-and-a-half per cent. Though the Commissioner referred to the percentages sold and mortgaged as if correct (see G. Young, CR Delhi's No. 2890, 12 December 1882, para. 94, *SR Delhi*, 1880) it is obvious that the district figure is irreconcilable with the figures given for the tahsils. The true figures appear to be twelve-and-a-half, seven,

THE PUNJAB TRADITION

and three-and-a-half per cent, with a district figure of seven-and-a-half per cent.
18 D. Ibbetson, *Karnal Revenue Rates Report*, 1877-8, paras 53-4, 140-1, 248-9.
19 D. Ibbetson, Assistant SO Karnal's No. 156, 19 May 1874, PP, Revenue, May 1875, 2A; *History of Services*, 1895, p. 74.
20 D. C. J. Ibbetson, *SR Panipat and Karnal*, 1880-2, paras 273-5.
21 R. Maconachie, *SR Delhi*, 1880, para. 227 and footnote on p. 207. See also: answer by R. Maconachie, SO Delhi, *Punjab Report* (Lahore 1878-9), pp. 332-4.
22 Remarks by T. Roberts, DC Gurgaon, in revenue report for 1878-9, quoted in PP, Revenue, March 1883, 1A.
23 Extracts from assessment reports of Firozpur, 1875, paras 13, 15, and of Nuh, 1876, paras 16, 25, quoted in F. C. Channing, *SR Gurgaon*, 1881, paras 170, 208, 212.
24 F. C. Channing, *SR Gurgaon*, 1881, para. 60 (this paragraph was written by J. Wilson).
25 *Ibid.*
26 Note by F. C. Channing, Settlement Sec. to FC, 15 August 1879, *Selections* (Lahore 1887), pp. 856-63, and F. C. Channing, *SR Gurgaon*, 1881, para. 294.
27 F. C. Channing, *SR Gurgaon*, 1881, paras 57, 297.
28 Remarks by J. Wilson, Assistant SO Gurgaon, *Punjab Report* (Lahore 1878-9), pp. 355-8; *History of Services*, 1910, p. 105.
29 E. P. Gurdon, Offg DC Ludhiana's No 184, 26 May 1874, PP, Revenue, May 1875, 2A; for Gurdon's career see E. P. Gurdon, DVJ Multan's No. —, December 1888, IP, Revenue (R), December 1891, 10-11A.
30 Remarks by E. P. Gurdon, DC Umballa, *ERR*, 1877-8, p. 8.
31 Remarks by J. W. MacNabb, as Offg CR Umballa, *ERR*, 1869-70, p. 20, and as CR Umballa, *ERR*, 1876-7, p. 10. For his career see Bengal Civil Service list in *New Annual Army List*, 1878.
32 Remarks by J. W. MacNabb, CR Umballa, *ERR*, 1877-8, p. 7.
33 *History of Services*, 1895, pp. 130-1.
34 S. S. Thorburn, *Bannu or our Afghan Frontier* (London 1876), p. vii.
35 *Ibid.*, p. 245.
36 *Ibid.*, pp. 50-1, 87, 95-101 and cf. p. 166.
37 *Ibid.*, p. 97.
38 *Ibid.*, p. 135 and see generally pp. 134-8.
39 *Ibid.*, pp. 38 (footnote), 111, 112, 126, 128, 132.
40 *Ibid.*, pp. 111-12.
41 *Ibid.*, pp. 123-34, esp. pp. 132-4.
42 *Ibid.*, pp. 127-8.
43 *Ibid.*, pp. 123-4.
44 *Ibid.*, pp. 131-2. The phrase quoted is from p. 131.
45 S. S. Thorburn, *SR Bannu*, 1878, paras 67, 196.

## NOTES

46 *Ibid.*, para. 68.
47 Remarks by E. G. Hastings, SO Kohat, *Punjab Report* (Lahore 1878–9), p. 540; extract from report by Hastings quoted in H. St G. Tucker, *SR Kohat*, 1883, para. 330.
48 E. G. Hastings, *SR Peshawar*, 1876, paras 318, 476–81.
49 E. G. Wace, *SR Hazara*, 1874, p. 185.
50 *History of Services*, 1888, p. 75.
51 In 1887 S. S. Thorburn asserted that the circumstances of the agricultural classes were incomparably easier in the Hazara district than in any of the other frontier districts with which he was acquainted, namely Bannu, Dera Ghazi Khan and Dera Ismail Khan. (He had not served in Peshawar or Kohat.) See remarks by S. S. Thorburn, DC Hazara, *ERR*, 1886–7, p. 56.
52 E. G. Wace, *SR Hazara*, 1874, pp. 84–7.
53 R. G. Thomson, *SR Jhelum*, 1881, para. 159 (referring to figures collected by Wace).
54 E. G. Wace, SO Jhelum's No. 214, 19 February 1877, PP, Home, March 1877, 12A, appendix.
55 E. G. Wace, SC's No. 1009, 5 September 1879, *Selections* (Lahore 1887), pp. 905–11.
56 *History of Services*, 1888, p. 9.
57 See, for instance, R. Temple, CR Lahore's No. 15, 23 January 1860, para. 3, *SR Gujranwala*, 1856.
58 Remarks by A. R. Bulman, DC Gujranwala, *ERR*, 1878–9, p. 19.
59 For the more complete statistics of later settlements see the assessment reports of the tahsils of the Jhang, Multan, Muzuffargarh and Dera Ghazi Khan districts, written in the last decade of the nineteenth century and the first decade of the twentieth century. Of course the statistics of land transfer in these assessment reports do not generally refer to the period from annexation to the 1870s. But they do show clearly that from the 1870s alienations were very extensive in these districts, compared to many other Punjab districts. There seems to be no reason therefore to question the assertions of the Settlement Officers of the 1870s.
60 H. St G. Tucker, *SR Dera Ismail Khan*, 1879, paras 704, 712.
61 F. W. R. Fryer, *SR Dera Ghazi Khan*, 1875, paras 124, 350.
62 According to Tupper his memorandum was written in 1873. See C. L. Tupper, *Punjab Customary Law* (Calcutta 1881), Vol. 3, p. 199. It follows from this that he wrote the memorandum while at Dera Ghazi Khan. Tupper was appointed to this district at the end of 1872 or the beginning of 1873 (cf. *History of Services*, 1890, p. 53 and *History of Services*, 1895, p. 136) and remained there till 1874. The question of extending the right of pre-emption to long-term usufructuary mortgages was raised in July 1873 by James Lyall.
63 Extract from Tupper's memorandum of 1873, C. L. Tupper, *Punjab Customary Law* (Calcutta 1881), Vol. 3, pp. 200–1.

64 C. L. Tupper, *Punjab Customary Law* (Calcutta 1881), Vol. 3, p. 199.
65 *Ibid.*
66 Tupper had heard Maine's lectures at Oxford, lectures later published in Maine's *Village-Communities in the East and West*. See C. L. Tupper 'India and Sir Henry Maine', *Journal of the Society of Arts*, Vol. XLVI, 18 March 1898, p. 390.
67 For some passages in Maine's publications before 1873 which suggest his influence on Tupper's view of political economy see: H. Maine, *Ancient Law* (Everyman's Library, London 1936), p. 179 (first published 1861); H. S. Maine, *Village-Communities in the East and West* (London 1872), pp. 196–7. Cf. also J. W. Burrow, *Evolution and Society* (Cambridge 1966), p. 154, where some later references to Maine's view of political economy are cited.
68 Extract from Tupper's memorandum of 1873, C. L. Tupper, *Punjab Customary Law* (Calcutta 1881), Vol. 3, p. 201.
69 Note, however, that in 1881 Tupper took exception to the statement that there were no village communities at all in the Dera Ghazi Khan district. C. L. Tupper, *Punjab Customary Law* (Calcutta 1881), Vol. 2, pp. 21–2.
70 W. E. Purser, *SR Montgomery*, 1874, pp. 128–9.
71 Extract from Multan settlement report, *circa* 1880, para. 56, enclosure to Offg Jnr Sec. to Govt's No. 231, 7 November 1888, PF 18. Cf. also C. A. Roe, *AR Shujabad*, 1877, paras 8, 24, 61, 82, 105, 119, 136 and C. A. Roe, *AR Lodhran*, 1878, paras 7–8, 19, 38, 40, 54, 70, 82.
72 *History of Services*, 1892, pp. 88–9.
73 On this particular point see E. O'Brien, *AR Alipur*, 1877, para. 48.
74 For O'Brien's general opinion see his remarks as SO Muzuffargarh, *Punjab Report* (Lahore 1878–9), pp. 498–500, and cf. E. O'Brien, *AR Sinanwan*, 1877, paras 53–4, 58–9 and E. O'Brien, *AR Alipur*, 1877, paras 48–9, 67, 78, 87.
75 E. B. Steedman, *AR Chiniot*, 1877, paras 43–5, 111–14, 157–8, 184, 188, 207–9, 234 and remarks by E. B. Steedman, SO Jhang, *Punjab Report* (Lahore 1878–9), p. 493.
76 For Lyall's views see following letters written by him as SC: No. 388, 13 October 1875, paras 7, 9, 15, *SR Dera Ghazi Khan*, 1875; No. 46M, 25 August 1876, paras 4–9, *SR Montgomery*, 1874; No. 144, 11 June 1877, para 2, *AR Sinanwan*, 1877; No. 66C, 15 December 1877, paras 7, 11, *AR Alipur*, 1877; No. 6C, 1 February 1878, paras 6, 16, *AR Chiniot*, 1877; No. 152, 20 June 1878, para. 5, *AR Shujabad*, 1877; No. 5, 6 January 1879, paras 2, 4, 19, 26, *AR Lodhran*, 1878; Lyall quoted in *SR Dera Ismail Khan*, 1879, para. 704 and in *SR Delhi*, 1880, footnote p. 207; note by J. B. Lyall, FC, 30 August 1879, *Selections* (Lahore 1887), pp. 839–45.
77 Note by J. B. Lyall, FC, 30 August 1879, *Selections* (Lahore 1887), pp. 839–45.

NOTES

78 Sec. to Govt's No. 155S, 10 July 1880 (Egerton's opinion), *Selections* (Lahore 1887), pp. 837-9.
79 Speech by R. E. Egerton, LG, 17 July 1879, Indian Legislative Council Proceedings, 1879, and see despatch cited in note 78.
80 Sec. to Govt's No. 459S, 17 September 1880 (Egerton's opinion), *Selections* (Lahore 1887), pp. 866-8.
81 *RR*, 1879-80, para. 65.
82 Proceedings of LG No. 339, 24 March 1881, paras 11-12, *RR*, 1879-80.
83 See 1881-2 correspondence and Jnr Sec. to Govt's No. 660-1246, 12 July 1882, PP, Foreign (G), July 1882, 3A.
84 See 1882-3 correspondence PP, Foreign (G), June 1883, 9A.
85 See generally revenue reports from 1880-1 to 1883-4; and the extracts from local reports and LG's reviews bound with these reports.
86 E. B. Steedman, *SR Jhang*, 1881, paras 168-9; *History of Services*, 1897, p. 118.
87 T. G. Walker, *AR Samrala*, 1881, para. 25; *History of Services*, 1895, p. 142.
88 J. A. L. Montgomery, *AR Una*, 1881, para. 26; J. A. L. Montgomery, *Papers connected with revenue rate report of Hoshiarpur*, 1882, para. 20; J. Montgomery, *AR Dasuya*, 1882, para. 20.
89 E. G. Wace, SC's No. 30C, 31 January 1881, para. 7, *AR Una*, 1881.
90 E. G. Wace, SC's No. 176, 10 July 1882, para. 7, *Papers connected with revenue rate report of Hoshiarpur*, 1882.
91 A. Kensington, *AR Garshankar*, 1882, para. 23.
92 E. G. Wace, SC's No. —, 5 September 1882, para. 12, *AR Garshankar*, 1882.
93 E. G. Wace, SC's No. 267, 26 September 1882, para. 7, *SR Jhang*, 1881.
94 *Ibid*.
95 Remarks by H. E. Perkins, CR Multan, *ERR*, 1881-2, pp. 35-6; cf. also his remarks as CR Rawalpindi, *ERR*, 1882-3, p. 103. For Perkins' limited experience of the south-west see *History of Services*, 1886, pp. 37-8; and for an informed officer's estimate of the extent of indebtedness in Muzaffargarh see O'Brien's writings cited in note 74.
96 C. A. McMahon, CR Hissar's No. 104, 18 June 1874, PP, Revenue, May 1875, 2A; and reference to McMahon in Proceedings of LG, 23 December 1874, para. 10, PP, Home, December 1874, 18A.
97 Remarks by C. A. McMahon, CR Hissar, *ERR*, 1876-7, pp. 4-6.
98 Remarks by C. A. McMahon, CR Amritsar, *ERR*, 1881-2, p. 19.
99 Remarks by C. A. McMahon, CR Amritsar, *ERR*, 1882-3, p. 73.
100 J. Wilson, *Scheme for the redemption of mortgages*, enclosure to T. Roberts, DC Gurgaon's No. 526, 5 December 1882, PP, Revenue (A), April 1883, 5A.
101 *History of Services*, 1891, p. 166.

102 G. G. Young, CR Delhi's No. 60, 8 January 1883, and his d.o., 7 March 1883, PP, Revenue (A), April 1883, 5A.
103 Snr Sec. to FC's No. 92, 24 January 1883 (Lyall's opinion), PP, Revenue (A), April 1883, 5A.
104 J. B. Lyall, FC's d.o., 19 March 1883, PP, Revenue (A), April 1883, 5A.
105 Snr Sec. to FC's No. 337, 15 March 1883 (Lyall's opinion), PP, Revenue (A), April 1883, 5A.
106 Under-Sec. to Govt's No. 104/504, 20 April 1883 (Aitchison's opinion), PP, Revenue (A), April 1883, 5A.
107 J. Wilson, *Report on the condition of the Jhajjar tahsil in the Rohtak district in December 1883*, n.d., esp. paras 46–54.
108 Note by H. W. Steel, DC (Rohtak), n.d., appendix 1 in Wilson's report, cited in note 107.
109 L. J. H. Grey, Offg DC Ferozepur's No. 85, 24 April 1874, PP, Revenue, May 1875, 2A. For Grey's career see F. and C. Grey (ed.), *Tales of our Grandfather* (London 1912), pp. v–viii.
110 Remarks by L. J. H. Grey, CR Hissar, *ERR*, 1882–3, p. 24 and H. Grey, Offg CR Hissar's No. 32, 31 January 1884, para. 6, PP, Revenue (R), October 1884, 13–14A.
111 H. Grey, Offg CR Hissar's No. 32, 31 January 1884, and see also extract from a note by H. Grey, Offg CR Hissar, 3 January 1884, PP, Revenue (R), October 1884, 13–14A.
112 Offg Snr Sec. to FC's No. 13C, 29 April 1884, PP, Revenue (R), October 1884, 13–14A.
113 Memorandum by W. E. Purser, SO Jullunder, 10 July 1884, PP, Revenue (R), October 1884, 13–14A, KW; Offg Sec. to Govt's No. 243, 24 October 1884, PP, Revenue (R), October 1884, 13–14A.
114 S. S. Thorburn, DC Dera Ismail Khan's No. 733, 16 November 1882, PP, Foreign (G), June 1883, 9A.
115 Remarks by S. S. Thorburn, DC Dera Ismail Khan, *ERR*, 1882–3, pp. 148, 150.
116 Note by S. S. Thorburn, DC Dera Ismail Khan, 29 June 1884, *Selections* (Lahore 1887), pp. 930–55.
117 E. L. Ommanney, Offg CR Derajat's No. 168, 26 April 1883, para. 9, PP, Foreign (G), June 1883, 9A. For Ommanney's career see C. E. Buckland, *Dictionary of Indian Biography* (London 1906), p. 323.
118 E. L. Ommanney, CR Derajat's No. 242, 15 July 1884, para. 2, *Selections* (Lahore 1887), p. 928. Ommanney repeatedly harked back to the incident of 1879. See E. L. Ommanney, CR Derajat's No. 535, 7 May 1888, para. 7, IP, Revenue (F), December 1888, 1–24A, and E. L. Ommanney, CR Peshawar's No. 49, 3 April 1889, para. 2, IP, Revenue (R), December 1891, 10–11A.
119 Remarks by E. L. Ommanney, CR Derajat, *ERR*, 1882–3, p. 143.
120 E. L. Ommanney, CR Derajat's No. 242, 15 July 1884, para. 2, *Selections* (Lahore 1887), pp. 928–9.

121 E. L. Ommanney, CR Derajat's No. 242, 15 July 1884, *Selections* (Lahore 1887), pp. 928–9.
122 C. E. Buckland, *Dictionary of Indian Biography* (London 1906), p. 283.
123 Offg Snr Sec. to FC's No. 1150, 8 October 1884, para. 7, *S R Jhang*, 1881.
124 For McMahon's old notion of the consequences of the restriction of credit see C. A. McMahon, CR Hissar's No. 104, 18 June 1874, paras 10–11, PP, Revenue, May 1875, 2A.
125 Offg Jnr Sec. to FC's No. 1189, 24 October 1884, *Selections* (Lahore 1887), pp. 923–8.
126 Jnr Sec. to Govt's No. 660–1246, 12 July 1882, PP, Foreign (G), July 1882, 3A.
127 Proceedings of LG No. 53, 14 March 1883, para. 8, *R R*, 1881–2.
128 Offg Jnr Sec. to Govt's Nos 501/1100 and 502/1100, 25 June 1883, PP, Foreign (G), June 1883, 9A; and Proceedings of LG No. 256, 15 November 1883, para. 9, *R R*, 1882–3.
129 Offg Jnr Sec. to Govt's No. 507, 22 May 1885, *Selections* (Lahore 1887), pp. 955–6.
130 Cf. on this point also Proceedings of LG No. 142, 17 July 1885, para. 19, *S R Jhang*, 1881.
131 Proceedings of LG No. 256, 24 December 1885, para. 5, *R R*, 1884–5. Local opinions on the correspondence initiated by Thorburn had been submitted to the Financial Commissioner's Office before December 1885, but there is no way of telling whether Aitchison had seen the local opinions. Officially they were not submitted to the Punjab Government till after Aitchison's departure.
132 C. Aitchison, *Lord Lawrence* (Oxford 1894), esp. pp. 193–4.
133 J. A. E. Miller, DJ Kangra's No. 1048, 5 August 1885, *Selections* (Lahore 1887), pp. 970–5. For Miller's career see *History of Services*, 1888, p. 89.
134 R. Clarke, Offg DC Delhi's No. 938, 6 August 1885, *Selections* (Lahore 1887), pp. 978–9. See *History of Services*, 1895, pp. 25–8 for Clarke's career.
135 For Ibbetson's career see *History of Services*, 1895, pp. 74–5.
136 See Ibbetson's own account of 1877–8, cited in note 18, and cf. Ibbetson's later memorandum paras 3–4, enclosed in D. Ibbetson, DC Rohtak's No. 65, 7 March 1889, IP, Revenue (R), December 1891, 10–11A. For an account of one part of one tahsil of the Karnal district in which transfers appear to have been more extensive see J. M. Douie, *A R Parganah Indri Tahsil Karnal*, 1886, para. 33.
137 See, for instance, D. Ibbetson, *Panjab Castes*, 1883, para. 356.
138 D. Ibbetson, Offg Director of Public Instruction's No. 1624, 12 August 1885, memorandum para. 8, *Selections* (Lahore 1887), p. 977.
139 Memorandum cited in preceding note, paras 8–12, *Selections* (Lahore 1887), pp. 976–8.

140 C. M. Rivaz, DC Kangra's No. 907, 7 July 1885, *Selections* (Lahore 1887), p. 962.
141 A. Anderson, Forest SO's No. —, 6 August 1885, *Selections* (Lahore 1887), pp. 982–3.
142 *History of Services*, 1895, pp. 112–13.
143 For Roe's views as discussed here and in succeeding paragraphs see: C. A. Roe, late Offg JC's No. 2339, 21 July 1885, *Selections* (Lahore 1887), pp. 967–9.
144 Roe's report of 1874 on Una, quoted in C. L. Tupper (ed.), *Punjab Customary Law* (Calcutta 1881), Vol. 2, p. 45.
145 Cf. Maine: 'Nobody is at liberty to attack several property and to say at the same time that he values civilisation. The history of the two cannot be disentangled. Civilisation is nothing more than a name for the old order of the Aryan world, dissolved but perpetually reconstituting itself under a vast variety of solvent influences, of which infinitely the most powerful have been those which have, slowly, and in some parts of the world much less perfectly than others, substituted several property for collective ownership.' (Rede lecture, 1875.) H. S. Maine, *Village-Communities in the East and West* (London 1876), p. 230.
146 On customary law in relation to land transfer see: S. Clifford, DJ Delhi's No. 251, 6 December 1888, para. 4, IP, Revenue (R), December 1891, 10–11A; opinion of Chatterji, JC, 1895, IP, Home (J), October 1897, 317–576A; opinion of Stogdon, JC, 9 March 1896, IP, Home (J), November 1898, 274–439A; opinion of Stogdon, JC, 29 February 1896, A. Christie, DVJ Sialkot's No. 111, 27 March 1896, para. 3 and opinion of Chatterji, 20 June 1896, IP, Revenue (LR), November 1898, 3–22A, Part 2.
147 Note by R. G. Thomson, Snr Sec. to FC, 21 October 1885, *Selections* (Lahore 1887), p. 1004.
148 G. Gordon Young, CR Jullunder's No. 2309, 1 August 1885, *Selections* (Lahore 1887), pp. 957–8.
149 F. W. R. Fryer, DC Hazara's No. 1363, 3 July 1885, Tucker's note with covering docket No. 867, 6 August 1887 [*sic* 1885], W. E. Purser, SO Jullunder's No. 226, 3 July 1885, J. Maconachie, DC Gurgaon's No. 513, 1 August 1885, *Selections* (Lahore 1887), pp. 963–6, 980–1.
150 For Wace's opinion as discussed in this and succeeding paragraphs see: note by Wace, 2nd FC, n.d., *Selections* (Lahore 1887), pp. 1006–10.
151 Note by Wace, 2nd FC, n.d., para. 2, *Selections* (Lahore 1887), p. 1007. Wace's generalisation was criticised by L. J. H. Grey. See Grey's article 'The ryot and the money-lender', November 1887, IP, Revenue (R), December 1891, 10–11A.
152 S. S. Thorburn, *Musalmans and Moneylenders in the Punjab* (Edinburgh 1886), pp. 1, 6, 79–92.
153 *Ibid.*, pp. 48–52, 56, 74, 88, 95–6.
154 *Ibid.*, pp. 100–5.

155 *Ibid.*, p. 103.
156 *Ibid.*, pp. 106–15, 139–53.
157 *History of Services*, 1911, pp. 65–6.
158 A. Kensington, *A R Garshankar*, 1882, para. 23; but cf. para. 25.
159 A. Kensington, *A R Naraingarh*, 1888, paras 17, 19.
160 Remarks by A. Kensington, SO North Umballa, in Extracts from annual agricultural statistics reports, 1885–6, IP, Revenue (R), December 1891, 10–11A.
161 A. Kensington, DC Umballa's No. 153, 5 February 1887, *Selections* (Lahore 1887), pp. 990–1.
162 *History of Services*, 1911, p. 31.
163 J. M. Douie, SO Karnal-Umballa's No. 316, 30 June 1885, *Selections* (Lahore 1887), pp. 983–4.
164 J. M. Douie, *A R Jagadhri*, 1887, paras 36, 38–40.
165 *RR*, 1882–3, para. 37 (quoting Bulman); remarks by A. R. Bulman, DC Umballa, *ERR*, 1883–4, p. 16.
166 A. R. Bulman, Offg CR Delhi's No. 223, 2 April 1887, *Selections* (Lahore 1887), pp. 986–7.
167 L. J. H. Grey, 'The ryot and his master', and 'The ryot and the money-lender', November 1887, IP, Revenue (R), December 1891, 10–11A.
168 See note 38.
169 S. S. Thorburn, *Musalmans and Moneylenders in the Punjab* (Edinburgh 1886), p. 87.
170 Sec. of State's No. 27, 24 March 1887, IP, Revenue (R), May 1887, 33A.
171 Offg Jnr Sec. to Govt's No. 231, 7 November 1888, para. 5, PF 18, p. 90.
172 Note by J. B. Lyall, LG, 2 August 1887; and marginal remarks by Lyall on notes by C. L. Tupper, 2 June 1887 and W. M. Young, 27 June 1887, PF 18, Notes, pp. 30–5.
173 Note by C. L. Tupper, 22 September 1887, PF 18, Notes, p. 42.
174 Note by M. W. Fenton, 2 April 1888, PF 18, Notes, pp. 42–57.
175 Note by H. C. Fanshawe, 9 July 1888, PF 18, Notes, pp. 57–65. See also the caustic comments on the copy of Thorburn's *Musalmans and Moneylenders in the Punjab* preserved in the West Pakistan Secretariat Library; and the manuscript correspondence in PP, Revenue, November 1888, 8–13A.
176 Note by H. C. Fanshawe, 9 July 1888, PF 18, Notes, p. 58.
177 Several of the assessment reports of the Umballa district were reviewed by Lyall at about the same time as he expressed his opinion on the question of indebtedness. See Offg Jnr Sec. to Govt's No. 146, 7 July 1888, *A R Pipli*, 1888, and No. 148, 7 July 1888, *A R Jagadhri*, 1887. Even Fanshawe considered the facts disclosed in the Umballa assessment reports rather disturbing. See note by H. C. Fanshawe, 9 July 1888, PF 18, Notes, p. 62.

178 Marginal remarks by Lyall on notes by M. W. Fenton, 2 April 1888, and H. C. Fanshawe, 9 July 1888, PF 18, Notes, pp. 43–4, 64.
179 Notes by J. B. Lyall, 17 July 1888 and 18 July 1887 [sic 1888], PF 18, Notes, pp. 65–7.
180 Notes by J. B. Lyall, 17 July 1888, 22 August 1888, and marginal remarks by Lyall on notes by M. W. Fenton, 3 August 1888 and H. C. Fanshawe, 8 August 1888, PF 18, Notes, pp. 65–6, 69, 72–3, 75–6.
181 The reforms on which opinions were requested were: courts should examine plaintiff before summoning defendant; real issues should be ascertained by oral examination of parties in one another's presence; provisions empowering courts to go behind bonds, separate principal from interest, decree only reasonable interest; compulsory arbitration with power to vary awards; court executing decree to have power to direct satisfaction of decree by instalments; sales in execution of decree to be conducted with more consideration; decrees against agriculturists to be executed through Collector; agriculturists not to be summoned to court at harvest time; extension of period of limitation; money-lenders obliged to grant receipts, statements of account and keeping of business-like accounts; extension of compulsory registration, system of village registrars; exclusion of legal practitioners from any grades of court, refusal of their costs in suits of less value than Rs 500; establishment of rural courts and conciliators; remission of half institution fees in cases compromised at first hearing; remission of fees in suits for redemption of land by agriculturists.
182 Offg Jnr Sec. to Govt's Nos 231–3, 7 November 1888, PF 18.
183 For the replies submitted in 1888–9 see IP, Revenue (R), December 1891, 10–11A.
184 For the general analysis which follows see: note by S. S. Thorburn, DC Dera Ismail Khan, 29 June 1884, paras 2, 3, 8, 9, 13, 15, 22, 27, 34, 35; E. L. Ommanney, CR Derajat's No. 242, 15 July 1884, paras 2, 5; J. A. E. Miller, DJ Kangra's No. 1048, 5 August 1885, paras 4–6; R. Clarke, Offg DC Delhi's No. 938, 6 August 1885; D. Ibbetson, Offg Director Public Instruction's No. 1624, 12 August 1885, para. 8, all in *Selections* (Lahore 1887), pp. 930, 931, 932, 933, 937, 938, 944–5, 948, 953–4, 928–9, 971, 979, 977; S. S. Thorburn, *Musalmans and Moneylenders in the Punjab* (Edinburgh 1886), pp. 1–2, 6, 13–14, 21–2, 29, 31, 32, 35, 37–8, 39–41, 52, 54, 57, 87, 88, 96, 97; E. L. Ommanney, CR Derajat's No. 535, 7 May 1888, para. 7, IP, Revenue (F), December 1888, 1–24A; notes by J. B. Lyall, LG, in July and August 1888, PF 18, Notes, pp. 65, 67, 73, 75–6; opinions of H. B. Beckett, T. J. Kennedy, E. P. Gurdon, J. W. Gardiner, M. L. Dames, L. W. Dane, S. S. Thorburn, J. C. Brown, J. Wilson, A. Kensington, W. A. Harris, C. M. Rivaz, D. Ibbetson, A. Anderson, L. J. H. Grey, E. L. Ommanney, J. R. Drummond, G. M. Ogilvie, C. R. Hawkins, in IP, Revenue (R), December 1891, 10–11A.

## NOTES

185 D. Ibbetson, Offg Director Public Instruction's No. 1624, 12 August 1885, para. 8, *Selections* (Lahore 1887), p. 977.
186 S. S. Thorburn, *Musalmans and Moneylenders in the Punjab* (Edinburgh 1886), pp. 39–40 and cf. p. 35.
187 Note by S. S. Thorburn, DC Dera Ismail Khan, 29 June 1884, paras 22, 35, *Selections* (Lahore 1887), pp. 944–5, 954.
188 T. J. Kennedy, Offg DC Montgomery's No. —, 31 December 1888, IP, Revenue (R), December 1891, 10–11A.
189 For the arguments of those who minimised the political danger see: C. A. Roe, late Offg JC's No. 2339, 21 July 1885, para. 4, *Selections* (Lahore 1887), p. 967; remarks by J. R. Maconachie, DC Gurgaon, *ERR*, 1887–8; opinions of J. B. Hutchinson, E. O'Brien, G. C. Walker, A. H. Benton, W. O. Clark, J. A. Grant, J. Bentinck, J. R. Maconachie, G. Knox, W. Coldstream, W. R. H. Merk, R. I. Bruce, R. M. Dane, C. R. Hawkins, G. R. Elsmie, W. M. Young, in IP, Revenue (R), December 1891, 10–11A.
190 G. C. Walker, SO Lahore's No. 21, 9 January 1889, IP, Revenue (R), December 1891, 10–11A.
191 Note by J. B. Lyall, LG, 26 June 1891, para. 1, IP, Revenue (R), December 1891, 10–11A.
192 For Government of India pressure and Punjab Government delays see IP, Revenue (R), May 1891, 1–8A and KW.
193 Note by J. B. Lyall, LG, 26 June 1891, IP, Revenue (R), December 1891, 10–11A; and marginal remarks by Lyall on note by H. C. Fanshawe, 22 April 1891, PF 18, Notes, pp. 223–37.
194 Note by H. C. Fanshawe, 22 April 1891, PF 18, Notes, pp. 233–4. Cf. note by P. P. Hutchins, 26 December 1890, para. 20, IP, Home (J), October 1891, 234–300A.
195 Offg Chief Sec. to Govt's No. 563S, 25 August 1891, IP, Revenue (R), December 1891, 10–11A.
196 D. Ibbetson, Offg Director Public Instruction's No. 1624, 12 August 1885, para. 11, *Selections* (Lahore 1887), pp. 977–8.
197 L. J. H. Grey, 'The ryot and the money-lender', November 1887, IP, Revenue (R), December 1891, 10–11A.
198 See opinions of G. Smyth, J. R. Maconachie, E. L. Ommanney, R. M. Dane, IP, Revenue (R), December 1891, 10–11A.
199 Offg Chief Sec. to Govt's No. 563S, 25 August 1891, para. 6, IP, Revenue (R), December 1891, 10–11A.
200 C. M. Rivaz, CR Lahore's No. 151, 21 February 1889, para. 4, IP, Revenue (R), December 1891, 10–11A.
201 Opinion by W. A. Harris, DJ Lahore, 6 February 1889, IP, Revenue (R), December 1891, 10–11A.
202 Marginal remark by J. B. Lyall, LG, on note by H. C. Fanshawe, 22 April 1891, PF 18, Notes, p. 232.
203 See note 199.
204 See note 199.

205 See note 199.
206 M. O'Dwyer, *India As I Knew It 1885-1925* (London 1926 ed.), p. 37.
207 See H. Maine, Memorandum on Mr Caird's report on the condition of India, 20 February 1880, W. Stokes (ed.), *Sir Henry Maine . . . Speeches and Minutes* (London 1892), p. 431 and G. Feaver, *From Status to Contract A Biography of Sir Henry Maine 1822-1888* (London 1969), p. 216.
208 R. Kumar, *Western India in the Nineteenth Century* (London 1968), p. 195.
209 *Ibid.*, p. 203.
210 *Ibid.*, p. 202.
211 *Ibid.*, pp. 203-15.
212 See, for instance, note by G. M. Ogilvie, CR Derajat, 1889, para. 9, IP, Revenue (R), December 1891, 10-11A.

CHAPTER IV

1 Central Provinces Govt's No. 195S, 25 July 1888, IP, Revenue (F), December 1888, 1-24A; Central Provinces Govt's No. 1466-212S, 11 November 1889, IP, Revenue (R), May 1891, 9-14A.
2 Bombay Govt's No. 3356, 25 June 1890, IP, Home (J), October 1891, 234-300A.
3 See notes by E. C. Buck of: 26 April 1889, IP, Revenue (R), May 1891, 15-18A, KW; 8 February 1890 (marginal notes), IP, Revenue (R), June 1890, 62-74A, KW; 27 December 1890, IP, Revenue (R), March 1891, 8-10A, KW; 9 February 1891, IP, Revenue (R), September 1893, 46-9A, KW1.
4 Marginal notes by P. P. Hutchins on note by J. P. Hewett, 23 August 1890, and on note by C. J. Lyall, 29 November 1890; note by P. P. Hutchins, 26 December 1890, all in IP, Home (J), October 1891, 234-300A, KW; note by P. P. Hutchins, 28 December 1890, IP, Revenue (R), May 1891, 9-14A, KW; marginal notes by P. P. Hutchins on notes by J. W. P. Muir-Mackenzie, 28 August 1891 and by E. C. Buck, 29 August 1891, and note by P. P. Hutchins, 1 September 1891, IP, Revenue (R), December 1891, 10-11A, KW.
5 Note by Lansdowne, 23 January 1890, IP, Revenue (R), May 1891, 1-8A, KW; notes by Lansdowne, 14 January 1891 and 18 February 1891, IP, Revenue (R), September 1893, 46-9A, KW.
6 Note by P. P. Hutchins, 26 December 1890, IP, Home (J), October 1891, 234-300A, KW; note by P. P. Hutchins, 28 December 1890, IP, Revenue (R), May 1891, 9-14A, KW.
7 Note by Lansdowne, 14 January 1891, and cf. note by P. P. Hutchins, 16 January 1891, IP, Revenue (R), September 1893, 46-9A, KW1.
8 Extract from P. P. Hutchins' d.o. to Secretary, 6 February 1891; and see later account given in note by P. P. Hutchins, 7 September 1891, both in IP, Home (J), October 1891, 234-300A, KW.

9 Note by E. C. Buck, 9 February 1891, IP, Revenue (R), September 1893, 46-9A, KW1.
10 See note by C. J. Lyall, Sec., Home Dept, 10 February 1891, IP, Home (J), October 1891, 234-300A.
11 Note by P. P. Hutchins, 15 February 1891, IP, Revenue (R), September 1893, 46-9A, KW1.
12 Note by Lansdowne, 18 February 1891, IP, Revenue (R), September 1893, 46-9A, KW1.
13 Order in Council, 20 February 1891, IP, Revenue (R), September 1893, 46-9A, KW1; and cf. Hutchins' later interpretation of the decision in his note of 7 September 1891, IP, Home (J), October 1891, 234-300A, KW.
14 Note by E. C. Buck, 29 August 1891, IP, Revenue (R), December 1891, 10-11A, KW; and see later account in note by E. C. Buck, 22 August 1893, IP, Revenue (G), November 1893, 1A, KW.
15 Note by A. E. Miller, 22 August 1891, IP, Home (J), October 1891, 234-300A, KW; note by P. P. Hutchins, 1 September 1891, IP, Revenue (R), December 1891, 10-11A, KW; notes by P. P. Hutchins, 7 September 1891, and by A. E. Miller, 15 September 1891, IP, Home (J), October 1891, 234-300A, KW.
16 Note by Lansdowne, 4 September 1891, IP, Revenue (R), December 1891, 10-11A, KW; note by Lansdowne, 16 September 1891, IP, Home (J), October 1891, 234-300A, KW; and cf. later account in note by C. J. Lyall, 10 March 1894, IP, Revenue (R), September 1894, 43-6A, KW4.
17 See later account in note by A. E. Miller, 15 March 1894, IP, Revenue (R), September 1894, 43-6A, KW4. And see Order in Council, 17 September 1891, IP, Revenue (R), September 1893, 46-9A, KW.
18 Resolution of 20 November 1891, IP, Revenue (R), September 1893, 46-9A.
19 J. B. Lyall to Lansdowne, 7 October 1891, IP, Home (J), October 1891, 234-300A, KW; Govt of India, Finance and Commerce Dept's No. 318, 2 December 1891, to Sec. of State, IP, Revenue (R), September 1893, 46-9A; note by J. P. Hewett, 3 March 1892, IP, Revenue (R), September 1893, 46-9A, KW1.
20 See reference to Home Dept office memorandum of 25 August 1892, in note by E. D. Maclagan, 19 May 1893, IP, Revenue (R), June 1893, 11-12A, KW.
21 Note by E. D. Maclagan, 13 September 1892, and marginal note by P. P. Hutchins, IP, Revenue (R), May 1893, 21A, KW; Govt of India's No. 2088-238, 16 September 1892 to Punjab Govt, IP, Revenue (R), May 1893, 21A; Govt of India's No. 2089-239, 16 September 1892 to Central Provinces Govt and Central Provinces Govt's No. 17C, 30 September 1892, IP, Revenue (R), May 1893,

18–19A; C. L. Tupper's d.o., 20 May 1893, IP, Revenue (R), May 1893, 21A, KW.
22 Note by E. D. Maclagan, 22 May 1893, IP, Revenue (R), June 1893, 11–12A, KW.
23 Note by C. H. T. Crosthwaite, 28 November 1892, IP, Revenue (R), September 1894, 43–6A, KW2.
24 Notes by C. B. Pritchard, 24 June 1893, D. Barbour, 21 October 1893, P. P. Hutchins, 25 October 1893, IP, Revenue (R), September 1894, 43–6A, KW3.
25 Note by E. C. Buck, 22 August 1893, IP, Revenue (G), November 1893, 1A, KW.
26 Notes by P. P. Hutchins, 22 August 1893, and A. E. Miller, 16 October 1893, IP, Revenue (G), November 1893, 1A, KW.
27 Note by Lansdowne, 24 August 1893, IP, Revenue (G), November 1893, 1A, KW.
28 See accounts in: note by E. D. Maclagan, 23 March 1894, IP, Revenue (R), April 1894, 1A, KW; note by F. M. W. Schofield, 3 October 1895, para. 6, IP, Revenue (LR), October 1895, 72–3A, KW4.
29 Note by Lansdowne, 3 January 1894, IP, Revenue (R), September 1894, 43–6A, KW3.
30 Note by A. P. MacDonnell, 27 April 1894, IP, Revenue (LR), May 1895, 11–14A, KW; Govt of India, Legislative Dept's No. 21, 2 May 1894 to Sec. of State for India, in 'Selections from Papers on Indebtedness and Land Transfer', IP, Revenue (LR), October 1895, 72–3A.
31 Note by C. J. Lyall, 18 January 1894, IP, Revenue (R), September 1894, 43–6A, KW3; Govt of India, Home Dept's Circular No. 5 (Judl)–607–615, 4 June 1894 in 'Selections from Papers on Indebtedness and Land Transfer', IP, Revenue (LR), October 1895, 72–3A; note by J. P. Hewett, 30 July 1894, IP, Revenue (R), September 1894, 43–6A, KW8.
32 Buck to Elgin, 30 June 1894, Elgin Papers, Correspondence with persons in India, Vol. 1, Part 1, No. 261.
33 MacDonnell to Elgin, 21 June 1894, Elgin Papers, Correspondence with persons in India, Vol. 1, Part 1, No. 240.
34 Elgin to Fowler, 17 July 1894, Wolverhampton Papers, Vol. 1, no number.
35 See notes 33 and 34; also MacDonnell to Babington Smith, 23 June 1894, and Elgin to MacDonnell, 27 June 1894, Elgin Papers, Correspondence with persons in India, Vol. 1, Part 1, No. 247, Part 2, No. 167.
36 Review by S. S. Thorburn, CR Rawalpindi, n.d., paras 4, 8, 12, *AR Gujranwala*, 1890; S. S. Thorburn, CR Rawalpindi's No. 2651, 12 September 1891, paras 2, 3, 8, 12, *AR Phalia*, 1891; review by S. S. Thorburn, CR Rawalpindi, n.d., paras 8, 13, *AR Shahpur*, 1891.

37 J. Wilson, *AR Shahpur*, 1891, paras 100–1, 104.
38 Note by J. B. Lyall, LG, 26 June 1891, para. 1, IP, Revenue (R), December 1891, 10–11A; review by C. M. Rivaz, FC, paras 4, 9–10, 16 (forwarding letter dated 5 October 1891), *AR Gujranwala*, 1890; Snr Sec. to FC's No. 718, 3 December 1891, para. 13, *AR Phalia*, 1891; Offg Rev. Sec. to Govt's No. 208, 11 December 1891, para. 9, *AR Gujranwala*, 1890; Offg Rev. Sec. to Govt's No. 14, 15 January 1892, para. 7, *AR Phalia*, 1891; review by W. M. Young, FC, paras 16, 31–2, 34, 37 (forwarding letter dated 2 July 1892), and Rev. Sec. to Govt's No. 99, 3 October 1892, paras 6, 8, *AR Shahpur*, 1891.
39 For Grey's views see letters written as Commissioner of Delhi division: No. 115A, 23 February 1888, *AR Jagadhri*, 1887; No. 219, 24 March 1888, *AR Naraingarh*, 1888; No. 510, 29 July 1889, IP, Revenue (R), December 1891, 10–11A; No. 626, 9 October 1889, *AR Bhiwani*, 1889 and footnote by Grey on p. 23 of this report; No. 456, 25 August 1890, para. 2, *AR Hansi, Hissar, Barwala, Fatehabad*, 1890; No. 544, 1 December 1892, Legislative Papers; No. 417, 1 October 1894, IP, Revenue (LR), June 1896, 28A.
40 A. Kensington, *AR Naraingarh*, 1888, para. 40; Snr Sec. to FC's No. 2398, 20 April 1888, paras 6, 17, and Offg Jnr Sec. to Govt's No. 148, 7 July 1888, para. 3, *AR Jagadhri*, 1887; memorandum by W. M. Young, 2nd FC, 1 October 1889, para. 12, IP, Revenue (R), December 1891, 10–11A; J. Wilson, *AR Jhelum and Bar Circles of Bhera*, 1890, paras 17, 20; review by W. M. Young, FC, para. 21 (forwarding letter dated 28 June 1890), *AR Bhiwani*, 1889; note by J. B. Lyall, LG, 26 June 1891, para. 1, IP, Revenue (R), December 1891, 10–11A; Offg Rev. Sec. to Govt's No. 516S, 2 August 1894, para. 4, IP, Revenue (LR), June 1896, 28A.
41 L. Dane, SO Gurdaspur's No. 4, 4 January 1889, IP, Revenue (R), December 1891, 10–11A; L. Dane, *AR Batala*, 1889, para. 118.
42 C. M. Rivaz, CR Lahore's No. 151, 21 February 1889, para. 4, IP, Revenue (R), December 1891, 10–11A.
43 C. M. Rivaz, CR Lahore's No. 668, 27 August 1889, para. 19, *AR Batala*, 1889.
44 Memorandum by G. R. Elsmie, 1st FC, 15 August 1889, para. 38, IP, Revenue (R), December 1891, 10–11A; review by W. M. Young, FC, para. 29 (forwarding letter dated 18 December 1889), *AR Batala*, 1889.
45 Jnr Sec. to Govt's No. 25, 29 January 1890, para. 9, *AR Batala*, 1889.
46 Marginal note by J. B. Lyall on note by H. C. Fanshawe, 22 April 1891, PF 18, Notes, pp. 232–3.
47 C. M. Rivaz, CR Lahore's No. 638, 5 August 1892, para. 16, *SR Gurdaspur*, 1892; L. Dane, SO Peshawar's No. 496, 14 August 1894, para. 7, IP, Home (J), October 1897, 317–576A.
48 S. S. Thorburn, CR Rawalpindi's No. 795/C.I.-6, 23 March 1895, para. 1, IP, Revenue (LR), June 1896, 28A.

49 The story can be traced in the following: J. Wilson, *AR Jhelum and Bar Circles of Bhera*, 1890, para. 17; correspondence printed with *AR Jhelum and Bar Circles of Bhera*, 1890, and Thorburn's reviews of *AR Daska*, 1890, *AR Gujrat*, 1890 and *AR Gujranwala*, 1890; L. W. Dane, *AR Shakargarh*, 1890, para. 30 and Rivaz's review, para. 4; J. Wilson, *AR Shahpur*, 1891, para. 110–11; correspondence printed with *AR Shahpur*, 1891, *AR Raya*, 1891; L. W. Dane, *SR Gurdaspur*, 1892, para. 63, and Rivaz's review para. 16; correspondence printed with *AR Zafarwal*, 1892.

50 Cf. review by C. M. Rivaz, 2nd FC, para. 4 (forwarding letter dated 26 March 1891), *AR Shakargarh*, 1890 and review by C. M. Rivaz, 2nd FC (forwarding letter dated 16 August 1893), *AR Zafarwal*, 1892, on this point.

51 Reviews by S. S. Thorburn, CR Rawalpindi: n.d., para. 4, *AR Gujranwala*, 1890; n.d., para. 5, *AR Shahpur*, 1891; n.d., para. 22, *AR Zafarwal*, 1892; 16 December 1893, para. 11, *AR Pasrur*, 1893; S. S. Thorburn, CR Rawalpindi's No. 795/C.I.–6, 23 March 1895, para. 13, IP, Revenue (LR), June 1896, 28A.

52 J. Wilson, *AR Shahpur*, 1891, para. 111.

53 C. M. Rivaz, CR Lahore's No. 151, 21 February 1889, para. 4, IP, Revenue (R), December 1891, 10–11A.

54 C. M. Rivaz, CR Lahore's No. 668, 27 August 1889, para. 19, *AR Batala*, 1889.

55 Rev. Sec. to Govt's No. 49, 16 March 1893, IP, Revenue (HB and AS), July 1893, 34–45A.

56 Offg Rev. Sec. to Govt's No. 516S, 2 August 1894, IP, Revenue (LR), June 1896, 28A.

57 For the 1894 discussion see correspondence in: IP, Revenue (LR), June 1896, 28A.

58 For the general views of Hutchinson and Robertson see: J. B. Hutchinson, DC Multan's No. 520, 7 July 1885, *Selections* (Lahore 1887), pp. 960–1; memorandum by J. B. Hutchinson, DC Multan (forwarded 15 December 1887), IP, Revenue (R), May 1891, 15–18A; J. B. Hutchinson, DC Multan's No. 645, 31 December 1888 and answer to questions by F. A. Robertson, AC, 1889, IP, Revenue (R), December 1891, 10–11A. For Massy see note 60.

59 For Young's general views see: memorandum by W. M. Young, 2nd FC, 1 October 1889, IP, Revenue (R), December 1891, 10–11A; review by W. M. Young, 2nd FC, para. 36 (forwarding letter dated 2 July 1892), *AR Shahpur*, 1891.

60 F. A. Robertson, DLR's No. 1557, 7 September 1894; J. B. Hutchinson, CR Lahore's No. 697, 4 October 1894; C. F. Massy, Offg CR Delhi's [*sic* Jullunder's] No. 2840–C/I.X.–4, 12 October 1894; note by W. M. Young, 1st FC, 28 February 1895, all in IP, Revenue (LR), June 1896, 28A.

## NOTES

61 L. J. H. Grey, CR Delhi's No. 417, 1 October 1894, IP, Revenue (LR), June 1896, 28A.
62 See opinions of E. B. Francis, H. P. P. Leigh, P. J. Fagan, E. B. Steedman and F. D. Cunningham, IP, Revenue (LR), June 1896, 28A.
63 L. W. Dane, SO Peshawar's No. 496, 4 August 1894, IP, Home (J), October 1897, 317–576A; J. A. L. Montgomery, Offg CR Rawalpindi's No. 2601, 17 September 1894; A. Anderson, DC Kangra's No. 1458, 26 September 1894; L. W. Dane, SO Peshawar's No. 590, 16 October 1894; S. S. Thorburn, CR Rawalpindi's No. 795/C.I.–6, 23 March 1895, all in IP, Revenue (LR), June 1896, 28A.
64 See Thorburn's opinion cited in note 63.
65 Note by C. M. Rivaz, 2nd FC, 26 March 1895, IP, Revenue (LR), June 1896, 28A.
66 F. D. Cunningham, DC Hazara's No. 2, 2 January 1889 and H. P. P. Leigh, Offg DC Kohat's No. 13, 4 April 1889, IP, Revenue (R), December 1891, 10–11A.
67 The Home Dept circular requested consideration of the following changes of law: to amend the law regarding usury so as to make it clear by a specific enactment to this effect that the courts, before awarding stipulated interest, shall be bound to enquire as to coercion, undue influence, fraud, or misrepresentation, wherever there is a reasonable suspicion of any of these; to provide in the Contract Act that taking an undue advantage of a debtor's simplicity or necessities shall, equally with the above causes, render an agreement voidable; by additions to the Evidence Act, to enable the court to require independent evidence of the transaction if it disbelieves or doubts the recorded consideration, and likewise to require proof of *bona fides* from the party who contracted when in a position of decided advantage.
68 Offg Rev. Sec. to Govt's No. 67, 19 July 1894, IP, Home (J), October 1897, 317–576A.
69 See opinions of L. J. H. Grey, H. M. M. Wood, G. W. Rivaz, C. A. Roe, F. C. Channing, J. R. Maconachie, G. M. Ogilvie, IP, Home (J), October 1897, 317–576A. Maconachie and Ogilvie probably felt Fitzpatrick's objection less strongly than the others.
70 See opinions of J. R. Maconachie, F. C. Channing and G. M. Ogilvie, IP, Home (J), October 1897, 317–576A.
71 See opinions of R. L. Harris, F. Field, M. L. Dames, E. B. Francis, E. B. Steedman, J. B. Hutchinson, W. O. Clark, J. A. L. Montgomery, C. F. Massy, A. Anderson, G. M. Ogilvie, IP, Home (J), October 1897, 317–576A.
72 J. B. Hutchinson, CR Lahore's No. 598, 13 August 1894; C. F. Massy, Offg CR Jullunder's No. 2553–U/I–23, 3 September 1894; J. R. Maconachie, DC Gurdaspur's No. 791, 14 November 1894, all in IP, Home (J), October 1897, 317–576A. See also C. F. Massy, Offg CR

Delhi's [sic Jullunder's] No. 2840–C/I.X.-4, 12 October 1894, para. 4, IP, Revenue (LR), June 1896, 28A.
73 A. Anderson, DC Kangra's No. 1477, 2 October 1894, IP, Home (J), October 1897, 317–576A. See also A. Anderson, DC Kangra's No. 1458, 26 September 1894, IP, Revenue (LR), June 1896, 28A.
74 E. B. Steedman, DC Simla's No. 1737, 10 August 1894, IP, Home (J), October 1897, 317–576A.
75 E. W. Parker, DVJ Jhelum's No. 693, 31 July 1894; C. S. Martindale, DVJ Ferozepur's No. 407, 10 August 1894; memorandum by H. A. Anderson, DVJ Derajat (forwarding letter dated 31 August 1894); opinion of F. C. Channing, JC, 2 October 1894; opinion of A. W. Stogdon, JC, 18 January 1895; opinion of P. C. Chatterji, JC (forwarded 19 January 1895), IP, Home (J), October 1897, 317–576A.
76 A. W. Stogdon, DVJ Delhi's No. 177, 17 August 1885, *Selections* (Lahore 1887), p. 970; F. C. Channing, DVJ Lahore's No. —, 2 January 1889 and A. W. Stogdon, DVJ Delhi's No. 2, 3 January 1889, IP, Revenue (R), December 1891, 10–11A.
77 J. R. Maconachie, DC Gurdaspur's No. 791, 14 November 1894, IP, Home (J), October 1897, 317–576A. For Maconachie's earlier opinion see: J. R. Maconachie, DC Gurgaon's No. 61, 11 March 1889, PP, Revenue (R), March 1891, 3–36A.
78 Note by D. Fitzpatrick, LG, 24 January 1895, IP, Home (J), October 1897, 317–576A.
79 Note by S. S. Thorburn, CR Rawalpindi, 8 March 1895, PP, Revenue (A), May 1895, 1–2A.
80 In a demi-official letter of 5 March 1895 to the Revenue Secretary of the Punjab Government it was mentioned that the Government of India was collecting information about agricultural indebtedness, and that one of the remedies proposed for it was that all transfers to non-agriculturists should be invalid unless specially sanctioned by Government officers. See E. D. Maclagan to R. G. Thomson, d.o., No. 697, 5 March 1895, IP, Revenue (LR), May 1895, 12C.
81 Rev. Sec. to Govt's No. 37, 8 May 1895, PP, Revenue (A), May 1895, 1–2A.
82 S. S. Thorburn, CR Rawalpindi's No. 1921, 24 June 1895, PP, Revenue (A), July 1895, 8–11A.
83 Offg Sec. to Govt of India, Legislative Dept's No. 589, 13 March 1895, FF, 441/72.
84 Many officers were consulted on this reference. The opinions are in FF, 441/72.
85 E. P. Henderson, Govt Advocate's No. 146/A, 16 August 1895, FF, 441/72.
86 J. M. Douie, DC Jullunder's No. 568, 10 June 1895; T. Troward, DVJ Amritsar's No. 461, 10 June 1895; C. G. Parsons, DC Umballa's No. 647R, 15 June 1895; S. S. Thorburn, CR Rawalpindi's No. 1843, 15 June 1895, all in FF, 441/6B.

NOTES

87 Offg Jnr Sec. to FC's No. 56C, 21 June 1895, para. 7, FF, 441/6B; note by C. M. Rivaz, 2nd FC, 12 July 1895 and Offg Jnr Sec. to FC's No. C/106, 17 July 1895, FF, 441/72.
88 Offg Sec. to Govt of India's Circular 24/75-1, 26 October 1895, IP, Revenue (LR), October 1895, 72-3A.
89 E. D. Maclagan, Note on Land Transfer and Agricultural Indebtedness in India, 18 March 1895, IP, Revenue (LR), October 1895, 72-3A.
90 D. Ibbetson, Memorandum on the restriction of the power to alienate interests in land, n.d., IP, Revenue (LR), October 1895, 72-3A. This memorandum appears to incorporate certain verbal amendments made at the instance of A. Mackenzie and with the consent of Ibbetson. See note by A. Mackenzie, 16 September 1895, IP, Revenue (LR), October 1895, 72-3A, KW1.
91 Note by D. Ibbetson, 22 August 1895, IP, Revenue (LR), October 1895, 72-3A, KW1.
92 Note by A. Mackenzie, 27 August 1895, IP, Revenue (LR), October 1895, 72-3A, KW1.
93 Note by Elgin, 12 September 1895, IP, Revenue (LR), October 1895, 72-3A, KW1. And see also: Elgin to Fowler, 11 June 1895, Wolverhampton Papers, Vol. 2, no number; Elgin to Hamilton, 16 October 1895, Hamilton Correspondence, D509/1; Elgin to MacDonnell, 29 October 1895, Elgin Papers, Correspondence with persons in India, Vol. 4, Part 2, No. 218.
94 Note by A. C. Trevor, 18 September 1895, IP, Revenue (LR), October 1895, 72-3A, KW1.
95 Cf. note by A. Mackenzie, 20 September 1895, IP, Revenue (LR), October 1895, 72-3A, KW1.
96 See note by A. Mackenzie cited in note 95; and notes by D. Ibbetson, 28 September 1895 and 2 October 1895, IP, Revenue (LR), October 1895, 72-3A, KW2 and 3.
97 Note by H. Brackenbury, 18 September 1895 and cf. note by D. Ibbetson, 2 October 1895, para. 8, IP, Revenue (LR), October 1895, 72-3A, KW1 and 3.
98 Offg Sec. to Govt of India's circular 24/75-1, 26 October 1895, IP, Revenue (LR), October 1895, 72-3A.
99 Deputy Sec. to Govt of India's No. 23 Judicial/1595, 31 October 1895, IP, Home (J), November 1895, 317-20A.
100 Offg Rev. Sec.'s No. 224, 3 December 1895, IP, Revenue (LR), June 1896, 28A.
101 Note by D. Fitzpatrick, LG, 26 December 1895, IP, Revenue (LR), November 1898, 3-22A.
102 J. R. Maconachie, DC Gurdaspur's No. 508G, 9 June 1896, IP, Revenue (LR), November 1898, 3-22A; and cf. earlier letters written as DC Gurdaspur: No. 791, 14 November 1894, IP, Home (J),

October 1897, 317–576A; No. 14G, 15 January 1896, IP, Revenue (LR), December 1896, 22–47A.
103 J. B. Hutchinson, CR Lahore's No. 250, 19 March 1896, IP, Revenue (LR), November 1898, 3–22A.
104 C. F. Massy, CR Jullunder's No. 460, 15 February 1896, IP, Revenue (LR), November 1898, 3–22A.
105 On the Sikh Jats see the author's 'Changes in Status and Occupation in Nineteenth-Century Panjab', in D. A. Low (ed.), *Soundings in Modern South Asian History* (London 1968), pp. 78–80.
106 E. B. Francis, DC, on furlough, No. —, 10 February 1896, IP, Revenue (LR), November 1898, 3–22A.
107 W. R. H. Merk, CR Peshawar's No. 223, 18 May 1896, IP, Revenue (LR), November 1898, 3–22A.
108 Opinion of C. A. Roe, Chief Judge, 2 February 1896, IP, Revenue (LR), November 1898, 3–22A.
109 F. A. Robertson, DLR's No. —, 28 April 1896, IP, Revenue (LR), November 1898, 3–22A.
110 See opinions of J. Frizelle, A. H. Diack, R. I. Bruce, J. A. Anderson, IP, Revenue (LR), November 1898, 3–22A.
111 R. Clarke, CR Delhi's No. 354, 13 August 1896, IP, Revenue (LR), November 1898, 3–22A.
112 S. S. Thorburn, Report on Peasant Indebtedness and Land Alienation to Money-lenders in parts of the Rawalpindi division, 1 May 1896, paras 53, 73–7, 86, IP, Revenue (LR), November 1898, 3–22A; S. S. Thorburn, CR Rawalpindi's No. 1472, 12 May 1896, IP, Home (J), November 1898, 274–439A; S. S. Thorburn, CR Rawalpindi's No. 259S, 9 September 1896, IP, Revenue (LR), November 1898, 3–22A.
113 A. Anderson, DC Kangra's No. 10C, 5 August 1896, IP, Revenue (LR), November 1898, 3–22A.
114 J. Wilson, *Report on the Revision of the Assessment of the Gurgaon district*, 1883, paras 10–11 and J. Wilson, *SR Sirsa*, 1884, para. 232.
115 J. Wilson, DC Rawalpindi's No. 47C, 20 August 1896, IP, Revenue (LR), November 1898, 3–22A.
116 J. G. Silcock, DC Jhelum's No. —, 13 April 1896, IP, Revenue (LR), November 1898, 3–22A.
117 Opinion of A. W. Stogdon, JC, 29 February 1896, and opinion of P. C. Chatterji, JC, 20 June 1896, IP, Revenue (LR), November 1898, 3–22A.
118 Note by C. M. Rivaz, 1st FC, 16 August 1896, and notes by C. L. Tupper, 2nd FC, 7 September and 11 September 1896, IP, Revenue (LR), November 1898, 3–22A.
119 Note by D. Fitzpatrick, LG, 1 January 1897, IP, Revenue (LR), November 1898, 3–22A.
120 Note by D. Fitzpatrick, LG, 5 March 1897. For this note and

correspondence on legislation similar to Deccan Act see: IP, Home (J), November 1898, 274–439A.

121 Notes by D. Ibbetson, 22 August 1896 and 29 August 1896; J. Woodburn, 2 September 1896; D. Ibbetson, 4 September 1896 (two notes), IP, Revenue (LR), November 1898, 3–22A, KW6.

122 Elgin to Hamilton, 28 April 1897, Hamilton Correspondence, D509/5.

123 S. S. Thorburn, CR Rawalpindi's No. 1790, 5 June 1897, PP, Revenue (A), September 1897, 1–7A; notes by M. W. Fenton, 17 July 1897 and W. M. Young, 23 August 1897, PF 190, pp. 218–19; J. Wilson, CR Rawalpindi's No. 3401, 11 November 1897 and Snr Sec. to FC's No. 743, 9 December 1897, PP, Revenue (A), February 1898, 3–8A; notes by M. W. Fenton, 16 December 1897, L. W. Dane, 20 December 1897, W. M. Young, 31 January 1898, PF 190, pp. 227–9.

124 Note by D. Ibbetson, 31 January 1898, IP, Revenue (LR), November 1898, 3–22A, KW6.

125 Note by C. M. Rivaz, 17 February 1898, IP, Revenue (LR), November 1898, 3–22A, KW6.

126 Note by J. Woodburn, 10 March 1898, IP, Revenue (LR), November 1898, 3–22A, KW6.

127 Note by Elgin, 22 March 1898, IP, Revenue (LR), November 1898, 3–22A, KW6; Elgin to Hamilton, 24 March 1898, Hamilton Correspondence, D509/10.

128 Offg Sec. to Govt of India's No. 570–27–17, 30 March 1898, IP, Revenue (LR), November 1898, 3–22A.

129 Notes by D. Ibbetson, 5 May 1898, C. M. Rivaz, 6 May 1898, Elgin, 6 May 1898, D. Ibbetson, 6 May 1898, IP, Revenue (LR), November 1898, 3–22A, KW6.

130 E. D. Maclagan, Note on Land Transfer and Agricultural Indebtedness in India, 18 March 1895, pp. 236–7, IP, Revenue (LR), October 1895, 72–3A.

131 For some brief references to British parallels see: J. Wilson, DC Rawalpindi's No. 47C, 20 August 1896, para. 7 and S. S. Thorburn, CR Rawalpindi's No. 259S, 9 September 1896, IP, Revenue (LR), November 1898, 3–22A.

132 N. G. Barrier, *The Punjab Alienation of Land Bill of 1900* (Durham, N. C., 1966), p. 97.

133 *Ibid.*, p. 98.

CHAPTER V

1 Notes by W. M. Young, LG, 7 and 9 April 1898, PF 190, p. 254.
2 Marginal remarks by W. M. Young, LG, on note by W. R. H. Merk, 9 May 1898, PF 190, pp. 255–7.
3 Note by M. W. Fenton, Rev. Sec., 16 June 1898, PF 190, p. 263.
4 Note by W. M. Young, LG, 22 June 1898, PF 190, p. 264.

5 Speech by W. M. Young, LG, in Indian Legislative Council, 19 October 1900, Legislative Papers.
6 On this point see note by W. M. Young, LG, 20 July 1898, IP, Revenue (LR), November 1898, 3-22A.
7 In what follows an attempt has been made to reconstruct the committee's discussions from the following sources: tabulated answers of officers (given before the committee sat); proceedings of Barnes Court committee, 1–2 July 1898; note by W. M. Young, LG, 20 July 1898, all in IP, Revenue (LR), November 1898, 3-22A. Additional sources are cited at the appropriate points.
8 Note by S. S. Thorburn, Offg FC, 5 February 1898, IP, Revenue (LR), June 1900, 24–5A; review by S. S. Thorburn, FC, 18 April 1898, para. 10, *AR Pind Dadan Khan*, 1897.
9 Note by L. W. Dane, Chief Sec., 20 December 1897, PF 190, pp. 228–9.
10 Cf. note by S. S. Thorburn, Offg FC, 5 February 1898, paras 2, 14, IP, Revenue (LR), June 1900, 24–5A.
11 Cf. note by C. L. Tupper, FC, 18 June [sic July] 1898, para. 9, FF, demi-official file, No. 28, KW, 441/50. This note suggests Tupper saw the proposed legislation very much as a measure directed against the money-lenders.
12 Cf. also note by S. S. Thorburn, FC, 10 May 1898, para. 8, PF 190, p. 358, where Thorburn indicated the need for safeguards to prevent the transfer of the business of money-lending and land-grabbing from professional lenders to agriculturist lenders, and to prevent wholesale expropriation of smaller proprietors by wealthy agricultural landlords.
13 J. A. L. Montgomery, Offg CR Rawalpindi's No. 2601, 17 September 1894, para. 5, IP, Revenue (LR), June 1896, 28A.
14 Note by J. M. Douie, 17 December 1895, paras 4, 6, PF 190, pp. 2–4.
15 Cf. note by S. S. Thorburn, FC, 10 May 1898, paras 6–7, PF 190, pp. 357–8.
16 Note by W. M. Young, LG, 20 July 1898, IP, Revenue (LR), November 1898, 3–22A.
17 Notes by C. M. Rivaz, 17 February and 13 June 1898; Order in Council, 15 July 1898, all in IP, Home (J), November 1898, 274–439A, KW. See also Elgin to Hamilton, 3 November 1898, Hamilton Correspondence, D509/12.
18 Note by C. M. Rivaz, 17 August 1898, IP, Revenue (LR), November 1898, 3–22A, KW6.
19 See Ibbetson to Elgin, 6 August 1898, Elgin Papers, Correspondence with persons in India, Vol. 10, Part 1, No. 63.
20 Notes by Elgin, 22 August and 1 September 1898, IP, Revenue (LR), November 1898, 3–22A, KW6; Elgin to Hamilton, 3 November 1898, Hamilton Correspondence, D509/12.
21 Notes by A. C. Trevor, J. Westland, E. H. H. Collen, M. D. Chalmers,

## NOTES

C. E. Nairne between 25 August and 23 October 1898, IP, Revenue (LR), November 1898, 3–22A, KW6.
22 Govt of India, Dept of Revenue and Agriculture's despatch to Sec. of State for India, No. 59 of 1898, 3 November 1898, para. 26, IP, Revenue (LR), November 1898, 3–22A, and notes by T. W. Holderness, Sec. Revenue Dept, 21 October 1898 and by C. M. Rivaz, 22 October 1898 in KW6 of this file.
23 Note by D. Fitzpatrick, 1 February 1899, and his suggestions for introductory remarks to proposed despatch; note by D. Fitzpatrick, 21 February 1899, all in IO, Dept of Revenue and Statistics Papers, 1898, Vol. 410, No. 2739; note by D. Fitzpatrick, 14 April 1899, IP, Revenue (LR), July 1899, 44–5A.
24 Hamilton to Curzon, 28 March 1899, Hamilton Correspondence, C126/1.
25 Minutes by C. H. T. Crosthwaite and P. P. Hutchins, 20 March 1899, IP, Revenue (LR), July 1899, 44–5A.
26 Crosthwaite to W. R. Lawrence, n.d., placed between letters of 18 May and 9 June 1899, Curzon Papers, Vol. 181, Part 1, No. 34.
27 Minutes by A. Lyall, 15 March 1899 and J. Edge, 13 April 1899, IP, Revenue (LR), July 1899, 44–5A.
28 Minute by J. Peile, 13 February 1899, IP, Revenue (LR), July 1899, 44–5A.
29 Notes by D. Fitzpatrick, 1 February and 21 February 1899, and Fitzpatrick's draft of 21 April 1899 of additional paragraph for despatch, IO, Dept of Revenue and Statistics Papers, 1898, Vol. 410, No. 2739; note by Fitzpatrick, 14 April 1899, IP, Revenue (LR), July 1899, 44–5A.
30 Cf. Hamilton to Elgin, 26 February 1897, Hamilton Correspondence, C125/2.
31 Hamilton to Curzon, 28 March 1899, Hamilton Correspondence, C126/1; and also Godley to Curzon, 24 March 1899, Curzon Papers, Vol. 181, Part 1, No. 22.
32 Cf. Rivaz to Curzon, 8 March 1899, Curzon Papers, Vol. 199, Part 1, No. 96 with Curzon to Hamilton, 9 March 1899, Curzon Papers, Vol. 158, Part 2, No. 9.
33 Hamilton to Curzon, 28 March 1899, Hamilton Correspondence, C126/1.
34 Godley to Curzon, 21 April 1899, Curzon Papers, Vol. 181, Part 1, No. 30; Hamilton to Curzon, 21 April 1899, Hamilton Correspondence, C126/1; Godley to Curzon, 3 May 1899, Curzon Papers, Vol. 158, Part 1, No. 15a; despatch from Secretary of State for India to Govt of India, No. 186, 27 April 1899, IP, Revenue (LR), July 1899, 44–5A.
35 Cf. Godley to Curzon, 3 May 1899, Curzon Papers, Vol. 158, Part 1, No. 15a, and also Crosthwaite to Lawrence, n.d., Curzon Papers, Vol. 181, Part 1, No. 34.

36 Note by C. M. Rivaz, 24 May 1899, IP, Revenue (LR), July 1899, 44–5A, KW.
37 Note by Curzon, 25 June 1899, IP, Revenue (LR), July 1899, 44–5A, KW; cf. Rivaz to Curzon, 3 May 1899, Curzon Papers, Vol. 199, Part 1, No. 178.
38 Notes by C. E. Dawkins, 30 June 1899, R. Gardiner, 1 July 1899, T. Raleigh, 1 July 1899, E. H. H. Collen, 3 July 1899, IP, Revenue (LR), July 1899, 44–5A, KW.
39 Order in Council, 7 July 1899, IP, Revenue (LR), July 1899, 44–5A, KW.
40 Rivaz to Curzon, 3 May 1899, Curzon Papers, Vol. 199, Part 1, No. 178.
41 Curzon to Hamilton, 12 July 1899, Curzon Papers, Vol. 158, Part 2, No. 30; and see also Curzon to Godley, 28 June 1899, Curzon Papers, Vol. 158, Part 2, No. 28b.
42 See Legislative Papers for the draft Alienation Bill.
43 These were as follows: existing and future conditional sales would be null and void; permanent alienations made without sanction would take effect as self-redeeming usufructuary mortgages; documents contravening the provisions of the Act would not be admitted to registration; any mortgagee or lessee who remained in possession after his term had expired could be ejected by the Deputy Commissioner on his own motion or on the application of the person entitled to possession.
44 Govt of India, Dept of Revenue and Agriculture's despatch to Sec. of State for India, No. 50, 27 July 1899, IP, Revenue (LR), July 1899, 44–5A; Telegram from Sec. of State for India to Viceroy, 13 September 1899, Legislative Papers; see also: IO, Dept of Revenue and Statistics Papers, 1899, Vol. 422, No. 2373, and Hamilton to Curzon, 3 August 1899, Hamilton Correspondence, C126/1.
45 Minute by D. Fitzpatrick, 3 November 1899, IO, Minutes of Dissent by Members of Council, 1881–1900, c/131.
46 Speech by C. M. Rivaz, in Legislative Council, 27 September 1899, Legislative Papers; Curzon to Hamilton, 27 September 1899, Curzon Papers, Vol. 158, Part 2, No. 43; Sec. to Govt of India's No. 1881, 28 September 1899, to Chief Sec. to Punjab Govt, Legislative Papers.
47 Remarks by J. R. Drummond, DC Gujranwala and by W. C. Renouf, DC Jullunder, *ERR*, 1895–6, pp. 47, 73; *RR*, 1896–7, para. 12b; remarks by C. L. Dundas, DC Shahpur, *ERR*, 1897–8, p. 24; W. S. Talbot, *AR Jhelum*, 18 July 1899, para. 52.
48 The account of public opinion on the Bill given in this and succeeding paragraphs is based on: note by S. S. Thorburn, FC, 8 November 1899, FF, 441/100A; Punjab correspondence of 1899–1900 and petitions, reports on petitions, pamphlets, letters, etc., in Legislative Papers; Selections from Punjab Native Papers, 1899–1900 (chiefly sections under heading 'Punjab Land Alienation Bill').

## NOTES

49 On these points see: note by C. L. Tupper, FC, 19 August 1900, FF, 441/100(3); *RR*, 1899–1900, para. 7; *RR*, 1900–1, para. 7.
50 For Punjab correspondence of 1899–1900 see Legislative Papers.
51 Young explained in the Legislative Council that he had chosen officers who not only understood the Bill, but also the real objections which underlay the critical opinions submitted to the Punjab Government. See speech of 22 June 1900, Legislative Papers.
52 Note by C. L. Tupper, FC, 5 February 1900 and Offg Jnr Sec. to FC's No. 258, 30 March 1900 in Punjab correspondence 1899–1900, Legislative Papers.
53 H. C. Fanshawe, CR Delhi's No. 70, 16 February 1900, Punjab correspondence 1899–1900, Legislative Papers.
54 See note by Raleigh cited in note 38 and speech by Edward Law in Legislative Council, 19 October 1900, Legislative Papers.
55 On Harnam Singh cf. *Rafiq-i-Hind*, 21 July 1900, Selections from Punjab Native Papers, 1900.
56 On Muhammad Hayat Khan see: remarks by S. S. Thorburn, DC Rawalpindi, *ERR*, 1888–9, p. 18; J. B. Lyall to Lansdowne, 7 October 1891, IP, Home (J), October 1891, 234–300A; Curzon to Godley, 4 July 1900, Curzon Papers, Vol. 159, Part 2, No. 41; *Rafiq-i-Hind*, 21 July 1900, Selections from Punjab Native Papers, 1900; speech by Muhammad Hayat Khan in Legislative Council, 19 October 1900, Legislative Papers.
57 Note by C. L. Tupper, FC, 5 February 1900, para. 6; H. C. Fanshawe, CR Delhi's No. 70, 16 February 1900, para. 8; memorandum by W. M. Young, LG, 15 May 1900, para. 8, all in Punjab correspondence 1899–1900, Legislative Papers; speech in Legislative Council by Muhammad Hayat Khan, 19 October 1900, Legislative Papers.
58 Cf. speech by C. M. Rivaz in Legislative Council, 10 August 1900, Legislative Papers.
59 The above interpretation of the reasons for the retention of the 'agriculturist' has been pieced together from the following sources: note by C. L. Tupper, FC, 5 February 1900, paras 2–4 and memorandum by W. M. Young, LG, 15 May 1900, para. 7, Punjab correspondence 1899–1900, Legislative Papers; later accounts given in draft of letter to Commissioners (Tupper's handwriting), 17 October 1900, para. 4, FF, 441/100 (4), and in note by D. Ibbetson, 11 January 1904, IP, Revenue (LR), March 1904, 14–15A, KW.
60 Note by T. Raleigh, 1 July 1899, para. 5, IP, Revenue (LR), July 1899, 44–5A, KW; note by C. L. Tupper, FC, 5 February 1900, paras 3, 6, 19, 20; H. C. Fanshawe, CR Delhi's No. 70, 16 February 1900, para. 8; Offg Jnr Sec. to FC's No. 258, 30 March 1900, para. 4, all in Punjab correspondence 1899–1900, Legislative Papers.
61 Rivaz to Tupper, 17 July 1900, FF, 441/100, KW, L.A., IV.

62 Memorandum by W. M. Young, LG, 15 May 1900, paras 9, 12, Punjab correspondence 1899–1900, Legislative Papers.
63 Note by C. L. Tupper, FC, 5 February 1900, paras 1, 5, Punjab correspondence 1899–1900, Legislative Papers.
64 Cf. speech in Legislative Council by Muhammad Hayat Khan, 19 October 1900, Legislative Papers.
65 The precise proposal made by Rivaz and refused by Young is not clear. That some such proposal as is referred to in the text was made is apparent from later references in: note by C. L. Tupper, FC, 30 April 1901, FF, 441/100(2), and note by W. M. Young, LG, 18 May 1901, PF 190, p. 1048.
66 Speech by C. M. Rivaz in Legislative Council, 10 August 1900, Legislative Papers.
67 Regarding the amendments in the mortgage restrictions cf. the following: note by C. L. Tupper, 2nd FC, 7 September 1896, paras 14–15, IP, Revenue (LR), November 1898, 3–22A; note by C. L. Tupper, FC, 5 February 1900, paras 9–11; H. C. Fanshawe, CR Delhi's No. 70, 16 February 1900, paras 5, 8; Offg Jnr Sec. to FC's No. 258, 30 March 1900, paras 2–3; note by W. M. Young, LG, 15 May 1900, paras 11, 14, all in Punjab correspondence 1899–1900, Legislative Papers; second speech by C. M. Rivaz in Legislative Council, 19 October 1900, Legislative Papers.
68 See later accounts: Tupper to Rivaz, 18 October 1900, FF, 442/1/00/6; speech by C. L. Tupper (on retrospective provisions relating to mortgages by conditional sale) in Legislative Council, 19 October 1900, Legislative Papers.
69 Report of Select Committee, 6 August 1900, minute of dissent by Harnam Singh, Ahluwalia, Bill as amended by report of Select Committee of 6 August 1900, all in Legislative Papers.
70 Curzon to Hamilton, 15 August and 24 October 1900, Curzon Papers, Vol. 159, Part 2, Nos 50 and 67; note by Curzon, 20 April 1905, IP, Revenue (LR), May 1905, 28–9B.
71 Telegrams dated 5, 11, 12, 14, 15, 18, 19 and 21 September 1900, Legislative Papers.
72 Note by C. L. Tupper, FC, 19 August 1900, FF, 441/100(3), and see later account in Jnr Sec. to FC's No. 225S, 13 August 1901, PF190, p. 1112.
73 Report of Select Committee, 2 October 1900, Legislative Papers.
74 Note by C. L. Tupper, FC, 5 October 1900, FF, 441/100(2); and see later reference in Jnr Sec. to FC's No. 225S, 13 August 1901, PF190, p. 1112.
75 On the above see: *Wakil*, 20 August and 3 September 1900, and *Rafiq-i-Hind*, 8 and 15 September 1900, Selections from Punjab Native Papers, 1900; K. B. Ahmed Shah, Judicial Extra Assistant Commissioner Gujranwala to Muhammad Hayat Khan, n.d.; Muhammad Hayat Khan to Rivaz and Douie, 14 September 1900;

Rivaz to Tupper, 14 September 1900; Douie to Tupper and Muhammad Hayat Khan, 15 September 1900; Tupper to Rivaz, 16 September 1900; Muhammad Shafi, Bar at Law, to Tupper, 18 September 1900, all in FF, 441/100, KW, L.A., IV; telegram from Sec. of State for India to Viceroy, 19 September 1900 and note by C. M. Rivaz, 21 September 1900, Legislative Papers; Rivaz to Tupper, 21 September 1900, FF, 441/100, KW, L.A., IV.
76 Cf. Douie to Tupper, 15 September 1900, FF, 441/100, KW, L.A., IV.
77 For the Bill as finally amended see Legislative Papers.
78 Note by C. L. Tupper, FC, 19 August 1900, FF, 441/100(3).
79 Notes by following (all members of conference of 10 September 1900 except Fanshawe): H. C. Fanshawe, 3 September 1900; Muhammad Hayat Khan, W. R. H. Merk, A. H. Diack, J. M. Douie, 10 September 1900; C. G. Parsons, H. A. Rose, 11 September 1900; E. D. Maclagan, 13 September 1900; C. L. Tupper, n.d.; and proceedings of conference, 10 September 1900, with remarks by A. H. Diack, 13 September 1900 and J. M. Douie, 14 September 1900, all in FF, 441/100(2).
80 Note by C. L. Tupper, FC, 5 October 1900, FF, 441/100(2).
81 Note by C. L. Tupper, FC, 24 October 1900, FF, 441/100(4).
82 Rev. and Financial Sec. to Govt's No. 117, 12 November 1900, and see also Nos 118–20, FF, 441/100 P.F.
83 Note by E. D. Maclagan, 18 March 1901, para. 19, referring to a demi-official letter from Rivaz, dated 30 November 1900, FF, 441/100(22).
84 The Punjab correspondence is in IP, Revenue (LR), May 1901, 11–12A.
85 Marginal remarks by W. M. Young, LG, on notes by E. D. Maclagan, 18 March 1901 and J. M. Douie, 26 March 1901; note by W. M. Young, LG, 5 April 1901, all in FF, 441/100(22); Revenue and Financial Sec. to Govt's No. 41, 16 April 1901, to Govt of India, IP, Revenue (LR), May 1901, 11–12A.
86 Note by C. L. Tupper, FC, 30 April 1901, FF, 441/100(2).
87 Notes by C. M. Rivaz, 26 April and Curzon, 7 May 1901, IP, Revenue (LR), May 1901, 11–12A; Curzon to Hamilton, 8 May 1901, Curzon Papers, Vol. 160, Part 2, No. 32.
88 Marginal note by C. L. Tupper, FC, 27 May 1901, on draft circular of May 1901, FF, 441/100(2).
89 T. R. Metcalf, *The Aftermath of Revolt India, 1857–1870* (Princeton 1964), p. 216.
90 *Ibid.*, p. 218.
91 E. Stokes, *The English Utilitarians and India* (Oxford 1959), p. 320.
92 Curzon to Hamilton, 24 October 1900, Curzon Papers, Vol. 159, Part 2, No. 67 and see also Curzon to Hamilton, 3 October 1900, Curzon Papers, Vol. 159, Part 2, No. 64.

## THE PUNJAB TRADITION

CHAPTER VI

1 A similar measure restricting alienations was passed a few years later for the North-West Frontier Province.
2 The account of the working of the Act which follows is based mainly on: *LAR*, from 1901 to 1907-8.
3 For the attitudes of agricultural tribes towards the Act see: *LAR*, from 1901 to 1907-8; H. A. Anderson, CR Jullunder's No. 3478, 19 September 1902, para. 3, FF, 441/100 (2½)A; copy of letter from SO Dera Ismail Khan, No. 831, 19 October 1902, para. 2, FF, 441/125; note by J. Wilson, 7 January 1904, IP, Revenue (LR), March 1904, 14-15A KW; H. J. Maynard, Commissioner of Excise's No. 23, 24 March 1904, para. 16, FF, 441/104A; E. R. Abbott, SO Jhang's No. 139, 10 October 1904, PF 190, p. 1310. Cf. also correspondence in FF, 441/100(22)A.
4 For this and succeeding paragraphs on notification of tribes see petitions and correspondence in: FF, 441/100 K. covers; 441/100(2); 441/100(2½)A; 441/100(4); 441/100(11)A; 441/100(13)A; 441/100(15); 441/100(22)A; and PF 190, pp. 1259-64, 1323, 1406-15, 1505-58.
5 P. D. Agnew, DC Rawalpindi's No. 96G, 21 May 1906, FF, 441/100(22)A; *LAR*, 1905-6, para. 22.
6 See: Selections from Punjab Native Papers, 1901-7 (sections headed 'Punjab Land Alienation Act'); *LAR*, from 1901 to 1907-8; copy of letter from SO Dera Ismail Khan, No. 831, 19 October 1902, para. 8, FF, 441/125; Chela Ram and Sant Ram, bankers, to DC Rawalpindi, 18 July 1903, FF, 441/105; H. J. Maynard, Commissioner of Excise's No. 23, 24 March 1904, and opinion by P. C. Chatterji, JC, 19 April 1904, FF, 441/104(A); Diwan Narendra Nath, DC Gujrat's No. 185, 10 August 1904, PF 190, p. 1315; extract from *Tribune*, 8 December 1904, FF, 441/104B.
7 Selections from Punjab Native Papers, 1901-7 (sections headed 'Punjab Land Alienation Act'); article by Mian Muhammad Shafi, barrister at law, 28 May 1903, FF, 441/104A (in pocket); Kazi Muhammad Aslam, DVJ Ferozepur's No. 336G, 29 June 1903, and report by Maulvi Imam-ud-Din Ahmad, pleader, 12 August 1902 [*sic* 1903], FF, 441/105; H. J. Maynard, Commissioner of Excise's No. 23, 24 March 1904, para. 16, FF, 441/104A; Shekh Asghar Ali, DC Muzuffargarh's No. 321, 19 October 1904, PF 190, pp. 1314-15.
8 W. M. Young, 'The Progress of the Panjab', *The Imperial and Asiatic Quarterly Review*, Third Series, Vol. XIX, Nos. 37 and 38, January-April 1905, pp. 66-7.
9 For this discussion see article cited in previous note, pp. 162-70.
10 For this paragraph and the next see: *LAR*, 1901 to 1907-8 and reviews of LG bound with these reports; J. A. L. Montgomery, CR Rawalpindi's No. 76, 8 January 1901 and Jnr Sec. to FC's No. 206, 5 March 1901 (C. L. Tupper), IP, Revenue (LR), July 1901, 51-8A; A. Anderson, CR Jullunder's No. 438, 3 February 1902, para. 3 and

# NOTES

J. A. L. Montgomery, CR Rawalpindi's No. 322, 8 February 1902, para. 5, IP, Home (J), October 1902, 225–6A; Curzon to Hamilton, 30 April 1902, Curzon Papers, Vol. 161, Part 2, No. 31; note by C. M. Rivaz, LG, 6 July 1902, FF, 441/105 KW; note by D. Ibbetson, 10 September 1902, IP, Home (J), October 1902, 225–6A, KW; note by T. G. Walker, CR Delhi, 10 October 1903; notes by C. L. Tupper, FC, 26 December 1903 and 14 February 1904; draft letter to Govt in Tupper's handwriting, 28 February 1904, all in FF, 441/105; A. Kensington, DVJ Lahore's No. 280, 5 April 1904, para. 4, FF, 441/104A; notes by J. Wilson, 12 April 1904, and D. Ibbetson, 18 April 1904, IP, Revenue (LR), April 1904, 39–40B; opinion by P. C. Chatterji, JC, 19 April 1904, FF, 441/104A; note by Curzon, 20 April 1905, IP, Revenue (LR), May 1905, 28–9B; opinion of H. P. P. Leigh, CR Multan, 21 February 1906, PF 190, p. 1478; note by J. M. Douie, 23 August 1906, FF, 441/100 KW, F.N.6, Vol. VI; opinion by A. Kensington, JC, 5 January 1907, and speech by C. M. Rivaz, LG, in Punjab Legislative Council, 21 February 1907, IP, Legislative, April 1907, 64–6A.

11 On this point see esp. discussions about abolition of 'agriculturist' in 1904 in PF 190; and in 1906–7 in IP, Legislative, April 1907, 64–6A.

12 *LAR*, 1907–8, para. 28.

13 Note by H. J. Maynard, 5 September 1898, with marginal remarks by W. M. Young, PF 18, pp. 1078–81.

14 See following letters on Bill by H. J. Maynard, DC Umballa: No. 233/1389 R, 25 November 1899; No. 246/1453 R, 5 December 1899; No. 252/1473 R, 8 December 1899; No. 19/92 R, 18 January 1900, all in Punjab correspondence 1899–1900, Legislative Papers. Maynard's No. 19/92 R, 18 January 1900, is summarised in Chapter I.

15 Opinion by H. J. Maynard, DC Umballa, 13 December 1901, para. 6, IP, Home (J), October 1902, 225–6A.

16 Note by H. J. Maynard, DC Umballa, 16 December 1900, IP, Revenue (LR), May 1901, 11–12A.

17 Maynard's opinion of 13 December 1901, para. 2, cited in note 15.

18 Maynard's opinion of 13 December 1901, paras 3–4, cited in note 15.

19 Maynard's opinion of 13 December 1901, para. 5, cited in note 15.

20 H. J. Maynard, Commissioner of Excise's No. 23, 24 March 1904, para. 14, FF, 441/104A.

21 Maynard's No. 23, 24 March 1904, para. 16, cited in note 20.

22 H. J. Maynard, DC Umballa's No. 437–2200 R, 24 December 1902, FF, 441/6D.

23 Maynard's No. 23, 24 March 1904, para. 17, cited in note 20.

24 Maynard's No. 23, 24 March 1904, para. 18, cited in note 20.

25 Maynard's No. 23, 24 March 1904, para. 19, cited in note 20.

26 H. J. Maynard, Commissioner of Excise's No. 273, 22 December 1904, para. 3, FF, 441/104, PF, Rev., KW.

27 H. J. Maynard, CR Lahore's No. 363, 31 July 1906, FF, 441/100(22)A.

28 H. J. Maynard, Offg CR Lahore's No. 570, 23 November 1906, para. 5, IP, Legislative, April 1907, 64–6A.
29 Maynard's No. 273, 22 December 1904, para. 2, cited in note 26.
30 Maynard's No. 570, 23 November 1906, para. 6, cited in note 28.
31 M. O'Dwyer, *India As I Knew It 1885–1925* (London 1926 ed.), p. 422.
32 L. Woolf, *Beginning Again An Autobiography of the Years 1911–1918* (London 1964), p. 228; L. Woolf, *Downhill All the Way An Autobiography of the Years 1919–1939* (London 1967), pp. 223–4, 227.
33 Related in M. Darling, *Apprentice to Power India 1904–1908* (London 1966), p. 128.
34 Minute by D. Ibbetson, 30 April 1907, para. 3, printed in V. C. Joshi (ed.), *Lajpat Rai Autobiographical Writings* (Delhi 1965), p. 228.
35 Marginal remark by T. G. Walker, FC, on note by L. H. Leslie-Jones, 31 October 1906, FF, 441/100(22)A.
36 J. Douie, *The Panjab, North-West Frontier Province and Kashmir* (Cambridge 1916), p. 102.
37 M. O'Dwyer, *India As I Knew It 1885–1925* (London 1926 ed.), p. 171.
38 *Ibid.*, p. 417.
39 *Ibid.*, p. 99.
40 Foreword by E. D. Maclagan to M. L. Darling, *The Punjab Peasant in Prosperity and Debt* (London 1925), pp. vii–viii.
41 H. K. Trevaskis, *The Land of the Five Rivers* (Oxford 1928), pp. 332–4.
42 H. Harcourt, *Sidelights on the Crisis in India* (London 1924), p. ix.
43 *History of Services*, 1911, cf. p. 29 and p. 82.
44 M. Darling, *Apprentice to Power India 1904–1908* (London 1966), p. 128.
45 See various books by Darling listed in bibliograpy.

# Appendix

DIVISIONS OF THE PUNJAB

From the time of the incorporation of the Delhi and Hissar divisions into the Punjab in 1858, the Province consisted of ten divisions under Commissioners.

| Divisions | Districts | Divisions | Districts |
|---|---|---|---|
| Delhi | Delhi | Lahore | Lahore |
|  | Gurgaon |  | Gujranwala |
|  | Karnal |  | Ferozepur |
| Hissar | Hissar | Rawalpindi | Rawalpindi |
|  | Rohtak |  | Jhelum |
|  | Sirsa |  | Gujrat |
|  |  |  | Shahpur |
| Umballa | Umballa | Multan | Multan |
|  | Ludhiana |  | Jhang |
|  | Simla |  | Montgomery |
|  |  |  | Muzuffargarh |
| Jullunder | Jullunder | Derajat | Dera Ismail Khan |
|  | Hoshiarpur |  | Dera Ghazi Khan |
|  | Kangra |  | Bannu |
| Amritsar | Amritsar | Peshawar | Peshawar |
|  | Gurdaspur |  | Hazara |
|  | Sialkot |  | Kohat |

The Thanesar district, which is not shown here, was broken up in 1862 and divided between Umballa and Karnal.

In 1884 these ten divisions were reduced to six, as follows (the Sirsa district being abolished and divided between Hissar and Ferozepur).

| Divisions | Districts | Divisions | Districts |
|---|---|---|---|
| Delhi | Delhi | Jullunder | Jullunder |
|  | Gurgaon |  | Hoshiarpur |
|  | Karnal |  | Kangra |
|  | Rohtak |  | Ferozepur |
|  | Hissar |  | Ludhiana |
|  | Umballa |  |  |
|  | Simla |  |  |

## THE PUNJAB TRADITION

| Divisions | Districts |
|---|---|
| Lahore | Gurdaspur |
| | Amritsar |
| | Lahore |
| | Jhang |
| | Montgomery |
| | Multan |
| Rawalpindi | Rawalpindi |
| | Jhelum |
| | Gujrat |
| | Shahpur |
| | Gujranwala |
| | Sialkot |
| Derajat | Muzuffargarh |
| | Dera Ghazi Khan |
| | Dera Ismail Khan |
| | Bannu |
| Peshawar | Peshawar |
| | Hazara |
| | Kohat |

These divisions remained practically unaltered until the creation of the North-West Frontier Province in 1901.

Throughout the book it has been found convenient to refer to particular parts of the Punjab as follows: south-eastern Punjab (Delhi, Gurgaon, Karnal, Rohtak, Hissar and Umballa districts); central Punjab (Ferozepur, Ludhiana, Jullunder, Hoshiarpur, Gurdaspur, Amritsar and Lahore districts); north-western Punjab (Rawalpindi, Jhelum, Gujrat, Shahpur, Gujranwala and Sialkot districts); south-western Punjab (Multan, Muzuffargarh, Jhang and Montgomery districts); the lower frontier (Dera Ismail Khan and Dera Ghazi Khan districts); and the upper frontier (Bannu, Kohat, Peshawar and Hazara districts). All references to districts here are to those existing from 1884.

# Bibliography

As far as primary sources are concerned, this bibliography lists only those sources, or classes of sources, which proved to be of immediate relevance.

RECORDS OF THE PUNJAB GOVERNMENT

West Pakistan Secretariat Records Office, Lahore. Punjab Government Civil Secretariat, Judicial Proceedings, 1856–68. Proceedings of the Punjab Government in (*a*) Judicial Department, 1869–71; (*b*) Revenue, Agriculture and Commerce Department, 1872–81 (unclassified); (*c*) Revenue and Agriculture Department, 1882–1900 (the most important branches are Revenue and Agriculture); (*d*) Home Department, 1872–1900 (unclassified until 1881, after that see Judicial branch); (*e*) Foreign Department, 1882–3 (General branch).

RECORDS OF THE FINANCIAL COMMISSIONER'S OFFICE, PUNJAB

West Pakistan Board of Revenue, Lahore. Financial Commissioner's Files under old head 441 and new head 442. Punjab Civil Secretariat Printed Files, Revenue, Nos 18, 172, 190.

RECORDS OF THE GOVERNMENT OF INDIA

Indian National Archives, New Delhi. Proceedings of the Government of India in (*a*) Revenue and Agriculture Department, 1888–1909 (the most important branches are Revenue and Land Revenue, but see also General, Famine and Horse-breeding and Agricultural Stock); (*b*) Home Department, 1870, 1891–1902 (Judicial branch); (*c*) Legislative Department, 1899–1907, including Papers relating to Act XIII of 1900. Selections from Punjab Native Papers, 1898–1907.

INDIA OFFICE RECORDS

Commonwealth Relations Office, London. (*a*) Department of Revenue and Statistics, 1898–9; (*b*) Judicial and Public Department, 1899–1900. Minutes of Dissent by Members of Council of India, 1881–1900.

PRIVATE PAPERS

ndia Office Library, Commonwealth Relations Office, London. Elgin Papers (MSS Eur. F. 84), Correspondence with persons in England and elsewhere, 1894–8, 5 vols; Correspondence with persons in India 1894–8, 10 vols. Wolverhampton Papers (MSS Eur. C. 145), Correspondence with Viceroy, 1894–5, 3 vols. Hamilton Correspondence, Letters to Elgin,

## THE PUNJAB TRADITION

C. 125, 3 vols; Letters to Curzon, C. 126, 1899–1903, 5 vols; D. 508 Private telegrams 1895–9; Letters from Elgin 1895–9, D. 509, 12 vols; Letters from Curzon 1899–1903, D. 510, 14 vols. Curzon Papers (MSS Eur. F. 111), Correspondence with Lord Salisbury, etc., 1899–1905, vols 158–64; Correspondence with persons in England and abroad, 1899–1905, vols 181–3; Correspondence with persons in India, 1899–1905, vols 199–211.

### PARLIAMENTARY PAPERS

House of Commons. 1854, LXIX, General report on Administration of Punjab for years 1849–50 and 1850–1; 1859, XVIII, General report on Administration of Punjab for years 1856–7 and 1857–8; 1870, LIII, Punjab Tenancy Act.

### OFFICIAL REPORTS AND PUBLICATIONS

The most extensive collection of Punjab reports is in the West Pakistan Board of Revenue Library, Lahore, which contains unpublished as well as published material. All sources listed below, which are not generally available, have been located in this Library.

*Assessment and Settlement Reports.* Over 150 settlement and assessment reports and collections of assessment correspondence have been consulted covering the period from the mid-nineteenth century to the early decades of the twentieth century.

### Annual and Quarterly Publications

*Annual Report on the Punjab Alienation of Land Act XIII of 1900* (Lahore 1902–9).
*Annual Report on the Revenue (or Land Revenue) Administration of the Punjab* (Lahore 1861–1902).
*History of Services of Gazetted Officers employed in the Punjab* (or similar titles, Lahore, various annual editions).
*Quarterly Civil List for the Punjab* (Lahore various editions).
*The New Annual Army List, Militia List and Indian Civil Service List* (or similar titles, London, various editions).

### Selections from Official Records

*Book Circular Orders issued by the Financial Commissioner for the Punjab in the Revenue Department for years 1858 to 1860*, Vol. 3.
*Circular Orders issued by the Board of Administration in the Revenue Department during the years 1849 to 1853* (Lahore 1855), Vol. 1.
*Punjab Government Records, Lahore Political Diaries 1847–1849*, Vol. V, *Political Diaries of Lieut. H. B. Edwardes, Assistant to the Resident at Lahore 1847–1849* (Allahabad 1911).
*Selections from the Public Correspondence of the Punjab Administration* (Lahore 1852–5), Vols 1 and 2.

## BIBLIOGRAPHY

*Selections from the Records of the Government of India*, No. XVIII, General Report on the Administration of the Punjab Territories from 1854–5 to 1855–6 inclusive (Calcutta 1856).
*Selections from the Records of the Government of the Punjab and its Dependencies*, New Series, No. XII, Current Rates of Interest on Loan Transactions in the Punjab (Lahore 1876); No. XIII, Papers regarding Alienation of Estates of Insolvent Proprietors to the Money-lending Class (Lahore 1876).
*Selections from the Records of the Office of the Financial Commissioner, Punjab*, New Series No. 11, No. 37, No. LXV, Papers on Indebtedness of Agriculturists in the Punjab and Foreclosure of Mortgage (Lahore 1887).

*Official and Semi-Official Treatises*
*Abstract Principles of Law circulated for the Guidance of Officers employed in the Administration of Civil Justice in the Punjab* (London 1865).
Baden-Powell, B. H., *The Land Systems of British India* (Oxford 1892), Vol. 2.
Cust, Robert, *Manual for the Guidance of Revenue Officers in the Punjab* (Lahore 1866).
Hunter, W. W., *The Imperial Gazetteer of India* (London 1886 ed.).
Hunter, W. W., *The Indian Empire: Its People, History, and Products* (London 1886 ed.).
Ibbetson, Denzil, *Panjab Castes; Being a reprint of the chapter on 'The Races, Castes and Tribes of the People' in the Report on the Census of the Panjab published in 1883 by the late Sir Denzil Ibbetson, K.C.S.I.* (Lahore 1916).
*Punjab Report in Reply to Inquiries issued by the Famine Commission* (Lahore 1878–9).
Roe, Charles Arthur and Rattigan, H. A. B., *Tribal Law in the Punjab, so far as it relates to right in ancestral land* (Lahore 1895).
Tupper, C. L., *Punjab Customary Law*, 3 vols (Calcutta 1881).

CONTEMPORARY WORKS
*Works by Punjab Officers*
Aitchison, Sir Charles, *Lord Lawrence and the Reconstruction of India under the Crown* (Oxford 1894).
An Old Punjaubee [H. W. H. Coxe], *The Punjaub and North-West Frontier of India* (London 1878).
Baden-Powell, B. H., *The Indian Village Community* (London 1896).
Baden-Powell, B. H., *The Origin and Growth of Village Communities in India* (London 1908 ed.).
Beames, John, *Memoirs of a Bengal Civilian* (London 1961).
Bowring, L., *Eastern Experiences* (London 1872).
Calvert, H., *The Wealth and Welfare of the Punjab: Being Some Studies in Punjab Rural Economics* (Lahore 1922).

Campbell, George, *India As It May Be; An Outline of a Proposed Government and Policy* (London 1853).
Campbell, Sir George, *Memoirs of My Indian Career*, 2 vols (London 1893).
Campbell, George, *Modern India: A Sketch of the System of Civil Government* (London 1852).
Cooper, Frederic, *The Crisis in the Punjab from the 10th of May until the Fall of Delhi* (London 1858).
Cust, Robert Needham, *Linguistic and Oriental Essays*, 3rd series (London 1891).
Cust, Robert Needham, *Memoirs of Past Years of a Septuagenarian* (Hertford 1899).
Cust, Robert Needham, *Pictures of Indian Life* (London 1881).
Darling, Malcolm Lyall, *At Freedom's Door* (London 1949).
Darling, Malcolm Lyall, *The Punjab Peasant in Prosperity and Debt* (London 1925 and 1947 ed.).
Darling, Malcolm Lyall, *Rusticus Loquitur or The Old Light and the New in the Punjab Village* (London 1930).
Darling, Malcolm Lyall, *Wisdom and Waste in the Punjab Village* (London 1934).
Darling, Sir Malcolm, *Apprentice to Power, India 1904–1908* (London 1966).
Douie, Sir James, *The Panjab, North-West Frontier Province and Kashmir* (Cambridge 1916).
Edwardes, Major Herbert B., *A Year on the Punjab Frontier in 1848–49*, 2 vols (London 1851 ed.).
Edwardes, Sir Herbert B., and Merivale, Herman, *Life of Sir Henry Lawrence* (London 1873 ed.).
Elsmie, G. R., *Thirty-Five Years in the Punjab 1858–1893* (Edinburgh 1908).
Forsyth, Ethel (ed.), *Autobiography and Reminiscences of Sir Douglas Forsyth* (London 1887).
Grey, Colonel L. J. H., *The India of the Future and its Defence* (London 1911 ed.).
Grey, F., and Grey, C. (ed.), *Tales of Our Grandfather or India since 1856* (London 1912).
Griffin, Lepel H., *The Rajas of the Punjab being the History of the Principal States in the Punjab and Their Political Relations with the British Government* (London 1873 ed.).
Harcourt, H., *Sidelights on the Crisis in India Being the Letters of an Indian Civilian and Some Replies of an Indian Friend* (London 1924).
Lawrence, Sir Henry Montgomery, *Essays, Military and Political Written in India* (London 1859).
Maynard, John, *The Russian Peasant: and other studies*, Book 1 (London 1942).

## BIBLIOGRAPHY

Maynard, Sir John, *Russia in Flux Before October* (New York 1962 ed.).
O'Dwyer, Sir Michael, *India As I Knew It 1885–1925* (London 1926 ed.).
Temple, Sir Richard, *James Thomason* (Oxford 1893).
Temple, Sir Richard, *Men and Events of My Time in India* (London 1882).
Temple, Sir Richard, *The Story of My Life*, 2 vols (London 1896).
Thorburn, S. S., *Bannu; or Our Afghan Frontier* (London 1876).
Thorburn, S. S., *Musalmans and Money-lenders in the Punjab* (Edinburgh 1886). The copy of this work used by the Punjab Government is in the West Pakistan Secretariat Library. Some of the marginal remarks made in the Secretariat were still legible.
Thorburn, S. S., *Problems of Indian Poverty* (London 1902).
Thorburn, S. S., *The Punjab in Peace and War* (London 1904).
Trevaskis, Hugh Kennedy, *The Land of the Five Rivers* (Oxford 1928).
Tupper, Charles Lewis, 'India and Sir Henry Maine', *Journal of the Society of Arts*, Vol. XLVI, 1898, pp. 390–9.
Tupper, Charles Lewis, *Our Indian Protectorate An Introduction to the Study of the Relations between the British Government and its Indian Feudatories* (London 1893).
Young, Sir W. Mackworth, 'The Progress of the Panjab', *The Imperial and Asiatic Quarterly Review*, Third Series, Vol. XIX, Nos 37 and 38, January–April 1905, pp. 48–76 and see further Proceedings of East India Association pp. 162–70 of this number.

*Other Contemporary Works*

Caird, Sir James, *India: The Land and the People* (London 1883).
Collings, Right Hon. Jesse, *Land Reform Occupying Ownership Peasant Proprietary and Rural Education* (London 1906).
Edwardes, Lady, *Memorials of the Life and Letters of Major-General Sir Herbert B. Edwardes*, 2 vols (London 1886).
Edwards, W., *Reminiscences of a Bengal Civilian* (London 1866).
Kay, Joseph, *Free Trade in Land* (London 1883 ed.).
Kaye, John William, *Lives of Indian Officers Illustrative of the History of the Civil and Military Services of India*, Vol. 2 (London 1867).
Maine, Sir Henry, *Ancient Law* (London 1917 ed.).
Maine, Sir Henry, *Lectures on the Early History of Institutions* (London 1875).
Maine, Sir Henry, *Village-Communities in the East and West* (London 1876 ed.).
Parry, E. Gambier, *Reynell Taylor* (London 1888).
Smith, R. Bosworth, *Life of Lord Lawrence*, 2 vols (London 1883 ed.).
Steel, Flora Annie, *The Garden of Fidelity Being the Autobiography of Flora Annie Steel 1847–1929* (London 1929).
Stokes, Whitley (ed.), *Sir Henry Maine . . . Speeches and Minutes* (London 1892).
Wilson, Lady, *Letters From India* (Edinburgh 1911).

OTHER WORKS

*Books*

Ballhatchet, Kenneth, *Social Policy and Social Change in Western India 1817–1830* (London 1957).

Barrier, Norman G., *The Punjab Alienation of Land Bill of 1900* (Durham N.C., 1966).

Beaglehole, T. H., *Thomas Munro and the Development of Administrative Policy in Madras 1792–1818* (Cambridge 1966).

Bearce, George D., *British Attitudes Towards India 1784–1858* (London 1961).

Black, R. D. Collison, *Economic Thought and the Irish Question 1817–1870* (Cambridge 1960).

Buckland, C. E., *Dictionary of Indian Biography* (London 1906).

Bullock, Alan, and Shock, Maurice (ed.), *The Liberal Tradition From Fox to Keynes* (London 1956).

Burn, W. L., *The Age of Equipoise A Study of the mid-Victorian Generation* (London 1964).

Burrow, J. W., *Evolution and Society A Study in Victorian Social Theory* (Cambridge 1966).

Clark, G. Kitson, *An Expanding Society Britain 1830–1900* (Melbourne 1967).

Clark, G. Kitson, *The Making of Victorian England* (London 1962).

Feaver, George, *From Status to Contract A Biography of Sir Henry Maine 1822–1888* (London 1969).

Frykenberg, Robert Eric, *Guntur District 1788–1848 A History of Local Influence and Central Authority in South India* (Oxford 1965).

Frykenberg, Robert Eric (ed.), *Land Control and Social Structure in Indian History* (Madison, Wisconsin 1969).

Gilbert, Martin, *Servant of India A Study of Imperial Rule from 1905 to 1910 as told through the correspondence and diaries of Sir James Dunlop Smith* (London 1966).

Gopal, S., *British Policy in India* (Cambridge 1965).

Guha, R., *A Rule of Property for Bengal* (Paris 1963).

Gupta, Sulekh Chandra, *Agrarian Relations and Early British Rule in India A Case Study of Ceded and Conquered Provinces (Uttar Pradesh)* (Bombay 1963).

Houghton, Walter E., *The Victorian Frame of Mind 1830–1870* (New Haven 1957).

Hutchins, F. G., *The Illusion of Permanence British Imperialism in India* (Princeton 1967).

Joshi, Vijaya Chandra (ed.), *Lajpat Rai Autobiographical Writings* (Delhi 1965).

Kopf, D., *British Orientalism and the Bengal Renaissance* (Berkeley 1969).

Kumar, Ravinder, *Western India in the Nineteenth Century A Study in the Social History of Maharashtra* (London 1968).

Low, D. A. (ed.), *Soundings in Modern South Asian History* (London 1968).
Lynd, Helen Merrell, *England in the Eighteen-Eighties Toward A Social Basis for Freedom* (London 1945).
MacDonagh, Oliver, *Ireland* (Englewood Cliffs, New Jersey 1968).
Metcalf, Thomas R., *The Aftermath of Revolt, India, 1857–1870* (Princeton 1964).
Moore, R. J., *Sir Charles Wood's Indian Policy 1853–66* (Manchester 1966).
Neale, Walter C., *Economic Change in Rural India, Land Tenure and Reform in Uttar Pradesh, 1800–1955* (New Haven 1962).
O'Malley, L. S. S., *The Indian Civil Service 1601–1930* (London 1965 ed.).
Perkin, Harold, *The Origins of Modern English Society 1780–1880* (London 1969).
Raj, Jagdish, *The Mutiny and British Land Policy in North India 1856–1868* (London 1965).
Seal, Anil, *The Emergence of Indian Nationalism Competition and Collaboration in the Later Nineteenth Century* (Cambridge 1968).
Somervell, D. C., *English Thought in the Nineteenth Century* (London 1929).
Spring, David, *The English Landed Estate in the Nineteenth Century: its Administration* (Baltimore 1963).
Stokes, Eric, *The English Utilitarians and India* (Oxford 1959).
Thompson, F. M. L., *English Landed Society in the Nineteenth Century* (London 1963).
Williams, Gertrude, *The State and the Standard of Living* (London 1936).
Wolpert, Stanley A., *Morley and India 1906–1910* (Berkeley 1967).
Woodruff, Philip, *The Men Who Ruled India*, 2 vols (London 1953–4).
Woof, Leonard, *Beginning Again An Autobiography of the Years 1911–1918* (London 1964).
Woolf, Leonard, *Downhill All the Way An Autobiography of the Years 1919–1939* (London 1967).
Young, G. M., *Victorian England Portrait of an Age* (London 1953 ed.).

*Articles*

Barrier, N. Gerald, 'The Punjab Disturbances of 1907: the response of the British Government in India to agrarian unrest', *Modern Asian Studies*, Vol. 1, Part 4, October 1967, pp. 353–83.
Barrier, N. Gerald, 'The Punjab Government and Communal Politics, 1870–1908', *The Journal of Asian Studies*, Vol. XXVII, No. 3, May 1968, pp. 523–39.
Barrier, Norman G., 'The Arya Samaj and Congress Politics in the Punjab, 1849–1908', *The Journal of Asian Studies*, Vol. XXVI, No. 3, May 1967, pp. 363–79.
Barrier, Norman G., 'The Formulation and Enactment of the Punjab

Alienation of Land Bill', *The Indian Economic and Social History Review*, Vol. II, No. 2, April 1965, pp. 145–65.

Black, R. D. Collison, 'Economic Policy in Ireland and India in the Time of J. S. Mill', *The Economic History Review*, 2nd series, Vol. XXI, No. 2, August 1968, pp. 321–36.

Chandra, Bipan, 'Reinterpretation of Nineteenth Century Indian Economic History', *The Indian Economic and Social History Review*, Vol. V, No. 1, March 1968, pp. 35–75.

Dumont, Louis, 'The "Village Community" from Munro to Maine' *Contributions to Indian Sociology*, No. IX, December 1966, pp. 67–89.

Hambly, G. R. G., 'Richard Temple and the Punjab Tenancy Act of 1868', *The English Historical Review*, Vol. LXXIX, No. CCCX, January 1964, pp. 47–66.

Hart, J., 'Nineteenth-Century Social Reform: A Tory Interpretation of History', *Past and Present*, No. 31, July 1965, pp. 39–61.

MacDonagh, O., 'The Nineteenth Century Revolution in Government: A Reappraisal', *The Historical Journal*, Vol. I, No. 1, 1958, pp. 52–67.

Mathur, Y. B., 'Judicial Administration of the Punjab, 1849–75', *Journal of Indian History*, Vol. XLIV, Part III, December 1966, pp. 707–36.

Matsui, Toru, 'On the Nineteenth-Century Indian Economic History— A Review of a "Reinterpretation" ', *The Indian Economic and Social History Review*, Vol. V, No. 1, March 1968, pp. 17–33.

McLane, John R., 'Peasants, Moneylenders and Nationalists at the end of the Nineteenth Century', *The Indian Economic and Social History Review*, Vol. 1, No. 1, July–September 1963, pp. 66–73.

Metcalf, Thomas R., 'The British and the Moneylender in Nineteenth-Century India', *The Journal of Modern History*, Vol. XXXIV, No. 4, December 1962, pp. 390–7.

Metcalf, Thomas R., 'The Influence of the Mutiny of 1857 on Land Policy in India', *The Historical Journal*, Vol. IV, No. 2, 1961, pp. 152–63.

Metcalf, Thomas R., 'The Struggle Over Land Tenure in India, 1860–1868', *The Journal of Asian Studies*, Vol. XXI, No. 3, May 1962, pp. 295–307.

Morris, Morris D., 'Towards a Reinterpretation of Nineteenth-Century Indian Economic History', *The Indian Economic and Social History Review*, Vol. V, No. 1, March 1968, pp. 1–15.

Morris, Morris D., 'Trends and Tendencies in Indian Economic History', *The Indian Economic and Social History Review*, Vol. V, No. 4, December 1968, pp. 319–88.

Myles, W. H., 'Sixty Years of Panjab Food Prices 1861–1920', *Indian Journal of Economics*, Vol. 6, Part 1, July 1925, pp. 1–52.

Naidis, M., 'John Lawrence and the Origins of the Punjab System, 1849–57', *Bengal Past and Present*, Vol. LXXX, No. 1, 1961, pp. 38–46.

Narain, Brij, 'Eighty Years of Punjab Food Prices 1841–1920', *Indian Journal of Economics*, Vol. 6, Part 4, April 1926, pp. 397–460.

Parris, H., 'The Nineteenth-Century Revolution in Government: A

Reappraisal Reappraised', *The Historical Journal*, Vol. III, No. 1, 1960, pp. 17–37.

Raychaudhuri, T., 'A Re-interpretation of Nineteenth Century Indian Economic History?', *The Indian Economic and Social History Review*, Vol. V, No. 1, March 1968, pp. 77–100.

Roberts, D., 'Jeremy Bentham and the Victorian Administrative State', *Victorian Studies*, Vol. 2, No. 3, March 1959, pp. 193–210.

Smith, B. C., 'Maine's Concept of Progress', *Journal of the History of Ideas*, Vol. XXIV, July–September 1963, No. 3, pp. 407–12.

# INDEX

*Entries to the Notes at the end of the book are indexed under the page on which the note is cited.*

Account books, 51, 70, 86, 305
Afghanistan, 169
Agitation, 1899–1900, for and against Punjab land legislation, 262, 263–5, 271, 281, 286
Agricultural banks, 136, 137
Agricultural credit, 33–4, 37, 98, 284; British attitudes to, 39, 44, 46, 47, 50, 51, 53, 66, 69, 72, 73, 82, 86, 87, 88, 89, 92, 95, 98, 110, 111, 112, 114, 131, 132, 138, 142–3, 145, 146, 148, 152, 154, 155, 156, 162, 176–9, 186, 187–8, 189, 203, 208, 211, 212, 215–16, 217–18, 230, 237–8, 246, 249, 251, 265, 266, 269, 274, 294; and light assessment, 77, 144, 202
Agricultural discontent, 185, 228, 263; British view of, 76, 125–6, 132, 141, 169–70, 175, 185, 203, 228, 241, 265
Agricultural indebtedness, 33–4, 38, 48, 96, 97; British attitudes to, 31, 48–9, 50, 51, 55, 66, 70, 71, 72, 75, 77, 81, 85, 86, 87–8, 91–2, 106, 108, 109–216 *passim*. *See also* Transfer of land, and under specific Punjab districts and divisions
Agricultural prices, 32, 33, 284
Agricultural prosperity, 71, 72, 76–7, 84, 85, 92–3, 95, 96–7, 109, 120, 132, 133, 139, 141, 157, 164, 180, 184, 186–7, 188, 189, 203, 207, 224, 286. *See also* Agricultural credit, Improvement, Land, market value of
Agricultural surplus, 32, 33
Agricultural tribes, differences in character of, 36, 37, 128; effect on British, 128, 138, 187, 189
Aitchison, Charles, 130, 131, 137, 140, 145–6, 160, 162, 321
Alienation, power of, *see* Transferability of individual interests in land
Alienation of land, *see* Transfer of land
Alipur tahsil, 48, 126–7
Amritsar district, 48

Amritsar division, 103, 112, 345
Anderson, Alexander, 149, 160, 168, 208, 210, 212, 227, 230, 274, 287
Anderson, H. A., 212–13
Anderson, J. A., 225
Aristocratic land policy, 33, 39, 40, 100–1, 103–4, 171, 292. *See also* Court of Wards, Encumbered estates
Army, Indian, 169, 170, 171
Aroras, 36, 235, 291
Ata Muhammad, 265
Attachment and sale of crops in execution of decree, 89, 121, 129, 145, 146, 149, 151

Banias, 36, 291
Bannu district, 60–1, 116–19
*Bannu or our Afghan Frontier*, 116–18
Bannu valley, 119
Barkley, D. G., 110
Barrier, N. G., 244, 305
Beadon, Major, 110–11
Bearce, G. D., 22
Bengal, 135
Benton, Alexander Hay, 70, 71, 111, 174
Birch, F. M., 84
Blyth, Mr, 92
Board of Administration, Punjab, 42–4, 46
Bombay Presidency, 221, 256; Government of, 166, 196, 242
Bond, power to go behind, 87, 105, 129, 148, 149, 167, 168, 174, 214–15, 253
Boulnois, Charles, 68, 73–4, 75, 79, 85, 91
Bowring, L., 101, 102, 106
Brackenbury, H., 221
Brandreth, Arthur, 11, 12, 31–3, 34, 35, 39–41, 66, 70, 75, 76, 78, 89, 94, 96, 97, 99, 100, 103, 104, 107, 110, 170, 298, 303

357

Brandreth, E. L., 54, 56, 60
Britain, 40, 76, 99, 148, 169, 193, 222, 235, 266, 296; relevance to Punjab and India of developments in, 18–20, 176, 179, 180–1, 192–3, 242–3, 279–80, 300; rural problems of, and Punjab, 20, 99, 144
British officers in India, role of general body of, 12–13; concept of schools of thought, 12, 14, significance of Indian experience of, 15; closeness of contact with Britain questioned, 19–20
British policy in India, thesis of European origins of, 15
British rule in India, British view of stability of, 106, 170–1, 314
Bruce, R. I., 225
Buck, Edward Charles, 196–201, 241, 242, 244
Bulman, A. R., 122, 158–9, 160
Bureaucracy, *see* British officers in India
Busk, Capt., 60

Campbell, George, 44–6, 48, 66, 88, 89, 101, 102, 105–6, 314
Central Provinces, 78, 233, 239, 242, 245, 254; Government of, 196, 199, 232, 237, 242
Central Punjab, 38, 249, 284, 346
Channing, Francis Chorley, 113, 114, 115, 211, 213
Chatterji, P. C., 213, 228–9
Chief Court, Punjab, 34, 67, 68, 85, 87, 90, 271
Cis-Sutlej division, 44, 60
Civil procedure, *see* Judicial system
Civilisation, British view of, 46, 66, 118, 141, 142, 150, 151, 155, 162–3, 164, 191
Clarke, Robert, 147, 148–9, 160, 168, 225–6, 247, 249, 250, 251, 274–5
Code of Civil Procedure, 34, 67–8, 70, 72, 73, 74
Coldstream, William, 111, 173
Communalism, and Punjab land legislation, 265, 271, 281–2
Contingencies, their bearing on general trends, 14, 18, 194–5, 245, 300–1
Contract Act, Indian, 34; proposed amendment of, 211–13, 253, 288, 331
Cooper, F., 102
Court of Wards, 215, 218
Coxe, H. W. H., 70, 83, 106, 314
Cracroft, J. E., 70, 110
Crosthwaite, Charles Hawkes Todd, 198, 199, 242, 256, 280
Cultural influences, 172, 184–5, 193, 299; diverse effects of, 22, 190
Cunningham, F. D., 208, 210, 275
Curzon, Lord, 242, 257, 259, 260, 262, 267, 270, 276–7, 278–9, 280
Cust, Robert Needham, 43, 51–2, 57, 58–9, 61–3, 66, 98, 102, 106
Customary law, 47, 53, 151, 228–9, 234, 238

Dane, Louis William, 168, 203, 204, 208, 209–10, 248, 250, 251, 287, 296
Darling, Malcolm Lyall, 297
Davies, Robert Henry, 54, 78, 79, 81–2, 83, 84–5, 91–3, 94, 95, 96, 97, 98
Davies, W. G., 110, 140
Deccan, 105, 128, 129, 135, 148, 211, 217
Deccan Agriculturists' Relief Act, 143, 191, 192, 205, 234; question of similar measure for Punjab, 129, 144–5, 147, 156, 157, 158, 159, 166–8, 173–6, 179, 180, 181–2, 207, 210, 222, 224, 226, 232, 240, 278, 324; influence on Punjab debate, 161, 181–2, 192, 193, 242; and Government of India, 196–9, 200, 222, 253
Delhi district, 113, 114, 315
Delhi division, 226, 345, 346
Dera Ghazi Khan district, 123, 125, 317, 318
Dera Ismail Khan district, 122–3, 262
Derajat division, 130–1, 142, 143, 145, 345, 346
Diack, A. H., 225
Differential assessment, 203–10, 215, 217, 222, 240, 248
Douie, James McCrone, 156, 157–8, 160, 168, 175, 215, 223, 247, 248, 249, 250, 251, 265, 266, 287, 296
Dunlop-Smith, J. R., 247, 248, 249, 250, 251

# INDEX

Eastern Punjab, 38, 167, 249. *See also* Central Punjab, South-eastern Punjab

Edge, John, 256

Edgeworth, M. P., 305

Edmonstone, George Frederick, 53, 307

Education, of agricultural class, 87–8, 97

Edwardes, Herbert Benjamin, 58–61, 66, 67, 101, 102, 106

Edwards, W., 74, 309

Egerton, Robert Eyles, 78, 80, 84, 91, 92, 93, 94, 109, 112, 128, 129, 130, 160, 161

Elgin, Lord, 201, 221, 239, 242, 243, 255

Elliott, Col., 71

Elsmie, G. R., 174, 204

Encumbered estates, 80, 83–4, 198, 199, 218

England, *see* Britain

*English Utilitarians and India, The*, 18

Entail, 20, 144, 193

Eurocentric bias in historiography of British India, 15–16, 19

Eviction, *see* Transfer of land, voluntary

Evidence Act, Indian, 34; proposed amendment of, 211, 213, 331

Evolution, social, 40, 125, 150–1, 164, 166, 177, 189, 190–1, 192, 300. *See also* Maine, Sir Henry, Natural law, Social Darwinism

Experience and opinion, 17, 21–2, 38–9, 40–1, 53, 66–7, 93–4, 110–28, 133–4, 141, 142, 146–9, 160–5, 177–8, 180, 184, 217–18, 300. *See also* Social influences

Fagan, P. J., 208

Famines, and land transfer, 60, 77, 109, 113, 114–15, 226, 232

Fanshawe, Herbert Charles, 113, 166, 266, 267, 268, 269, 275, 323

Fendall, Colonel, 76, 79–80

Ferozepur district, 139, 224

Firozpur tahsil, 114–15

Fitzpatrick, Dennis, 199, 200, 202, 203, 204, 205–6, 209, 210–11, 212, 213–14, 216, 222–3, 224, 225, 231–2, 239–42, 243, 245, 246, 251, 252, 256, 257, 258, 261, 269, 277, 278, 280, 286

Fluctuating assessment, 81, 82, 127, 128, 129, 139, 140, 143, 166, 197, 201–2

Foreclosure of mortgage, 44

Formal authority, scholarly preoccupation with, 12, 13, 15, 16, 18–20, 23, 192; significance of, 13, 182, 194–5, 224, 225, 240, 242, 244, 278–80

Forsyth, Thomas Douglas, 63–4, 67, 91

Francis, E. B., 208, 224

Free trade in land, 21

Freedom of contract, 69, 92, 114, 147, 150, 152, 154, 168. *See also* Bond, Deccan Agriculturists' Relief Act, Transferability of individual interests in land

Frizelle, J., 225

Frontier districts, of Punjab, 36, 38, 60–1, 102, 106, 141, 142, 155. *See also* Lower frontier, Upper frontier

Fryer, F. W. R., 123, 152

Frykenberg, R., 16

Gardiner, R., 259–60

Garshankar tahsil, 156–7

Gopal, S., 12

Government in India, portrayed as landlord of soil, 76, 83, 86, 96, 99, 158, 312

Government of India, 12, 74, 128, 214; and early Punjab protective policy, 42, 43, 50–1, 306; role in land transfer debate, 166, 175, 196–201, 213, 216–22, 225, 232–9, 240, 242–5, 246, 253–6, 277

Grey, L. J. H., 139, 159, 160, 168, 175, 177–8, 202–3, 208, 209–10, 211, 213

Griffin, Lepel Henry, 70, 102, 106

Guha, R., 15

Gujranwala district, 37, 48, 51, 52, 79, 121–2, 306

Gujranwala tahsil, 306

Gujrat district, 55–6, 76–7

Gurdaspur district, 48, 54, 79–80, 94

Gurdon, E. P., 115

Gurgaon district, 113, 114–15, 135–6, 185

359

Hambly, G. R. G., 103
Hamilton, Lord, 257, 258, 278–9, 280
Harcourt, H., 297
Harnam Singh, 266–7, 270, 271, 272, 279
Harris, W. A., 179
Hastings, E. G., 120
Hazara district, 120–1, 143, 317
Heavy assessment, policy of, 202–3, 209–10, 217
Henderson, E. P., 215
Hissar division, 60, 77, 345
Historical method, in British-Indian history, 11–23, 192, 279
Hoshiarpur district, 57, 58, 78, 84, 86, 92, 94, 111, 132, 133, 156–7, 185
Hutchins, F. G., 22
Hutchins, P. P., 175–6, 197, 198, 199, 253, 256, 257, 280
Hutchinson, J. B., 207, 208, 212, 224

Ibbetson, Denzil, 113–14, 125, 130, 147–9, 160, 161, 162, 163, 168, 169, 175, 176–7, 178, 180, 201, 216–21, 223, 233–8, 239, 242, 243–6, 251, 252, 254, 261, 271, 277, 283, 287, 296
Imprisonment for debt, 85, 89, 145, 146
Improvement, 40, 56, 65, 66, 89, 109–10, 132, 189; of land, 33, 37, 38–9, 46, 59, 69, 72, 73, 89, 92, 98, 117, 155–6, 164, 178, 207, 256; of material conditions of Punjab, 64, 71, 75, 96
Indebtedness, *see* Agricultural indebtedness
*India as it may be*, 44, 45–6
India Office, and land transfer debate, 12, 165, 256–8, 261, 271, 278–9, 280
Indian National Congress, 296
Indian states, 177–8, 180, 202–3, 217
Individualism, 141, 142, 151, 154–5
Influence and authority, various senses of theme of, 13, 15, 18
Influences, underlying, 15, 184–95, 298–301; and contingencies, 18, 194–5, 245, 300–1; distinguished from impersonal forces, 18; inter-relationships of 22, 184–94, 298–300, diverse effects of, 22, 298. *See also* Cultural influences, Social influences

Insolvency, 84, 85, 180
Intellectual influences, 17, 40, 99, 118, 125, 160, 162, 163–4, 180, 183, 188–94, 243, 279, 288, 295, 297, 299–300; treatment of in British–Indian historiography, 16, 18–20, 21, 192, 279; formal and informal, 18–20, 21, 23, 96, 133, 141, 154; need for verifying, 19, 20–1, 192; need to examine in social context, 21–2, 189, 191, 193, 300; diverse effects of, 22, 190–1, 193, 241, 300; political significance of, 300. *See also* Britain, Civilisation, Evolution, Freedom of contract, Improvement, Individualism, *Laissez-faire*, Maine (Sir Henry), Political economy, Progress, Social Darwinism
Intellectual tradition, new, *see* Punjab tradition
Interest rates, 34, 59, 79, 83, 86, 89, 92, 98, 121, 145–6, 148, 177, 179, 181, 217–18, 237–8; and civil courts, 79, 82, 87, 97, 150, 154, 167, 174, 211, 212, 214–15, 331. *See also* Bond
Ireland, 20, 135, 148, 191, 192–3, 257, 279

Jagadhri tahsil, 157–8
Jews, in Russia and eastern Europe, 156, 179
Jhajjar tahsil, 134, 140
Jhang district, 80–1, 83, 85, 127, 131–2, 141, 317
Jhansi Encumbered Estates Act, 134
Jhelum district, 32, 33, 37, 100, 104, 121, 213, 214, 228, 241, 263, 265
Judicial system, 34–5, 43, 44, 49, 150; British attitudes to, 34, 44, 45, 49, 50, 57, 70, 76, 77, 78, 79, 86, 95, 117, 121, 126, 129, 134, 138, 142–3, 145, 146, 147, 148, 149, 150, 152, 153–4, 156, 162, 166, 168, 169, 174, 175, 181, 191, 197, 215, 216, 286. *See also* Attachment and sale of crops, Bond, Code of Civil Procedure, Contract Act, Customary law, Deccan Agriculturists' Relief Act, Evidence Act, Imprisonment for debt, Interest rates, Limitation law, Punjab Civil Code, Transfer of land, compulsory

# INDEX

Jullunder district, 54, 78, 92, 110
Jullunder division, 57, 81, 83, 274, 345, 346

Kangra district, 64, 227
Karnal district, 113, 114, 147, 157
Kensington, Alfred, 133, 156–7, 160, 168, 203, 275
Khatris, 36, 54, 122, 235, 291
Kohat district, 119–20, 210
Kumar, R., 16, 191–2

Labour party, British, 296
Lahore district, 76–7, 265
Lahore division, 51–2, 345, 346
*Laissez-faire*, 20, 21, 89, 91, 93, 95–6, 99, 136, 145, 146, 164, 189, 190, 191, 193, 205–6, 207, 241, 264, 279, 300. *See also* Freedom of contract
Lake, Edward John, 57, 58, 64, 67
Land, communal and individual interests in, 32, 37, 142, 151, 166, 185; and British attitudes, 45, 56, 117–18, 142, 147–8, 150–1, 154–5, 165–6, 183, 185, 190, 191. *See also* Transferability of individual interests in land, Village communities
Land, market value of, 33, 34, 37, 65, 67, 98, 284; and British attitudes, 46, 52, 54, 55, 56, 59, 62, 64, 65, 66, 71, 73, 78, 87, 89, 92, 95, 96, 98, 109, 112, 117, 132, 133, 137, 138, 177, 178, 187, 202, 203, 207, 251
Land alienation, *see* Transfer of land
Land Alienation Act, Punjab, *see* Punjab Alienation of Land Act
Land Alienation Bill committees, 264, 271
*Land and the Law in India, The*, 192
Landlord policy, *see* Aristocratic land policy
Lansdowne, Lord, 197, 198, 199, 200, 221, 242, 243
Law, *see* Judicial system
Law, Edward, 266
Lawrence, Henry, 42, 101, 106
Lawrence, John, 11, 42, 46, 47, 50, 51, 52, 56, 101–2, 106, 305
Leigh, H. P. P., 208, 210
Limitation law, 49, 51, 85, 88, 97, 120–1, 145, 146, 151, 168, 288

Lindsay, Charles Robert, 73, 79, 85–7, 91, 94, 96, 97
Lower frontier, 37, 121–2, 125, 127–8, 346
Ludhiana district, 48, 132, 262
Lyall, Alfred, 256
Lyall, James Broadwood, 80, 83, 90, 109, 112, 114, 123, 127–8, 136–7, 162, 164, 165–8, 174, 175–6, 179–80, 181–3, 190, 196, 198, 200, 202, 203, 204, 239, 286

MacDonnell, Anthony Patrick, 199, 200, 201, 242, 244
Mackenzie, Alexander, 196, 221, 242
Mackenzie, Hector, 55–6, 66, 67
Maclagan, E. D., 216, 297
McLeod, Donald Friell, 52, 57, 61, 69, 72–3, 75
McMahon, Charles Alexander, 92, 111, 134–5, 144–5, 160, 161
MacNabb, J. W., 115–16
Maconachie, Robert, 113, 114, 152, 173, 211, 212, 213, 224, 230
Madras Presidency, 197
Maine, Sir Henry, 118, 124, 150, 166, 179, 180, 190, 191–2, 322
Mansel, Charles, 42
*Manual for the Guidance of Revenue Officers in the Punjab*, 59, 62
Martindale, C. S., 212–13
Marwat, 117–19
'Masses', British notion of political importance of, 81–2, 101, 102, 146, 169, 170–1, 299
Massy, C. F., 207, 208, 210, 212, 224
Maynard, Herbert John, 11, 12, 33, 35, 38–41, 288–95, 296, 297, 298, 303
Mayo, Lord, 74
Melvill, Philip Sandys, 55, 56, 67, 71–2, 78–9, 87–90, 94, 97, 98, 99, 107
Merk, W. R. H., 224, 247, 262, 274–5
Metcalf, T. R., 103, 279, 309–10
Mill, J. S., 312
Miller, A. E., 198, 199
Miller, J. A. E., 147, 160
*Modern India*, 44–5
Montagu-Chelmsford reforms, 296
Montgomery, J. A. L., 208, 247, 248, 249, 250, 251, 275, 287

361

Montgomery, Robert, 42, 47, 56–7, 58, 61
Montgomery district, 80–1, 84, 85, 125–6
Moore, R. J., 103–4, 313
Mortgage by conditional sale, 157, 226, 234, 248, 254, 261, 263, 266, 268–9, 270, 271, 272
Muhammad Hayat Khan, 267, 269, 271
Muhammad Shafi, 271
Muharram Ali Chishti, 265
Multan district, 80, 85, 126, 207, 317
Multan division, 76, 80, 345
Munro, A. A., 76
*Musalmans and Money-lenders in the Punjab*, 154–6, 165, 197
Mutiny of 1857, *see* Revolt of 1857
Muzaffargarh district, 48, 52, 85, 126–7, 134, 317

Naesmyth, James, 60, 77
Naraingarh tahsil, 157
Narrative history, 18, 23. *See also* Contingencies
Natural law, 138, 144, 145, 150, 207. *See also* Political economy
North India, 46, 77, 104, 105, 136, 253
North-West Frontier Province, 283, 341
North-Western India, 218
North-Western Provinces, 42, 44, 45, 51, 52, 53, 54, 57, 59, 60, 68, 72–3, 74, 75, 83, 100, 104, 196, 198, 218, 232, 233, 237, 239, 242, 245, 256, 266, 307; influence on Punjab protective policy, 31, 42–3, 44, 47, 67, 105
North-western Punjab, 38, 121–2, 226, 346

O'Brien, Edward, 126–7, 173
O'Dwyer, Michael Francis, 297
Ogilvie, G. M., 168, 175, 211, 213
Ommanney, E. L., 143, 160, 320
Oudh Talukdars' Act, 80
Ouseley, Gore, 79, 91, 92, 109

Parker, E. W., 212–13
Parsons, C. G., 215
Peile, James, 256–7
Perkins, H. E., 111–13, 134, 160

Peshawar district, 120
Peshawar division, 224, 345, 346
Political economy, 35, 40, 46, 56, 60, 66–7, 72, 82, 85, 92, 95–6, 97, 99, 124–5, 138, 147, 149, 151, 161, 189, 191, 193, 200, 205–6, 207, 222, 225, 243, 265, 277, 279, 282; and early protective policy, 44, 47, 50, 53, 56, 58–9, 62, 63, 65, 95; and new intellectual tradition, 69, 75, 89, 98–9, 176–81, 184, 186, 187, 205, 287. *See also* Freedom of contract, *Laissez-faire*
Pre-emption, 44, 46, 47, 53, 55–6, 62–5, 67, 75, 83, 90–1, 95, 98, 99, 105, 114, 123–4, 125, 127, 134, 139, 147, 221, 225, 226, 248, 254, 255, 290–3
Prinsep, Edward, 103
Progress, 40, 65, 66, 99, 117, 125, 141, 142, 155, 189, 190, 191,
Protective policy, early, 31, 56, 68, 69, 89, 124, 180, 184; its inception, 42, 43–7; significance of 43, 98, 105–7; and revolt of 1857, 49–53; divergent attitudes, 53–6; challenged and maintained, 57–67, 96; perpetuated, 67, 72, 75, 80, 91, 95, 97, 107, 287. *See also* Pre-emption, Transfer of land, compulsory
Punjab, effectiveness of British administration in, 16; agricultural history of, 32, 33; ownership of land of, 32, 36, 37, 131; agricultural systems of, 36, 37; description of society of, 36; tenancy debate in, 103
Punjab Alienation of Land Act, official discussions (1895–1901) leading to introduction of, 216–62, 265–82; economic and administrative implications of restrictions, 217–18, 230, 232, 237–8, 241, 246, 248–9, 251, 253, 256, 258, 260, 265, 266, 269, 270, 273, 274, 276, 277; political implications of restrictions, 218, 222, 230, 231, 234 237, 245, 248–9, 251, 253, 256, 257, 258, 259, 260, 277, 278; restrictions and non-agriculturists, 218, 221, 223, 231, 234–5, 236, 245–6, 251–2, 257, 258, 259–60, 265, 267–8, 281, 282; restrictions on temporary transfer, 219, 223, 226, 227, 229, 232, 233–4,

Punjab Alienation of Land Act—*cont.* 238, 239, 248, 250–1, 253–4, 261, 265–6, 269–70, 271; restrictions on permanent transfer, 219–20, 223, 226–7, 228, 229, 232, 234, 237, 238, 239, 251–2, 254–5, 260, 261, 269; social scope of restrictions, 219–20, 223, 226–7, 229, 230, 231, 234–6, 246, 247, 250–2, 253–5, 257, 258, 259–60, 261, 265, 266, 267–9, 272–7, 280–1, 282, 336; role of revenue authorities, 220, 223, 229, 230, 232, 236–7, 238, 239, 247–8, 251, 252, 254, 255, 256, 257, 259, 261, 265, 267; hypothecation of crops, 220, 252, 255, 261, 266, 270; retrospective effect, 220–1, 234, 248, 254, 261, 265, 266, 268–9, 270; enforcement, 221, 261, 338; geographical scope of restrictions, 221, 222–3, 224, 225, 226, 228, 229, 230, 231, 237–8, 240, 246, 247–50, 252–3, 255, 256–7, 258, 259, 260, 261, 265, 278–9; pre-emption, 221, 225, 226, 248, 254, 255; assessment of public opinion and agitation, 221, 222, 223, 230, 231, 234–5, 245–6, 248–9, 253, 256, 258, 262, 281–2; mortgage by conditional sale, 226, 234, 248, 254, 261, 266, 268–9, 270, 271, 272; sale of land in execution of decree, 252, 255, 261, 268

Punjab Alienation of Land Act, XIII of 1900, introduction of, 283; intellectual origins of, 20, 279–80, 300; communal implications of, 281–2; working of, 283–6; amendment of, 283, 287, 294, 295; and public opinion 284–6, 290–1; British attitudes to, 286–7, 288–95; and new political vision, 288–95

Punjab Alienation of Land Bill, versions of, 260–1, 267–70, 271–2; British attitudes to, 35, 38–9, 265–73; and public opinion, 262–5, 271

Punjab Civil Code, 1854, 46–7

Punjab committee (Barnes Court committee), 1898, 247–53, 258, 260, 261, 273, 278, 280

Punjab Laws Act, 1872, 84, 90

Punjab officers, 42; role of general body of, 12–13, 41, 182, 239–40, 277, 278, 301; varied local experience of, 17, 38, 165. *See also* Experience and opinion, Trends

Punjab society, fragmented constitution of, 36; effects on British, 128, 153, 179, 180, 186, 187. *See also* Agricultural tribes

Punjab tradition, 11, 31, 39–41, 100–8, 293; and loyalty of village India, 11, 31, 40, 81–2, 100, 101–2, 103, 104, 105, 106, 107, 108, 169–70, 171, 172, 184, 193, 194, 217, 246, 296–7, 299, 301; and indebtedness and land transfer, 11–12, 15, 31, 39–40, 98, 99–100, 107–8, 170, 172, 184, 185–6, 189, 193, 194, 298–9; division into periods, 11–12, 35, 76, 98, 100, 107, 298–9, 301; unorthodox views, 32–3, 35, 39–40, 173, 288–95; and non-agricultural society, 35, 169, 171–2, 173, 218, 245–6, 281, 287, 293, 296, 299; new intellectual tradition, 41, 69, 75, 89, 98–9, 176–81, 186, 193, 194, 280, 301; old and new political tradition, 171, 172, 173, 184–6, 193, 245, 296, 299, 301; and alienation legislation, 195, 245, 246, 265, 277, 287, 301; and political agitation, 217, 245–6, 281, 297; influence of new political tradition, 295–7, 301. *See also* Cultural influences, Influence and authority, Influences, Intellectual influences, 'Masses', Social influences

Purser, W. E., 113, 125–6, 140, 152

*Rafiq-i-Hind*, 265
Raleigh, T., 259–60, 266, 268
Rawalpindi district, 267
Rawalpindi division, 345, 346
Redemption of mortgages, schemes for, 88, 135–6, 137
Registration of bonds, 51
Revenue system, 32, 33, 42–3, 49, 100, 172, 284, 302; British attitudes to, 32–3, 55, 70, 76, 78, 81, 82, 102, 115, 117, 118–19, 123, 126, 127, 128, 129, 135, 136, 138, 139, 142, 143, 152, 153, 154, 156, 162, 171, 172, 175, 178, 196, 201–10, 286. *See also* Differential

Revenue system—*cont.*
assessment, Fluctuating assessment, Heavy assessment, and Transfer of land, compulsory
Revolt of 1857, 33, 101, 102, 103, 104–5, 106, 305; and attitudes to land transfer, 49–53, 54–6, 70, 72–3, 74, 75, 76, 81–2, 83, 106, 107–8, 170
Rivaz, Charles Montgomery, 149, 160, 168, 175, 179, 202, 204, 205, 209, 215, 229, 230, 231, 233, 238, 239, 242, 246, 253–5, 257, 258–9, 260, 261, 266, 267, 268, 269, 270, 271, 273, 274, 276–7, 278, 279, 280–2, 285, 287, 296
Roberts, T., 114
Robertson, F. A., 207, 208, 225, 230
Roe, Charles Arthur, 126, 130, 149–51, 159, 162–3, 164, 174, 189, 190, 211, 224–5, 247
Rohtak district, 113, 137, 139
Russia, 169

Saunders, L. S., 76–7
Sawan Mal, 76
Seal, A., 12
Shahpur district, 61, 202, 228
Silcock, J. G., 168, 175, 213–14, 228, 230, 231
Simla district, 283
Simson, David, 68–9, 73–4, 75, 98
Smyth, T. W., 84
Social Darwinism, 73, 95, 128, 139, 144, 149–50, 153, 158, 187, 189, 190, 205
Social influences, 15, 31, 99, 105, 127–8, 130, 153, 154, 165, 171–2, 174, 184–8, 190, 193, 212; ignored in British-Indian historiography, 15–16, 17, 18, 20; and social history, 16–17; methods of ascertaining, 16–18; particular and general, 17, 171–2; need to examine in context, 17, 21, 97, 99–100, 170, 184–5, 188–9, 193, 299, 300; direct and indirect, 17, 165, 221, 243, 280; and contingencies, 18, 194–5, 245, 300–1; and orthodox British intellectual tradition, 21, 95, 188–90, 193, 194, 207, 300; and formal thinkers, 21–2,
96, 191; and new intellectual tradition, 22, 40–1, 89, 176–81, 186, 193, 194, 205, 217–18, 300; diverse effects of, 22, 96–7, 161–2, 163, 184, 186, 193, 194, 287–8; relative importance of, 22, 99, 189, 194, 298, 299, 300–1. *See also* Agricultural credit, Agricultural discontent, Agricultural indebtedness, Agricultural prosperity, Agricultural tribes, Experience and opinion, Punjab society, Transfer of land
South-eastern Punjab, 37, 113–16, 128, 134, 141, 218, 226, 227–8, 249, 346
South-western Punjab, 37, 47–8, 76, 80–1, 122, 125–8, 141, 150, 153, 166, 317, 346
State action, 99, 147, 193
Steedman, E. B., 127, 131–2, 155, 159, 160, 208, 210, 212
Steel, H. W., 139
Stogdon, A. W., 213, 228–9
Stokes, E., 12, 15, 18, 279

Talbot, W. S., 265
Taylor, Reynell, 80, 102
Temple, Richard, 47, 49, 52, 53–4, 101, 102, 105–6
Thanesur district, 60, 345
Thomason, James, 101
Thorburn, Septimus Smet, 116–19, 130, 140–3, 146, 154–6, 160, 161, 162, 163, 164, 165, 168, 175, 182–3, 185, 190, 201, 204, 205, 208–9, 210, 213–14, 215, 226–7, 230, 232, 243, 247, 248, 249, 250, 251, 262, 286, 317, 336
Thornton, Edward, 50, 51, 53, 57–8, 104, 305
Thornton, T. H., 91
Tighe, Captain, 59, 64–5, 67, 77–8
Transfer of land, compulsory, 44, 98; for debt in execution of civil decrees, 34–5, 44, 45, 46, 47, 50–1, 52–3, 57–9, 67–75, 85, 86, 95, 105, 111–12, 150, 180, 252, 253, 255, 261; for arrears of revenue, 45, 51–2, 59, 78, 150; at instance of Settlement Officer, 51, 306. *See also* Mortgage by conditional sale

## INDEX

Transfer of land, voluntary, 16, 34, 35, 43, 48, 49, 60, 65, 80, 85, 94, 95, 99, 109–10, 131, 133, 160, 168, 185–6, 201, 226, 263, 283–4; political significance of, 11–12, 31, 33, 40, 44, 62, 76, 78, 81–2, 83, 84, 85, 86, 90, 93, 94–5, 97, 98, 100, 108, 110, 119, 132, 135, 140–1, 143, 146–7, 149, 154, 163, 167, 168–73, 174, 175, 181, 183–4, 200, 201, 204–5, 216–17, 218, 219, 221, 222, 224, 225, 226, 228, 241, 277, 278, 288–9, 292–3, 296, 314; and British intellectual tradition, 11–12, 40–1, 83, 85–6, 89, 98–9, 143, 155–6, 163–4, 176, 180; local variations in, 17, 35–8, 48, 76–8, 93–4, 97, 110–28 *passim*, 167, 185, 187, 284, 317; early British restrictions on, 31, 43–4, 47, 53, 61–2, 63, 67; early British attitudes to, 31, 43–9, 51–3, 54–6, 59–63, 65, 66, 105; under Sikh and early British rule, 37, 48, 60–1, 117, 128; later British attitudes to, 38–9, 76–100, 107–8, 109–246 *passim*; injustice of, 78, 90, 138, 186, 227–8; eviction and retention of old owners, 90, 110–11, 159, 173; and communal differences, 128, 155, 167, 169, 185; financial implications of, 132, 186, 196. *See also* Agricultural indebtedness, *and under* specific Punjab districts and divisions

Transferability of individual interests in land, 32, 34, 37, 53, 142; British attitudes to, 35, 40, 45–6, 52, 53–6, 59, 60, 61, 62–3, 64, 66, 88–90, 91, 92, 97, 110, 124, 131–2, 133, 135, 136, 137, 138–9, 142, 144, 148, 149, 150–1, 152, 154–6, 159–60, 162, 165–6, 175, 179, 184, 190, 191, 195, 196, 197, 198, 199, 200, 203, 204, 205, 210, 212–13, 214, 215, 216, 217–21, 300. *See also* Customary law, Entail, Land, communal and individual interests in, Punjab Alienation of Land Act, Punjab Alienation of Land Bill

Trends, general, in official opinion, 13, 14, 31, 41, 107, 130, 160–1, 183–4, 195, 201, 215–16, 239–40, 242, 243

245, 265, 277, 278, 280, 281, 283, 286, 287, 298, 301
Trevaskis, H. K., 297
Trevor, A. C., 221, 255, 261, 266, 267, 268
Troward, T., 215
Tucker, H. St G., 122–3, 152
Tupper, Charles Lewis, 99, 123–5, 130, 166, 180, 229–30, 247–8. 249, 250, 251, 252, 266, 267, 268, 269, 270, 271, 272, 275–6, 277, 287, 317, 318, 336

Umballa district, 37, 38–9, 43, 48, 55, 59, 77–8, 115–16, 156, 157–9, 166–7, 173, 185, 251
Umballa division, 345
Upper frontier, 37, 38, 48, 116–21, 173, 346

*Vesh* tenure, 117–18, 142
Village communities, 36, 125, 147, 150, 185; British attitudes to, 42, 43–6, 56, 62, 63, 66, 68, 75, 88, 123–4, 158, 203, 218, 220, 226, 234, 251, 254, 259, 318. *See also* Protective policy
*Village-Communities in the East and West*, 118, 322
Village servants, 171, 272, 274, 275, 285

Wace, Edward George, 120–1, 130, 132–4, 152–4, 160, 162, 163–4, 193
Wakefield, G. E., 80, 83, 312
Walker, G. C., 173, 247, 248–9, 250, 251, 275
Walker, T. G., 132, 296
Waterfield, W. G., 76–7
West, Raymond, 192
*Western India in the Nineteenth Century*, 16
Western Punjab, 142, 154–5, 167, 169, 171, 275. *See also* North-western Punjab, South-western Punjab
Wilson, James, 115, 135–6, 137–9, 141, 159, 160, 161, 162, 164, 168, 175, 183, 185, 201–2, 203, 204, 205, 227–8, 230, 232, 243, 265, 275, 287

Woodburn, John, 238–9, 243
Wynyard, W., 53

Young, George Gordon, 136, 151–2, 164, 203

Young, R., 83–4
Young, William Mackworth, 173, 174, 180, 189, 202, 203, 204, 207, 208, 232–3, 246, 247, 252–3, 260, 261, 266, 267, 268, 269, 270, 272–4, 276, 277–8, 280–2, 286, 288, 338

**DO NOT REMOVE OR MUTILATE CARD**

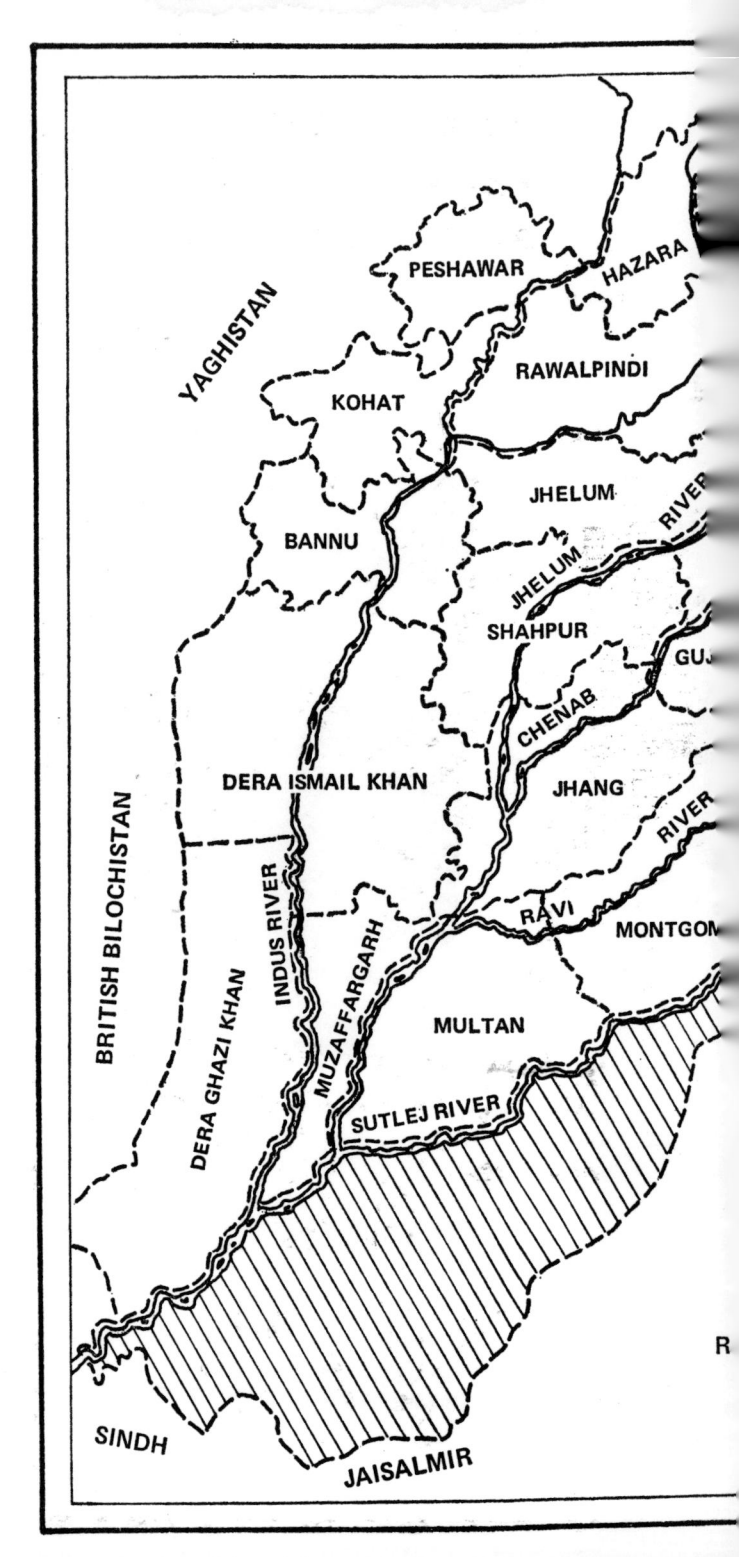